Microsized and Nanosized Carriers for Nonsteroidal Anti-Inflammatory Drugs

Microsized and Nanosized Carriers for Nonsteroidal Anti-Inflammatory Drugs

Formulation Challenges and Potential Benefits

Edited by

Bojan Čalija
Department of Pharmaceutical Technology and Cosmetology,
Faculty of Pharmacy, University of Belgrade,
Belgrade, Serbia

ACADEMIC PRESS

An imprint of Elsevier
elsevier.com

Academic Press is an imprint of Elsevier
125 London Wall, London EC2Y 5AS, United Kingdom
525 B Street, Suite 1800, San Diego, CA 92101-4495, United States
50 Hampshire Street, 5th Floor, Cambridge, MA 02139, United States
The Boulevard, Langford Lane, Kidlington, Oxford OX5 1GB, United Kingdom

Notices
Knowledge and best practice in this field are constantly changing. As new research and experience broaden our understanding, changes in research methods, professional practices, or medical treatment may become necessary.

Practitioners and researchers must always rely on their own experience and knowledge in evaluating and using any information, methods, compounds, or experiments described herein. In using such information or methods they should be mindful of their own safety and the safety of others, including parties for whom they have a professional responsibility.

To the fullest extent of the law, neither the Publisher nor the authors, contributors, or editors, assume any liability for any injury and/or damage to persons or property as a matter of products liability, negligence or otherwise, or from any use or operation of any methods, products, instructions, or ideas contained in the material herein.

Library of Congress Cataloging-in-Publication Data
A catalog record for this book is available from the Library of Congress

British Library Cataloguing-in-Publication Data
A catalogue record for this book is available from the British Library

ISBN: 978-0-12-804017-1

For information on all Academic Press publications
visit our website at https://www.elsevier.com/

Working together
to grow libraries in
developing countries

www.elsevier.com • www.bookaid.org

Publisher: Mica Haley
Acquisition Editor: Kristine Jones
Editorial Project Manager: Tracy Tufaga
Production Project Manager: Sue Jakeman
Designer: Mark Rogers

Typeset by Thomson Digital

Contents

3. Microemulsions and Nanoemulsions as Carriers for Delivery of NSAIDs

Ljiljana Đekić, Marija Primorac

4. Diversity and Functionality of Excipients for Micro/Nanosized Drug Carriers

Jela Milić, Bojan Čalija, Sanela M. Đorđević

8. Natural and Modified Silica-Based Materials as Carriers for NSAIDs

Danina Krajišnik, Aleksandra Daković, Jelena Janićijević, Jela Milić

List of Contributors

Bojan Čalija, Department of Pharmaceutical Technology and Cosmetology, Faculty of Pharmacy, University of Belgrade, Belgrade, Serbia

Nebojša Cekić, Faculty of Technology, University of Niš; R&D Sector, DCP Hemigal, Leskovac, Serbia

Aleksandra Daković, Institute for the Technology of Nuclear and Other Mineral Raw Materials, Belgrade, Serbia

Ljiljana Đekić, Department of Pharmaceutical Technology and Cosmetology, Faculty of Pharmacy, University of Belgrade, Belgrade, Serbia

Sanela M. Đorđević, Department of Pharmaceutical Technology and Cosmetology, Faculty of Pharmacy, University of Belgrade, Belgrade, Serbia

Tanja M. Isailović, Department of Pharmaceutical Technology and Cosmetology, Faculty of Pharmacy, University of Belgrade, Belgrade, Serbia

Jelena Janićijević, Department of Pharmaceutical Technology and Cosmetology, Faculty of Pharmacy, University of Belgrade, Belgrade, Serbia

Danina Krajišnik, Department of Pharmaceutical Technology and Cosmetology, Faculty of Pharmacy, University of Belgrade, Belgrade, Serbia

Ana Micov, Department of Pharmacology, Faculty of Pharmacy, University of Belgrade, Belgrade, Serbia

Jela Milić, Department of Pharmaceutical Technology and Cosmetology, Faculty of Pharmacy, University of Belgrade, Belgrade, Serbia

Caroline O'Sullivan, Department of Process, Energy & Transport Engineering, Cork Institute of Technology, Cork, Ireland

Uroš Pecikoza, Department of Pharmacology, Faculty of Pharmacy, University of Belgrade, Belgrade, Serbia

Marija Primorac, Department of Pharmaceutical Technology and Cosmetology, Faculty of Pharmacy, University of Belgrade, Belgrade, Serbia

Snežana D. Savić, Department of Pharmaceutical Technology and Cosmetology, Faculty of Pharmacy, University of Belgrade, Belgrade, Serbia

Radica Stepanović-Petrović, Department of Pharmacology, Faculty of Pharmacy, University of Belgrade, Belgrade, Serbia

Marija N. Todosijević, Department of Pharmaceutical Technology and Cosmetology, Faculty of Pharmacy, University of Belgrade, Belgrade, Serbia

Maja Tomić, Department of Pharmacology, Faculty of Pharmacy, University of Belgrade, Belgrade, Serbia

Sonja Vučen, School of Pharmacy, University College Cork, Cork, Ireland

Editor Biography

Bojan Čalija was born in Sarajevo (Bosnia and Herzegovina). He graduated from the Faculty of Pharmacy, University of Belgrade in 2007. In 2013, he received his PhD in Pharmaceutical Technology at the Faculty of Pharmacy, University of Belgrade with his PhD thesis entitled *"Functionality of chitosans in formulation of alginate–chitosan microparticles as carriers for nonsteroidal antiinflammatory drugs."* He completed postgraduate academic specialist studies in Industrial Pharmacy at the Faculty of Pharmacy, University of Belgrade in 2015.

During his Master's and PhD studies, he was awarded with the scholarships of the Ministry of Science and Technology of Republic of Srpska and the Ministry of Education and Culture of Republic of Srpska. In 2009, as a DAAD scholar, he was a guest researcher at the Department of Pharmaceutical Technology at the University of Technology Carolo-Wilhelmina in Braunschweig (Germany).

Since 2007, Bojan Čalija has been employed at the Faculty of Pharmacy, University of Belgrade as a teaching associate, teaching assistant, and assistant professor within the Department of Pharmaceutical Technology and Cosmetology. His teaching activities are involved in the Integrated Academic Studies for Pharmaceutical Technology I, Pharmaceutical Technology II, Novel Pharmaceutical Dosage Forms, as well as Doctoral Studies in Pharmaceutical Technology and Specialist Studies in Industrial Pharmacy and Pharmaceutical Technology.

From 2008 to 2010, he was engaged in the national project of technological development: *"Development and characterization of colloidal carriers for nonsteroidal anti-inflammatory drugs."* Since 2011, Bojan Čalija has participated in the national project of technological development: *Development and characterization of micro and nano drug delivery systems for nonsteroidal anti-inflammatory drugs"* and in the project of basic research: *"Synthesis of molecules with anti-inflammatory and cardio protective activity: structural modifications, modeling, physicochemical characterization and formulational investigation."* From 2010 through 2012, he was engaged in the international Tempus project: *"Postgraduate Qualification in Pharmacy—The Way Forward."*

His research is focused on formulation and characterization of polymeric microparticulate drug carriers.

Bojan Čalija is the author or the coauthor of more than 70 original articles, professional papers, and short communications papers. He is a peer reviewer for several international scientific journals.

He is the coauthor of one textbook in the field of Pharmaceutical Technology, one workbook, and one multimedia publication in the field of Industrial Pharmacy.

Preface

In recent decades, various drug carriers have been developed to overcome limitations associated with use of conventional drug delivery systems, such as low bioavailability, insufficient stability, high drug plasma fluctuations, lack of selectivity for target tissues, frequent administration, and low patient compliance. Owing to their tailorable properties and small size, micro- and nanosized entities are nowadays the most intensively investigated drug carriers. Rapid expansion of research in this field has been driven by utilization of materials with improved functional properties, along with employment of innovative preparation and characterization techniques.

Nonsteroidal anti-inflammatory drugs (NSAIDs) are one of the most commonly used groups of medications worldwide. These drugs are widely used for the treatment of pain, inflammation, fever, and thrombosis. However, their use is related to some serious gastrointestinal, cardiovascular, and renal adverse effects. Some of these drugs have short half-lives, so frequent administration is required to maintain optimal blood concentration levels for a longer period of time. Limited absorption and low bioavailability are also frequently related to the oral administration of some NSAIDs. Encapsulation/entrapment of NSAIDs in micro- and nanosized carriers could be used to overcome these limitations. Nevertheless, development of a drug carrier with desirable characteristics is a complex process involving selection of appropriate encapsulation/entrapment material, encapsulation/entrapment procedure, and adjustment of optimal encapsulation/entrapment conditions. Only careful selection of encapsulation/ entrapping materials and techniques with respect to the structure, physicochemical, pharmacodynamic, and pharmacokinetic properties of the drug, and the route of administration may result in the overall improvement of the therapeutic efficacy of NSAIDs.

This book gives the reader a comprehensive overview of formulation strategies of different micro- and nanosized carriers intended for oral, dermal, and transdermal administration of NSAIDs in one resource, including particulate carriers (microparticles, nanoparticles, and porous inorganic materials) and soft colloidal carriers (microemulsions and nanoemulsions). It also discusses the latest research on advances and limitations of both micro- and nanosized drug carriers and NSAIDs. Special attention is paid to the functionality of polymers, silica-based materials, and natural surfactants as potential excipients for micro- and nanosized drug carriers.

Practical solutions for improving overall therapeutic efficacy of NSAIDs have been included throughout this book and may also apply to the formulation of micro- and nanosized carriers containing other drugs that exhibit similar physicochemical, biopharmaceutical, and pharmacokinetic characteristics. Therefore, we hope this book will serve as a useful resource for graduate students, professors, and researchers in the pharmaceutical sciences, especially in Pharmaceutical Technology.

Bojan Čalija
Department of Pharmaceutical Technology and Cosmetology,
Faculty of Pharmacy, University of Belgrade,
Belgrade, Serbia

Chapter 1

Clinical Uses of Nonsteroidal Anti-Inflammatory Drugs (NSAIDs) and Potential Benefits of NSAIDs Modified-Release Preparations

Maja Tomić, Ana Micov, Uroš Pecikoza, Radica Stepanović-Petrović
Department of Pharmacology, Faculty of Pharmacy, University of Belgrade, Belgrade, Serbia

1.1 NONSTEROIDAL ANTI-INFLAMMATORY DRUGS

The first record about the use of decoctions/extracts of willow bark/leaves for musculoskeletal pain was 3500 years ago in the Ebers papyrus. Hippocrates, Celsus, Pliny the Elder, Dioscorides, and Galen all recommended decoctions of parts of willow and other plants containing salicylate for rheumatic pain and/or fever. Salicylic acid was isolated in 1836 (by Pina) and synthesized in 1860 (by Kolbe). The first nonsteroidal anti-inflammatory drug (NSAID)—acetylsalicylic acid, was synthesized in 1897 (by Hoffmann) in an attempt to improve palatability of salicylic acid. Acetylsalicylic acid was the first drug tested in animals in an industrial setting, and after human studies it was marketed as aspirin in 1899 (Brune and Hinz, 2004; Vane, 2000).

At the present time, there are more than 50 different NSAIDs on the global market (Rang et al., 2015b). They are the most frequently used medications for their analgesic, anti-inflammatory, and antipyretic therapeutic properties, and aspirin also for its antiplatelet/cardioprotective action. Their wide use could be illustrated by the data that in the United States in 2010 more than 29 million adults (12.1%) were regular NSAIDs users (used NSAID at least 3 times per week for more than 3 months) and around 43 million adults (19.0%) were regular users of aspirin. Compared with 2005, an overall increase of 41% in NSAID use and 57% in aspirin use was observed (Zhou et al., 2014).

Microsized and Nanosized Carriers for NSAIDs. http://dx.doi.org/10.1016/B978-0-12-804017-1.00001-7

1.1.1 Classification and Mechanism of Action

1.1.1.1 Classification

NSAIDs are traditionally classified by their chemical structure on derivatives of salicylic acid (e.g., aspirin), acetic and phenylacetic acids (e.g., indomethacin, ketorolac, diclofenac), propionic acid (e.g., ibuprofen, ketoprofen, naproxen), fenamic acid (e.g., mefenamic acid), and enolic acid (e.g., piroxicam, meloxicam) (Table 1.1). After the development of the selective cyclooxygenase (COX)-2 inhibitors, the classification according to the relative inhibition of COX isoenzymes emerged and became widely accepted (FitzGerald and Patrono, 2001; Frölich, 1997; Hawkey, 1999). According to this criterion NSAIDs are classified into nonselective, traditional NSAIDs (tNSAIDs) that inhibit both COX-1 and COX-2, and COX-2 selective NSAIDs, colloquially termed coxibs. However, several older NSAIDs (e.g., diclofenac, meloxicam, nimesulide) exert some degree of COX-2 selectivity similar to the first coxib—celecoxib. Therefore these drugs are sometimes more accurately termed as COX-2 selective NSAIDs, although this has not been used commonly (Grosser et al., 2011; Rang et al., 2015b).

NSAIDs could also be classified on basis of their pharmacokinetic properties, that is, plasma $t_{1/2}$ (Section 1.1.2).

Paracetamol (acetaminophen) is conventionally separated from the NSAID group and classified as a *nonopioid analgesic* or *analgesic–antipyretic*. It shares many properties with tNSAIDs relevant to its clinical action (e.g., analgesic and antipyretic action) but it has some important differences. It is largely devoid of anti-inflammatory activity, and its mechanism of action appears to be only partly related to COX-inhibition (Borazan and Furst, 2015; Grosser et al., 2011).

1.1.1.2 COX Isoforms and Their Roles

COX-1 and COX-2 are closely related (they share >60% sequence identity) and catalyze the same reaction—the formation of prostaglandins (PG)s PGG_2 and PGH_2 from arachidonic acid (Fig. 1.1). Arachidonic acid is released from membrane phospholipids by phospholipase A_2, which is activated by various stimuli (inflammatory, physical, chemical, and mitogenic). PGG_2 and PGH_2 are cyclic endoperoxides, unstable intermediates that are converted by tissue (relatively) specific enzymes to PGs (PGE_2, $PGF_{2\alpha}$, PGD_2, and PGI_2), and to thromboxane A_2 (TxA_2) collectively named prostanoids (FitzGerald and Patrono, 2001; Smyth et al., 2011). Tissue specificity is illustrated by the examples of TxA_2, that is the dominant COX-1 product in platelets, and PGE_2, that is the dominant COX-2 product in macrophages (Smyth et al., 2011).

The expression of COX-1 and COX-2 and their roles in the body are mostly different (Grosser et al., 2011; Rang et al., 2015b; Smyth et al., 2009).

COX-1 is a predominantly constitutive enzyme widely expressed in most tissues including gastrointestinal (GI) mucosa, platelets, endothelium, kidneys, and uterus (Frölich, 1997; Jouzeau et al., 1997; Smyth et al., 2011). It has a

TABLE 1.1 Classification of NSAIDs According to Chemical Structure, COX Selectivity and Pharmacokinetic Characteristics (Brune and Zeilhofer, 2006; Grosser et al., 2011; Rang et al., 2015b; The electronic Medicines Compendium (eMC), 2016; Warner et al., 1999)

Drug	Chemical structure	COX selectivity	Pharmacokinetics			
			Elimination half-life ($t_{1/2}$)	Protein binding (%)	Oral bioavailability (%)	Renal elimination (%)
Aspirin (acetylsalicylic acid)	Salicylate	Weakly COX-1 selective	~20 min	80–90	20–70	90–100
Diclofenac	Acetic acid derivatives	Weakly COX-2 selective	1–2 h	99	30–80	65
Indomethacin		Weakly COX-1 selective	2.5 h	90	90–100	60
Ketorolac		Highly COX-1 selective	4–6 h	99	—	91
Ibuprofen	Propionic acid derivatives	Nonselective	2–4 h	99	80–100	100
Naproxen		Weakly COX-1 selective	14 h	99	~95	~100
Ketoprofen		Weakly COX-1 selective	2 h	98	~90	75–90
Flurbiprofen		Very COX-1 selective	6 h	99	—	—
Piroxicam	Enolic acid derivatives	Weakly COX-2 selective	45–50 h	99	~100	—
Meloxicam		Moderately COX-2 selective	15–20 h	99	~100	50
Mefenamic acid	Fenamate	Weakly COX-2 selective	3–4 h	>90	—	52
Celecoxib	Diaryl heterocyclic NSAID	Moderately COX-2 selective	6–12 h	97	20–60	27
Etoricoxib	Bipyridine derivative	Very COX-2 selective	~22 h	>90	~80–90	70
Paracetamol (acetaminophen)	Para aminophenol derivative	Weak and similar affinity for COX-1 and COX-2	2 h	20–50	70–100	90–100

COX, Cyclooxygenase.

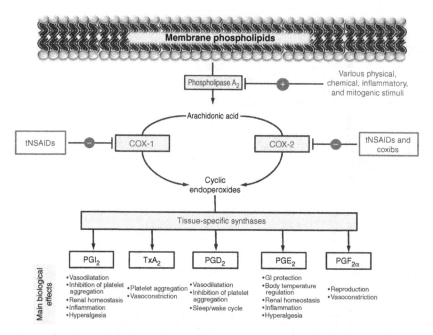

FIGURE 1.1 Biosynthesis and main biological activities of prostanoid mediators and the site of action of NSAIDs (Brune and Patrignani, 2015; FitzGerald and Patrono, 2001; Rang et al., 2015a; Smyth et al., 2011). Abbreviations: *COX*, cyclooxygenase; *GI*, gastrointestinal; *tNSAIDs* traditional nonsteroidal anti-inflammatory drugs; *PG*, prostaglandin; *TxA$_2$*, thromboxane A$_2$.

"housekeeping" role, as it is principally involved in tissue homeostasis. In gastric mucosa, COX-1 is responsible for the synthesis of PGE$_2$ and PGI$_2$, which exert cytoprotective effects on several aspects of gastric function such as an increase of bicarbonate and mucus secretion, reduction of gastric acid and pepsin secretion, and maintaining adequate blood flow to mucosa. They also promote the secretion of protective mucus in the duodenum (Cryer, 2001; Grosser et al., 2011; Rang et al., 2015d; Smyth et al., 2011). Inhibition of the GI PGs production is regarded as the cause of the most frequent and potentially most dangerous side effects of tNSAIDs—gastric/duodenal ulceration and bleeding (Cryer, 2001) (Section 1.1.4.1).

In platelets, COX-1 is essential for the synthesis of TxA$_2$, which stimulates platelet aggregation and vasoconstriction, and thus exerts hemostatic/thrombogenic effect. Pharmacological inhibition of TxA$_2$ synthesis leads to the inhibition of platelet aggregation. That is the mechanism responsible for the protective effect of aspirin against arterial thrombosis where platelet aggregation is a dominant process. In the endothelium, COX-1 activation leads to the production of prostacyclin (PGI$_2$) that inhibits platelet aggregation and exerts vasodilator action. Both effects contribute to its antithrombogenic action (Frölich, 1997; Rang et al., 2015a; Smyth et al., 2011). In the kidney, PGE$_2$ and

PGI_2 influence several functions, including total renal blood flow, distribution of renal blood flow, Na^+ and water reabsorption, and renin release. It is known now that both COX-1 and COX-2 are involved in the regulation of kidney functions (Frölich, 1997; Rang et al., 2015c; Smyth et al., 2009, 2011). Inhibition of COXs in the kidneys is associated with an increased risk of peripheral edema and sodium retention. In the uterus, COX-1 produces $PGF_{2\alpha}$, PGE_2, and PGI_2 that play roles in menstruation and initiation of parturition, but the contribution of COX-2 is also implicated (Frölich, 1997; Rang et al., 2015c; Smyth et al., 2011).

COX-2 is a predominantly inducible enzyme, considered to be mainly responsible for the production of prostanoids in inflammation (FitzGerald and Patrono, 2001; Hawkey, 1999; Rang et al., 2015b). Although COX-2 has a major role, COX-1 also contributes in the initial stage of inflammation (Grosser et al., 2011; McAdam et al., 2000).

One of the main stimuli for COX-2 induction is cytokines (such as interleukin-1, IL-1 and tumor necrosis factor-α, TNF-α) (Rang et al., 2015b; Smyth et al., 2009, 2011). Inflammation, which is a normal response to any tissue injury, may be exaggerated or sustained without clear benefit and thus become a cause of common bothersome symptoms of many diseases—pain and edema. PGE_2 and PGI_2 are primary PGs that mediate inflammation. They increase local blood flow and vascular permeability, causing edema, and reduce the threshold to nociceptor stimulation, causing their sensitization (a phenomenon called peripheral sensitization), that manifests as increased sensitivity to painful stimuli (hyperalgesia) (Pulichino et al., 2006). Thus, inhibition of PGs synthesis by NSAIDs is responsible for their anti-inflammatory (antiedematous) and analgesic action. It should be noted that there is also a central component of analgesic action of NSAIDs, related to inhibition of PGs (dominantly PGE_2 produced by COX-1 and COX-2) that facilitate transmission of pain impulses in the spinal cord (central sensitization) (Grosser et al., 2011; Vanegas and Schaible, 2001).

COX-2 is also involved in genesis of fever. In conditions such as infection or malignancy, cytokines (e.g., IL-1, IL-6) and interferons act as endogenous pyrogens inducing COX-2 in the preoptic hypothalamic area (Engblom et al., 2003). Released PGE_2 acts on the hypothalamus and sets the thermoregulatory center to a higher point, causing elevation of body temperature. NSAIDs inhibit this response by reducing PGE_2 synthesis (Grosser et al., 2011).

Altogether, COX-1 and COX-2 contribute to the generation of prostanoids involved in homeostatic as well as inflammatory functions, but the relative contribution of these isoenzymes differs: COX-1 is more involved in homeostasis and COX-2 is more involved in inflammation.

1.1.1.3 NSAIDs Mechanism of Action

Most currently available tNSAIDs act as reversible inhibitors of both COX-1 and COX-2. Aspirin is an exception as it acetylates, that is, irreversibly inhibits COX-1 and COX-2. The relative potency against the two isoforms differs among the individual tNSAIDs (Table 1.1). The inhibition of COX-2 mediates, in large part, the anti-inflammatory, analgesic, and antipyretic actions of tNSAIDs, while the concomitant inhibition of COX-1 largely (but not exclusively) accounts for GI adverse effects (Grosser et al., 2011; Rang et al., 2015b).

With that in mind, selective COX-2 inhibitors (coxibs) were developed (FitzGerald and Patrono, 2001; Hawkey, 1999). These were indeed associated with considerably (but not completely) reduced GI toxicity, but the adverse effects associated with COX-2 inhibition in the cardiovascular (CV) system resulted in the withdrawal of some coxibs (rofecoxib, valdecoxib) or severe restriction of use of others (e.g., celecoxib).

The mechanism of action of paracetamol (acetaminophen) is still not completely known. At typical used doses, it only partly ($\sim$50%) inhibits COX-1 and COX-2. It exerts analgesic and antipyretic action, but has very weak anti-inflammatory activity. The poor anti-inflammatory effect of paracetamol could, at least in part, be explained by its inactivation at sites of inflammation that usually contain increased concentrations of leukocyte-generated peroxides (Boutaud et al., 2002). It is also suggested that COX inhibition by paracetamol could be especially pronounced in the central nervous system, explaining its antipyretic and analgesic efficacy (Boutaud et al., 2002; Mallet and Eschalier, 2010; Rang et al., 2015b). Some mechanisms other than COX inhibition, have been also proposed to account for the analgesic effect of paracetamol (i.e., involvement of serotonergic and endocannabinoid systems) (Mallet and Eschalier, 2010). Paracetamol is associated with a considerably reduced incidence of GI adverse effects compared to tNSAIDs.

1.1.2 Pharmacokinetic Properties

The chemical diversity of NSAIDs yielded a broad range of pharmacokinetic properties, but there are several common characteristics. The majority of NSAIDs are weak organic acids that are absorbed well after oral administration. In the acid environment of the stomach, acidic NSAIDs are dominantly in nonionized form so they are, in minor part, absorbed through the stomach wall. The major place of NSAIDs absorption is small intestine, due to its extremely large surface area. Food does not substantially influence their bioavailability.

The majority of NSAIDs are extensively metabolized—some by phase I and consequently phase II reactions and some by direct glucuronidation (phase II) alone. The NSAIDs are dominantly metabolized in the liver, by CYP3A or CYP2C families of P450 enzymes. The most important route of final elimination is renal excretion, but almost all NSAIDs undergo biliary excretion and reabsorption (enterohepatic circulation), to some degree. The degree of lower GI tract irritation correlates with the degree of enterohepatic circulation (Borazan and Furst, 2015). According to the half-lives, NSAIDs can be classified as the ones with shorter $t_{1/2}$ (<6 h, e.g., diclofenac, aspirin, ibuprofen) and longer $t_{1/2}$ (>10 h, e.g., celecoxib, naproxen, oxicams) (Table 1.1).

Most NSAIDs are highly bound to plasma proteins (95–99%) (Table 1.1), thus have the potential to displace other drugs that could result in clinically meaningful interactions (Section 1.1.5). NSAIDs are generally widely distributed throughout the body. They readily penetrate arthritic joints as well as central nervous system. It has been suggested that NSAIDs with more acidic functional groups (e.g., ibuprofen, diclofenac) tend to accumulate at the sites of inflammation. This could explain the fact that those NSAIDs could remain in the synovial fluid longer than could be expected according to their half-lives (Brune et al., 2010; Brune and Patrignani, 2015).

1.1.2.1 Biopharmaceutical/Pharmacokinetic Considerations of Topically Administered NSAIDs

Multiple NSAIDs are marketed in formulations for topical application on joints and muscles. Today there is substantial evidence that this route of administration can ensure effective local concentrations, which are predominantly the result of skin permeation, direct diffusion, and local blood redistribution of the drug, with low concomitant plasma levels (Brunner et al., 2005; Dehghanyar et al., 2004; Efe et al., 2014; Mills et al., 2005; Altman and Barthel, 2011; Rannou et al., 2016). That could ensure efficacy in localized treatment of pain and edema, while minimizing systemic drug exposure and consequently its systemic adverse effects.

In a study with healthy male volunteers (12 participants), Brunner et al. (2005) compared the bioavailability of diclofenac with respect to subcutaneous adipose and skeletal muscle tissue after repeated topical and oral administration of equivalent daily doses. Participants were first on topical treatment (48 mg of diclofenac was applied 3 times daily for 3 days onto a defined area of the thigh), and then, after a 14-day wash-out period, they were treated orally with 50 mg of diclofenac, 3 times daily for 3 days). Measurement of unbound drug concentrations in target tissues (by microdialysis) showed that the relative bioavailability of diclofenac was substantially higher after topical than after oral administration (324 and 209%, respectively) whereas relative plasma bioavailability was 50-fold lower. Maximum plasma concentrations were approximately 250-fold lower after topical compared with oral drug application (Brunner et al., 2005).

In a recent study, Efe et al. (2014) measured diclofenac concentrations in synovial tissue, synovial fluid, and plasma (by liquid chromatography), after topical application of diclofenac sodium gel in patients with joint effusions planned for total knee arthroplasty due to osteoarthritis. A total of 39 patients were randomized to 2- or 3-times daily application of diclofenac sodium gel to knees requiring surgery over a treatment period of 3 days. Within 8 h after the last application, total knee arthroplasty was conducted, and the diclofenac concentrations were determined in target tissues. The median diclofenac concentration was approximately 10- to 20-fold higher in synovial tissue than in synovial fluid or plasma in both treatment groups suggesting that diclofenac penetrates the skin locally and reaches the desired target tissue.

TABLE 1.2 Percutaneous Absorption of Topically Administered NSAIDs (Rannou et al., 2016)

NSAID (concentration in topical preparation, %)	Percutaneous absorption (%)
Diclofenac (1)	6
Etofenamate (5)	21
Flufenamic acid (2.5)	2
Ibuprofen (5)	5
Indomethacin (1)	1
Ketoprofen (2.5)	1
Salicylic acid (2)	1–23

Available data suggest that bioavailability of commonly used NSAIDs following topical application, ranges from 1% to 7% (Table 1.2). Etofenamate, due to its favorable physicochemical characteristics, exerted higher potential for percutaneous penetration (>20%), and accumulation in the target tissues (Walde, 1987).

Findings of these biopharmaceutical/pharmacokinetic studies are in accordance with the findings of preclinical (Table 1.6) as well as clinical studies and metaanalysis (Chou et al., 2011; Lin et al., 2004; Simon et al., 2009; Tugwell et al., 2004) that demonstrate analgesic and/or anti-inflammatory efficacy of topically applied NSAIDs. As some authors find that skin penetration of NSAIDs can be highly variable (Dehghanyar et al., 2004; Müller et al., 1997), finding a more convenient way for delivery of topical NSAIDs is of great clinical importance.

1.1.3 Therapeutic Actions and Uses

All NSAIDs (including selective COX-2 inhibitors) are anti-inflammatory, analgesic, and antipyretic, with the exception of paracetamol, which is largely devoid of anti-inflammatory activity. Aspirin (in particular dose range) possess antiplatelet properties.

The combined analgesic and anti-inflammatory effects make NSAIDs especially useful for symptomatic relief of acute/chronic painful and/or inflammatory conditions. The main clinical application of NSAIDs is in the treatment of musculoskeletal disorders (chronic that include osteoarthritis and rheumatoid arthritis, and acute that include acute gout and various injuries). NSAIDs are also widely used in the management of headaches, dental and postoperative pain, and dysmenorrhea (Brayfield, 2014; Grosser et al., 2011). Given in single dose or in short-term intermittent therapy, NSAIDs can relieve pain of mild to moderate intensity. It may take up to 3 weeks until their full anti-inflammatory action develops. It is generally thought that there are only small differences in anti-inflammatory/analgesic activity between individual NSAIDs and the choice is largely empirical. Effects in individual patients vary widely. However, when making a choice, the NSAID with low risk of GI toxicity should be preferred and the lowest effective dose should be used. If a patient fails to respond to one NSAID, another drug may be efficacious (Brayfield, 2014).

Coxibs are reserved for patients with a history or with a high risk of serious GI problems that are/could be related to use of tNSAIDs, provided that they have low CV risk (Brayfield, 2014; Grosser et al., 2011).

NSAIDs are usually given orally, with or after food. Some of them can be given by intramuscular (e.g., diclofenac, ketorolac, ketoprofen, piroxicam) or intravenous (e.g., diclofenac, ketorolac) route. Some NSAIDs are applied topically (as creams/gels/solutions/patches) or rectally (as suppositories). There are also ophthalmic NSAID preparations (eye drops) for the inhibition of miosis during operations and ocular inflammation after operations, and some other indications (Brayfield, 2014).

Paracetamol is one of the most commonly used analgesic–antipyretic agents and a component of many over-the-counter (OTC) preparations for headache, toothache, and cold and flu remedies. The drug is available in monocomponent preparations or in fixed-dose combinations containing other analgesics (including aspirin and codeine/dihydrocodeine), caffeine (that potentiates the effects of analgesics, Sawynok, 2011), antihistamines, decongestants, antitussives, expectorants, and antiemetics (e.g., metoclopramide), for acute migraine treatment. Paracetamol is an alternative to ibuprofen as an analgesic–antipyretic agent and to NSAIDs in treating symptoms in osteoarthritis. It is not a suitable substitute for NSAIDs in chronic rheumatic conditions with pronounced inflammation, such as rheumatoid arthritis. Due to its favorable safety profile, it is especially suitable for use in children and the elderly (Brayfield, 2014; Grosser et al., 2011).

Commonly used therapeutic doses of some NSAIDs are presented in Table 1.3.

1.1.3.1 Musculoskeletal Disorders

1.1.3.1.1   Osteoarthritis

Osteoarthritis is the most common joint disorder and is the second most common cause of permanent disability in adults. About 60% people older than 65 years have the symptoms related to osteoarthritis (Felson, 2015; Hunter and Felson, 2006; Sarzi-Puttini et al., 2005).

Osteoarthritis is characterized by a degeneration of articular cartilage together with changes in subchondral bone, mild to moderate intraarticular inflammation and outgrowth of bone at the joint margins (osteophytes). These changes result in structural and functional failure of joints. Osteoarthritis commonly affects knees,

TABLE 1.3 Commonly Used Doses of Selected NSAIDs (British Medical Association, Royal Pharmaceutical Society of Great Britain, 2014; Grosser et al., 2011; The electronic Medicines Compendium (eMC), 2016)

NSAID	Daily dosage[a] (mg)
Aspirin (acetylsalicylic acid)	Anti-inflammatory/analgesic/antipyretic: usually 500–1000; max. 3000 Cardioprotection: usually 75–100; max. 325
Diclofenac	75–150
Indomethacin	50–200
Ketorolac	Max. 40
Ibuprofen	Usually 200–1200; max. 2400
Naproxen	500–1250
Ketoprofen	100–200
Flurbiprofen	150–300
Piroxicam	10–20
Meloxicam	7.5–15
Mefenamic acid	1500
Celecoxib	200–400
Etoricoxib	30–120
Paracetamol (acetaminophen)	Usually 500–1500; max. 4000

[a]Limited dosing information is given. The stated doses are those used in adults, by the peroral route. For additional dosing information, refer to the product information literature.

hips, joints of (cervical and lumbosacral) spine, first metatarsal phalangeal joint (joint at the base of the foot toe), and the joints in hands (distal and proximal interphalangeal joints and the base of the thumb) (Felson, 2015). Typically osteoarthritis presents as joint pain, which is exacerbated by activity and relieved by rest, transient stiffness (in the morning or after rest) and reduced mobility.

The current therapeutic strategy in osteoarthritis is to relieve pain and to maintain joint function (Felson, 2015; Hunter and Felson, 2006). Nonpharmacologic measures are an important treatment modality that is directed to reduction of the load of the affected joint(s) and symptom relief. These include education, exercise, weight reduction in obese and maintenance of reduced weight, bracing, physiotherapy, transcutaneous electrostimulation therapy (TENS), acupuncture, and others (Sharma, 2016). Most clinical guidelines for treatment of osteoarthritis recommend paracetamol as the initial analgesic for pain treatment, while oral NSAIDs are universally recommended in patients with persistent symptoms that have not responded adequately to paracetamol. However, in clinical trials, paracetamol has been shown to be less effective than NSAIDs in patients with osteoarthritis (Pelletier et al., 2016; Towheed et al., 2006; Williams et al., 1993). It is suggested that NSAIDs could produce about 30% greater improvement of pain than high-dose paracetamol (Felson, 2015). Thus, NSAIDs can be considered as the first-line treatment, besides paracetamol. For pain in osteoarthritis that could not be relieved with NSAIDs and/or paracetamol, or if those treatments are not well tolerated, opioid analgesics (tramadol) or antidepressants (duloxetine) can be tried (Goodwin et al., 2009; Felson, 2015).

Systemic use of NSAIDs is commonly related to GI side effects, and also bears a risk of CV and renal toxicity (Section 1.1.4). Considering that osteoarthritis generally affects older persons and that the use of medicines for symptom relief is usually long-term, the risk of side effects is substantial.

GI toxicity could be prevented/reduced by concomitant use of gastroprotective agents (e.g., proton pump inhibitors, Section 1.1.4.1). Another way to minimize the incidence of GI as well as other systemic side effects is to use NSAIDs topically. Clinical trials have demonstrated that topical NSAIDs applied on the skin of the affected knee or hands (but not the hip) are slightly less efficacious than oral NSAIDs preparations, but have far fewer side effects (Felson, 2015). Topical NSAIDs can cause local skin irritation on the place of application (redness, burning, or itching sensation) in up to 40% of patients (Felson, 2015), thus developing of new topical formulations with better tolerability is important for the improvement of osteoarthritis treatment.

1.1.3.1.2 Rheumatoid Arthritis

Rheumatoid arthritis is a common chronic systemic inflammatory disease that results in progressive disability and increased mortality. Autoimmune reaction-mediated inflammation of the synovial membrane leads to its proliferation, causing erosion of the cartilage and bone, that is, irreversible joint damage. Affected joints become swollen, painful, deformed, and stiff. The earliest involved joints are typically the small joints of the hands and feet, usually in a symmetric distribution. Systemic manifestations include general malaise, fatigue, weight loss, fever, and anemia (O'Dell, 2004).

NSAIDs provide symptomatic relief from pain and inflammation in rheumatoid arthritis. They do not alter the progression of the disease and additional antirheumatic drugs (disease-modifying antirheumatic drugs, DMARDs, e.g., methotrexate, sulfasalazine, immunosuppressants, anticytokines, and other biopharmaceuticals) are needed to prevent/delay irreversible joint damage (O'Dell, 2004; Shah and St. Clair, 2015). Since joint damage occurs early at the course of the disease, rapid diagnosis and institution of DMARD treatment is crucial. Addition of glucocorticoids to DMARD therapy may be useful in early disease to control synovitis, and to suppress the progression of the disease until DMARDs begin to work (e.g., 6–8 weeks for methotrexate).

NSAIDs are particularly helpful during the first few weeks until a definitive diagnosis of rheumatoid arthritis can be established and treatment with DMARDs is started. Later in the course of the disease, they are considered to be an adjunctive therapy for management of symptoms uncontrolled by other measures (Shah and St. Clair, 2015). Both tNSAIDs and COX-2 selective NSAIDs are efficacious and are well tolerated for short treatment periods (O'Dell, 2004). Chronic use in rheumatoid arthritis should be avoided. Topical NSAIDs may provide slight relief of pain, but their role in rheumatoid arthritis treatment is unclear (Brayfield, 2014).

1.1.3.2 Mild to Moderate Pain

When employed as analgesics, NSAIDs are usually effective only against pain of low to moderate intensity, such as *dental pain* or headaches. They are particularly effective when inflammation has caused peripheral and/or central sensitization of pain perception.

Postoperative pain or another acute pain arising from inflammation is controlled well by NSAIDs (with the exception of high intensity pain). They are used with opioids in the management of severe pain such as cancer pain and are particularly effective in bone pain of malignant origin (Brayfield, 2014; Grosser et al., 2011). NSAIDs lack efficacy in neuropathic pain.

Primary *dysmenorrhea*, characterized by cramps during menstruation, is known to be caused by PGs released by the endometrium in the luteal phase of the menstrual cycle. NSAIDs are the treatment of choice in this condition (Marjoribanks et al., 2003). NSAIDs are taken at the onset of discomfort and continued for a few days while the symptoms persist. A systematic review that compared several NSAIDs and paracetamol concluded that ibuprofen appeared to have the best risk–benefit ratio in dysmenorrhea and was the preferred analgesic. Naproxen, mefenamic acid, and aspirin were also effective, but the limited data on paracetamol did not show such clear benefits (Zhang and Li Wan Po, 1998).

NSAIDs and paracetamol are often tried first for the symptomatic treatment of various types of *headache* including *tension-type headache (TTH) and migraine*. TTH and migraine are the most common headaches in the general population. Disorders in the nociceptive system occur in both types of headache, while skeletal muscle and vascular mechanisms are important in TTH and migraine, respectively. The peripheral and/or central release of PGs has been implicated in sensitization involved in the pathogenesis of TTH (Bendtsen and Fernández-de-la-Peñas, 2011), while this is less well understood in migraine. In the treatment of episodic TTH, NSAIDs and paracetamol are the drugs of first choice (Bendtsen et al., 2010, 2012). In migraine attack, NSAIDs/paracetamol and triptans consist the first therapeutic line (Bendtsen et al., 2012; Evers et al., 2009). NSAIDs can also be combined with triptans for more efficacious and/or prolonged pain relief in acute migraine (naproxen–sumatriptan fixed combination is now available) (Grosser et al., 2011). The choice of the drug depends on the effectiveness of analgesics used in previous attacks and severity of the attacks (stratified approach). Concomitant antiemetic–prokinetic drug (i.e., metoclopramide or domperidone) is recommended in migraine attack treatment to aid relief of the associated nausea and to accelerate the propulsion of orally administered analgesics through the stomach and thus improve their efficacy (Bendtsen et al., 2012; Evers et al., 2009).

1.1.3.3 Fever

Antipyretic therapy is reserved for patients in whom fever in itself may be deleterious and for those who experience substantial relief when the fever is lowered. Paracetamol, ibuprofen, and aspirin are the main antipyretics used in clinical practice. Paracetamol is usually the antipyretic of choice in infants and children but ibuprofen is an effective alternative. Aspirin is generally contraindicated in children (<16 years old) because of the possible link between its use and the development of Reye's syndrome (Brayfield, 2014; Grosser et al., 2011).

1.1.3.4 Cardioprotection (Aspirin)

Aspirin is widely used for secondary prevention of CV events. In this indication it reduces the risk of serious vascular events by 20–25%. It irreversibly inhibits platelet COX-1, and thus completely suppresses TxA_2 formation in the affected thrombocyte until the end of its lifetime (8–10 days). It is usually administered at doses 75–100 mg once daily, in long-term prophylaxis. Higher doses (160–325 mg) are needed for rapid platelet inhibition (i.e., in acute coronary syndrome) (Weitz, 2015).

Placebo-controlled trials revealed that low-dose aspirin increases the incidence of serious GI bleeds, reflecting not just suppression of platelet thromboxane, but also reduction of gastroepithelial PGE_2 and PGI_2 (Grosser et al., 2011).

Due to their reversible COX inhibition and relatively short $t_{1/2}$, most other tNSAIDs are not thought to have a significant cardioprotective effect (García Rodríguez et al., 2004). Data suggest that cardioprotection can be lost when combining low-dose aspirin with ibuprofen (Catella-Lawson et al., 2001), so it is generally advised that ibuprofen should be administered at least 2 h after aspirin. Moreover, diclofenac in a dose of 150 mg daily, and ibuprofen in a dose of 2.4 g daily are associated with an increased risk of thrombotic events (Section 1.1.4.2).

1.1.4 Adverse Effects

The burden of side effects among NSAIDs is generally high, most probably reflecting the fact that they are used extensively in the vulnerable elderly population, for rheumatic disease, that usually necessitates large doses and sustained treatment.

Adverse effects that could complicate therapy with NSAIDs are presented in Table 1.4. The most frequent are GI and CV side effects. There are differences between NSAID subclasses or individual medicines in the potential of producing particular side effect. For example, COX-2 selective drugs have much less GI toxic potential than tNSAIDs, and among individual tNSAIDs, there are differences in the risk of GI toxicity (Section 1.1.4.1).

TABLE 1.4 Side Effects of NSAIDs (Brayfield, 2014; Grosser et al., 2011; Rang et al., 2015b, 2015c, 2015d)

System	Side effects manifestations
GI	Abdominal discomfort or pain, nausea, diarrhea, anorexia, gastric erosions/ulcers[a], GI hemorrhage[a], perforation/obstruction
CV	Closure of ductus arteriosus, myocardial infarction[b], stroke[b], thrombosis[b]
Renal	Salt and water retention, edema, decreased effectiveness of antihypertensive and diuretic medications, worsening of renal function in renal/cardiac and cirrhotic patients, decreased urate excretion (especially with aspirin), hyperkalemia, interstitial nephritis, nephrotic syndrome, hematuria
Central nervous system	Headache, vertigo, dizziness, nervousness, tinnitus, depression, confusion, drowsiness, insomnia, hyperventilation (salicylates), visual disturbances
Hemato-logical	Anemia, thrombocytopenia, neutropenia, eosinophilia, agranulocytosis[c], inhibited platelet activation[a], propensity for bruising[a], increased risk of hemorrhage[a]
Reproduc-tive (female)	Reduced fertility (reversible on stopping treatment), prolongation of gestation, inhibition of labor
Hypersensi-tivity	Vasomotor rhinitis, angioneurotic edema, urticaria, asthma, flushing, hypotension, rarely: shock, hepatotoxicity, aseptic meningitis (patients with systemic lupus erythematosus may be particularly susceptible)

[a]*Side effects decreased with COX-2-selective NSAIDs.*
[b]*Except with the low-dose aspirin.*
[c]*Most frequently related with the use of pirazolones (e.g., phenylbutazone).*

Age is generally correlated with an increased risk of developing serious adverse reactions to NSAIDs, and caution is needed in choosing a lower starting dose for elderly patients (Grosser et al., 2011). It is generally advised that systemic NSAIDs should be used in low doses and for a shortest period of time.

Unlike NSAIDs, paracetamol is well tolerated and rarely produces side effects. However, acute overdosage can cause severe, even fatal hepatic damage, and the number of accidental or deliberate poisonings with paracetamol is growing. Chronic use of less than 2 g/day is not typically associated with hepatic dysfunction, but overuse of acetaminophen-containing narcotic and OTC combination products has led to increased awareness of the possibility of toxicity (Grosser et al., 2011; Rang et al., 2015b). The maximal daily dose of paracetamol for adults is 4 g/day (2 g/day for chronic alcoholics) (Grosser et al., 2011).

1.1.4.1   Gastrointestinal Side Effects

GI side effects are the most common side effects of NSAIDs. They include dyspepsia, nausea, anorexia, bloating, GI bleeding, and ulcer disease. Gastric or duodenal ulcers are estimated to occur in 15–30% of regular users, and about 30–40% of patients experience upper GI side effects so severe that they need to discontinue the medication (Felson, 2015; Grosser et al., 2011). It is important to note that major GI side effects may occur in patients who do not complain of GI symptoms, for example, in one study in patients hospitalized due to GI bleeding, 81% had no premonitory symptoms (Felson, 2015).

Damage of the *upper GI tract* (stomach or duodenum) by NSAIDs can be induced by at least two mechanisms. Inhibition of COX-1 in the cells of gastric mucosa depresses cytoprotective PGs that inhibit acid secretion by the stomach, enhance mucosal blood flow, and promote the secretion of cytoprotective mucus in duodenum. Inhibition of PGI_2 and PGE_2 synthesis makes the stomach more susceptible to damage and can occur with oral, parenteral, or rectal administration of NSAIDs (Aabakken, 1992; Grosser et al., 2011). Another mechanism is local irritation from contact of orally administered NSAID with the gastric mucosa (Bjorkman, 1996). Local irritation allows back diffusion of acid into the gastric mucosa and induces tissue damage. However, the incidence of GI adverse events is not significantly reduced by formulations that reduce drug contact with the gastric mucosa, such as enteric coating, suggesting that the contribution of direct irritation to the overall risk is minor (Derry and Loke, 2000; García Rodríguez et al., 2001; Grosser et al., 2011).

The risk of upper GI complications associated with some individual NSAIDs is presented in Fig. 1.2.

NSAIDs have also been associated with the damage of the *lower GI tract* (distal small intestine or colon) (Aabakken, 1992; Gleeson et al., 1996; Evans et al., 1997; Rahme and Bernatsky, 2010). The rate of lower GI bleeding events is believed to be about a third of that of upper GI bleeding. The mechanisms of the NSAID-induced lower GI tract damage have not been widely studied and remain poorly characterized. However, as the data suggest that the degree of lower GI tract irritation correlates with the degree of NSAIDs/their metabolites enterohepatic circulation (Borazan and Furst, 2015), the action of NSAIDs on lower GI mucosa could be local. The preventive strategies are also not understood—proton pump inhibitors are not known to prevent or to heal lower GI bleeding (Rahme and Bernatsky, 2010). It should be noted here that aspirin and some other NSAIDs (e.g., piroxicam and coxibs) have demonstrated protective effect against colorectal cancer in some patients (Croswell et al., 2015). The mechanism of this action is not known (Section 1.2.1).

Current strategies for minimizing the risk of GI side effects of NSAIDs are:

- avoiding taking two NSAIDs;
- taking NSAID with or after food;
- taking gastroprotective medicines (in patients with a high risk), such as proton pump inhibitors and H_2 blockers (that reduce gastric acid secretion) or misoprostol (a PGE_1 analog, that mimics gastroprotective effects of natural PGs) (Naesdal and Brown, 2006; Vonkeman and van de Laar, 2010);

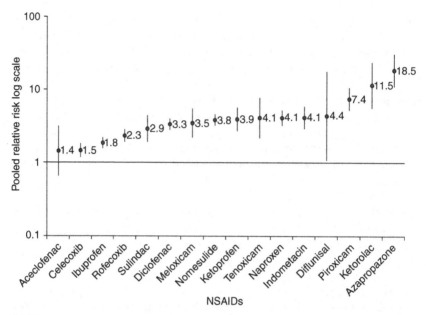

FIGURE 1.2   Pooled relative risks and 95% confidence intervals (CIs) of upper GI complications associated with the use of individual NSAIDs. *Vertical bars* denote 95% CIs. *(Reprinted with permission from Castellsague J, Riera-Guardia N, Calingaert B, Varas-Lorenzo C, Fourrier-Reglat A, Nicotra F, Sturkenboom M, Perez-Gutthann S, Safety of Non-Steroidal Anti-Inflammatory Drugs (SOS) Project: Individual NSAIDs and upper gastrointestinal complications: a systematic review and meta-analysis of observational studies (the SOS project),* Drug Saf *35:1127–1146, 2012, Copyright (2012) Springer International Publishing)*

- administering NSAIDs topically, as drug plasma concentrations are markedly lower after topical than after systemic administration. There is evidence that this route of NSAID administration was not associated with GI bleeding and perforation (Evans et al., 1995; Simon, 2013).

One more possibility for reducing GI and other systemic dose-dependent side effects of NSAIDs is to combine them with another classic (e.g., opioids) or adjuvant analgesics (e.g., anticonvulsants, antidepressants). There is substantial preclinical evidence that NSAIDs produce synergistic or additive interactions with anticonvulsants/antidepressants when reducing pain in inflammation (Hurley et al., 2002; Jones et al., 2007; Stepanović-Petrović et al., 2011; Tomić et al., 2013). Additive and synergistic interactions enable usage of considerably lower doses of components in combination than in monotherapy, with maintained or even augmented analgesia and lowered incidence of drug-specific side effects. There is also some clinical evidence about superior analgesia of NSAID–antidepressant/anticonvulsant combinations than that of monotherapy in treatment of inflammatory pain (Frakes et al., 2011; Gilron et al., 2005) Combining analgesics from different pharmacological classes represents a concept of *multimodal analgesia*, which has a great importance in treating chronic pain states (Gilron et al., 2013).

1.1.4.2 Cardiovascular Side Effects

Based on the data from clinical and epidemiological studies (Cannon et al., 2006; Hernández-Díaz et al., 2006; Kearney et al., 2006; McGettigan and Henry, 2006) it is known that all NSAID use can, to varying degrees, be associated with a small increase in risk of *thrombotic events* (e.g., myocardial infarction and stroke), especially when used in high doses long term. Coxibs, diclofenac (150 mg daily), and ibuprofen (2.4 g daily) are associated with an increased risk of thrombotic events. The increased risk for diclofenac is similar to that of licensed doses of etoricoxib. Naproxen (1 g daily) is associated with a lower thrombotic risk, and low doses of ibuprofen (1.2 g daily or less) have not been associated with an increased risk of myocardial infarction.

The increased CV risk is explained by the reduction of COX-2-derived PGI_2 formed in dysfunctional vasculature (i.e., with atherosclerotic lesions), that opposes the effect of prothrombotic stimuli (Grosser et al., 2006). The risk of CV adverse events appears to be influenced by characteristics of the patient (presence of CV risk factors) and of the drug (degree of COX-2 selectivity, dose, and treatment duration). Thus, COX-2 selective inhibitors should not be given to patients with increased CV risk, and the lowest possible dose of NSAIDs should be prescribed for the shortest possible period of time.

It is also well documented that NSAIDs can *elevate arterial blood pressure* (Johnson et al., 1994). NSAIDs have little effect on blood pressure in normotensive subjects, but in patients with hypertension NSAIDs could further elevate the blood pressure and reduce the effectiveness of antihypertensives (Section 1.1.5). The rise in blood pressure by NSAIDs could be explained by suppression of renal PGI_2 and PGE_2 involved in arterial pressure homeostasis (Grosser et al., 2006).

1.1.4.3 Renal Side Effects

NSAIDs can affect renal function. Higher risk exists in patients with heart failure, reduced circulation, cirrhosis or renal vascular disease, patients receiving diuretics, or the elderly. NSAIDs can induce renal disorders after systemic, and even after topical use (O'Callaghan et al., 1994).

Evidence on renal toxicity due to COX-2 selective inhibitors is less extensive, but it appears they have renal effects similar to those of the tNSAIDs (Noroian and Clive, 2002; Perazella and Tray, 2001). ACE inhibitors and angiotensin receptor antagonists can also produce renal impairment and concomitant use with NSAIDs should be undertaken with great care (Loboz and Shenfield, 2005).

Long-term use of (usually high doses of) NSAIDs has been associated with analgesic nephropathy. It is a condition of slowly progressive renal failure, decreased concentrating capacity of the renal tubule, and sterile pyuria. If recognized on time, NSAIDs withdrawal permits recovery of renal function (Grosser et al., 2011).

1.1.5 Interactions

NSAIDs interact with several classes of medicines by means of either pharmacokinetic or pharmacodynamic mechanisms (Table 1.5). The most important interactions are with antihypertensive agents (that result in the reduction of their efficacy); ACE inhibitors (that increase the risk of renal toxicity); aspirin, other antiplatelet, and anticoagulant agents (that increase the risk of bleeding); aspirin (that result in the reduction of its cardioprotective effects); and methotrexate (that results in an increased risk of methotrexate toxicity, in patients with RA). Some other clinically meaningful interactions are presented in Table 1.5.

TABLE 1.5 Overview of the More Important Pharmacokinetic and Pharmacodynamic Interactions of NSAIDs (Baxter, 2010; British Medical Association, Royal Pharmaceutical Society of Great Britain, 2014; Grosser et al., 2011)

Combination	Effect	Comment/(probable) mechanism of interaction
NSAIDs + ACE inhibitors	Increased risk of renal impairment	Both PGs (synthesis inhibited by NSAIDs) and angiotensin II (synthesis inhibited by ACE inhibitors) are important for maintaining normal renal perfusion. In patients whose kidneys are under perfused, NSAIDs and ACE inhibitors, when used together, may cause further deterioration in renal function. This interaction is also seen with angiotensin II receptor antagonists (sartans) and NSAIDs.
	Reduced hypotensive effect	ACE inhibitors reduce blood pressure, at least in part, by preventing the breakdown of kinins that stimulate the production of vasodilator and natriuretic PGs. Therefore, NSAIDs might reduce the effect of ACE inhibitors by blocking the production of PGs. Another mechanism of this interaction is the same as with all other antihypertensives.
NSAIDs + other antihypertensive drugs	Reduced hypotensive effect	NSAID use may lead to salt and water retention and thus antagonize the effects of antihypertensive medication.
NSAIDs + low-dose aspirin	Increased risk of GI bleeding	The damaging effects of low-dose aspirin and NSAIDs on the GI tract appear to be additive.
	Possibly reduced cardioprotective effects of low-dose aspirin	The cardioprotective effects of low-dose aspirin are attributed to its ability to irreversibly inhibit COX-1 in platelets and consequently block the production of TxA_2. Other NSAIDs that are COX-1 inhibitors also possess this effect, but it is more short-lived, as they bind reversibly to COX-1. Therefore NSAIDs can competitively inhibit the binding of aspirin to platelets.

TABLE 1.5 Overview of the More Important Pharmacokinetic and Pharmacodynamic Interactions of NSAIDs (Baxter, 2010; British Medical Association, Royal Pharmaceutical Society of Great Britain, 2014; Grosser et al., 2011) (cont.)

Combination	Effect	Comment/(probable) mechanism of interaction
NSAIDs + corticosteroids	Increased risk of GI bleeding and ulceration	Both groups of agents inhibit the production of cytoprotective PGs in the GI mucosa.
NSAIDs + selective serotonin reuptake inhibitors (SSRI) or venlafaxine	Increased risk of bleeding	SSRIs and venlafaxine can lead to serotonin depletion in platelets by blocking its reuptake from the bloodstream. This leads to impairment of hemostatic function and increases the risk of bleeding. This risk is further enhanced by NSAIDs, which also impair platelet function by interfering with the synthesis of TxA_2.
NSAIDs + warfarin	Increased risk of bleeding	This interaction could be both because almost all tNSAIDs temporarily suppress normal platelet function and because some NSAIDs also increase warfarin blood levels (by interfering with its metabolism and/or displacing warfarin from its binding site on plasma proteins).
NSAIDs + other anticoagulants (e.g., dabigatran, heparin, low-molecular weight heparins)	Increased risk of bleeding	This interaction could be because almost all tNSAIDs temporarily suppress normal platelet function by interfering with the synthesis of TxA_2.
NSAIDs + methotrexate	Increased methotrexate toxicity	NSAIDs probably reduce the excretion of methotrexate. Additionally, many NSAIDs are highly bound to plasma proteins and may displace methotrexate from its binding site.
NSAIDs + sulfonylurea hypoglycemic agents	Increased hypoglycemic effect	Certain NSAIDs can increase levels of sulfonylurea agents by interfering with their metabolism and/or displacing them from their binding sites on plasma proteins.
NSAIDs + lithium	Increased lithium toxicity	Certain NSAIDs can reduce the renal excretion of lithium.

Abbreviations: ACE, angiotensin-converting enzyme; COX, cyclooxygenase; GI, gastrointestinal; TxA_2, thromboxane A_2.

1.2 POTENTIAL BENEFITS OF NSAIDS MODIFIED-RELEASE PREPARATIONS

As stated before, one of the most common therapeutic uses of NSAIDs is in chronic treatment of musculoskeletal disorders. With use of relatively high doses, for prolonged periods of time and in elderly population, the incidence of NSAIDs side effects, especially on GI system, is relatively high. Thus, a major challenge for improving therapy with NSAIDs is the reduction of GI side effects. The risk of other side effects (CV or renal) could be minimized by careful evaluation of propensity to develop particular side effect for each patient, and choosing the NSAID with lower risk for inducing such effects and limiting its use to a lowest effective dose and for a shortest period of time.

Besides the use of gastroprotective agents (proton pump inhibitors, H_2 blockers, and misoprostol), that is generally recommended as the first-line strategy for preventing/reducing GI side effects of NSAIDs (Grosser et al., 2011; Naesdal and Brown, 2006; Vonkeman and van de Laar, 2010), topical NSAIDs administration is another possibility of reducing not only their GI, but all systemic side effects. There is substantial evidence that topical NSAIDs offer comparable level of symptom relief as oral NSAIDs in patients with hand or knee OA, with greatly reduced plasma concentrations and systemic side effects (Altman and Barthel, 2011; Rannou et al., 2016; Section 1.2.2).

The rationale for developing *oral modified-release drug-delivery systems* is mainly the prolongation of drugs effect with aim of: (1) reducing the frequency of dosing and improving patient compliance and (2) reducing systemic adverse effects, by means of lowered peak plasma concentrations. While patient compliance is undoubtedly improved with such formulations, reduction of systemic adverse effects with modified-release oral preparations is debatable and seems to depend on the mechanism underlying particular side effect of a particular (class of) drug (Florence and Jani, 1994). In recent times, *modified-release drug-delivery systems for local administration* are also developed, with aim of: (1) minimizing systemic adverse effects and drug–drug interactions, (2) prolonging the action of the drug (thus improving patient compliance), (3) improving release and/or penetration of the drug into the target tissue, and (4) improving local tolerability of the preparation.

The use of oral modified-release NSAIDs preparations is well established, and is especially important for NSAIDs with short half-lives (e.g., diclofenac, ibuprofen). However, developing NSAID modified-release preparations for local administration is the area of intensive research. Modified-release NSAIDs preparations for topical (Table 1.6) and some other local routes [e.g., *intraarticular* (Edwards, 2011; Türker et al., 2008), *ophthalmic* (Das et al., 2012; Ibrahim et al., 2013)] have been developed and tested for their efficacy and tolerability.

In the further text, available data from preclinical and/or clinical studies comparing the therapeutic and/or side effects of modified-release and conventional NSAIDs preparations for oral and topical routes of administration will be discussed, aiming to address the potential benefits of modified-release preparations.

1.2.1   Oral NSAIDs Modified-Release Preparations

It is known that the damage of the upper GI tract involves systemic (inhibition of cytoprotective PG synthesis in GI mucosa) and local mechanisms (irritation due to direct contact of the drug with GI mucosa). Clinical trials have demonstrated that preparations that release NSAIDs (ketoprofen, indomethacin, diclofenac) into small intestine do not have significantly improved gastric tolerability, in comparison with conventional formulations (Bakshi et al., 1993; Collins et al., 1988; Rhymer et al., 1982; Swift et al., 1992). There also appears to be no convincing evidence that the risk of major GI bleeding associated with low-dose aspirin (75 mg daily) is reduced by using enteric-coated or modified-release formulations rather than soluble aspirin (Derry and Loke, 2000; García Rodríguez et al., 2001). Having also in mind that upper GI damage could occur with parenteral and rectal NSAIDs administration as well (Aabakken, 1992; Grosser et al., 2011), systemic mechanism is considered to be a dominant factor in NSAIDs-induced upper GIT damage, and modified-release formulation approaches could not reduce it to a substantial extent.

Mechanism of lower GI tract damage is less well understood, but it could be, at least in part, of local nature, as the degree of lower GI tract irritation correlates with the degree of NSAID/their metabolites enterohepatic circulation (Borazan and Furst, 2015). To that end, it seems possible that modified-release formulations that prolong the contact of NSAIDs with intestinal mucosa could increase the toxicity to distal GI regions (Davies, 1999). Interestingly, aspirin, as well as some other NSAIDs (e.g., piroxicam and coxibs), have been studied with regard to their potential to reduce the formation of adenomatous polyps and colorectal cancer prevention (it is considered that most colorectal cancers develop from adenomatous polyps). Epidemiological studies suggest that frequent use of aspirin is associated with as much as 50% reduction of the risk of colonic cancer (Kune et al., 2007). Two randomized controlled studies (Physician's Health Study and Women's Health Study) demonstrated a significant risk reduction for colonic adenoma incidence with aspirin, in persons with previous history of adenomas (Croswell et al., 2015). The mechanism of this action is currently not known (it is proposed to be related to COX-2 inhibition), and this area requires further investigation, directed both on possible harms and benefits of NSAIDs in the lower GI tract.

Taken together, it can be concluded that NSAIDs-induced upper GI damage could not be relieved by modified-release formulation approaches in clinically significant extent, while the data on the lower GI tract damage is not clear. From the standpoint of NSAIDs treatment GI safety, there is no convincing evidence that modified-release preparation offer an advantage over standard preparations.

1.2.2   Topical NSAIDs Modified-Release Preparations

Topical NSAIDs exerted efficacy comparable to that of oral NSAIDs in relieving symptoms of knee and hands OA, with superior safety profile (Chou et al., 2011; Lin et al., 2004; Simon et al., 2009; Tugwell et al., 2004; Felson, 2015) and they

TABLE 1.6 Animal Studies Comparing Efficacy of Conventional and Modified-Release Topical NSAID Preparations

NSAID	Modified-release topical NSAID preparation	Animal models of inflammation	Findings	References
Diclofenac	Ternary solvent system, microemulsion	Carrageenan-induced paw edema in rats	Selected ternary solvent system showed higher activity than commercial preparation	Escribano et al. (2003)[a]
Ibuprofen	Microemulsion	Carrageenan-induced paw hyperalgesia and edema in rats	Selected microemulsion was more efficacious than the reference hydrogel in exerting antihyperalgesic effects in prophylactic treatment, whereas they were comparable in therapeutic treatment as well as in producing antiedematous effect in both protocols	Djekic et al. (2015)[b]
Naproxen	Microemulsion	Carrageenan-induced paw edema in rats	Selected microemulsion showed higher anti-edematous activity than commercial gel formulation	Okur et al. (2011)[c]
Tenoxicam	Microemulsion-based topical hydrogel	Xylene-induced ear edema in mice; carrageenan-induced paw edema in rats; cotton pellet granuloma test in rats	Microemulsion-based hydrogels showed superior efficacy in controlling inflammation as compared to conventional topical dosage forms	Goindi et al. (2016)[d]
Meloxicam	Nanostructured-lipid carriers gel	Carrageenan-induced paw edema in rats	Meloxicam nanostructured lipid gel showed higher anti-edematous effect than conventional meloxicam gel	Khurana et al. (2013)[e]

[a]Escribano E, Calpena AC, Queralt J, Obach R, Doménech J: Assessment of diclofenac permeation with different formulations: anti-inflammatory study of a selected formula, Eur J Pharm Sci 19:203–210, 2003.
[b]Djekic L, Martinovic M, Stepanović-Petrović R, Tomić M, Micov A, Primorac M: Design of block copolymer costabilized nonionic microemulsions and their in vitro and in vivo assessment as carriers for sustained regional delivery of ibuprofen via topical administration, J Pharm Sci 104:2501–2512, 2015.
[c]Okur UN, Apaydın S, Karabay Yavaşoğlu NÜ, Yavaşoğlu A, Karasulu HY: Evaluation of skin permeation and anti-inflammatory and analgesic effects of new naproxen microemulsion formulations, Int J Pharm 416:136–144, 2011.
[d]Goindi S, Narula M, Kalra A: Microemulsion-based topical hydrogels of tenoxicam for treatment of arthritis, AAPS PharmSciTech, 17:597-606, 2016.
[e]Khurana S, Jain NK, Bedi PM: Development and characterization of a novel controlled release drug delivery system based on nanostructured lipid carriers gel for meloxicam, Life Sci 93:763–772, 2013.

are therefore recommended in international and national guidelines as an early treatment option in this indication (Rannou et al., 2016). The most favorable data exist for topical diclofenac. There is no strong evidence about the efficacy of topical NSAIDs in other chronic musculoskeletal painful conditions, including rheumatoid arthritis (Brayfield, 2014; Derry et al., 2012). In acute conditions such as sprains, strains, and overuse injuries, topical NSAIDs also provided good levels of pain relief probably similar to that of oral NSAID preparations. Formulations of diclofenac, ibuprofen, and ketoprofen provided the best effects (Derry et al., 2015).

Topical NSAIDs can cause local skin irritation on the place of application (Felson, 2015). It is also known that skin penetration of NSAIDs can be highly variable (Dehghanyar et al., 2004; Müller et al., 1997), and that formulation can substantially influence clinical efficacy (Derry et al., 2012). Therefore, improving topical NSAIDs preparations is important way to improve the treatment of acute and chronic musculoskeletal disorders.

Novel formulations of modified-release topical NSAIDs preparations are being extensively developed, characterized, and examined for their efficacy and tolerability. Studies in animal models of inflammation showed their greater or comparable efficacy in comparison with conventional topical preparations (Table 1.6), with favorable safety profile.

1.3 CONCLUSIONS

NSAIDs are widely used for treating musculoskeletal disorders, mild to moderate pain and fever, and aspirin also for secondary CV prevention. Adverse effects limit their use; the most common are effects on GI and CV systems. They may be prevented by performing risk assessments for each patient, choosing a NSAID with low risk for the particular side effect, and limiting its dosage and treatment duration. Gastroprotective agents are recommended for gastroduodenal ulcers prevention. Topical NSAID application offers a possibility for minimization of all systemic NSAIDs side effects, as well as drug–drug interactions. Evidence supports their use in hands and knees osteoarthritis, and probably also for acute musculoskeletal pain. They can cause local skin irritation. Modified-release oral preparations improve patient compliance, and are especially important for short-acting NSAIDs. Topical modified-release preparations could improve efficacy and tolerability of NSAIDs topical treatment, and patient compliance.

ACKNOWLEDGMENT

This work was realized within the framework of the project 175045 supported by the Ministry of Education, Science and Technological Development of Republic of Serbia.

REFERENCES

Aabakken L: Review article: non-steroidal, anti-inflammatory drugs the extending scope of gastrointestinal side effects, *Aliment Pharmacol Ther* 6:143–162, 1992.

Altman RD, Barthel HR: Topical therapies for osteoarthritis, *Drugs* 71:1259–1279, 2011.

Bakshi R, Ezzet N, Frey L, Lasry D, Salliere D: Efficacy and tolerability of diclofenac dispersible in painful osteoarthrosis, *Clin Rheumatol* 12:57–61, 1993.

Baxter K, editor: *Stockley's drug interactions*, ed 9, London, 2010, Pharmaceutical Press.

Bendtsen L, Birk S, Kasch H, Aegidius K, Sørensen PS, Thomsen LL, Poulsen L, Rasmussen MJ, Kruuse C, Jensen R: Danish Headache Society: Reference programme: diagnosis and treatment of headache disorders and facial pain. Danish Headache Society, 2nd Edition, *J Headache Pain* 13(Suppl 1):S1–S29, 2012.

Bendtsen L, Evers S, Linde M, Mitsikostas DD, Sandrini G, Schoenen J: EFNS: EFNS guideline on the treatment of tension-type headache—report of an EFNS task force, *Eur J Neurol* 17:1318–1325, 2010.

Bendtsen L, Fernández-de-la-Peñas C: The role of muscles in tension-type headache, *Curr Pain Headache Rep* 15:451–458, 2011.

Bjorkman DJ: Nonsteroidal anti-inflammatory drug-induced gastrointestinal injury, *Am J Med* 101:25S–32S, 1996.

Borazan NH, Furst DE: Nonsteroidal anti-inflammatory drugs, disease-modifying antirheumatic drugs, nonopioid analgesics, and drugs used in gout. In Katzung BG, Trevor AJ, editors: *Basic & clinical pharmacology, international edition*, ed 13, McGraw-Hill Education, 2015, pp 618–641.

Boutaud O, Aronoff DM, Richardson JH, Marnett LJ, Oates JA: Determinants of the cellular specificity of acetaminophen as an inhibitor of prostaglandin H(2) synthases, *Proc Natl Acad Sci USA* 99:7130–7135, 2002.

Brayfield A, editor: *Martindale: the complete drug reference*, slp ed 38, London, 2014, Pharmaceutical Press.

British Medical Association, Royal Pharmaceutical Society of Great Britain: *British National Formulary (BNF)*, Number 68, London, 2014, British Medical Association and Royal Pharmaceutical Society of Great Britain.

Brune K, Hinz B: The discovery and development of anti-inflammatory drugs, *Arthritis Rheum* 50:2391–2399, 2004.

Brune K, Patrignani P: New insights into the use of currently available non-steroidal anti-inflammatory drugs, *J Pain Res* 8:105–118, 2015.

Brune K, Renner B, Hinz B: Using pharmacokinetic principles to optimize pain therapy, *Nat Rev Rheumatol* 6:589–598, 2010.

Brune K, Zeilhofer HU: Antipyretic analgesics: basic aspects. In McMahon SB, Koltzenburg M, editors: *Wall & Melzack's textbook of pain*, Philadelphia, 2006, Elsevier Churchill Livingstone, pp 459–469.

Brunner M, Dehghanyar P, Seigfried B, Martin W, Menke G, Müller M: Favourable dermal penetration of diclofenac after administration to the skin using a novel spray gel formulation, *Br J Clin Pharmacol* 60:573–577, 2005.

Cannon CP, Curtis SP, FitzGerald GA, Krum H, Kaur A, Bolognese JA, Reicin AS, Bombardier C, Weinblatt ME, van der Heijde D, Erdmann E, Laine L: MEDAL Steering Committee: Cardiovascular outcomes with etoricoxib and diclofenac in patients with osteoarthritis and rheumatoid arthritis in the Multinational Etoricoxib and Diclofenac Arthritis Long-term (MEDAL) programme: a randomised comparison, *Lancet* 368:1771–1781, 2006.

Catella-Lawson F, Reilly MP, Kapoor SC, Cucchiara AJ, DeMarco S, Tournier B, Vyas SN, FitzGerald GA: Cyclooxygenase inhibitors and the antiplatelet effects of aspirin, *N Engl J Med* 345:1809–1817, 2001.

Chou R, McDonagh MS, Nakamoto E, Griffin J: *Analgesics for osteoarthritis: an update of the 2006 comparative effectiveness review*, Rockville, MD, 2011. Available from http://www.ncbi.nlm.nih.gov/pubmedhealth/PMH0016485/pdf/PubMedHealth_PMH0016485.pdf

Collins AJ, Davies J, Dixon AS: A prospective endoscopic study of the effect of Orudis and Oruvail on the upper gastrointestinal tract in patients with osteoarthritis, *Br J Rheumatol* 27:106–109, 1988.

Croswell JM, Brawley OW, Kramer BS: Prevention and early detection of cancer. In Kasper DL, Fauci AS, Hauser SL, Longo DL, Jameson JL, Loscalzo J, editors: *Harrison's principles of internal medicine*, ed 19, New York, 2015, McGraw-Hill Education, pp 475–483.

Cryer B: Mucosal defense and repair. Role of prostaglandins in the stomach and duodenum, *Gastroenterol Clin North Am* 30:877–894, 2001, v–vi.

Das S, Bellare JR, Banerjee R: Protein based nanoparticles as platforms for aspirin delivery for ophthalmologic applications, *Colloids Surf B* 93:161–168, 2012.

Davies NM: Sustained release and enteric coated NSAIDs: are they really GI safe? *J Pharm Pharm Sci* 2:5–14, 1999.

Dehghanyar P, Mayer BX, Namiranian K, Mascher H, Müller M, Brunner M: Topical skin penetration of diclofenac after single- and multiple-dose application, *Int J Clin Pharmacol Ther* 42:353–359, 2004.

Derry S, Loke YK: Risk of gastrointestinal haemorrhage with long term use of aspirin: meta-analysis, *BMJ* 321:1183–1187, 2000.

Derry S, Moore RA, Gaskell H, McIntyre M, Wiffen PJ: Topical NSAIDs for acute musculoskeletal pain in adults, *Cochrane Database Syst Rev* 6:CD007402, 2015.

Derry S, Moore RA, Rabbie R: Topical NSAIDs for chronic musculoskeletal pain in adults, *Cochrane Database Syst Rev* 9:CD007400, 2012.

Edwards SH: Intra-articular drug delivery: the challenge to extend drug residence time within the joint, *Vet J* 190:15–21, 2011.

Efe T, Sagnak E, Roessler PP, Getgood A, Patzer T, Fuchs-Winkelmann S, Peterlein CD, Schofer MD: Penetration of topical diclofenac sodium 4% spray gel into the synovial tissue and synovial fluid of the knee: a randomised clinical trial, *Knee Surg Sports Traumatol Arthrosc* 22:345–350, 2014.

Engblom D, Saha S, Engström L, Westman M, Audoly LP, Jakobsson PJ, Blomqvist A: Microsomal prostaglandin E synthase-1 is the central switch during immune-induced pyresis, *Nat Neurosci* 6:1137–1138, 2003.

Evans JM, McMahon AD, McGilchrist MM, White G, Murray FE, McDevitt DG, MacDonald TM: Topical non-steroidal anti-inflammatory drugs and admission to hospital for upper gastrointestinal bleeding and perforation: a record linkage case-control study, *BMJ* 311:22–26, 1995.

Evans JM, McMahon AD, Murray FE, McDevitt DG, MacDonald TM: Non-steroidal anti-inflammatory drugs are associated with emergency admission to hospital for colitis due to inflammatory bowel disease, *Gut* 40:619–622, 1997.

Evers S, Afra J, Frese A, Goadsby PJ, Linde M, May A, Sándor PS: European Federation of Neurological Societies: EFNS guideline on the drug treatment of migraine—revised report of an EFNS task force, *Eur J Neurol* 16:968–981, 2009.

Felson DT: Osteoarthritis. In Kasper DL, Fauci AS, Hauser SL, Longo DL, Jameson JL, Loscalzo J, editors: *Harrison's principles of internal medicine*, ed 19, New York, 2015, McGraw-Hill Education, pp 2226–2233.

FitzGerald GA, Patrono C: The coxibs, selective inhibitors of cyclooxygenase-2, *N Engl J Med* 345:433–442, 2001.

Florence AT, Jani PU: Novel oral drug formulations. Their potential in modulating adverse effects, *Drug Saf* 10:233–266, 1994.

Frakes EP, Risser RC, Ball TD, Hochberg MC, Wohlreich MM: Duloxetine added to oral nonsteroidal anti-inflammatory drugs for treatment of knee pain due to osteoarthritis: results of a randomized, double-blind, placebo-controlled trial, *Curr Med Res Opin* 27:2361–2372, 2011.

Frölich JC: A classification of NSAIDs according to the relative inhibition of cyclooxygenase isoenzymes, *Trends Pharmacol Sci* 18:30–34, 1997.

García Rodríguez LA, Hernández-Díaz S, de Abajo FJ: Association between aspirin and upper gastrointestinal complications: systematic review of epidemiologic studies, *Br J Clin Pharmacol* 52:563–571, 2001.

García Rodríguez LA, Varas-Lorenzo C, Maguire A, González-Pérez A: Nonsteroidal anti-inflammatory drugs and the risk of myocardial infarction in the general population, *Circulation* 109:3000–3006, 2004.

Gilron I, Jensen TS, Dickenson AH: Combination pharmacotherapy for management of chronic pain: from bench to bedside, *Lancet Neurol* 12:1084–1095, 2013.

Gilron I, Orr E, Tu D, O'Neill JP, Zamora JE, Bell AC: A placebo-controlled randomized clinical trial of perioperative administration of gabapentin, rofecoxib and their combination for spontaneous and movement-evoked pain after abdominal hysterectomy, *Pain* 113:191–200, 2005.

Gleeson MH, Lim SH, Spencer D: Non-steroidal anti-inflammatory drugs, salicylates, and colitis, *Lancet* 347:904–905, 1996.

Goodwin JL, Kraemer JJ, Bajwa ZH: The use of opioids in the treatment of osteoarthritis: when, why, and how? *Curr Rheumatol Rep* 11:5–14, 2009.

Grosser T, Fries S, FitzGerald GA: Biological basis for the cardiovascular consequences of COX-2 inhibition: therapeutic challenges and opportunities, *J Clin Invest* 116:4–15, 2006.

Grosser T, Smith EM, FitzGerald GA: Anti-inflammatory, antipyretic and analgesic agents; pharmacotherapy of gout. In Brunton LL, Chabner BA, Knollmann BC, editors: *Goodman & Gilman's the pharmacological basis of therapeutics*, ed 12, New York, 2011, McGraw-Hill Medical Publishing Division, pp 959–1004.

Hawkey CJ: COX-2 inhibitors, *Lancet* 353:307–314, 1999.

Hernández-Díaz S, Varas-Lorenzo C, García Rodríguez LA: Non-steroidal anti-inflammatory drugs and the risk of acute myocardial infarction, *Basic Clin Pharmacol Toxicol* 98:266–274, 2006.

Hunter DJ, Felson DT: Osteoarthritis, *BMJ* 332:639–642, 2006.

Hurley RW, Chatterjea D, Rose Feng M, Taylor CP, Hammond DL: Gabapentin and pregabalin can interact synergistically with naproxen to produce antihyperalgesia, *Anesthesiology* 97:1263–1273, 2002.

Ibrahim MM, Abd-Elgawad AE, Soliman OA, Jablonski MM: Nanoparticle-based topical ophthalmic formulations for sustained celecoxib release, *J Pharm Sci* 102:1036–1053, 2013.

Johnson AG, Nguyen TV, Day RO: Do nonsteroidal anti-inflammatory drugs affect blood pressure? A meta-analysis, *Ann Intern Med* 121:289–300, 1994.

Jones CK, Peters SC, Shannon HE: Synergistic interactions between the dual serotonergic, noradrenergic reuptake inhibitor duloxetine and the non-steroidal anti-inflammatory drug ibuprofen in inflammatory pain in rodents, *Eur J Pain* 11:208–215, 2007.

Jouzeau JY, Terlain B, Abid A, Nédélec E, Netter P: Cyclo-oxygenase isoenzymes. How recent findings affect thinking about nonsteroidal anti-inflammatory drugs, *Drugs* 53:563–582, 1997.

Kearney PM, Baigent C, Godwin J, Halls H, Emberson JR, Patrono C: Do selective cyclo-oxygenase-2 inhibitors and traditional non-steroidal anti-inflammatory drugs increase the risk of atherothrombosis? Meta-analysis of randomised trials, *BMJ* 332:1302–1308, 2006.

Kune GA, Kune S, Watson LF: Colorectal cancer risk, chronic illnesses, operations and medications: case control results from the Melbourne Colorectal Cancer Study. 1988, *Int J Epidemiol* 36:951–957, 2007.

Lin J, Zhang W, Jones A, Doherty M: Efficacy of topical non-steroidal anti-inflammatory drugs in the treatment of osteoarthritis: meta-analysis of randomised controlled trials, *BMJ* 329:324, 2004.

Loboz KK, Shenfield GM: Drug combinations and impaired renal function—the 'triple whammy', *Br J Clin Pharmacol* 59:239–243, 2005.

Mallet C, Eschalier A: Pharmacology and mechanism of action of acetaminophen. In Beaulieu P, Lussier D, Porreca F, Dickenson AH, editors: *Pharmacology of pain*, Seattle, 2010, IASP Press, pp 65–85.

Marjoribanks J, Proctor ML, Farquhar C: Nonsteroidal anti-inflammatory drugs for primary dysmenorrhoea, *Cochrane Database Syst Rev* 4:CD001751, 2003.

McAdam BF, Mardini IA, Habib A, Burke A, Lawson JA, Kapoor S, FitzGerald GA: Effect of regulated expression of human cyclooxygenase isoforms on eicosanoid and isoeicosanoid production in inflammation, *J Clin Invest* 105:1473–1482, 2000.

McGettigan P, Henry D: Cardiovascular risk and inhibition of cyclooxygenase: a systematic review of the observational studies of selective and nonselective inhibitors of cyclooxygenase 2, *JAMA* 296:1633–1644, 2006.

Mills PC, Magnusson BM, Cross SE: Penetration of a topically applied nonsteroidal anti-inflammatory drug into local tissues and synovial fluid of dogs, *Am J Vet Res* 66:1128–1132, 2005.

Müller M, Mascher H, Kikuta C, Schäfer S, Brunner M, Dorner G, Eichler HG: Diclofenac concentrations in defined tissue layers after topical administration, *Clin Pharmacol Ther* 62:293–299, 1997.

Naesdal J, Brown K: NSAID-associated adverse effects and acid control aids to prevent them, *Drug Saf* 29:119–132, 2006.

Noroian G, Clive D: Cyclo-oxygenase-2 inhibitors and the kidney: a case for caution, *Drug Saf* 25:165–172, 2002.

O'Callaghan CA, Andrews PA, Ogg CS: Renal disease and use of topical non-steroidal anti-inflammatory drugs, *BMJ* 308:110–111, 1994.

O'Dell JR: Therapeutic strategies for rheumatoid arthritis, *N Engl J Med* 350:2591–2602, 2004.

Pelletier JP, Martel-Pelletier J, Rannou F, Cooper C: Efficacy and safety of oral NSAIDs and analgesics in the management of osteoarthritis: evidence from real-life setting trials and surveys, *Semin Arthritis Rheum* 45:S22–S27, 2016.

Perazella MA, Tray K: Selective cyclooxygenase-2 inhibitors: a pattern of nephrotoxicity similar to traditional nonsteroidal anti-inflammatory drugs, *Am J Med* 111:64–67, 2001.

Pulichino AM, Rowland S, Wu T, Clark P, Xu D, Mathieu MC, Riendeau D, Audoly LP: Prostacyclin antagonism reduces pain and inflammation in rodent models of hyperalgesia and chronic arthritis, *J Pharmacol Exp Ther* 319:1043–1050, 2006.

Rahme E, Bernatsky S: NSAIDs and risk of lower gastrointestinal bleeding, *Lancet* 376:146–148, 2010.

Rang HP, Ritter JM, Flower RJ, Henderson G, editors: Local hormones 1: histamine and the biologically active lipids. In *Rang & Dale's pharmacology. International edition*, ed 8, London, 2015a, Elsevier Churchill Livingstone, pp 212–221.

Rang HP, Ritter JM, Flower RJ, Henderson G, editors: Anti-inflammatory and immunosuppressant drugs. In *Rang & Dale's pharmacology. International edition*, ed 8, London, 2015b, Elsevier Churchill Livingstone, pp 317–334.

Rang HP, Ritter JM, Flower RJ, Henderson G, editors: The kidney and urinary system. In *Rang & Dale's Pharmacology. International Edition*, ed 8, London, 2015c, Elsevier Churchill Livingstone, pp 367–379.

Rang HP, Ritter JM, Flower RJ, Henderson G, editors: The gastrointestinal tract. In *Rang & Dale's Pharmacology. International Edition*, ed 8, London, 2015d, Elsevier Churchill Livingstone, pp 367–379.

Rannou F, Pelletier JP, Martel-Pelletier J: Efficacy and safety of topical NSAIDs in the management of osteoarthritis: evidence from real-life setting trials and surveys, *Semin Arthritis Rheum* 45:S18–S21, 2016.

Rhymer AR, Hart CB, Daurio C: A double-blind trial comparing indomethacin sustained release capsules (Indocid-R) with indomethacin capsules in patients with rheumatoid arthritis, *Rheumatol Rehabil* 21:101–106, 1982.

Sarzi-Puttini P, Cimmino MA, Scarpa R, Caporali R, Parazzini F, Zaninelli A, Atzeni F, Canesi B: Osteoarthritis: an overview of the disease and its treatment strategies, *Semin Arthritis Rheum* 35(1 Suppl 1):1–10, 2005.

Sawynok J: Caffeine and pain, *Pain* 152:726–729, 2011.

Shah AE, St. Clair WE: Rheumatoid arthritis. In Kasper DL, Fauci AS, Hauser SL, Longo DL, Jameson JL, Loscalzo J, editors: *Harrison's principles of internal medicine*, ed 19, New York, 2015, McGraw-Hill Education, pp 2136–2149.

Sharma L: Osteoarthritis year in review 2015: clinical, *Osteoarthritis Cartilage* 24:36–48, 2016.

Simon LS: Nonsteroidal anti-inflammatory drugs and their risk: a story still in development, *Arthritis Res Ther* 15(Suppl 3):S1, 2013.

Simon LS, Grierson LM, Naseer Z, Bookman AA, Zev Shainhouse J: Efficacy and safety of topical diclofenac containing dimethyl sulfoxide (DMSO) compared with those of topical placebo, DMSO vehicle and oral diclofenac for knee osteoarthritis, *Pain* 143:238–245, 2009.

Smyth EM, Grosser T, FitzGerald GA: Lipid-derived autacoids: eicosanoids and platelet-activating factor. In Brunton LL, Chabner BA, Knollmann BC, editors: *Goodman & Gilman's the pharmacological basis of therapeutics*, ed 12, New York, 2011, McGraw-Hill Medical Publishing Division, pp 937–958.

Smyth EM, Grosser T, Wang M, Yu Y, FitzGerald GA: Prostanoids in health and disease, *J Lipid Res* 50(Suppl):S423–S428, 2009.

Stepanović-Petrović RM, Tomić MA, Vučković SM, Poznanović G, Ugrešić ND, Prostran MŠ, Bošković B: Pharmacological interaction between oxcarbazepine and two COX inhibitors in a rat model of inflammatory hyperalgesia, *Pharmacol Biochem Behav* 97:611–618, 2011.

Swift GL, Arnold J, Williams GT, Williams BD, Rhodes J, Khan F: A comparison of upper gastrointestinal mucosal damage by standard and delayed-release indomethacin, *Aliment Pharmacol Ther* 6:717–725, 1992.

The electronic Medicines Compendium (eMC), 2016. Available from https://www.medicines.org.uk/emc

Tomić MA, Micov AM, Stepanović-Petrović RM: Levetiracetam interacts synergistically with nonsteroidal analgesics and caffeine to produce antihyperalgesia in rats, *J Pain* 14:1371–1382, 2013.

Towheed TE, Maxwell L, Judd MG, Catton M, Hochberg MC, Wells G: Acetaminophen for osteoarthritis, *Cochrane Database Syst Rev* 1:CD004257, 2006.

Tugwell PS, Wells GA, Shainhouse JZ: Equivalence study of a topical diclofenac solution (pennsaid) compared with oral diclofenac in symptomatic treatment of osteoarthritis of the knee: a randomized controlled trial, *J Rheumatol* 31:2002–2012, 2004.

Türker S, Erdoğan S, Ozer YA, Bilgili H, Deveci S: Enhanced efficacy of diclofenac sodium-loaded lipogelosome formulation in intra-articular treatment of rheumatoid arthritis, *J Drug Target* 16:51–57, 2008.

Vane JR: The fight against rheumatism: from willow bark to COX-1 sparing drugs, *J Physiol Pharmacol* 51:573–586, 2000.

Vanegas H, Schaible HG: Prostaglandins and cyclooxygenases in the spinal cord, *Prog Neurobiol* 64:327–363, 2001.

Vonkeman HE, van de Laar MAFJ: Nonsteroidal anti-inflammatory drugs: adverse effects and their prevention, *Semin Arthritis Rheum* 39:294–312, 2010.

Walde HJ: Konzentration von Etofenamat in intra- und periartikulären Geweben nach perkutaner Applikation beim Menschen.Topische Behandlung mit nicht- steroidalen Antirheumatika. 4. Int. Etofenamat-Symposium vom 18-21.6.1987 in Stresa, Italien: pmi-Verlag Frankfurt/Main, Derneue Weg, 1987, pp S91–S94.

Warner TD, Giuliano F, Vojnovic I, Bukasa A, Mitchell JA, Vane JR: Nonsteroid drug selectivities for cyclo-oxygenase-1 rather than cyclo-oxygenase-2 are associated with human gastrointestinal toxicity: a full in vitro analysis, *Proc Natl Acad Sci USA* 96:7563–7568, 1999.

Weitz JI: Antiplatelet, anticoagulant, and fibrinolytic drugs. In Kasper DL, Fauci AS, Hauser SL, Longo DL, Jameson JL, Loscalzo J, editors: *Harrison's principles of internal medicine*, ed 19, New York, 2015, McGraw-Hill Education, pp 745–760.

Williams HJ, Ward JR, Egger MJ, Neuner R, Brooks RH, Clegg DO, Field EH, Skosey JL, Alarcón GS, Willkens RF, et al: Comparison of naproxen and acetaminophen in a two-year study of treatment of osteoarthritis of the knee, *Arthritis Rheum* 36:1196–1206, 1993.

Zhang WY, Li Wan Po A: Efficacy of minor analgesics in primary dysmenorrhoea: a systematic review, *Br J Obstet Gynaecol* 105:780–789, 1998.

Zhou Y, Boudreau DM, Freedman AN: Trends in the use of aspirin and nonsteroidal anti-inflammatory drugs in the general U.S. population, *Pharmacoepidemiol Drug Saf* 23:43–50, 2014.

Chapter 2

Polymeric Microparticles and Inorganic Micro/Nanoparticulate Drug Carriers: An Overview and Pharmaceutical Application

Danina Krajišnik*, Bojan Čalija*, Nebojša Cekić**

*Department of Pharmaceutical Technology and Cosmetology, Faculty of Pharmacy, University of Belgrade, Belgrade, Serbia; **Faculty of Technology, University of Niš; R&D Sector, DCP Hemigal, Leskovac, Serbia

2.1 INTRODUCTION

A number of limitations associated with use of conventional drug delivery systems have led to the development of various micro- and nanosized drug carriers, such as microparticles, nanoparticles, micelles, liposomes, virosomes, nanocomplexes, polymer–drug conjugates, and dendrimers. These carriers are designed with aim to improve therapeutic outcomes and/or reduce drug's adverse effects, by providing protection of the entrapped drug against in vivo degradation, accumulation in pathological areas, releasing drug in desired manner, improving drug solubility and/or reducing its immunogenicity (Hafner et al., 2014; Lam and Gambari 2014; Torchilin, 2012). Additionally, small sizes make these carriers suitable for different routes of administration allowing their direct administration at site of action. Design of an effective delivery system comprises a thorough understanding of the drug, the disease, and the target site (Mahato and Narang, 2012), as well as materials and techniques available for their preparation (Tran et al., 2011).

Rapid progress in material science has contributed to the significant advancement in this field in the last two decades. A wide variety of materials of both natural and synthetic origin with diverse physicochemical properties are nowadays available for preparation of micro- and nanosized drug carriers. Among them, biodegradable polymers are of particular importance due to biocompatibility,

Microsized and Nanosized Carriers for NSAIDs. http://dx.doi.org/10.1016/B978-0-12-804017-1.00002-9
31

versatility, and possibility of functionalization (Freiberg and Zhu, 2004). The latter means that they can be designed or mixed with other materials to meet the specific requirements, such as stability, acceptable size, morphology, encapsulation efficiency, and drug loading capacity or sensitivity to biological stimuli (Elsabahy and Wooley, 2012). Polymeric microparticles are excellent example of how these materials can be employed to improve therapeutic outcomes and patient compliance of some well-known drugs via modified release and/or direct application on the site of action.

Recently, structured porous inorganic materials have also received considerable attention in this field. High chemical and mechanical stability under the array of physiological conditions along with hydrophilic character, high surface-to-volume ratio and tailorable structure (Arruebo, 2012; Perioli and Pagano, 2012; Wu et al., 2011) are some of the characteristics important for their application in drug delivery. For these reasons, many porous inorganic materials are currently being investigated, such as silica-based micro- or mesoporous materials, mesoporous carbons, porous silicon, ceramic, and carbon-based nanotubes, aluminosilicates and layered silicates (Arruebo, 2012; Perioli and Pagano, 2012; Siefker et al., 2014; Wang et al., 2015). Organized porosity of these materials allows the release of their protected cargo (adsorbed or encapsulated drug, gene, or protein) in different manner (immediate and sustained drug delivery) or under the influence of various biological stimuli (stimuli-responsive and targeted drug delivery). Possibility of pore-wall functionalization of several representatives of these materials [i.e., mesoporous silica nanoparticles (MSNs)] which affects drug capacity, polarity, and drug-release properties is another advantage making them particularly interesting as potential drug carriers (Argyo et al., 2014; Arruebo, 2012; Chen et al., 2016).

This chapter briefly reviews characteristics, methods of preparation/functionalization, and pharmaceutical application of polymeric microparticles and inorganic micro/nanoparticulate carries, useful for a subsequent understanding of their application for delivery of nonsteroidal anti-inflammatory drugs discussed in Chapters 5 and 8.

2.2 POLYMERIC MICROPARTICLES AS DRUG CARRIERS

In general, a term microparticles is used to describe particles with a diameter between 1 and 1000 µm (Singh et al., 2010). From a morphological standpoint, two general types of microparticles can be distinguished: microcapsules, consisting of clearly defined solid, liquid, or gaseous drug-containing core and surrounding shell material (reservoir system), and microspheres, in which drug is dissolved or dispersed throughout the solid matrix (matrix system) (Fig. 2.1) (Nordstierna et al., 2010; Singh et al., 2010).

The commonly used microencapsulating agents are polymers of both natural and synthetic origin. In recent years, attention has been focused on

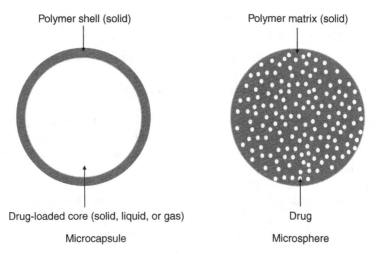

Microcapsule   Microsphere

FIGURE 2.1   Schematic representation of two general types of microparticles.

microparticles consisting natural, nontoxic, biodegradable, biocompatible, low cost, and abundant polymers, such as polysaccharides (e.g., starch, alginate, pectin, dextran, pullulan, and gums) and proteins (e.g., albumin, gelatin, collagen, gluten) (Prajapati et al., 2015; Tonessen and Karlsen, 2002; Yang et al., 2015). Among semisynthetic encapsulating polymers, the most frequently used are chitosan and cellulose derivatives, such as carboxymethylcellulose (CMC), carboxymethylcellulose sodium (NaCMC) and ethylcellulose (EC) (Huang et al., 2006). Synthetic biodegradable microencapsulating polymers are aliphatic poly(ester)s consisting of lactic and glycolic acid, as well as copolymer poly(lactic-co-glycolic acid) (PLGA), poly(3-hydroxybutyrate) (PHB), and poly(ε-caprolactone) (PCL) (Lassalle and Ferreira, 2007; Prajapati et al., 2015; Versypt et al., 2013), whereas PLGA represents the "gold standard" of biodegradable polymers having widespread commercial application in drug delivery systems (Wischke and Schwendeman, 2008).

2.2.1   Microencapsulation Techniques

Microencapsulation is a term that represents range of techniques for microparticles production, that is, techniques used to encase solids, liquids, or gases inside matrix or shell, mainly consisting of biodegradable polymeric materials (Ghosh, 2006). Continuous improvement of these techniques can be ascribed to the strict requirements of regulatory authorities related to use of organic solvents and surface active agents, as well as the nature of new active pharmaceutical ingredients. That is, a number of these actives, such as biological drugs/biopharmaceutics, exhibit high sensitivity to the environmental conditions. Selection of optimal microencapsulation technique depends on the characteristics of the both polymer and drug and requires the following considerations:

- possible influence of microencapsulation procedure on stability and pharmacodynamic activity of the drug (Tran et al., 2011),
- drug encapsulation efficiency and loading (Tran et al., 2011; Yeo and Park, 2004),
- desired size, shape, surface properties, and dispersibility of microparticles (easy administration to the target site) (Bock et al., 2011; Prajapati et al., 2015),
- desired drug release profiles in order to increase therapeutic efficacy and/or minimize side effects (Prajapati et al., 2015; Tran et al., 2011),
- batch-to-batch reproducibility (Bock et al., 2011),
- feasibility for large-scale production (Puel et al., 2006; Tran et al., 2011), and
- process-cost, complexity, and environmental safety aspects.

Depending on nature of the microparticles formation mechanism, microencapsulation techniques can be classified into three categories: chemical, physicochemical, and physicomechanical (Jamekhorshid et al., 2014; Lam and Gambari, 2014). Brief overview of common microencapsulation techniques, their main advantages, and drawbacks are given in Table 2.1.

2.2.1.1 Chemical Microencapsulation Techniques

The most common chemical techniques are interfacial and in situ polymerization (Ghosh, 2006; Jyothi et al., 2010).

Interfacial polymerization. This method involves polymerization of two reactive monomers, each soluble in one phase of an emulsion, at water/oil emulsion interfaces (Arshady, 1989; Jyothi et al., 2010). Depending on the type of emulsion (oil-in-water or water-in-oil), it can be used for encapsulation of various core materials, including hydrophobic and hydrophilic drugs, as well as their solutions in water or in water-immiscible liquids. If the resulting polymer is soluble in the emulsion droplets, this process leads to the formation of microspheres. Otherwise, the polymer forms shell around droplets which results in the microcapsule formation (Arshady, 1989). The main disadvantage of this method is related to the use of potentially toxic organic solvent and monomers and their complete removal from the final product (Finch and Bodmeier, 2000; Vemmer and Patel, 2013).

In situ polymerization. Like interfacial polymerization, this method is based on polymerization of two reactive monomers. However, both the monomers used for in situ polymerization are soluble in the continuous phase of emulsion, so the polymerization takes place in continuous phase. The monomers first form low molecular weight prepolymer. As the prepolymer grows, it deposits on the surface of dispersed core material, resulting in formation of microcapsules (Brown et al., 2003; Jyothi et al., 2010). This method is particularly suitable for encapsulation of liquid actives or their solutions (Thies, 1996).

TABLE 2.1 Common Microencapsulation Techniques and Their Main Advantages/Disadvantages

Group	Technique	Advantages	Disadvantages	References
Chemical	Interfacial polymerization	High encapsulation efficiency Easy product recovery	Possible reaction between reagent and active Difficult to control polymerization	Yeo et al. (2001) Desai and Park (2005)
	In situ polymerization	Easy product recovery	Difficult removal of chemicals	Brown et al. (2003)
Physicochemical	Coacervation	Applicable to encapsulation of all actives dispersible in liquid Controllable particle size	Expensive and complex technique Possible particles agglomeration Requires additional crosslinking Difficult scaling-up for industrial production	Desai and Park (2005) Dubey et al. (2009) Yeo et al. (2001)
	Ionic gelation	Mild reaction conditions	High microparticles permeability	Fundueanu et al. (1999) Yeo et al. (2001)
Physicomechanical	Spray drying	Available for industrial application One-step, closed procedure Time effective Allows production of microparticles under aseptic conditions	Possible polymorphic transformations Low production yield (considerable drug loss due to sticking to the chamber wall) Polymers can be used in limited concentration since high viscosity liquids cannot be sprayed	Park and Yeo (2007) Yeo et al. (2001)
	Fluidized-bed coating technique	Available for industrial application Controllable process parameters	Liquids can be encapsulated only if previously absorbed onto porous solids Possible particles agglomeration	Desai and Park (2005) Fang and Bhandari (2012)
	Solvent evaporation/ extraction	Allows encapsulation of low molecular weight actives	Use of organic solvents	Prajapati et al. (2015) Yeo et al. (2001)

2.2.1.2 Physicochemical Microencapsulation Techniques

The most often used physicochemical microencapsulation techniques are coacervation/phase separation, ionic gelation, and sol–gel encapsulation (Jamekhorshid et al., 2014; Jyothi et al., 2010).

Coacervation/phase separation. Coacervation is among the oldest encapsulation techniques and the first one used for the industrial production of microcapsules (Jyothi et al., 2010). It is based on phase separation of a homogeneous polymer solution into two phases, one dense and rich in polymer (coacervate) and the other liquid with low polymer content (Park and Yeo, 2007). Depending on the number of the polymers involved, coacervation can be simple or complex. Simple coacervation is based on use of only one polymer and the phase separation can be triggered by polymer desolvation, usually by addition of inorganic salts, nonsolvents, temperature change (Park and Yeo, 2007; Jyothi et al., 2010). On the other hand, complex coacervation involves addition of oppositely charged polymer to the polymer solution and ability of these polymers to interact in water and form polymer-rich phase. Given that formation of the coacervates is based on electrostatic interactions, pH value of reaction medium is critical process parameter (Burgess and Hickey, 2007; Park and Yeo, 2007). Microparticles obtained by coacervation usually require additional stabilization by crosslinking or thermal treatment (Burgess and Hickey, 2007; Jyothi et al., 2010).

Ionic gelation. This method is based on the ability of polyelectrolytes to crosslink in the presence of oppositely charged ions and form hydrogels (Lam and Gambari, 2014). It has been used for encapsulation of various actives by using polyanions, such as alginates, gellan gum, CMC, and polycations, such as chitosan, as polymeric gelling agents (Prajapati et al., 2015). Several approaches have been proposed to obtain more or less spherical crosslinked microparticles, including emulsification and extrusion techniques.

In emulsification technique water insoluble salt of crosslinking ions is dispersed in solution/dispersion of drug in polymer solution. Thereafter, this phase is emulsified in appropriate oil phase containing lipophilic emulsion stabilizer until W/O emulsion is formed. Then, organic acid soluble in oil phase is added under stirring to release crosslinking ions from the insoluble salt, causing gelling of aqueous polymer solution and subsequent formation of microparticles (Reis et al., 2006)

Extrusion techniques are based on drop-wise addition of drug dispersion/solution in polyelectrolyte solution into gelling bath containing counter ions. What distinguishes them is the way of droplets formation. Depending on the way of droplets formation and enhancements of the dropping into gelling bath, four techniques can be differentiated:

- Coaxial air-flow (AirJet technique) where generation of single droplets happens at the nozzle tip while the dropping is enhanced with laminar flow of air coming out from concentric outer nozzle (Cekić et al., 2007; Prusse et al., 2008).

- Electrostatic technique differs from previous one only by the way enhancement of dropping is accomplished (Bugarski et al., 1994). Here electric field is utilized for that purpose, strength of which can greatly influence droplet size, apart from nozzle diameter and flow rate. Electrostatic and AirJet techniques are limited to lab-scale applications (Prusse et al., 2008).
- Vibration technique utilizes vibration applied on laminar fluid jet which breaks into droplet if the right frequency is applied (Heinzen et al., 2002). Microparticles size is adjusted by the nozzle diameter, viscosity of the fluid, and frequency of vibrations applied. Vibration technique could be used for larger scale applications when multinozzle modification is applied (Prusse et al., 2008).
- JetCutter technique generates droplets by cutting the liquid jet by rotating cutting wires. This technique has the highest throughput and is best one suitable for scaling-up to industrial level of production (Prusse et al., 2008).

This technique is fast, relatively simple, and allows microparticles formation in aqueous environment at room temperature. On the other hand, the main drawback is low mechanical strength and high permeability of microparticles (Lam and Gambari, 2014). For further stabilization, microparticles obtained by ionic gelation are usually reinforced by polyelectrolyte complexation with oppositely charged polyelectrolytes (Fig. 2.2) (Calija et al., 2013; Cekic et al., 2009).

FIGURE 2.2   Scanning electron micrograph of naproxen-loaded Ca-alginate microparticles reinforced with oligochitosan via polyelectrolyte complexation.

2.2.1.3 Physicomechanical Microencapsulation Techniques

Commonly used physicomechanical techniques are spray drying, fluid-bed coating, solvent evaporation, pan coating, and centrifugal techniques (Ghosh, 2006; Jyothi et al., 2010; Jamekhorshid et al., 2014).

Spray drying. This technique is widely used in food, chemical, pharmaceutical, and biochemical industries for various applications, including microencapsulation (Gharsallaoui et al., 2007; Sollohub and Cal, 2010). Basically, it is a continuous one-step and close-system process where drug is dissolved or dispersed in concentrated polymer solution and sprayed into hot gaseous medium of the spray dryer chamber (Lam and Gambari, 2014; Park and Yeo, 2007). As a consequence of solvent evaporation, the polymer rapidly solidifies around drug particles, which results in formation of either microspheres or polynuclear microparticles (Jyothi et al., 2010; Lam and Gambari, 2014).

Fluidized-bed coating technique. This technique, also known as air-suspension technique involves suspension of active material in high-velocity air stream followed by spraying with polymer solution, melt or dispersible (coating medium) (Burgess and Hickey, 2007). Solidification and subsequent microparticles formation is simply achieved by solvent evaporation or cooling. The coating medium can be introduced in fluid bed chamber from the top, bottom, and tangentially (Jyothi et al., 2010). Possible agglomeration of particles is one of the main drawbacks of this technique (Fang and Bhandari, 2012).

Solvent evaporation. In this method, drug is dissolved or dispersed in the polymer solution in volatile organic solvent. Thereafter, the mixture is emulsified in water containing emulsifying agent to obtain emulsion. Once the emulsion is formed, the organic solvent is removed by evaporation at elevated temperatures. As a consequence of solvent evaporation, polymer shrinks around the drug forming microcapsules (Lam and Gambari, 2014; Prajapati et al., 2015).

2.2.2 Characteristics of Polymeric Microparticles

Depending on the field of application of polymeric microparticles and on their nature, characterization may vary to a certain extent, but the following properties are of particular importance: particles size and size distribution, morphology, drug loading, encapsulation efficiency, physicochemical state of the drug and the polymer, drug release profile, and particles degradation.

Microparticles size affects in vivo performance and determines possible routes of administration. Particles ranging between 1 and 5 µm are ideal targeting systems for vaccines and immunomodulators and exhibit efficient disposition in the respiratory tract upon pulmonary administration (Rawat et al., 2008; Wattendorf et al., 2008). Particles smaller than 25 µm in diameter are used in ocular systems, due to eye sensitivity on presence of larger particles (Florence and Siepmann, 2009). Particles ranging from 10 to 250 µm in diameter are small enough to be easily administered via intramuscular or subcutaneous injection by using standard needles and large enough to avoid uptake by macrophage cells (Tran et al., 2011). Size dependency was confirmed for gastrointestinal adsorption and deposition of microparticles in the inflamed regions of lower parts of GIT (Lamprecht et al., 2001; Wei et al., 2008). Besides, particles size is inversely proportional to the surface area, so the small size makes them more available for adsorption/desorption (Dubey et al., 2009). Smaller particles have larger surface area accessible for functionalization, which is commonly used to improve binding to target tissues (Kohane, 2007). On the other hand, smaller particles aggregate more easily. It was found that microparticles size affects drug loading, porosity, and drug release rate, which is also important for potential application of these drug carriers (Siepmann et al., 2004). Therefore, wide or multimodal size distribution of microparticles may cause significant variability in particles in vivo performance. To address this problem, significant efforts have been lately devoted to the development of techniques for production of uniform-size or monodispersed microparticles (Tran et al., 2011).

Drug loading or loading capacity, which is usually expressed as mass percentage of drug to total mass of dried microparticles, is another important characteristic for the potential use (Ye et al., 2010). Generally, high drug loadings are desirable, especially if the particles are intended for prolonged delivery of drugs with high therapeutic doses (Freiberg and Zhu, 2004; Ye et al., 2010). Encapsulation efficiency describes what percentage of the starting amount of drug is successfully entrapped in the microparticles (Ye et al., 2010). The higher the encapsulation efficiency, the lesser is the loss of drug during encapsulation procedure. Therefore, high values of encapsulation efficiency are highly desirable. Drug loading and encapsulation efficiency depend on numerous factors, including the nature of drug and polymer, their starting concentrations and microencapsulation conditions/technique (Jain 2000; Park and Yeo, 2007). Influence of many factors, as well as their interaction, make prediction and control of encapsulation efficiency and drug loading quite difficult (Calija et al., 2011). From the industry standpoint, both drug loading and encapsulation efficiency are critical parameters, especially if the actives are highly expensive substances, such as proteins.

The drug release rate from polymeric microparticles is key feature for their potential application. It is determined by properties of both drug and polymer, especially by polymer solubility and biodegradability, drug/polymer ratio, distribution of the drug within particles, size, surface area, and porosity of microparticles and microencapsulation conditions/technique (Burgess and Hickey, 2007; Calija et al., 2011; Yang et al., 2000).

2.2.3 Pharmaceutical Application of Polymeric Microparticles

Application of polymeric microparticles as carriers for various active pharmaceutical ingredients, including drugs, genes, and cells has been extensively studied in the last few decades. Owing to their small size, these carriers can be easily administered via different routes, such as: oral (Adebisi and Conway, 2011), buccal (Sudhakar et al., 2006), ocular (Addo et al., 2015), nasal (Chaturvedi et al., 2011, topical (Lam and Gambari, 2014), and pulmonary (El-Sherbiny et al., 2010) and parenteral (Shi and Li, 2005). The possibility of direct administration of the encapsulated drug to the site of action allows dose reduction and subsequent minimization of side effects (Siepmann and Siepmann, 2006).

Microencapsulation is a useful strategy to solve in vitro and in vivo drug stability issues or to prevent unwanted drug–excipients interactions in the final formulation. Depending on the properties of encapsulating polymer and microencapsulation conditions, microparticles can extend shelf-life of various actives through their protection from ambient conditions, such as moisture, oxygen, light, and temperature during processing and storage (Abbas et al., 2012). Moreover, this approach is useful for protection of highly sensitive actives, such as peptides, proteins, and cells, from enzymatic degradation and immune response upon administration (Hernández et al., 2010; Tan et al., 2010).

Encapsulation of powders into microparticles can be useful solution for manufacturing complications related with dusting, hygroscopicity, and poor flowability of powders (Desai and Park, 2005). Unpleasant taste of some drugs can be efficiently masked by microencapsulation, usually in suspensions or tablets as final dosage forms (Ayenew et al., 2009; Sohi et al., 2004). Microencapsulation of sticky, viscous liquids into solids of appropriate spherical morphology can further improve technical operations, such as filling, mixing, and tableting (Burgess and Hickey, 2007).

The leading reason for microencapsulation is to achieve modified, in most cases sustained drug release. Slow release of encapsulated drug in a controlled manner allows reduction of dosage frequency, which is especially convenient for drugs with a short half-life, reduces fluctuations of drug–plasma concentrations, and therefore, minimizes side effects, improves patient compliance and overall therapeutic outcome. All commercially available drug-loaded polymeric microparticles, presented in Table 2.2 are intended for sustained drug delivery. These drugs are mainly intended for intramuscular or subcutaneous administration with dosage frequency approximately from 2 weeks to 4 months.

Microparticles can be designed to target specific area in the body. This can be achieved by using polymers sensitive to internal stimuli (e.g., pH, ionic strength, temperature), surface functionalization with site-specific ligands (active targeting) or by external stimuli to direct microparticles to the target area (physical targeting) (Park et al., 2010).

Cell microencapsulation is a promising alternative for conventional transplantation therapy without immune rejection and effective strategy for treatment of chronic diseases by sustained release of de novo synthesized therapeutic products of encapsulated cells (Hernández et al., 2010; Murua et al., 2008). The microparticles used for cell encapsulation should allow entry of nutrients and exit of cell products and provide protection of cells from the environmental conditions and immune response of the host (Hernández et al., 2010).

TABLE 2.2 List of Some Marketed Polymeric Microparticles Drug Products

Drug/active substance	Trade name	Company	Polymer	Microencapsulation technique[a]	Particle size (μm)	Indication
Buserelin acetate	Suprecur	Sanofi-Aventis	PLGA	Spray drying	N/A	Infertility, endometriosis
Lanreotide acetate	Somatuline LA	Ipsen	PLGA	Spray drying/phase separation	N/A	Acromegaly
Leuprolide acetate	Lupron Depot	TAP	PLGA	Double emulsion (w/o/w)	~8	Prostate cancer, endometriosis
Minocycline hydrochloride	Arestin	OraPharma	PLGA	Phase separation	20–60	Periodontitis
Naltrexone	Vivitrol	Alkermes	PLGA	Emulsion (o/w)	<100	Alcohol dependence, prevention of relapse to opioid dependence
Octreotide acetate	Sandostatin LAR	Novartis	PLGA	Emulsion/phase separation	1–250	Acromegaly
Risperidone	Risperdal Consta	Janssen	PLGA	Double emulsion (w/o/w)	N/A	Schizophrenia, bipolar disorder
Triptorelin pamoate	Trelstar Depot	Watson Pharma	PLGA	Spray drying	<200	Prostate cancer

N/A, information not available.
[a]Different techniques have been described in patents for some drugs.

Microparticles have also significant potential for vaccine delivery. An obvious advantage is their size, which is similar to the pathogens (O'Hagan et al., 2006). Second, depending on the size, they can be uptaken by macrophage cells (<5 μm) or directly by dendritic cells (1–3 μm). Besides, multiple copies of antigens can be attached on their surface, which is important for activation of B cells (O'Hagan et al., 2006).

2.3 POROUS INORGANIC MATERIALS AS DRUG CARRIERS

Porous solids are of scientific and technological interest because of their ability to interact with atoms, ions, and molecules not only at their surfaces, but throughout the bulk of the material (Davis, 2002). Porous materials play vital roles in many fields of science and technology and have attracted much attention as a useful platform for advanced functional material design (Xu et al., 2013). So far, extensive use of these materials in the industry was based on their ion exchange, adsorption (for selective separation), and catalytical properties (Hennion, 2000; Ohji and Fukushima, 2012; Pera-Titus, 2014; Schmidt, 2009; Shen et al., 2015; Vázquez and Paull, 2010; Xie et al., 2010; Zou et al., 2002). Porous materials have become also important for biomedical applications due to their excellent intrinsic properties (Davis, 2002; Dorozhkin, 2010; Lee and Shin, 2007; Maccauro et al., 2009; McInnes and Voelcker, 2009; Meek et al., 2011; Santos et al., 2011; Volodkin, 2014; Wang, 2009).

During the last two decades, there has been an increase in investigations related to biomedical application of porous materials particularly as drug carriers due to their excellent intrinsic and functional properties. High surface area and well-defined surface properties, tailorable and uniform pores size with narrow distributions, and possibility of pore-wall functionalization which permits hosting of molecules of interest, that is, drugs followed by their release in a more reproducible and predicable manner are some of the essential characteristics relevant for this application (Andersson et al., 2004; Arruebo, 2012; Heikkilä et al., 2007b; Li et al., 2004; Mizushima et al., 2006; Shivanand and Sprockel, 1998; Song et al., 2005; Takahashi et al., 2005, Wu et al., 2011). Furthermore, some structured porous materials can be configured as micro- and nanoparticulated systems, fibers, monoliths, coatings, etc. opening up their application for diverse biomedical application (Chung and Park, 2007; Della Rocca et al., 2011; Garg et al., 2012; Lee and Shin, 2007; Ojha et al., 2008).

2.3.1 Characteristics of Porous Inorganic Materials Used in Drug Delivery

The distribution of sizes, shapes, and volumes of the void spaces in porous materials directly relates to their ability to perform the desired function in a particular application (Davis, 2002). Classification of pores is one of the basic requisites of comprehensive characterization of porous solids. There are various

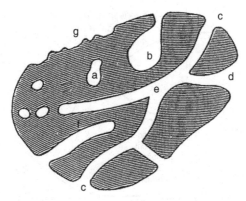

FIGURE 2.3   Schematic pores classification, according to their availability to surroundings.
a, Closed pores; *b, f*, pores open only at one end; *c, d, g*, open pores; *e*, open at two ends (through)
pores. *(Modified from IUPAC—Rouquerol J, Avnir D, Fairbridge CW, Everett DH, Haynes JH,
Pernicone N, Ramsay JDF, Sing KSW, Unger KK: Recommendations for the characterization of
porous solids (technical report),* Pure Appl Chem *66:1739–1758, 1994; Reprinted from Zdravkov
BD, Čermák JJ, Šefara M, Janků J: Pore classification in the characterization of porous materials:
a perspective,* Cent Eur J Chem *5:385–395, 2007, with permission from Springer)*

categorizations of pores described in the literature, but it is difficult to give a
consistent global classification of porous substances including catalysts, adsorbents, oxides, carbons, zeolites, organic polymers, soils, etc. A useful attempt,
at classification is based on pore origin, structure, size, and accessibility to surroundings (Fig. 2.3).

With respect to their origin and structure, pores are categorized into *intra-
particle* pores and *interparticle* pores (Kaneko, 1994). Pores can also be classified according to their accessibility to surroundings (Fig. 2.3). An open is one
which is connected to the external surface of the material and allows the pas-
sage of molecules or ions from the surroundings through the solid in contrast to
the closed pored that is within the solid which is not connected to the external
surface and hence is isolated. Although the closed pore is not associated with
adsorption and permeability of molecules, it influences the mechanical properties of solid materials. Some may be open only at one end, so they are then
described as blind (i.e., dead-end, or saccafe) pores, while others may be open
at two ends (through pores) (Rouquerol et al., 1994; Zdravkov et al., 2007).

The "pore size" is a property of major importance in practical applications
of porous materials, but it is even less susceptible to precise definition. There
are various categories of pore sizes described in the literature. According to the
International Union of Pure and Applied Chemistry (IUPAC) porous materials
are classified into three categories in relation to pore diameter, namely microporous (with pores <2.0 nm), mesoporous (with pores in the range of 2.0–50 nm),
and macroporous (with pores >50 nm) (Rouquerol et al., 1994).

On the basis of their origin, porous structures can be classified into organic, inorganic, and organic–inorganic composites (Arruebo, 2012). The main

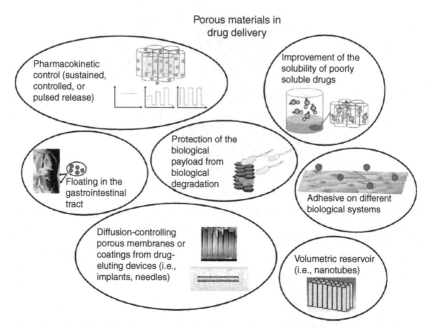

FIGURE 2.4 **Schematic overview of some of the advantages described for porous materials in drug delivery applications.** *(Reprinted from Arruebo M: Drug delivery from structured porous inorganic materials, Wires Nanomed Nanobiol 4:16–30, 2012, with permission from John Wiley and Sons)*

advantages of using a structured porous material in drug delivery applications including their ability: (1) to achieve a sustained, controlled, pulsed, or stimuli-responsive drug release; (2) to improve the solubility of poorly soluble drugs; (3) to float in the gastrointestinal tract; (4) to adhere to different biological systems; (5) to protect the biological payload from physiological degradation; (6) to act as a volumetric reservoir (i.e., nanotubes, nanocapsules); or (7) to act as a diffusion-controlling porous membrane or coating in drug-eluting devices (i.e., implants, needles), are summarized in Fig. 2.4. When considering the potential use of structured porous materials for the aforementioned purposes their attributes, such as nature, size, physicochemical, and functional properties as well as toxicity and biocompatibility are taken into account.

A wide range of inorganic porous materials has been used as excipients [according to European Pharmacopoeia (Ph. Eur. 8.0) an excipient (auxiliary substance) is any constituent of a medicinal product that is not an active substance] in pharmaceutical preparations because they have certain desirable physical and physicochemical properties, such as high adsorption capacity, specific surface area, swelling capacity, and reactivity to acids. Other important properties are dispersivity in water, hygroscopicity, unctuosity, thixotropy, slightly alkaline reaction (pH), plasticity, opacity, color, and nontoxicity to humans. Based on these characteristics inorganic porous materials, such as hydroxylapatite, bentonite, attapulgite, magnesium trisilicate, porous silicon dioxide, kaolin, or talc are used in various pharmaceutical preparations and technologies as adsorbents, glidants, desiccants, anticaking agent, suspending and thickening agents, tablet and capsule diluents, viscosity-increasing agents, coating agents, etc. (Carretero and Pozo, 2009; Rowe et al., 2012).

In recent years, many types of inorganic porous materials, such as mesoporous silicas, hydroxyapatites, tricalcium phosphates, mesoporous carbons, porous silicon, mesoporous organosilicates, calcium silicates, ceramic and carbon-based nanotubes, aluminosilicates, and layered silicates have shown numerous possibilities for biomedical application, due to their high chemical and mechanical stability under an array of physiological conditions and low susceptibility to microbiological contamination (Arruebo, 2012; Chen et al., 2016; Li and Shi, 2014; Mamaeva et al., 2013; Siefker et al., 2014, Xu et al., 2013).

Porous structures with prescribed structural, surface, and morphological properties can be obtained by various techniques. Template-based synthesis is the most popular method by using either soft templates (i.e., organic-based molecules, supramolecules, molecular associations, vesicles, ionic liquids, colloidal crystals, air bubbles, etc.), hard templates (i.e., porous sacrificial solids whose pores are filled with the material of interest and dissolved to reveal the desired porous structure), or a combination of the both to achieve hierarchical porous structures (Arruebo, 2012; Zhao et al., 2006). Porous network characteristics of these materials are important for their practical applications in active substance/drug adsorption, loading capacity, and afterward drug release. Dependent on the material used, there are several methods of drug loading described in the literature: simple mixing, drug adsorption, solvent evaporation, loading under high pressure, vacuum process, stirring in drug solution or suspension, layer-by-layer adsorption, etc.

In the following paragraphs an overview of porous inorganic materials application in biomedical field is given, with particular reference to their use as drug carriers.

2.3.2   Structured Porous Inorganic Materials Used in Drug Delivery: An Overview

Among the inorganic matrices suitable for drug delivery application, ordered mesoporous silica materials and layered double hydroxides (LDHs) found considerable attention (Pasqua, 2011; Perioli and Pagano, 2012; Rojas et al., 2015; Titinchi et al., 2014; Vallet-Regí et al., 2013). These materials are able to act as host for organic molecules (guests), such as drugs, forming inorganic–organic hybrids (Ambrogi et al., 2007; Ambrogi et al., 2012; Choy et al., 2007; Oh et al., 2013; Park et al., 2008; Tammaro et al., 2007; Van Speybroeck et al., 2009).

The term "mesoporous silica structures" was firstly used to describe zeolite–silica gel mixtures with a well-defined and uniform porosity (diameter $\sim$20–200 Å)

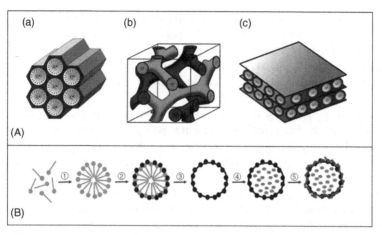

FIGURE 2.5 (A) Structures of mesoporous M41S materials: (a) MCM-41 (*2D hexagonal,* space group *p6mm*), (b) MCM-48 (*cubic,* space group *Ia3d*), and (c) MCM-50 (*lamellar,* space group *p2*). (B) Synthesis and functionalization of MSNs with further encapsulation of cargo molecules. Surfactant was first dissolved in aqueous solution to form micelles and self-assemble with defined geometry (①), attracted silicates *(black dots)* to produce mesostructured silicate–surfactant complexes (②), followed by the removal of templating surfactant to yield mesoporous silica (③). MSNs can be further loaded with cargo molecules *(red dots)* (④) and the surface can be functionalized with functional groups or ligands *(shown in purple)* (⑤). *(Part A, reprinted with permission from Hoffmann F, Cornelius M, Morell J, Fröba M: Silica-based mesoporous organic–inorganic hybrid materials,* Angew Chem Int Ed *45:3216–3251, 2006, with permission from John Wiley and Sons; part B, reproduced from Tao Z: Mesoporous silica-based nanodevices for biological applications,* RSC Adv *4:18961–18980, 2014, with permission of The Royal Society of Chemistry)*

(Mieville, 1972). In addition to IUPAC, a functional definition of mesoporous compounds is given by Arends et al. (1997) as those with a pore diameter ranging from 1.5 to 10 nm (Pasqua, 2011). Since the discovery of M41S family of ordered mesoporous silica materials (Fig. 2.5A) in 1990s (Beck et al., 1992; Kresge et al., 1992), synthesis and applications of mesoporous solids have received intensive attention, initially in the field of separation, catalysis, sensors, and devices, due to their highly ordered structures, larger pore size, and high surface area.

In general, mesoporous silica materials (also designated in the literature as well as MSNs, size typically <500 nm) are synthesized via a template-directed method (Kresge et al., 1992) in the presence of a supramolecular assembled surfactant that acts as a structure-directing template (Wang et al., 2015). MSNs are obtained after removal of the structure directing agent (by calcination or extraction) leading to opening of the porosity and eventually formation of MSNs with regular arrays of uniform channels (Beck et al., 1992; Kresge et al., 1992). By tuning the synthesis conditions and/or by variation of the reactants elongated MSNs with tunable aspect ratios can be synthesized (Huang et al., 2011) providing yet another means for optimization of the particle technology for biological applications. A synthesis of MCM-41, as representative of the first structurally ordered mesoporous materials is given in Fig. 2.5B.

MSNs typically have a high specific surface area (600–1000 m^2/g) and a high pore volume (0.6–1.0 mL/g), which allows high levels of drug loadings to be achieved. Characteristic pore dimensions of MSNs are 2–4 nm, but recent advances have made it possible to synthesize MSNs with pore dimensions as large as 30 nm (Gao et al., 2009; Kim et al., 2011), which makes these materials compatible with molecular dimensions ranging from small molecular drugs to larger proteins (Mamaeva et al., 2013).

MCM-41 (*M*obil *C*omposition of *M*atter No. 41) material is characterized by its very high surface area, of up to 1400 m^2/g, the homogeneously sized pores, with diameters of 1.5–20 nm, which are arranged hexagonally and a very high pore volume ($\sim$1 cm^3/g) (Fig. 2.4B). The pore walls of the silica have a thickness of 1–1.3 nm, and for this reason MCM-41 does not possess high thermal, chemical, or hydrothermal stability (Pasqua, 2011). Additionally, the pore wall structure consists of a disordered network of siloxane bridges and free silanol groups (Brühwiler and Calzaferri, 2004) that could act as reacting nuclei for molecule binding and for derivatization (Perioli and Pagano, 2012). This aspect is important because of the possibility to modify the surface characteristics through functionalization in order to make these materials able to store molecules with different lipophilicity/hydrophilicity degree and to obtain a controlled release (Wang, 2009), or any improved property with regard to application concerns (Tao, 2014).

The SBA (*S*anta *B*arbara *A*morphous) families of materials are another representative of highly ordered mesoporous materials (Zhao et al. 1998a; Zhao et al. 1998b), that were synthesized in an acid medium by the use of commercially nonionic triblock copolymer surfactant. Among a variety of SBA materials, SBA-15 (2D hexagonal) immediately attracted a lot of attention for the application in drug delivery field. SBA-15 silica is a combined micro- and mesoporous material with hexagonally ordered tunable uniform mesopores (4–14 nm) (Celer et al., 2006), with a very narrow pore size distribution. Additionally, it exhibits attractive features, including large mesopore size and volume, high specific surface area and connectivity between adjacent mesopores through pores (micropores and narrow mesopores) present in the walls of the primary (ordered) mesopores. The mesoporous silica pore walls are thicker (3–6 nm) than those of MCM-41 and consequently have higher hydrothermal stability. The surface of SBA-15 is hydrophilic and weakly negatively charged (<-0.08 C/m^2) (Salis et al., 2010) under physiological conditions. The properties of SBA-15 materials can be tailored by tuning the synthesis parameters, such as the temperature, pH, electrolytes, cosurfactants, and so on. Several other morphologies have been obtained, such as gyroids, rods, fibers, and spheres of different diameters. The internal (up to $\sim$1800 m^2/g) (Colilla et al., 2007) and external surfaces of SBA-15 (Fig. 2.6) provide easily accessible silanol groups that can be functionalized through the use of silane chemistry, thereby providing an avenue to modify the surface chemistry (Pasqua, 2011; Perioli et Pagano, 2012; Siefker et al., 2014).

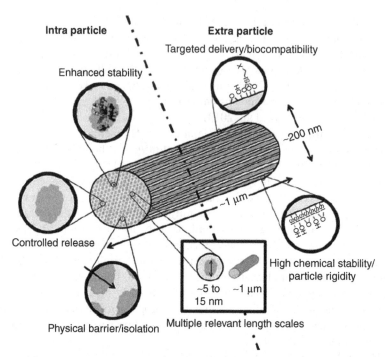

FIGURE 2.6   Intra- and extraparticle aspects of SBA-15. Design aspects of SBA-15 are illustrated, highlighting their possible application to address intra- and extraparticle challenges. *(Reprinted from Siefker J, Karande P, Coppens MO: Packaging biological cargoes in mesoporous materials: opportunities for drug delivery, Exp Opin Drug Deliv 11:1781–1793, 2014, with permission from Taylor & Francis)*

The synthesis of MCM-41 and SBA materials was significant in the development of multifunctional inorganic materials and initiated a wave of research on fabrication of novel mesoporous materials with high-ordered structures, such as MSU (*M*ichigan *S*tate *U*niversity) (Bagshaw et al., 1995), HMS (*H*exagonal *M*esoporous *S*ilica) (Tanev and Pinnavaia, 1995), TUD-1 (*T*echnische *U*niversiteit *D*elft) (Heikkilä et al., 2007a; Jansen et al., 2001), MCFs (*M*esostructured *C*ellular *F*oams) (Schmidt-Winkel et al., 1999), FSM (*F*olded *S*heet *M*esoporous) (Tozuka et al., 2005), or HMMs (*H*ollow-*S*tructured *M*esoporous *M*aterials) (Li and Shi, 2014).

Among the inorganic nanomaterials studied, LDHs are considered as the most biocompatible nanoconstructs (Liang et al., 2014) and have received considerable attention in recent years (Kuthati et al., 2015). Layered compounds with positively charged layers, the so-called LDHs, also known very often as *hydrotalcite-like systems*, derived from the natural hydroxycarbonate of Mg and Al (discovered in Sweden in 1842) or *anionic clays* due to the similarities shared with cationic clays, attracted a lot of attention for their biomedical application owing to its unique properties (Ambrogi et al., 2001; Costantino and Nocchetti, 2001; Costantino et al., 2008; Kuthati et al., 2015; Ladewig et al., 2009; Rives et al., 2013, Rives et al., 2014; Xu et al., 2006).

LDHs constitute a large family of materials with general formula $[M(II)_{1-x}M(III)_x(OH)_2]^{x+}(A^{n-}_{x/n})^{x-}\,mS$, where M(II) is a divalent metal cation (usually Mg, Zn), M(III) is a trivalent metal cation (usually Al, Fe), generally M(II)/M(III) = 2, A^{n-} is an exchangeable inorganic or organic anion, and m are the moles of solvent S, usually water, cointercalated per mole of compound (Costantino et al., 2008; Perioli and Pagano, 2012). In Fig. 2.7, the structure of hydrotalcite-like compounds (HTlc) shown is similar to that of the mineral brucite $(Mg(OH)_2)$ in which each layer is obtained by the edge concatenation of different $Mg(OH)_6$ octahedra (Allmann, 1968).

The isomorphic substitution of the divalent cations by trivalent cations in brucite-like layers $(M^{II}(OH)_2)$ creates a positive layer charge, thus LDHs/HTlc can accommodate charge-compensating anions in the interlayer region, where hydration water molecules are also accommodated (Costantino et al., 2008; Oh et al., 2009). An intercalated anion can be replaced by via ion-exchange

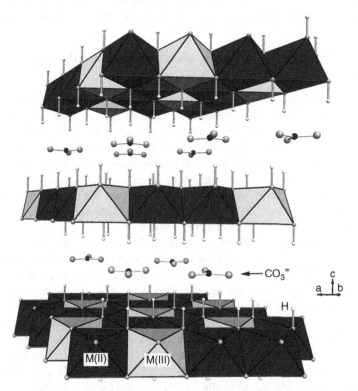

FIGURE 2.7 **Schematic illustration of the HTlc structure in carbonate form.** *(Reprinted from Costantino U, Ambrogi V, Nocchetti M, Perioli L: Hydrotalcite-like compounds: versatile layered hosts of molecular anions with biological activity,* Micropor Mesopor Mater *107:149–160, 2008, with permission from Elsevier)*

mechanism, with consequent variation of the interlayer distance (Perioli and Pagano, 2012). It is a unique property that the anions, such as Cl^- and NO_3^- in the interlayer can be readily exchanged with CO_3^{2-}, SO_4^{2-}, and many other organic (biomolecular) anions (Xu et al., 2006; Rives et al., 2014).

HTlc are present in nature, not in large quantity, but they can be easily synthesized in laboratory at high level of purity, moreover are cheap, eco-compatible green materials and can be organically modified with a variety of organic anions (Oh et al., 2012; Pucciariello et al., 2007; Rives et al., 2013). The main routes most frequently followed for synthesis of these materials, among the many ways proposed are coprecipitation, anion exchange, the reconstitution, hydrothermal, and microwave treatments (Rives et al., 2014). This versatility in the chemical composition leads to many and different potential applications. The current interest in LDHs is founded on several properties, such as acid-based properties, so-called *memory effect* (the ability to recover their original layered structure when mixed oxides, previously prepared by calcination of some LDHs at moderate temperatures, are put in contact with solutions containing anions) and anion exchange capacity (AEC), usually larger than that shown by cationic clays, ranging between 2 and 4 mEq/g (Rives et al., 2013; Rives et al., 2014).

2.3.3 Pharmaceutical Application of Structured Porous Inorganic Materials

Due to their advantageous structural properties, such as a high internal surface area and pore volume, tunable pore sizes, colloidal stability, and the possibility to specifically functionalize the inner pore system and/or the external particle surface, structured porous inorganic materials have attracted substantial attention in recent years for diverse biomedical applications including bioimaging for diagnostics, biosensing, biocatalysis, bone repair and scaffold engineering, and drug delivery (Fig. 2.4) (Argyo et al., 2014; Arruebo, 2012; Chen et al., 2016; Colilla and Vallet-Regi, 2013; Li and Shi, 2014; Mamaeva et al., 2013; Tarn et al., 2013; Wang et al., 2015; Xu et al., 2013).

Since the first report about using MCM-41 as nanocarrier for ibuprofen (Vallet-Regi et al., 2001), numerous investigations have been done in this area, developing different types of MSNs with varying porous structure and functionality for immediate, sustained, or controlled/targeted drug delivery for various routes of application (Chen et al., 2016; Wang, 2009; Yang et al., 2012). The development of mesoporous silica-based stimuli-responsive controlled drug delivery systems has attracted increasing attention (Chen et al., 2016). MSN-based stimuli-responsive controlled drug delivery systems (CDDSs) have been developed by applying controls, such as "gatekeepers" over the pore entrance. The drugs cannot leak out from silica carriers unless the drug-loading system is exposed to external stimuli, such as pH, redox potential, temperature, photoirradiation, or enzymes, which trigger the removal of the gatekeepers (Fig. 2.8) (Wang et al., 2015).

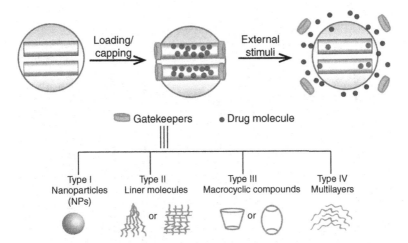

FIGURE 2.8 Different gatekeepers on the pore outlets of MSNs for stimuli-responsive CDDSs. *(Reprinted from Wang Y, Zhao Q, Han N, Bai L, Li J, Liu J, Che E, Hu L, Zhang Q, Jiang T, Wang S: Mesoporous silica nanoparticles in drug delivery and biomedical applications, Nanomed Nanotechnol 11:313–327, 2015, with permission from Elsevier)*

Biomedical applications of MSNs, including MSN-based biotherapeutic agent delivery (such as protein, peptides, and genes), MSN-assisted bioimaging [magnetic resonance (MR) imaging and fluorescent imaging] and MSNs as bioactive materials for tissue regeneration are undergoing intensive study (Arruebo, 2012; Mamaeva et al., 2013; Tao, 2014; Wang, 2009; Wang et al., 2015). Other representatives of inorganic mesoporous materials, such as porous silicon, mesoporous Al_2O_3, TiO_2, carbon or hydroxyapatite, have also been intensively studied for their utilization in formulations of poorly water-soluble drugs in order to enhance their dissolution and permeation behavior (Jiang et al., 2012; Kapoor et al., 2009; Kinnari et al., 2011; Perioli and Pagano, 2012; Wang et al., 2010; Xu et al., 2013; Zhao et al., 2012b,c; Zhu et al., 2014).

Based on the previously discussed characteristics of mesoporous inorganic materials, a summary of the type, modification/functionalization and their applications as drug carriers is provided in Table 2.3.

Along with investigations related to biomedical application of various silica-based nanomaterials, there are numerous studies concerning their biocompatibility and safety assessment (Di Pasqua et al., 2008; Heikkilä et al., 2010; Mamaeva et al., 2013; Hudson et al., 2008; Petushkov et al., 2010; Xu et al., 2013). The results from the literature underscore the importance of careful materials characterization since the toxicity depends on the particle size, porosity, shape, surface area, surface functionalization, and surface treatment (Petushkov et al., 2010). Furthermore, since the toxicity may vary based on the cell line, concentration, and exposure time in a complex way (Petushkov et al., 2010),

TABLE 2.3 Examples of Literature Reports on Inorganic Mesoporous Materials as Drug Carriers

Inorganic drug carrier		Drug/active substance	Modification/functionalization	Remarks/application	References
Mesoporous silicon and silica	MCM-41	Ibuprofen	None	Modified drug release/oral drug delivery	Andersson et al. (2004), Charnay et al. (2004), Vallet-Regí et al. (2001)
	MCM-41	Rutin	Functionalization with aminopropyl groups	Topical application	Berlier et al. (2013a)
	MCM-41	Quercetin	Functionalization with n-octyl triethoxysilane	Topical application	Berlier et al. (2013b)
	MCM-41	Trolox (6-hydroxy-2,5,7,8 tetramethylchromane-2-carboxylic acid)	None	Topical application	Gastaldi et al. (2012)
	MCM-41	Econazole nitrate	None	Topical application	Ambrogi et al. (2010)
	MCM-48	Ibuprofen Erythromycin	None	Modified drug release/oral drug delivery	Izquierdo-Barba et al. (2005)
	MCM-41 Si-MCM-41	Captopril	Silylation of MCM-41 surface with (trimethylchlorosilane, TMCS)	Modified drug release/oral drug delivery	Qu et al. (2006)
	Si-MCM-41	Acetylsalicylic acid	Aminopropyl surface modification via solvothermal process	Modified drug release/oral drug delivery	Zeng et al. (2005)

SBA-16	Indomethacin	None	Improved delivery of a poor water soluble drug/oral drug delivery	Hu et al. (2011)
SBA-15	Indomethacin Glibenclamide	None	Enhanced oral absorption of poorly soluble weakly acidic drugs/oral drug delivery	van Speybroeck et al. (2011)
TUD-1	Ibuprofen	None	Drug delivery with fast release property for poorly soluble drug	Heikkilä et al. (2007a)
FSM-16	Flurbiprofen	None	Solid dispersions of flurbiprofen in FSM-16 were prepared by solvent evaporation and sealed-heating; dissolution improvement of poorly water soluble drug/oral drug delivery	Tozuka et al. (2005)
Porous silicon (PSi) Thermally carbonized porous silicon (TCPSi) Thermally oxidized porous silicon (TOPSi) Thermally hydrocarbonized porous silicon (THCPSi)	Ibuprofen	None	Improved dissolution rate of a poor water soluble drug/oral drug delivery	Limnell et al. (2007)

(Continued)

TABLE 2.3 Examples of Literature Reports on Inorganic Mesoporous Materials as Drug Carriers (*cont.*)

Inorganic drug carrier		Drug/active substance	Modification/ functionalization	Remarks/application	References
	MCM-41, SBA-15, expanded SBA-15, FDU-12, and SBA-16 Hierarchical zeolites with additional mesoporosity (h-ZSM-5 and h-BETA zeolites)	Methylprednisolone hemisuccinate	None	Modified drug release/nasal drug delivery	García-Muñoz et al. (2014)
	Colloidal mesoporous silica (CMS)	Heparin	Functionalization of the outer nanoparticle surface with aminopropyl groups	Injectable drug delivery system	Argyo et al. (2012)
	Mesoporous silica nanoparticles (MSN)	Insulin	MSNs coated with low molecular weight chitosan	An injectable controlled release carrier of insulin	Elsayed et al. (2014)
Other mesoporous materials	Fibrous ordered mesoporous carbon (FOMC)	Celecoxib	None	Enhanced drug loading; improved dissolution rate; enhanced oral bioavailability; reduced gastric damage/oral drug delivery	Zhao et al. (2012a)
	Uniform mesoporous carbon spheres (UMCS) FOMC	Lovastatin	None	Improved dissolution rate of a poor water soluble drug/ oral drug delivery	Zhao et al. (2012b)

Hydroxycarbonate apatite (HCA)	Carvedilol	None	Oral delivery of poorly soluble drugs	Zhao et al. (2012c)
Amorphous mesoporous titania (APMT) Anatase mesoporous titania (ATMT)	Carvedilol	None	Carrier for poorly water-soluble drugs/oral drug delivery	Jiang et al. (2012)
Mesoporous alumina	Ibuprofen	Aminopropyltrimethoxysilane (APTMS) Methyltrimethoxysilane (MTMS) 2,3-Dihydroxynaphthalene (DN)	Surface functionalization (hydrophobic vs. hydrophilic groups) influenced drug loadings and rate of release/sustained drug delivery	Kapoor et al. (2009)

the long-term biocompatibility and cytotoxicity of these materials should be systematically investigated and classified in the future (Xu et al., 2013).

The versatility of LDHs to intercalate different drug families has been shown and attracted a great deal of interest for their potential as drug carriers for oral, topical, ocular, and parenteral drug delivery (Cao et al., 2011; Choi and Choy, 2011; Kwak et al., 2004; Leroux and Taviot-Guého, 2005; Rives et al., 2013; Rives et al., 2014; Singh et al., 2015; Tammaro et al., 2009). Besides LDHs, natural layered compounds, such as smectites (*cationic clays*) have been explored and utilized in drug delivery system for therapeutic application because drug or gene molecules can be safely encapsulated in the interlayer of clays via intercalative ion exchange process (Aguzzi et al., 2007; Chrzanowski et al., 2013; Rodrigues et al., 2013; Yang et al., 2016). Recently, such inorganic delivery systems have received growing attention because their inertness and low toxicity gives rise to safety and stability in biosystems. Furthermore, the hybridization of drug with clays offers the fascinating features, such as controlled and sustained release, improved water-solubility, and even protective and targeted delivery (Rodrigues et al., 2013; Yang et al., 2016). In addition to clays, other representatives of ordered porous materials, such as zeolites and diatomaceous earth (diatomite) have been intensively investigated (both unmodified and modified) as potential drug carriers for oral and topical applications (Aw et al., 2012; Bariana et al., 2013; Bonferoni et al. 2007; Cerri et al. 2004; Janićijević et al., 2015; Krajišnik et al., 2013; Losic et al., 2010; Milić et al., 2014; Ninan et al., 2014; Vilaça et al., 2013).

Microneedles made of inorganic porous materials including porous silicon (Chen et al., 2008; Ji et al., 2006) and calcium phosphates (Shirkhanzadeh, 2005) have been proposed as transdermal drug delivery systems. Transdermal patches made of functionalized carbon nanotube-based membranes have also been demonstrated as effective systems enabling controlled drug delivery to the skin by applying a small electrical bias to create a programmable drug delivery (Strasinger et al., 2009). The electroconductive nature of carbon nanotubes allowed easy application of iontophoresis in transdermal drug delivery for both water soluble or insoluble drugs (Degim et al., 2010).

2.4 CONCLUSIONS

Due to their biocompatibility, versatility, and favorable physicochemical characteristics, both polymeric and structured porous inorganic materials are good candidates for a wide range of pharmaceutical applications, including their use for preparation of micro- and nanosized particulate drug carriers. The most common reason for encapsulation/entrapment of drugs in both polymeric microparticles and structured porous inorganic micro/nanosized particulate carriers is to achieve modified, that is, sustained or prolonged drug release. Slow release of drug from these carriers allows reduction of dosage frequency, reduces fluctuations of its plasma concentrations, and therefore, minimizes side effects, improves patient compliance and overall therapeutic outcome. Besides, these particulate carriers can be tailored to exhibit sensitivity to biological stimuli (e.g., pH, ionic strength, temperature, redox potential, temperature, photoirradiation, or enzymatic activity) and can be used to target specific areas in the body.

As can be seen from this brief review, numerous techniques are nowadays available for preparation of these particulate drug carriers. The optimal preparation technique and preparation conditions have to be considered with respect to the properties of drug, starting material(s) and desired characteristics of drug carrier. The special attention should be paid to drug loading and encapsulation/entrapment efficiency, size, shape, surface properties, and possible influence of preparation procedure on stability and pharmacodynamic activity of the drug.

Recent research efforts in this field of biomedicine have been particularly focused on modification/functionalization of these drug carriers with aim to improve their overall in vivo performance.

ACKNOWLEDGMENT

This work was realized within the framework of the projects TR 34031 and ON172018 supported by the Ministry of Education, Science and Technological Development of Republic of Serbia.

REFERENCES

Abbas S, Da Wei C, Hayat K, Xiaoming Z: Ascorbic acid: microencapsulation techniques and trends—a review, *Food Rev Int* 28:343–374, 2012.

Addo RT, Yeboah KG, Siwale RC, Siddig A, Jones A, Ubale RV, Akande J, Nettey H, Patel NJ, Addo E, D'Souza MJ: Formulation and characterization of atropine sulfate in albumin–chitosan microparticles for in vivo ocular drug delivery, *J Pharm Sci* 104:1677–1690, 2015.

Adebisi A, Conway BR: Gastroretentive microparticles for drug delivery applications, *J Microencapsul* 28:689–708, 2011.

Aguzzi C, Cerezo P, Viseras C, Caramella C: Use of clays as drug delivery systems: possibilities and limitations, *Appl Clay Sci* 36:22–36, 2007.

Allmann R: The crystal structure of pyroaurite, *Acta Cryst* Part B24:972–977, 1968.

Ambrogi V, Fardella G, Grandolini G, Perioli L: Intercalation compounds of hydrotalcite-like anionic clays with anti-inflammatory agents: I. Intercalation and in vitro release of ibuprofen, *Int J Pharm* 220:23–32, 2001.

Ambrogi V, Perioli L, Marmottini F, Giovagnoli S, Esposito M, Rossi C: Improvement of dissolution rate of piroxicam by inclusion into MCM-41 mesoporous silicate, *Eur J Pharm Sci* 32:216–222, 2007.

Ambrogi V, Perioli L, Pagano C, Latterini L, Marmottini F, Ricci M, Rossi C: MCM-41 for furosemide dissolution improvement, *Micropor Mesopor Mater* 147:343–349, 2012.

Ambrogi V, Perioli L, Pagano C, Marmottini F, Moretti M, Mizzi F, Rossi C: Econazole nitrate-loaded MCM-41 for an antifungal topical powder formulation, *J Pharm Sci* 99:4738–4745, 2010.

Andersson J, Rosenholm J, Areva S, Lindén M: Influences of material characteristics on ibuprofen drug loading and release profiles from ordered micro- and mesoporous silica matrices, *Chem Mater* 16:4160–4167, 2004.

Arends IWCE, Sheldon RA, Wallau M, Schuchardt U: Oxidative transformations of organic compounds mediated by redox molecular sieves, *Angew Chem Int Ed* 36:1144–1163, 1997.

Argyo C, Cauda V, Engelke H, Rädler J, Bein G, Bein T: Heparin-coated colloidal mesoporous silica nanoparticles efficiently bind to antithrombin as an anticoagulant drug delivery system, *Chem Eur J* 18:428–432, 2012.

Argyo C, Weiss V, Bräuchle C, Bein T: Multifunctional mesoporous silica nanoparticles as a universal platform for drug delivery, *Chem Mater* 26:435–451, 2014.

Arruebo M: Drug delivery from structured porous inorganic materials, *Wires Nanomed Nanobiol* 4:16–30, 2012.

Arshady R: Preparation of microspheres and microcapsules by interfacial polycondensation techniques, *J Microencapsul* 6:13–28, 1989.

Aw MS, Simovic S, Yu Y, Addai-Mensah J, Losic D: Porous silica microshells from diatoms as biocarrier for drug delivery applications, *Powder Technol* 223:52–58, 2012.

Ayenew Z, Puri V, Kumar L, Bansal AK: Trends in pharmaceutical taste masking technologies: a patent review, *Rec Pat Drug Deliv Formul* 3:26–39, 2009.

Bagshaw SA, Prouzet E, Pinnavaia TJ: Templating of mesoporous molecular sieves by nonionic polyethylene oxide surfactants, *Science* 269:1242–1244, 1995.

Bariana M, Aw MS, Kurkuri M, Losic D: Tuning drug loading and release properties of diatom silica microparticles by surface modifications, *Int J Pharm* 443:230–241, 2013.

Beck JS, Vertuli JC, Roth WJ, Leonowicz ME, Kresge CT, Schmitt KD, Chu C, Olson DH, Sheppard EW, McCullen SB, Higgins JB, Schlenker JL: A new family of mesoporous molecular sieves prepared with liquid crystal templates, *J Am Chem Soc* 114:10834–10843, 1992.

Berlier G, Gastaldi L, Sapino S, Miletto I, Bottinelli E, Chirio D, Ugazio E: MCM-41 as a useful vector for rutin topical formulations: synthesis, characterization and testing, *Int J Pharm* 457:177–186, 2013a.

Berlier G, Gastaldi L, Ugazio E, Miletto I, Iliade P, Sapino S: Stabilization of quercetin flavonoid in MCM-41 mesoporous silica: positive effect of surface functionalization, *J Colloid Interface Sci* 1:109–118, 2013b.

Bock N, Woodruff MA, Hutmacher DW, Dargaville TR: Electrospraying, a reproducible method for production of polymeric microspheres for biomedical applications, *Polymers* 3:131–149, 2011.

Bonferoni MC, Cerri G, de' Gennaro M, Juliano C, Caramella C: Zn^{2+}-exchanged clinoptilolite-rich rock as active carrier for antibiotics in anti-acne topical therapy. In-vitro characterization and preliminary formulation studies, *Appl Clay Sci* 36:95–102, 2007.

Brown EN, Kessler MR, Sottos NR, White SR: In situ poly (urea-formaldehyde) microencapsulation of dicyclopentadiene, *J Microencapsul* 20:719–730, 2003.

Brühwiler D, Calzaferri G: Molecular sieves as host materials for supramolecular organization, *Micropor Mesopor Mater* 72:1–23, 2004.

Bugarski B, Li Q, Goosen MFA, Poncelet D, Neufeld RJ, Vunjak G: Electrostatic droplet generation: mechanism of polymer droplet formation, *AIChE J* 40:1026–1031, 1994.

Burgess D, Hickey A: Microsphere technology and applications. In Swarbrick J, editor: *Encyclopedia of pharmaceutical technology*, New York, 2007, Informa Healthcare, pp 2328–2338.

Calija B, Cekic N, Savic S, Daniels R, Markovic B, Milic J: pH-sensitive microparticles for oral drug delivery based on alginate/oligochitosan/Eudragit® L100-55 "sandwich" polyelectrolyte complex, *Colloids Surf B* 110:395–402, 2013.

Calija B, Cekic N, Savic S, Krajisnik D, Daniels R, Milic J: An investigation of formulation factors affecting feasibility of alginate–chitosan microparticles for oral delivery of naproxen, *Arch Pharm Res* 34:919–929, 2011.

Cao F, Wang Y, Ping Q, Liao Z: Zn-Al-NO₃-layered double hydroxides with intercalated diclofenac for ocular delivery, *Int J Pharm* 404:250–256, 2011.

Carretero MI, Pozo M: Clay and non-clay minerals in the pharmaceutical industry. Part I. Excipients and medical applications, *Appl Clay Sci* 46:73–80, 2009.

Cekic ND, Milic JR, Savic SD, Savic MM, Jovic Z, Daniels R: Influence of the preparation procedure and chitosan type on physicochemical properties and release behavior of alginate–chitosan microparticles, *Drug Dev Ind Pharm* 35:1092–1102, 2009.

Cekić ND, Savic SD, Milic JR, Savic MM, Jovic Z, Malesevic M: Preparation and characterisation of phenytoin-loaded alginate and alginate–chitosan microparticles, *Drug Deliv* 14:483–490, 2007.

Celer EB, Kruk M, Zuzek Y, Jaroniec M: Hydrothermal stability of SBA-15 and related ordered mesoporous silicas with plugged pores, *Mater Chem* 16:2824–2833, 2006.

Cerri G, de Gennaro M, Bonferoni MC, Caramella C: Zeolites in biomedical application: Zn-exchanged clinoptilolite-rich rock as active carrier for antibiotics in anti-acne topical therapy, *Appl Clay Sci* 27:141–150, 2004.

Charnay C, Bégu S, Tourné-Péteilh C, Nicole L, Lerner DA, Devoisselle JM: Inclusion of ibuprofen in mesoporous templated silica: drug loading and release property, *Eur J Pharm Biopharm* 57:533–540, 2004.

Chaturvedi M, Kumar M, Pathak K: A review on mucoadhesive polymer used in nasal drug delivery system, *J Adv Pharm Technol Res* 2:215–222, 2011.

Chen S, Hao X, Liang X, Zhang Q, Zhang C, Zhou G, Shen S, Jia G, Zhang J: Inorganic nanomaterials as carriers for drug delivery, *J Biomed Nanotechnol* 12:1–27, 2016.

Chen B, Wei J, Tay FEH, Wong YT, Iliescu C: Silicon microneedle array with biodegradable tips for transdermal drug delivery, *Microsyst Technol* 14:1015–1019, 2008.

Choi SJ, Choy JH: Layered double hydroxide nanoparticles as target-specific delivery carriers: uptake mechanism and toxicity, *Nanomedicine* 6:803–814, 2011.

Choy JH, Choi SJ, Oh JM, Park T: Clay minerals and layered double hydroxides for novel biological applications, *Appl Clay Sci* 36:122–132, 2007.

Chrzanowski W, Kim SY, Abou Neel EA: Biomedical applications of clay, *Aust J Chem* 66:1315–1322, 2013.

Chung HJ, Park TG: Surface engineered and drug releasing pre-fabricated scaffolds for tissue engineering, *Adv Drug Deliv Rev* 59:249–262, 2007.

Colilla M, Balas F, Manzano M, Vallet-Regí M: Novel method to enlarge the surface area of SBA-15, *Chem Mater* 19:3099–3101, 2007.

Colilla M, Vallet-Regi M: Smart drug delivery from silica nanoparticles. In Alvarez-Lorenzo C, Concheiro A, editors: *Smart materials for drug delivery, vol 2*, Cambridge, 2013, The Royal Society of Chemistry, pp 63–89.

Costantino U, Ambrogi V, Nocchetti M, Perioli L: Hydrotalcite-like compounds: versatile layered hosts of molecular anions with biological activity, *Micropor Mesopor Mater* 107:149–160, 2008.

Costantino U, Nocchetti M: Layered double hydroxides and their intercalation compounds in photochemistry and in medicinal chemistry. In Rives V, editor: *Layered double hydroxides: present and future*, New York, 2001, Nova Science Publisher Inc., pp 383–411.

Davis ME: Ordered porous materials for emerging applications, *Nature* 417:813–821, 2002.

Degim IT, Burgess DJ, Papadimitrakopoulos F: Carbon nanotubes for transdermal drug delivery, *J Microencapsul* 27:669–681, 2010.

Della Rocca J, Liu D, Lin W: Nanoscale metal-organic frameworks for biomedical imaging and drug delivery, *Acc Chem Res* 44:957–968, 2011.

Desai KG, Park HJ: Recent developments in microencapsulation of food ingredients, *Dry Technol* 23:1361–1394, 2005.

Di Pasqua AJ, Sharma KK, Shi YL, Toms BB, Ouellette W, Dabrowiak JC, Asefa T: Cytotoxicity of mesoporous silica nanomaterials, *J Inorg Biochem* 102:1416–1423, 2008.

Dorozhkin SV: Bioceramics of calcium orthophosphates, *Biomaterials* 31:1465–1485, 2010.

Dubey R, Shami TC, Rao KUB: Microencapsulation technology and applications, *Def Sci J* 59:82–95, 2009.

Elsabahy M, Wooley KL: Design of polymeric nanoparticles for biomedical delivery applications, *Chem Soc Rev* 41:2545–2561, 2012.

Elsayed A, Al-Remawi M, Maghrabi I, Hamaidi M, Jaber N: Development of insulin loaded mesoporous silica injectable particles layered by chitosan as a controlled release delivery system, *Int J Pharm* 461:448–458, 2014.

El-Sherbiny IM, McGill S, Smyth HD: Swellable microparticles as carriers for sustained pulmonary drug delivery, *J Pharm Sci* 99:2343–2356, 2010.

Fang Z, Bhandari B: Encapsulation techniques for food ingredient systems. In Bhandari B, Roos YH, editors: *Food materials science and engineering*, West Sussex, 2012, Wiley-Blackwell, pp 320–344.

Finch CA, Bodmeier R: Microencapsulation, Ullmann's encyclopedia of industrial chemistry. Weinheim, 2000, Wiley-VCH Verlag GmbH & Co.

Florence A, Siepmann J: *Modern pharmaceutics, volume 2: applications and advances*, ed 5, Boca Raton, 2009, CRC Press.

Freiberg S, Zhu XX: Polymer microspheres for controlled drug release, *Int J Pharm* 282:1–8, 2004.

Fundueanu G, Nastruzzi C, Carpov A, Desbrieres J, Rinaudo M: Physico-chemical characterization of Ca-alginate microparticles produced with different methods, *Biomaterials* 20:1427–1435, 1999.

Gao F, Botella P, Corma A, Blesa J, Dong L: Monodispersed mesoporous silica nanoparticles with very large pores for enhanced adsorption and release of DNA, *J Phys Chem B* 113:1796–1804, 2009.

García-Muñoz RA, Morales V, Linares M, Gonzáles PE, Sanz R, Serrano DP: Influence of the structural and textural properties of ordered mesoporous materials and hierarchical zeolitic supports on the controlled release of methylprednisolone hemisuccinate, *J Mater Chem B* 2:7996–8004, 2014.

Garg T, Singh O, Arora S, Murthy RSR: Scaffold: a novel carrier for cell and drug delivery, *Crit Rev Ther Drug* 29:1–63, 2012.

Gastaldi L, Ugazio E, Sapino S, Iliade P, Miletto I, Berlier G: Mesoporous silica as a carrier for topical application: the Trolox case study, *Phys Chem Chem Phys* 14:11318–11326, 2012.

Gharsallaoui A, Roudaut G, Chambin O, Voilley A, Saurel R: Applications of spray-drying in microencapsulation of food ingredients: an overview, *Food Res Int* 40:1107–1121, 2007.

Ghosh SK: Functional coatings and microencapsulation: a general perspective. In Ghosh SK, editor: *Functional coatings: by polymer microencapsulation*, Weinheim, 2006, Wiley-VCH Verlag GmbH & Co. KGaA.

Hafner A, Lovrić J, Lakoš GP, Pepić I: Nanotherapeutics in the EU: an overview on current state and future directions, *Int J Nanomed* 9:1005–1023, 2014.

Heikkilä T, Salonen J, Tuura J, Hamdy M, Mul G, Kumar N, Salmi T, Murzin D, Laitinen L, Kaukonen A: Mesoporous silica material TUD-1 as a drug delivery system, *Int J Pharm* 331:133–138, 2007a.

Heikkilä T, Salonen J, Tuura J, Kumar N, Salmi T, Murzin DY, Hamdy MS, Mul G, Laitinen L, Kaukonen AM, Hirvonen J, Lehto VP: Evaluation of mesoporous TCPSi, MCM-41, SBA-15, and TUD-1 materials as API carriers for oral drug delivery, *Drug Deliv* 14:337–347, 2007b.

Heikkilä T, Santos HA, Kumar N, Murzin DY, Salonen J, Laaksonen T, Peltonen L, Hirvonen J, Lehto VP: Cytotoxicity study of ordered mesoporous silica MCM-41 and SBA-15 microparticles on Caco-2 cells, *Eur J Pharm Biopharm* 74:483–494, 2010.

Heinzen C, Marison I, Berger A, von Stockar U: Use of vibration technology for jet break-up for encapsulation of cells, microbes and liquids in monodisperse microcapsules, *Landbauforschung Völkenrode* 241:19–25, 2002.

Hennion MC: Graphitized carbons for solid-phase extraction, *J Chromatogr A* 885:73–95, 2000.

Hernández RM, Orive G, Murua A, Pedraz JL: Microcapsules and microcarriers for in situ cell delivery, *Adv Drug Deliv Rev* 62:711–730, 2010.

Hu Y, Wang J, Zhi Z, Jiang T, Wang S: Facile synthesis of 3D cubic mesoporous silica microspheres with a controllable pore size and their application for improved delivery of a water-insoluble drug, *J Colloid Interface Sci* 363:410–417, 2011.

Huang HJ, Yuan WK, Chen XD: Microencapsulation based on emulsification for producing pharmaceutical products: a literature review, *Dev Chem Eng Miner Process* 14(3/4):515–544, 2006.

Huang X, Li L, Liu T, Hao N, Liu H, Chen D, Tang F: The shape effect of mesoporous silica nanoparticles on biodistribution, clearance, and biocompatibility in vivo, *ACS Nano* 5:5390–5399, 2011.

Hudson SP, Padera RF, Langer R, Kohane DS: The biocompatibility of mesoporous silicates, *Biomaterials* 29:4045–4055, 2008.

Izquierdo-Barba I, Martinez Á, Doadrio AL, Pérez-Pariente J, Vallet-Regí M: Release evaluation of drugs from ordered three-dimensional silica structures, *Eur J Pharm Sci* 26:365–373, 2005.

Jain RA: The manufacturing techniques of various drug loaded biodegradable poly(lactide-*co*-glycolide) (PLGA) devices, *Biomaterials* 21:2475–2490, 2000.

Jamekhorshid A, Sadrameli SM, Farid M: A review of microencapsulation methods of phase change materials (PCMs) as a thermal energy storage (TES) medium, *Renew Sust Energy Rev* 31:531–542, 2014.

Janićijević J, Krajišnik D, Čalija B, Nedić Vasiljević B, Dobričić V, Daković A, Antonijević MD, Milić J: Modified local diatomite as potential functional drug carrier—a model study for diclofenac sodium, *Int J Pharm* 496:466–474, 2015.

Jansen JC, Shan Z, Marchese L, Zhou W, van der Puil N, Maschmeyer T: A new templating method for three-dimensional mesopore networks, *Chem Commun*:713–714, 2001.

Ji J, Tay FEH, Miao J, Iliescu C: Microfabricated microneedle with porous tip for drug delivery, *J Micromech Microeng* 16:958–964, 2006.

Jiang H, Wang T, Wang L, Sun C, Jiang T, Cheng G, Wang S: Development of an amorphous mesoporous TiO_2 nanosphere as a novel carrier for poorly water-soluble drugs: effect of different crystal forms of TiO_2 carriers on drug loading and release behaviors, *Micropor Mesopor Mater* 153:124–130, 2012.

Jyothi NV, Prasanna PM, Sakarkar SN, Prabha KS, Ramaiah PS, Srawan GY: Microencapsulation techniques, factors influencing encapsulation efficiency, *J Microencapsul* 27:187–197, 2010.

Kaneko K: Determination of pore size and pore distribution. 1. Adsorbents and catalysts, *J Membr Sci* 96:59–89, 1994.

Kapoor S, Hegde R, Bhattacharyya AJ: Influence of surface chemistry of mesoporous alumina with wide pore distribution on controlled drug release, *J Control Release* 140:34–39, 2009.

Kim MH, Na HK, Kim YK, Ryoo SR, Cho HS, Lee KE, Jeon H, Ryoo R, Min DH: Facile synthesis of monodispersed mesoporous silica nanoparticles with ultralarge pores and their application in gene delivery, *ACS Nano* 5:3568–3576, 2011.

Kinnari P, Mäkilä E, Heikkilä T, Salonen J, Hirvonen J, Santos HA: Comparison of mesoporous silicon and non-ordered mesoporous silica materials as drug carriers for itraconazole, *Int J Pharm* 414:148–156, 2011.

Kohane DS: Microparticles and nanoparticles for drug delivery, *Biotechnol Bioeng* 96:203–209, 2007.

Krajišnik D, Daković A, Malenović A, Djekić L, Kragović M, Dobričić V, Milić J: An investigation of diclofenac sodium release from cetylpyridinium chloride-modified natural zeolite as a pharmaceutical excipient, *Micropor Mesopor Mater* 167:94–101, 2013.

Kresge CT, Leonowicz ME, Roth WJ, Vartuli JC, Beck JS: Ordered mesoporous molecular sieves synthesized by a liquid-crystal template mechanism, *Nature* 359:710–712, 1992.

Kuthati Y, Kankala RK, Lee CH: Layered double hydroxide nanoparticles for biomedical applications: current status and recent prospects, *Appl Clay Sci* 112–113:100–116, 2015.

Kwak SY, Kriven WM, Wallig MA, Choy JH: Inorganic delivery vector for intravenous injection, *Biomaterials* 25:5995–6001, 2004.

Ladewig K, Zhi PX, Gao QL: Layered double hydroxide nanoparticles in gene and drug delivery, *Expert Opin Drug Deliv* 6:907–922, 2009.

Lam PL, Gambari R: Advanced progress of microencapsulation technologies: in vivo and in vitro models for studying oral and transdermal drug deliveries, *J Control Release* 178:25–45, 2014.

Lamprecht A, Schäfer U, Lehr CM: Size-dependent bioadhesion of micro- and nanoparticulate carriers to the inflamed colonic mucosa, *Pharm Res* 18:788–793, 2001.

Lassalle V, Ferreira ML: PLA nano- and microparticles for drug delivery: an overview of the methods of preparation, *Macromol Biosci* 7:767–783, 2007.

Lee SH, Shin H: Matrices and scaffolds for delivery of bioactive molecules in bone and cartilage tissue engineering, *Adv Drug Deliv Rev* 59:339–359, 2007.

Leroux F, Taviot-Guého C: Fine tuning between organic and inorganic host structure: new trends in layered double hydroxide hybrid assemblies, *J Mater Chem B* 15:3628–3642, 2005.

Li Y, Shi J: Hollow-structured mesoporous materials: chemical synthesis, functionalization and applications, *Adv Mater* 26:3176–3205, 2014.

Li ZZ, Wen LX, Shao L, Chen JF: Fabrication of porous hollow silica nanoparticles and their applications in drug release control, *J Control Release* 98:245–254, 2004.

Liang R, Wei M, Evans DG, Duan X: Inorganic nanomaterials for bioimaging, targeted drug delivery and therapeutics, *Chem Commun* 50:14071–14081, 2014.

Limnell T, Riikonen J, Salonen J, Kaukonen A, Laitinen L, Hirvonen J, Lehto V: Surface chemistry and pore size affect carrier properties of mesoporous silicon microparticles, *Int J Pharm* 343:141–147, 2007.

Losic D, Yu Y, Aw MS, Simovic S, Thierry B, Addai-Mensah J: Surface functionalisation of diatoms with dopamine modified iron-oxide nanoparticles: toward magnetically guided drug microcarriers with biologically derived morphologies, *Chem Commun* 46:6323–6325, 2010.

Maccauro G, Iommetti PR, Muratori F, Raffaelli L, Manicone PF, Fabbriciani C: An overview about biomedical applications of micron and nano size tantalum, *Recent Pat Biotechnol* 3:157–165, 2009.

Mahato RI, Narang AS: *Pharmaceutical dosage forms and drug delivery*, ed 2, Boca Raton, 2012, CRC Press.

Mamaeva V, Sahlgren C, Lindén M: Mesoporous silica nanoparticles in medicine—recent advances, *Adv Drug Deliv Rev* 65:689–702, 2013.

McInnes SJP, Voelcker NH: Silicon-polymer hybrid materials for drug delivery, *Future Med Chem* 1:1051–1074, 2009.

Meek ST, Greathouse JA, Allendorf MD: Metal-organic frameworks: a rapidly growing class of versatile nanoporous materials, *Adv Mater* 23:249–267, 2011.

Mieville RL: Measurement of microporosity in the presence of mesopores, *J Colloid Interface Sci* 41:371–373, 1972.

Milić J, Daković A, Krajišnik D, Rottinghaus GE: Modified natural zeolites–functional characterization and biomedical application. In Tiwari A, editor: *Advanced healthcare materials*, Hoboken, Salem, 2014, John Wiley & Sons, Inc., Scrivener Publishing LLC, pp 361–403.

Mizushima Y, Ikoma T, Tanaka J, Hoshi K, Ishihara T, Ogawa Y, Ueno A: Injectable porous hydroxyapatite microparticles as a new carrier for protein and lipophilic drugs, *J Control Release* 110:260–265, 2006.

Murua A, Portero A, Orive G, Hernández RM, de Castro M, Pedraz JL: Cell microencapsulation technology: towards clinical application, *J Control Release* 132:76–83, 2008.

Ninan N, Muthiah M, Bt.Yahaya NA, Park IK, Elain A, Wong TW, Thomas S, Grohens Y: Antibacterial and wound healing analysis of gelatin/zeolite scaffolds, *Colloid Surf B* 115:244–252, 2014.

Nordstierna L, Abdalla AA, Nordin M, Nydén M: Comparison of release behaviour from microcapsules and microspheres, *Prog Org Coat* 69:49–51, 2010.

O'Hagan DT, Singh M, Ulmer JB: Microparticle-based technologies for vaccines, *Methods* 40:10–19, 2006.

Oh JM, Biswick TT, Choy JH: Layered nanomaterials for green materials, *J Mater Chem* 19:2553–2563, 2009.

Oh JM, Park DH, Choi SJ, Choy JH: LDH nanocontainers as bio-reservoirs and drug delivery carriers, *Recent Pat Nanotechnol* 6:200–217, 2012.

Oh YJ, Choi G, Choy YB, Park JW, Park JH, Lee HY, Yoon YJ, Chang HC, Choy JH: Aripiprazole-montmorillonite: a new organic–inorganic nanohybrid material for biomedical applications, *Chem Eur J* 19:4869–4875, 2013.

Ohji T, Fukushima M: Macro-porous ceramics: processing and properties, *Int Mater Rev* 57:115–131, 2012.

Ojha SS, Stevens DR, Hoffman TJ, Stano K, Klossner R, Scott MC, Krause W, Clarke LI, Gorga RE: Fabrication and characterization of electrospun chitosan nanofibers formed via templating with polyethylene oxide, *Biomacromolecules* 9:2523–2529, 2008.

Park JK, Choy YB, Oh JM, Kim JY, Hwang SJ, Choy JH: Controlled release of donepezil intercalated in smectite clays, *Int J Pharm* 59:198–204, 2008.

Park JH, Saravanakumar G, Kim K, Kwon IC: Targeted delivery of low molecular drugs using chitosan and its derivatives, *Adv Drug Deliv Rev* 62:28–41, 2010.

Park K, Yeo Y: Microencapsulation technology. In Swarbrick J, editor: *Encyclopedia of pharmaceutical technology*, New York, 2007, Informa Healthcare, pp 2315–2327.

Pasqua L: *Update on silica-based mesoporous materials for biomedical applications*, Shawbury, Shrewsbury, Shropshire, 2011, iSmithers Rapra Publishing.

Pera-Titus M: Porous inorganic membranes for CO_2 capture: present and prospects, *Chem Rev* 114:1413–1492, 2014.

Perioli L, Pagano C: Inorganic matrices: an answer to low drug solubility problem, *Expert Opin Drug Deliv* 9:1559–1572, 2012.

Petushkov A, Ndiege N, Salem AK, Larsen SC: Toxicity of silica nanomaterials: zeolites, mesoporous silica, and amorphous silica nanoparticles, Fishbein JC, editor: *Advances in molecular toxicology*, vol 4, New York, 2010, Elsevier, pp 223–266.

Prajapati VD, Jani GK, Kapadia JR: Current knowledge on biodegradable microspheres in drug delivery, *Expert Opin Drug Deliv* 12:1283–1299, 2015.

Prusse U, Bilancetti L, Bučko M, Bugarski B, Bukowski J, Gemeiner P, Lewinska D, Manojlović V, Massart B, Nastruzzi C, Nedovič V, Poncelet D, Siebenhaar S, Tobler L, Tosi A, Vikartovská A, Vorlop KD: Comparison of different technologies for alginate beads production, *Chem Pap* 62:364–374, 2008.

Pucciariello R, Tammaro L, Villani V, Vittoria V: New nanohybrids of poly (ε-caprolactone) and a modified Mg/Al hydrotalcite: mechanical and thermal properties, *J Polym Sci Pol Phys* 45:945–954, 2007.

Puel F, Briançon S, Fessi H: Industrial technologies and scale-up. In Benita S, editor: *Microencapsulation: methods and industrial applications*, New York, 2006, Taylor & Francis, pp 149–182.

Qu F, Zhu G, Huang S, Li S, Qiu S: Effective controlled release of captopril by silylation of mesoporous MCM-41, *ChemPhysChem* 7:400–406, 2006.

Rawat A, Majumder QH, Ahsan F: Inhalable large porous microspheres of low molecular weight heparin: in vitro and in vivo evaluation, *J Control Release* 128:224–232, 2008.

Reis CP, Neufeld RJ, Vilela S, Ribeiro AJ, Veiga F: Review and current status of emulsion/dispersion technology using an internal gelation process for the design of alginate particles, *J Microencapsul* 23:245–257, 2006.

Rives V, del Arco M, Martín C: Layered double hydroxides as drug carriers and for controlled release of non-steroidal anti-inflammatory drugs (NSAID): a review, *J Control Release* 169:28–39, 2013.

Rives V, del Arco M, Martín C: Intercalation of drugs in layered double hydroxides and their controlled release: a review, *Appl Clay Sci* 88–89:239–269, 2014.

Rodrigues LADS, Figueiras A, Veiga F, de Freitas RM, Nunes LC, da Silva Filho EC, da Silva Leite CM: The systems containing clays and clay minerals from modified drug release: a review, *Colloid Surf B* 103:642–651, 2013.

Rojas R, Bedoya DA, Vasti C, Giacomelli CE: LDH nanoparticles: synthesis, size control and applications in nanomedicine. In Sherman IT, editor: *Layered double hydroxides (LDHs): synthesis, characterization and applications*, New York, 2015, Nova Science Publisher Inc., pp 101–120.

Rouquerol J, Avnir D, Fairbridge CW, Everett DH, Haynes JH, Pernicone N, Ramsay JDF, Sing KSW, Unger KK: Recommendations for the characterization of porous solids (Technical Report), *Pure Appl Chem* 66:1739–1758, 1994.

Rowe C, Sheskey PJ, Cook WG, Fenton ME: *Handbook of pharmaceutical excipients*, ed 7, London, 2012, Pharmaceutical Press.

Salis A, Parsons DF, Boström M, Medda L, Barse B, Ninham BW, Monduzzi M: Ion specific surface charge density of SBA-15 mesoporous silica, *Langmuir* 26:2484–2490, 2010.

Santos HA, Salonen J, Bimbo LM, Lehto VP, Peltonen L, Hirvonen J: Mesoporous materials as controlled drug delivery formulations, *J Drug Deliv Sci Technol* 21:139–155, 2011.

Schmidt W: Solid catalysts on the nanoscale: design of complex morphologies and pore structures, *ChemCatChem* 1:53–67, 2009.

Schmidt-Winkel P, Lukens WW, Zhao D, Yang P, Chmelka BF, Stucky GD: Mesocellular siliceous foams with uniformly sized cells and windows, *J Am Chem Soc* 121:254–255, 1999.

Shen Y, Fang Q, Chen B: Environmental applications of three-dimensional graphene-based macrostructures: adsorption, transformation, and detection, *Environ Sci Technol* 49:67–84, 2015.

Shi Y, Li LL: Current advances in sustained-release systems for parenteral drug delivery, *Expert Opin Drug Deliv* 2:1039–1058, 2005.

Shirkhanzadeh M: Microneedles coated with porous calcium phosphate ceramics: effective vehicles for transdermal delivery of solid trehalose, *J Mater Sci Mater Med* 16:37–45, 2005.

Shivanand P, Sprockel OL: A controlled porosity drug delivery system, *Int J Pharm* 167:83–96, 1998.

Siefker J, Karande P, Coppens MO: Packaging biological cargoes in mesoporous materials: opportunities for drug delivery, *Expert Opin Drug Deliv* 11:1781–1793, 2014.

Siepmann J, Faisant N, Akiki J, Richard J, Benoit JP: Effect of the size of biodegradable microparticles on drug release: experiment and theory, *J Control Release* 96:123–134, 2004.

Siepmann J, Siepmann F: Microparticles used as drug delivery systems. In Richtering W, editor: *Smart colloidal materials*, Berlin, 2006, Springer, pp 15–21.

Singh MN, Hemant KS, Ram M, Shivakumar HG: Microencapsulation: a promising technique for controlled drug delivery, *Res Pharm Sci* 5:65–77, 2010.

Singh NK, Nguyen QV, Kim BS, Lee DS: Nanostructure controlled sustained delivery of human growth hormone using injectable, biodegradable, pH/temperature responsive nanobiohybrid hydrogel, *Nanoscale* 7:3043–3054, 2015.

Sohi H, Sultana Y, Khar RK: Taste masking technologies in oral pharmaceuticals: recent developments and approaches, *Drug Dev Ind Pharm* 30:429–448, 2004.

Sollohub K, Cal K: Spray drying technique: II. Current applications in pharmaceutical technology, *J Pharm Sci* 99:587–597, 2010.

Song SW, Hidajat K, Kawi S: Functionalized SBA-15 materials as carriers for controlled drug delivery: influence of surface properties on matrix-drug interactions, *Langmuir* 21:9568–9595, 2005.

Strasinger CL, Scheff NN, Wu J, Hinds BJ, Stinchcomb AL: Carbon nanotube membranes for use in the transdermal treatment of nicotine addiction and opioid withdrawal symptoms, *Subst Abuse* 3:31–39, 2009.

Sudhakar Y, Kuotsu K, Bandyopadhyay AK: Buccal bioadhesive drug delivery—a promising option for orally less efficient drugs, *J Control Release* 114:15–40, 2006.

Takahashi T, Yamada Y, Kataoka K, Nagasaki Y: Preparation of a novel PEG-clay hybrid as a DDS material: dispersion stability and sustained release profiles, *J Control Release* 107:408–416, 2005.

Tammaro L, Costantino U, Bolognese A, Sammartino G, Marenzi G, Calignano A, Tetè S, Mastrangelo F, Califano L, Vittoria V: Nanohybrids for controlled antibiotic release in topical applications, *Int J Antimicrob Agents* 29:417–423, 2007.

Tammaro L, Costantino U, Nocchetti M, Vittoria V: Incorporation of active nano-hybrids into poly(ε-caprolactone) for local controlled release: antifibrinolytic drug, *Appl Clay Sci* 43:350–356, 2009.

Tan ML, Choong PF, Dass CR: Recent developments in liposomes, microparticles and nanoparticles for protein and peptide drug delivery, *Peptides* 31:184–193, 2010.

Tanev PT, Pinnavaia TJ: A neutral templating route to mesoporous molecular sieves, *Science* 267:865–867, 1995.

Tao Z: Mesoporous silica-based nanodevices for biological applications, *RSC Adv* 4:18961–18980, 2014.

Tarn D, Ashley CE, Xue M, Carnes EC, Zink JI, Brinker CJ: Mesoporous silica nanoparticles nanocarriers: biofunctionality and biocompatibility, *Acc Chem Res* 46:792–801, 2013.

Thies C: A survey of microencapsulation processes. In Benita S, editor: *Methods and industrial applications*, New York, 1996, Marcel Dekker, pp 133–154.

Titinchi SJJ, Singh MP, Abbo HS, Green IR: Advanced materials for biomedical application and drug delivery. In Tiwari A, editor: *Advanced healthcare materials*, Hoboken, Salem, 2014, John Wiley & Sons, Inc., Scrivener Publishing LLC, pp 49–85.

Tonessen HH, Karlsen J: Alginate in drug delivery systems, *Drug Dev Ind Pharm* 28:621–630, 2002.

Torchilin VP: Multifunctional nanocarriers, *Adv Drug Deliv Rev* 64:302–315, 2012.

Tozuka Y, Wongmekiat A, Kimura K, Moribe K, Yamamura S, Yamamoto K: Effect of pore size of FSM-16 on the entrapment of flurbiprofen in mesoporous structures, *Chem Pharm Bull* 53:974–977, 2005.

Tran VT, Benoît JP, Venier-Julienne MC: Why and how to prepare biodegradable, monodispersed, polymeric microparticles in the field of pharmacy? *Int J Pharm* 407:1–11, 2011.

Vallet-Regí M, Garcia MM, Colilla M: Biomedical applications of mesoporous ceramics: drug delivery, Smart materials and bone tissue engineering. Boca Raton, 2013, CRC Press.

Vallet-Regi M, Rámila A, del Real RP, Pérez-Pariente J: A new property of MCM-41: drug delivery system, *Chem Mater* 13:308–311, 2001.

Van Speybroeck M, Barillaro V, Thi TD, Mellaerts R, Martens J, Van Humbeeck J, Vermant J, Annaert P, Van Den Mooter G, Augustijns P: Ordered mesoporous silica material SBA-15: a broad-spectrum formulation platform for poorly soluble drugs, *J Pharm Sci* 98:2648–2658, 2009.

van Speybroeck M, Mellaerts R, Thi TD, Martens JA, Van Humbeeck J, Annaert P, Van den Mooter G, Augustijns P: Preventing release in the acidic environment of the stomach via occlusion in ordered mesoporous silica enhances the absorption of poorly soluble weakly acidic drugs, *J Pharm Sci* 100:4864–4876, 2011.

Vázquez M, Paull B: Review on recent and advanced applications of monoliths and related porous polymer gels in micro-fluidic devices, *Anal Chim Acta* 668:100–113, 2010.

Vemmer M, Patel AV: Review of encapsulation methods suitable for microbial biological control agents, *Biol Control* 67:380–389, 2013.

Versypt AN, Pack DW, Braatz RD: Mathematical modeling of drug delivery from autocatalytically degradable PLGA microspheres—a review, *J Control Release* 165:29–37, 2013.

Vilaça N, Amorim R, Machado AF, Parpot P, Pereira MFR, Sardo M, Rocha J, Fonseca AM, Neves IC, Baltazar F: Potentiation of 5-fluorouracil encapsulated in zeolites as drug delivery systems for in vitro models of colorectal carcinoma, *Colloid Surf B* 112:237–244, 2013.

Volodkin D: $CaCO_3$ templated micro-beads and -capsules for bioapplications, *Adv Colloid Interface* 207:306–324, 2014.

Wang S: Ordered mesoporous materials for drug delivery, *Micropor Mesopor Mater* 117:1–9, 2009.

Wang F, Hui H, Barnes TJ, Barnett C, Prestidge CA: Oxidized mesoporous silicon microparticles for improved oral delivery of poorly soluble drugs, *Mol Pharm* 7:227–236, 2010.

Wang Y, Zhao Q, Han N, Bai L, Li J, Liu J, Che E, Hu L, Zhang Q, Jiang T, Wang S: Mesoporous silica nanoparticles in drug delivery and biomedical applications, *Nanomed Nanotechnol* 11:313–327, 2015.

Wattendorf U, Coullerez G, Vörös J, Textor M, Merkle HP: Mannose-based molecular patterns on stealth microspheres for receptor-specific targeting of human antigen-presenting cells, *Langmuir* 24:11790–11802, 2008.

Wei W, Wang LY, Yuan L, Yang XD, Su ZG, Ma GH: Bioprocess of uniform-sized crosslinked chitosan microspheres in rats following oral administration, *Eur J Pharm Biopharm* 69:878–886, 2008.

Wischke C, Schwendeman SP: Principles of encapsulating hydrophobic drugs in PLA/PLGA microparticles, *Int J Pharm* 364:298–327, 2008.

Wu C, Wang Z, Zhi Z, Jiang T, Zhang J, Wang S: Development of biodegradable porous starch foam for improving oral delivery of poorly water soluble drugs, *Int J Pharm* 403:162–169, 2011.

Xie Z, Liu Z, Wang Y, Yang Q, Xu L, Ding W: An overview of recent development in composite catalysts from porous materials for various reactions and processes, *Int J Mol Sci* 11:2152–2187, 2010.

Xu W, Riikonen J, Lehto VP: Mesoporous systems for poorly soluble drugs, *Int J Pharm* 453:181–197, 2013.

Xu ZP, Zeng QH, Lu GQ, Yu AB: Inorganic nanoparticles as carriers for efficient cellular delivery, *Chem Eng Sci* 61:1027–1040, 2006.

Yang YY, Chung TS, Bai XL, Chan WK: Effect of preparation conditions on morphology and release profiles of biodegradable polymeric microspheres containing protein fabricated by double-emulsion method, *Chem Eng Sci* 55:2223–2236, 2000.

Yang P, Gai S, Lin J: Functionalized mesoporous silica materials for controlled drug delivery, *Chem Soc Rev* 41:3679–3698, 2012.

Yang J, Han S, Zheng H, Dong H, Liu J: Preparation and application of micro/nanoparticles based on natural polysaccharides, *Carbohydr Polym* 123:53–66, 2015.

Yang JH, Lee JH, Ryu HJ, Elzatahry AA, Alothman ZA, Choy JH: Drug–clay nanohybrids as sustained delivery systems, *Appl Clay Sci*, 2016.

Ye M, Kim S, Park K: Issues in long-term protein delivery using biodegradable microparticles, *J Control Release* 146:241–260, 2010.

Yeo Y, Baek N, Park K: Microencapsulation methods for delivery of protein drugs, *Biotechnol Bioproc E* 6:213–230, 2001.

Yeo Y, Park K: Control of encapsulation efficiency and initial burst in polymeric microparticle systems, *Arch Pharm Res* 27:1–12, 2004.

Zdravkov BD, Čermák JJ, Šefara M, Janků J: Pore classification in the characterization of porous materials: a perspective, *Cent Eur J Chem* 5:385–395, 2007.

Zeng W, Qian XF, Zhang YB, Yin J, Zhu ZK: Organic modified mesoporous MCM-41 through solvothermal process as drug delivery system, *Mater Res Bull* 40:766–772, 2005.

Zhao D, Feng J, Huo Q, Melosh N, Fredrickson GH, Chmelka BF, Stucky GD: Triblock copolymer syntheses of mesoporous silica with periodic 50 to 300 angstrom pores, *Science* 279:548–552, 1998a.

Zhao D, Huo Q, Feng J, Chmelka BF, Stucky GD: Nonionic triblock and star diblock copolymer and oligomeric sufactant syntheses of highly ordered, hydrothermally stable, mesoporous silica structures, *J Am Chem Soc* 120:6024–6036, 1998b.

Zhao P, Jiang H, Jiang T, Zhi Z, Wu C, Sun C, Zhang J, Wang S: Inclusion of celecoxib into fibrous ordered mesoporous carbon for enhanced oral bioavailability and reduced gastric irritancy, *Eur J Pharm Sci* 45:639–647, 2012a.

Zhao XS, Su F, Yan Q, Guo W, Bao XY, Lv L, Zhou Z: Templating methods for preparation of porous structures, *J Mater Chem* 16:637–648, 2006.

Zhao P, Wang L, Sun C, Jiang T, Zhang J, Zhang Q, Sun J, Deng Y, Wang S: Uniform mesoporous carbon as a carrier for poorly water soluble drug and its cytotoxicity study, *Eur J Pharm Biopharm* 80:535–543, 2012b.

Zhao Q, Wang T, Wang J, Zheng L, Jiang T, Cheng G, Wang S: Fabrication of mesoporous hydroxycarbonate apatite for oral delivery of poorly water-soluble drug carvedilol, *J Non Cryst Solids* 358:229–235, 2012c.

Zhu W, Wan L, Zhang C, Gao Y, Zheng X, Jiang T, Wang S: Exploitation of 3D face-centered cubic mesoporous silica as a carrier for a poorly water soluble drug: influence of pore size on release rate, *Mater Sci Eng C* 34:78–85, 2014.

Zou H, Huang X, Ye M, Luo Q: Monolithic stationary phases for liquid chromatography and capillary electrochromatography, *J Chromatogr A* 954:5–32, 2002.

Chapter 3

Microemulsions and Nanoemulsions as Carriers for Delivery of NSAIDs

Ljiljana Đekić, Marija Primorac
Department of Pharmaceutical Technology and Cosmetology, Faculty of Pharmacy, University of Belgrade, Belgrade, Serbia

3.1 INTRODUCTION

Nonsteroidal anti-inflammatory drugs (NSAIDs) is a general term that refers to a heterogeneous group of organic acids with analgesic, antipyretic, anti-inflammatory, and platelet inhibitory actions. Well-known NSAIDs, such as ibuprofen, ketoprofen, diclofenac, etodolac, and celecoxib, are widely available in pharmaceutical dosage forms for peroral administration. They are extensively used for treatment of acute and chronic inflammation and mild to moderate pain associated with dysmenorrhea, headache, migraine, postoperative and dental pain, musculoskeletal injuries, and rheumatic diseases (Aronson, 2016; Sweetman, 2009). These drug substances are classified in the class 2 of the FDAs Biopharmaceutics Classification System (BCS) of drugs (FDA, 2015) due to their low solubility and high permeability. Ibuprofen, ketoprofen, diclofenac, celecoxib, and etodolac are usually described as practically insoluble in water hydrophobic weakly acidic substances. According to the DrugBank database, the water solubility data experimentally determined are: 21 mg/L (ibuprofen), 51 mg/L (ketoprofen), 2.37 mg/L (diclofenac), 3.3 mg/L (celecoxib), and 16 mg/L (etodolac) with the log P values 3.97, 3.12, 4.51, 3.9, and 2.5, respectively, and pK_a values 4.91, 3.12, 4.15, 3.5, and 4.65, respectively (DrugBank, 2015). Ibuprofen ((RS)-2-(4-Isobutylphenyl) propionic acid) and ketoprofen ((RS)-2-[3-(benzoyl)phenyl]propanoic acid) are usually administered as the racemic compounds, but pharmaceutical preparations containing only the (S)-(+)-enantiomer (dexibuprofen and dexketoprofen, respectively) are available in some countries. Ibuprofen and ketoprofen are usually given as the free acids but various salts (lysine and sodium) are also in use. Ibuprofen

Microsized and Nanosized Carriers for NSAIDs. http://dx.doi.org/10.1016/B978-0-12-804017-1.00003-0

does not exhibit genuine polymorphism. However, it has a tendency toward slight crystal lattice modification, which may also affect its dissolution behavior. Ketoprofen can exist as two polymorphs. No data were found in the literature as to whether the polymorphic form of ketoprofen-free acid affects dissolution performance or bioavailability (BA) (Potthast et al., 2005; Shohin et al., 2012). Diclofenac (2-[(2,6-dichlorophenyl)amino]-benzeneacetic acid) is used mainly as sodium and potassium salts. Their polymorphs were not reported (Chuasuwan et al., 2009). Celecoxib (4-[5-(4-methylphenyl)-3-trifluoromethyl)-1H-pyrazoyl-1-yl]benzensulfonamide) exists in three polymorphic forms (I, II, and III) and a solid-state interconversion between the forms at ambient conditions has not been observed (Subramanian et al., 2004). There is no evidence of polymorphism in etodolac (2-[(1RS)-1,8-diethyl-1,3,4,9-tetrahydropyrano[3,4-*b*] indole-1-yl] acetic acid) (Barakat, 2009; Raja Sekharan et al., 2014). NSAIDs are highly permeable drugs. Moreover, NSAIDs increase permeability of gastrointestinal tract (GIT) membrane promoting their own transport, particularly upon oral administration of high doses or long-term usage, and likely increasing the risk for gastrointestinal (GI) side effects and the damage of the GI membrane (Patil et al., 2004). Absorption of NSAIDs is rapid. Strengths of immediate release (IR) oral solid dosage forms with ibuprofen range from 200 to 800 mg with linear pharmacokinetics in the dose range of 200–400 mg. The permeability of ibuprofen in GIT is high and an absolute BA is about 100%. The maximum plasma concentration achieves within 1–2 h (Potthast et al., 2005). Food intake affects the absorption rate of ibuprofen, likely due to food induced pH elevation in the stomach resulting in earlier in vivo dissolution of ibuprofen. According to the present regulations, ibuprofen is a BCS class 2 drug with high permeability and pH-dependent solubility, that is, low solubility at pH 1.2 and 4.5 and high solubility at pH 6 (Alvarez et al., 2011). The single dose for ketoprofen in IR solid oral dosage forms (tablets and capsules) ranges from 25 to 100 mg. Ketoprofen is mainly absorbed in the small intestine and peak plasma concentrations (C_{max}) are reached within 1–2 h (T_{max}) after administration of a single dose. Ketoprofen shows dose linearity over a dose range of 50–200 mg. BA for 100 mg capsules is 92%. Yazdanian et al. (2004) classified ketoprofen as BCS class 1, but this was based only on pH 7.4 solubility. Wu and Benet (2005) also assigned ketoprofen to BCS class 1 with regard to its disposition characteristics to estimate permeability. Another opinion is that ketoprofen is a borderline case between BCS classes 1 and 2. When administered with food in conventional form, the total BA of ketoprofen remains unchanged, but the absorption rate is slowed by 1–2 h (Patil et al., 2005). Dosage range of diclofenac salts for IR solid oral dosage forms is from 12.5 to 50 mg. Diclofenac is 100% absorbed after oral administration, proportional with the dose within the range 25–150 mg. Administration with food can extend the lag time (t_{lag}) of drug absorption, thereby increasing the time to maximum concentration (t_{max}) and decreasing the maximum concentration (C_{max}), but without a significant effect on the extent of oral absorption (Chuasuwan et al., 2009). Diclofenac potassium and diclofenac sodium are both BCS class 2 drugs with high permeability through the intestinal membrane. Food does not have a significant effect on the extent of oral absorption of diclofenac sodium or diclofenac potassium. Diclofenac potassium is claimed to dissolve faster, and hence absorbed faster than the sodium salt and is recommended for the treatments that need fast onset of action, mainly for its analgesic properties (Chuasuwan et al., 2009). Celecoxib is a hydrophobic and highly permeable drug belonging to BCS class 2 with t_{max} about 3 h after oral administration (Subramanian et al., 2004).

Poor solubility of the NSAIDs is a main obstacle for rapid onset of action. For this class of compounds, dissolution in the environmental lumen is the rate-controlling step in the absorption process (Barakat, 2009). Also, low aqueous solubility leads to high variability in absorption after oral administration of some NSAIDs (e.g., celecoxib). Therefore, there is a permanent interest to enhance the aqueous solubility and dissolution rate of NSAIDs in order to achieve faster onset of action and to minimize the absorption variability. Encapsulation of NSAIDs in colloidal nanodispersions, such as microemulsions and nanoemulsions represents a promising strategy with the significant potential for enhancement of BA. Currently, the growing attention is on development of preconcentrates of microemulsions and nanoemulsions, that is, self-microemulsifying drug-delivery systems (SMEDDS) and self-nanoemulsifying drug-delivery systems (SNEDDS), respectively, due to their easy preparation, superior physical stability and drug encapsulation capacity. Generally, the results of numerous studies demonstrate that formulation of poorly soluble drugs in SMEDD/SNEDDS is one of the most promising approach for increase of solubilization of poorly soluble drugs in biological milieu and manipulation of their biodistribution and absorption in order to achieve the enhancement of BA (Agrawal et al., 2012; Djekic and Primorac 2010; Fatouros et al., 2007; Gupta et al., 2013; Humberstone and Charman, 1997; Koushik et al., 2013; Pouton, 2000, 2006; Pouton and Porter, 2008). Recently, several studies have reported potential of SMEDDS/SNEDDS for enhancement in BA of poorly soluble NSAIDs (Barakat, 2009; Raja Sekharan et al., 2014; Patil et al., 2004, 2005; Subramanian et al., 2004). This chapter describes the development approach and NSAIDs oral delivery potential of microemulsions, nanoemulsions, and their preconcentrates (SMEDDS and SNEDDS, respectively).

3.2 MICROEMULSIONS AND NANOEMULSIONS AS DRUG-DELIVERY CARRIERS

Nanoemulsions are oil-in-water or water-in-oil emulsions with droplet size in the range of 50–1000 nm (preferably from 100 to 500 nm). In literature, such systems are also referred as *miniemulsions*, *ultrafine emulsions*, and *submicron emulsions*. Microemulsions are isotropic, transparent systems which contain spherical droplets of water phase or oil phase, with diameter of average size from 10 to 100 nm, dispersed in a continuous oil or water phase, respectively,

TABLE 3.1 Main Characteristics of Microemulsions and Nanoemulsions

System	Microemulsions	Nanoemulsions
Appearance	Transparent	Opalescent or opaque
Droplet size	<150 nm	0.2–1 μm
Interfacial area	~200 m^2/g	~15 m^2/g
Interfacial tension	~10^{-2}–10^{-3} mN/m	~1–50 mN/m
Stability	Thermodynamically stable systems	Kinetically stable systems

and with the monomolecular film of surfactant(s) at the water/oil interface (Anton and Vandamme, 2011; Djekic, 2012; Ezrahi et al., 1999; Fanun, 2011; Kahlweit, 1999; Mason et al., 2006; Sjöblom et al., 1996; Strey, 1994). The main differences between microemulsions and nanoemulsions regarding their physical stability, appearance, and microstructure are summarized in (Table 3.1).

Microemulsions are transparent, while nanoemulsions and emulsions are opalescent or opaque. The area of the surfactant film at the oil–water interface and interfacial tension of microemulsions is higher, more than 10 times and up to 1000 times, respectively, than the values of the corresponding parameters for nanoemulsions. Therefore, the capacity for solubilization of poorly soluble substances in microemulsons is usually higher in comparison to the nanoemulsions. The key difference between microemulsions and nanoemulsions is related to their physical stability. Microemulsions are thermodynamically stable systems, while nanoemulsions are thermodynamically unstable, yet kinetically stable systems. Thermodynamically equilibrated state provides long-term stability of microemulsion formulations. On the other hand, introduction of thermal and/or mechanical energy in the system (i.e., mixing and heating) is usually required for preparation of nanoemulsions. Phase separation after a certain period of time after preparation of nanoemulsions is inevitable (Anton and Vandamme, 2011). Production of nanoemulsions is commonly based on high-energy processes in high-pressure piston homogenizers and microfluidizers. Droplet size and physical stability of nanoemulsions depend on a number of factors: physical–chemical properties and concentration of ingredients, the applied production process and the equipment performances, the order of addition of different phases, temperature and speed and duration of emulsification, and homogenization, storage conditions (e.g., temperature, light) (Anton and Vandamme, 2011). Novel low-energy procedures based on the principles of self-emulsification or phase inversion are suitable for preparation of nanoemulsions with very fine droplets without heating and mixing at low speed. Formation of nanoemulsions and microemulsions is formulated in well-optimized mixtures of an oil phase, a surfactant, a cosurfactant, and an aqueous phase, and within a specified range of concentrations form spontaneously, is thermodynamically favored process, and generally does not require the significant input of heat, stirring, or homogenization (Anton and Vandamme, 2011; McClements, 2012; Sole et al., 2010; Wennerström et al., 2006). The design of such nanodispersions, with the ability to form almost spontaneously from the corresponding preconcentrates (SMEDDS and SNEDDS) upon mixing with the aqueous media on mild agitation in vitro or with the fluids in the GIT lumen under digestive motility, represents an important current concept for oral administration of poorly soluble drugs. SMEDDS and SNEDDS are isotropic solutions of drug substances in the homogeneous mixtures of surfactants, oils, and hydrophilic cosolvents (Djekic and Primorac, 2010; Gursoy and Benita, 2004; Porter et al., 2008; Pouton, 2000, 2006; Pouton and Porter, 2008). SMEDDS and SNEDDS are more suitable for production, storage, and application than microemulsions and nanoemulsions. SNEDDS and SMEDDS are classified as Type III lipid formulations for oral administration of drugs, according to *The Lipid Formulation Classification System* (LFCS) proposed by Pouton (2000), and they usually comprise up to 80% of oil phase, 20–50% of surfactants (HLB > 11), and 20–50% of cosolvents. The compositions of the preconcentrates may vary in terms of the type and concentration of the used excipients, which create a difference regarding their dispersibility in the biological environment and availability of the active substance for absorption. SNEDDS typically contain a higher concentration of the oil (up to 40%) and a lower proportion of the hydrophilic surfactants and cosolvents (up to 40%). SMEDDS are more hydrophilic, have lower oil content (up to 20%) and higher concentrations of surfactants and cosolvents (up to 50%). SMEDDS disperse spontaneously and the dispersion process is relatively fast and unaffected by the influence of food and endogenous factors, such as digestion of lipids and secretion of bile and pancreatic juice. In addition, since the surface of the oil–water interface film is inversely proportional to the diameter of the droplets of the dispersed oil phase, it is considered that the SMEDDSs provide a large capacity for solubilizing of poorly soluble drug substances and rapid drug release, which are prerequisites for improvement of their absorption (Huiling et al., 2013; Kuentz, 2012; Porter et al., 2008; Pouton, 2006). The self-dispersion process is spontaneous and large surface area of an in situ formed nanocarrier is available for solubilization of poorly soluble substances as well as their in vivo release. Such features make self-microemulsifying and self-nanoemulsifying systems particularly useful in oral delivery of poorly soluble drugs (Mrsny, 2012; Khamkar, 2011). Solubilization of poorly soluble substances provides the drug concentration in the carrier and at the site of absorption for several times greater than their solubility. Furthermore, ingredients such as surfactants and oils can increase permeability of biological membranes leading to an increase in the extent of the drug absorption. The smaller oil droplets provide a large interfacial area for pancreatic lipase to hydrolyze triglycerides and thereby promote the rapid release of the drug and/or formation of mixed micelles of bile salts containing the drug (O'Driscoll, 2002). The surfactants used are known to improve the BA by various mechanisms, including (1) improvement in drug dissolution, (2) increase in intestinal epithelial permeability, (3) increase in tight-junction permeability, (4) inhibition of the efflux of drug substances through the P-glycoprotein, and/or (5) metabolic degradation of drug substances in the enterocytes/intestinal epithelium under the influence of CYP450 enzyme (Fatouros et al., 2007; O'Driscoll, 2002). A major drawback of microemulsions and low-energy produced nanoemulsions as well as their preconcentrates SMEDDS and SNEDDS, respectively, is a relatively high surfactant content and potential for irritation at the site of application. In addition, many factors in vivo, including the volume and pH of GIT fluids as well as presence of food, may affect structure and stability of the nanocarriers, thereby compromising their drug-delivery potential (Jankovic et al., 2016).

The lipid formulations concept, including SMEDDS and SNEDDS, is already established as an important approach for improvement of oral delivery of poorly soluble drugs. Several studies carried out were aimed to design the carriers of microemulsion or nanoemulsion type (often generated from the corresponding SMEDDS and SNEDDS, respectively) for oral administration of NSAIDs and to evaluate their performances in terms of impact on the release of the drug from the carrier formed in vitro and/or in situ, as well as absorption and BA of the model substances, such as ibuprofen (Djekic et al., 2013a; Mercuri et al., 2011), ketoprofen (Patil et al., 2004, 2005), diclofenac (Attama et al., 2003), celecoxib (Subramanian et al., 2004), and etodolac (Barakat, 2009). In the other parts of this chapter are commented composition and NSAIDs delivery profiles of these types of drug-delivery systems.

3.3 DESIGN AND CHARACTERIZATION OF BIOCOMPATIBLE MICROEMULSION/NANOEMULSION DRUG-DELIVERY SYSTEMS

Development of microemulsions and nanoemulsions, as well as their preconcentrates, requires careful selection of excipients and their concentrations, which are appropriate to solubilize the entire dose of the drug, provide the solubilized state, and optimal drug-release kinetic during the absorption in the GIT. Despite a great number of oils, surfactants, and cosurfactants, available in the current market as pharmaceutical excipients approved for oral administration, the selection of the components suitable for self-dispersing formulations is a huge challenge due to lack of systematic investigations of the effect of formulation parameters, such as chemical structure and relative amounts of the components, on microemulsion/nanoemulsion formation and properties (Sprunk et al., 2012). The main criteria for selection of excipients are pharmaceutical acceptability, biocompatibility, physicochemical stability, mutual miscibility, and compatibility as well as solubility and compatibility of the excipients with the drug substance. Frequently chosen components of the oil phase are: vegetable oils (e.g., corn oil, olive oil, peanut oil, rapeseed oil, sesame oil, soybean oil, coconut or palm seed oil); hydrogenated vegetable oils (e.g., Lubritab, Akofine, Sterotex,

Dynasan P60, Softisan 154, Suppocire, Cutina HR, Sterotex HM, Hydrocote, Lipo); partial glycerides (Capmul MCM, Geleol, Imwitor 191, Cutina GMS, Tegin, Precirol ATO 5, Peceol, Maisine 35-1, Compritol 888 ATO). The surfactants involved in the SMEDDS formulations are from the class of nonionic tensides that have been reported as safe for oral administration in concentrations relevant for stabilization of microemulsions/nanoemulsions, such as polyoxylglycerides (Labrasol, Labrafil-s, and Gelucire-s), ethoxylated glycerides derived from castor oil (Cremophor EL, RH40, or RH60), and esters of fatty acids and alcohols (e.g., Plurol Oleique CC497, Capryol 90, Lauroglycol 90, Mirj 45, Mirj 52, Solutol HS15, Span 80, Span20, Tween 80, Tween 20). Furthermore, the nonionic tensides are less affected by pH and changes in ionic strength. Among the polyoxyethylene-based surfactants, Labrasol and Cremophor EL are well-characterized pharmaceutical excipients as solubility and absorption enhancers. Hydrophilic cosolvents, such as low-molecular weight macrogols (polyethylene glycols, PEGs) (e.g., macrogol 300, macrogol 400), ethanol, propylene glycol, glycerol, and diethylene glycol monoethyl ether, are common ingredients of SMEDDS and SNEDDS. These molecules may increase solubility of the drug and facilitate dispersion of the preconcentrate and formation of the microemulsion/nanoemulsion carriers. However, in some cases, there is a certain risk for irritation of GI mucosa and relatively high chemical reactivity. For instance, PEGs contain peroxide impurities, as well as secondary products formed by autooxidation, which can compromise chemical stability of the oils and a drug substance. PEGs, also, due to their hygroscopicity, may affect hard gelatin capsules integrity. Oxidability issue is also the important factor in selection of oil. Therefore, although the physical stability of the SMEDDS and SNEDDS preconcentrates is superior compared to ready-to-use microemulsions and nanoemulsions, respectively, the preconcentrates are more susceptible for oxidation. Thus, hydrogenated vegetable oils are preferable as most resistant to oxidative degradation. In some cases, where chemical and/or physical stability issues occur at the room temperature, low storage temperatures (2–8°C) are required (Hauss, 2007; Jannin et al., 2008; Kommuru et al., 2001; Pouton, 2000; Sha et al., 2005; Strickley, 2004).

The important task for formulators is to develop the formulation with the drug loading capacity equivalent to the therapeutical dose. Therefore, generally accepted approach for screening of the excipients is determination of the drug solubility in pure excipients (e.g., oils, surfactants) or, preferable, in the mixture of the ingredients of the formulation (Fanun, 2009b; Jannin et al., 2008; Kang et al., 2004; Kommuru et al., 2001; Patel and Sawant, 2007; Rane and Anderson, 2008; Ying et al., 2008; Zhang et al., 2004). In most cases, the acceptance or rejection of the excipients was based exclusively on the available literature or experimentally obtained data on the drug solubility (Fanun, 2009a; Jankovic et al., 2016; Mrsny, 2012; Pouton, 2000). Triglycerides have high solvent capacity for more hydrophobic drugs (log $P > 4$). Solvent capacity for less hydrophobic drugs can be improved by blending triglycerides with mixed monoglycerides and diglycerides. The hydrophilic surfactants and cosolvents may increase the solvent capacity for drugs with intermediate log P ($2 <$ log $P < 4$) which have limited solubility in both water and lipids (Pouton, 2000). The drug solubility in the formulation may be significantly different and insufficient for uploading the therapeutic dose of the drug substance in a suitable unit dosage form (Rane and Anderson, 2008). That shifts the focus on testing the solubility from the individual excipients to the mixtures of the excipients (Jankovic et al., 2016). For example, Subramanian et al. (2004) developed SMEDDS comprising combination of polysorbate 80, polysorbate 20, and PEG-8 caprylic/ capric glycerides. It was determined that the solubility of celecoxib in mixture of polysorbate 80 and C8/C10 diesters of propylene glycol increased from 93.6 to 298.3 mg/mL as the ratio of polysorbate 80 to C8/C10 diesters of propylene glycol increased from 1:4 to 4:1. On the other hand, the solubility of celecoxib in the mixture of polysorbate 20 and propylene glycol monocaprylic ester increased from 112.2 to 247.2 mg/mL as the ratio of polysorbate 20 to propylene glycol monocaprylic ester increased from 1:4 to 3:1, but further increase in polysorbate 20 content resulted in decrease in celecoxib solubility.

The concentrations of ingredients of preconcentrates required for self-microemulsification or self-nanoemulsification are often adjusted by performing extensive and time-consuming phase behavior studies in surfactants/ cosolvents/oil/water systems, including identification of different thermodynamically stable phases as a function of concentrations of the constituents, temperature and pressure (Alany et al., 2009; Djekic, 2012; Djekic et al., 2012; Friberg and Aikens, 2009; Kahlweit, 1999; Sjöblom et al., 1996). Phase behavior studies collect information about mutual solubility of the excipients and their concentration ranges which correspond to formation of different phases including nanoemulsions and microemulsions. For instance, the investigations of Djekic et al. (2012) revealed that the surfactant-to-cosurfactant mass ratio and molar volume of oil are important formulation factors in development of microemulsions. Phase behavior of such systems is very complex and may be affected by numerous factors and the extensive evaluation of the relationship between physicochemical characteristics of the excipients and phase behavior of the multicomponent systems is still a difficult task.

The recent studies pointed that development of microemulsion/nanoemulsion carriers and their preconcentrates requires a more convenient experimental approach that should include qualitative and quantitative optimization regarding their dispersibility and drug solubilization capacity upon administration (Djekic et al., 2013a; Djekic and Primorac, 2014; Jankovic et al., 2016). Preconcentrates of microemulsions and nanoemulsions are usually administered orally in soft and hard capsules or as oral solutions, often diluted with water or fruit juice before taking. In vitro characterization of these aspects of the systems after water phase dilution is suitable for assessment of drug solubilization capacity and differentiation of self-microemulsifying systems from self-nanoemulsifying systems (Anton and Vandamme, 2011). The study of Djekic et al. (2013a) evaluated the influence of the type and concentration of the oil phase and surfactant-to-cosurfactant mass ratio on self-microemulsifying ability of the microemulsion preconcentrates comprising PEG-8 caprylic/capric glycerides (the surfactant), PEG-40 hydrogenated castor oil (the cosurfactant) (at surfactant-to-cosurfactant mass ratios varied from 0.11 up to 9.0), and 10 or 20% w/w of the oil (medium-chain triglycerides or olive oil). The dispersibility assessment in neutral and acidic media included droplet size and zeta potential analysis. The microemulsification ability was observed in systems prepared with medium-chain triglycerides at surfactant-to-cosurfactant ratios 2.33 and 1.0 (in the mixtures containing 10% of the oil) and 0.43 and 0.11 (when 20% of the oil was used). The charge of the droplets of these formulations was negative, however these samples were suitable for incorporation of cationic lipid oleyl amine, providing the positive zeta potential, which is preferred for absorption in the GI environment. The obtained results indicated that medium-chain triglycerides were generally more suitable oil for microemulsification process in comparison with olive oil, which comprises long-chain triglycerides, and at the lower investigated concentration. Furthermore, the ability of the PEG-8 caprylic/capric glycerides/PEG-40 hydrogenated castor oil/medium-chain triglycerides mixtures to form microemulsions was diminished in the acidic medium. In this study, only formulations, which passed the dispersibility test in both double-distilled water and acidic media, were considered as microemulsion preconcentrates which were used for further evaluation as potential carriers for oral delivery of ibuprofen. For further assessment were selected two series of potential SMEDDS prepared with 10% of ibuprofen loading and 10 or 20% of the oil. Characterization of the investigated formulations included evaluation of self-microemulsification ability and in vitro drug release. Formation of oil-in-water microemulsions with the average droplet size (Z-ave) below 100 nm, was observed in dispersions prepared with 10% of medium-chain triglycerides, within the entire investigated range of the surfactant-to-cosurfactant mass ratio. These formulations were classified as SMEDDS. Results of characterization pointed out the importance of type and concentration of the oil, as well as the concentration of the surfactants, for self-microemulsification ability of the investigated systems (Djekic and Primorac, 2014; Mercuri et al., 2011). Mercuri et al. (2011) investigated the mechanism of emulsification, the droplet size of the resulting nanoemulsions and emulsions and the effect of ibuprofen (6%) on the emulsification process of self-emulsifying drug-delivery systems composed of 65% soybean oil, 17.5% Span 80, and 17.5% Tween 80 (w/w) by using optical microscope employing polarizing optics and droplet size measurement by laser light-scattering technique. The self-emulsification process was characterized in different aqueous media and by using three different methods: (1) by gently inverting volumetric flask, (2) in USP dissolution apparatus II, and (3) by using the in vitro Dynamic Gastric Model (DGM) of the human stomach (developed at the Institute of Food Research, Norwich, United Kingdom) which is able to replicate its digestive functions of transforming the bolus into chyme (Marciani et al., 2003, 2006, 2009). The investigation showed different emulsification processes in the presence and absence of the drug, which was also manifested in different droplet sizes. The first process involves the budding off or erosion of material from the surface of larger droplets (Fig. 3.1), involving the presence of lamellar liquid crystalline phases whose presence was confirmed by the establishment of pseudoternary phase diagrams. The second involves distortion and breakup of the larger particles (Fig. 3.2). While some differences were observed

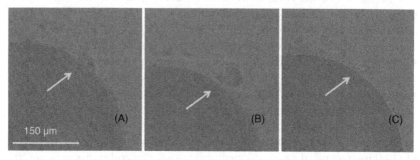

FIGURE 3.1 Photomicrographs of the SEDDS placebo in contact with AGJ_{wp} observed using polarized light microscopy (Leica DM LS2; ×4 magnification). Images show the interface during ejection, as indicated by the *arrows* (images A–C taken over 8 s). Bar = 150 µm. *(Reprinted with permission from Mercuri A, Passalacqua A, Wickham MS, Faulks RM, Craig DQ, Barker SA: The effect of composition and gastric conditions on the self-emulsification process of ibuprofen-loaded self-emulsifying drug delivery systems: a microscopic and dynamic gastric model study,* Pharm Res 28:1540–1551, 2011)

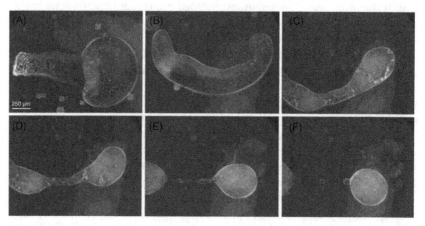

FIGURE 3.2 Photomicrographs showing injection of a droplet of the ibuprofen-loaded SEDDS formulation into 0.1 N HCl under polarized light (Olympus BX60). The pictures show that self-emulsification occurs through a process whereby the droplet entirely becomes distorted and breaks down into individual droplets. Formation of lamellar liquid crystals is also observed. Images were taken over a period of 300 s. Bar = 250 µm. *(Reprinted with permission from Mercuri A, Passalacqua A, Wickham MS, Faulks RM, Craig DQ, Barker SA: The effect of composition and gastric conditions on the self-emulsification process of ibuprofen-loaded self-emulsifying drug delivery systems: a microscopic and dynamic gastric model study,* Pharm Res 28:1540–1551, 2011)

depending on the aqueous medium used, the key factor influencing mechanism appeared to be the presence of ibuprofen, which was also shown to influence the liquid crystalline phases. It is suggested that the surface activity of the drug may well be of relevance to these observations, but overall, the study has clearly shown that the drug must be considered as a contributing factor to the emulsification properties of the SEDDS. A trend of decreasing size with the drug addition was noted, again suggesting the influence of the drug on the emulsification process. The DGM studies indicated that the SEDDS generated fine droplets, which remained stable within the gastric environment for up to 2 h, irrespective of the presence of the drug. It was proposed that the vigor of the mechanical movement of the stomach supersedes the formulation effects, leading to a small, uniform-size distribution irrespective of the presence of the drug. In this study it was concluded that while the drug may alter the emulsification process and mechanism, in a biological environment such effects may be superseded by the mechanical movement of the stomach (Mercuri et al., 2011).

Barakat (2010) performed formulation of etodolac-loaded SNEDDS, which were optimized by evaluating their ability to self-nanoemulsify when introduced to an aqueous medium under gentle agitation, and by determination of the droplet size of the resulting emulsion. A series of SNEDDS formulations prepared by varying concentrations of the surfactant (Labrasol) (20–40%), the cosurfactant (Transcutol P, Lauroglycol 90, or Capryol 90) (10–30%), and the oil (Labrafac WL1349, Labrafil M 1944 CS, or Labrafil M 2125) (30%). Etodolac was dispersed into the mixture of oil and surfactant–cosurfactant at the level of 20% w/w. The efficiency of self-nanoemulsification was assessed. The droplet size distribution of the nanoemulsions upon dilution with purified water was determined by photon correlation spectroscopy. Lipophilic surfactants with HLB < 10 (Capryol 90, Lauroglycol 90) were capable of promoting some emulsification of the oil, but the resulting emulsions are normally crude in terms of size. Hydrophilic surfactants with HLB > 10 (Labrasol, Transcutol P), on the other hand, provide fine, uniform emulsion droplets (Lacy and Embleton, 1997). The characterization of emulsification process revealed better visual grading and smaller droplet size values resulting when the formulations were dispersed in the acidic medium. The droplet size analysis showed that increasing the surfactant concentration (from 20 to 40% w/w) in SNEDDS formulations decreased the mean droplet size of the nanoemulsion formed (Fig. 3.3). The smallest droplet size was observed when Lauroglycol 90 or Capryol 90 were used as cosurfactants, likely as the result of more surfactant being available to stabilize the oil–water interface and form a better, close-packed film at the oil–water interface (Levy and Benita, 1990). Droplet size decreased as the surfactant-to-cosurfactant ratio increased. An optimized formulation of SNEDDS composed of 20% etodolac, 30% oil Labrafac WL1349, 10% Lauroglycol 90, and 40% Labrasol (Barakat, 2010).

Attama et al. (2003) evaluated the liquefaction time for self-emulsifying systems with 50 mg of diclofenac which was formulated as tablets. The surfactant-to-oil mass ratios were 1:14 (batch 1), 2:13 (batch 2), 3:12 (batch 3), 4:11 (batch 4), and 5:10 (batch 5). The tablet melt time (liquefaction time) was recorded

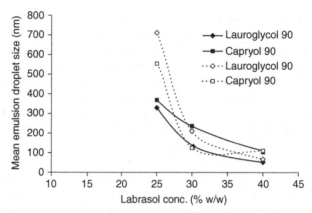

FIGURE 3.3   Effect of surfactant (Labrasol) concentration on mean emulsion droplet diameter. Water *(dashed lines)*, 0.1 M HCl *(solid lines)*. *(Reprinted with permission from Barakat NS: Enhanced oral bioavailability of etodolac by self-emulsifying systems: in-vitro and in-vivo evaluation,* J Pharm Pharmacol *62:173–180, 2010)*

using a thermometer with attached tablet in simulated gastric fluid (SGF) without pepsin, maintained at 37 ± 1°C. The important drawback of the test was the absence of agitation, thus the liquefaction times were fairly high compared to disintegration standards for compressed uncoated tablets. The authors indicated that at GI conditions, however, GI motility will likely lower the liquefaction time, resulting in faster emulsification and penetration of the aqueous fluid into tablet interior, ensuring drug release even before tablet integrity fails. Nevertheless, the diclofenac self-emulsifying tablets showed acceptable tablet properties.

Relevant literature describes a growing interest for development of new strategies for more comprehensive design of microemulsion- and nanoemulsion-forming systems. Computer programs based on artificial intelligence concepts are proving to be distinctive utilities for this purpose. Nonlinear mathematical approaches, such as experimental design, artificial neural networks (ANN), genetic algorithms, and/or neuro-fuzzy logic represent promising tools for in silico modeling of formulation procedures in development of drug carriers. There are several reports of the design of SMEDDS/SNEDDS based on phase-behavior studies upgraded with the experimental design approach (Krstić et al., 2015; Sprunk et al., 2012). There are particular examples related with the development of SMEDDS and SNEDDS for oral delivery of NSAIDs. Subramanian et al. (2004) developed SMEDDS comprising the combination of polysorbate 80 (the surfactant), polysorbate 20 (the cosurfactant), and PEG-8 caprylic/capric glycerides (the oil). The surfactant-to-oil ratio of 3:1 and 2:1 was selected to construct the phase diagrams. The monophasic zones produced by the present systems were high at 3:1 ratio of surfactant to oil. The homogeneous mixture consisting of polysorbate 20, propylene glycol monocaprylic ester, and PEG-8 caprylic/capric glycerides, produced larger region of monophasic zone than mixture containing polysorbate 80, C8/C10 diesters of propylene glycol and PEG-8 caprylic/capric glycerides. Mixtures composed of polysorbate 80, C8/C10 diesters of propylene glycol, and PEG-8 caprylic/capric glycerides were able to solubilize higher amounts of the drug than the mixtures of polysorbate 20, propylene glycol monocaprylic ester, and PEG-8 caprylic/capric glycerides. Hence, the latter were selected for further optimization, since it possessed low viscosity, high self-emulsification region, and better spontaneity. Composition of SMEDDS was optimized using simplex lattice mixture design. In this design, five design points and three check points were generated using Design Expert software. Based on the pseudoternary diagram the concentrations of the components were selected. Dissolution efficiency (DE), $t_{85\%}$, absorbance of diluted SMEDDS formulation and solubility of celecoxib in diluted formulation were chosen as response variables. The results indicate that celecoxib had little effect on the formation of microemulsions. The SMEDDS formulation optimized via mixture design consisted of 49.5% PEG-8 caprylic/capric glycerides, 40.5% mixture of polysorbate 20 and propylene glycol monocaprylic ester (3:1), and 10% celecoxib, showed significantly higher rate and extent of absorption than conventional capsule and thus had the potential to minimize the variability in absorption and to provide rapid onset of action of celecoxib. Patil et al. (2004) assessed the effect of concentrations of cosurfactant and gelling agent on emulsification process (i.e., time required for complete emulsification, viscosity, and the droplet size) and in vitro drug diffusion of gelled self-emulsifying ketoprofen-loaded system by using 3^2 factorial design. The investigated system consisted of diesters of caprylic/capric acids (the oil), C8/C10 mono/diglycerides (the cosurfactant), polysorbate 20 (the surfactant), and colloidal silicon oxide (the gelling agent). Multiple regression analysis data and response surfaces obtained using Unistat software, showed that liquid crystal phase viscosity increased significantly with increasing amount of silicon dioxide, which in turn caused an increase in average droplet size of resultant emulsion and slower drug diffusion. Moreover, it was demonstrated that although C8/C10 mono/diglycerides had no effect on average droplet size, it increased drug diffusion from the formulation. Although it was observed that the entire drug was released within 5–10 min from each SEDDS formulated, ketoprofen release was highly dependent on liquid crystal phase formed at the interface, since it is likely to affect the angle of curvature of the droplet formed and the resistance offered for partitioning of drug into aqueous media. The in vitro diffusion of drug from liquid crystal phases was directly proportional to C8/C10 mono/diglycerides concentration and was inversely proportional to colloidal silicon oxide concentration. The study revealed that resultant drug diffusion from the formulation was the net result of these two variables acting in opposite directions.

ANN models were introduced as useful tools for accurate differentiation and prediction of the regions of different colloidal systems, including biocompatible microemulsions and nanoemulsions, from the qualitative and quantitative composition of multicomponent formulations of surfactant/cosolvent/oil/water type (Djekic et al., 2011a, 2013b). Although in silico formulation is not a substitute for laboratory experiments, the results of current efforts clearly demonstrate a potential to shorten the time necessary to find optimal quantitative and qualitative composition. Also, this strategy is capable of generating new potential microemulsion/nanoemulsion-forming systems. For the purpose of development of biocompatible microemulsion carriers for ibuprofen and diclofenac sodium, Djekic (2012) performed a phase-behavior study of the pseudoternary systems Labrasol/cosurfactant/oil/water by construction of pseudoternary phase diagrams at different surfactant-to-cosurfactant mass ratios. Furthermore, in order to elucidate the influence of oil and cosurfactant on the efficiency of such complex mixtures to generate microemulsions, suitable ANN models were developed. Phase-behavior study pointed that the cosurfactant PEG-40 hydrogenated castor oil demonstrated optimal solubilization power compared to the other cosurfactants, at surfactant-to-cosurfactant mass ratios in the range from 0.67 to 1.5. The data obtained from the phase-behavior study were used to generate inputs (surfactant-to-cosurfactant mass ratios and surfactant + cosurfactant-to-oil mass ratios) and an output for ANN training (microemulsion area border) by employing software program *Statistica Neural Networks* (StatSoft, Inc., Tulsa, Oklahoma, USA). The architectures of the generated ANNs were the multilayer perceptron (MLP) network with 4 layers; the generalized regression neural network (GRNN) with 27 hidden units in the second layer (with negative exponential activation and radial postsynaptic function), 2 units in the third layer, and 1 output unit in the fourth layer; the radial basis function (RBF) network. The prediction ability of the generated ANNs for the microemulsion area border in the investigated systems was above 90%. Systematic experimental approach carried out in this study enable to assess combined influences of the formulation variables on microemulsion formation in multicomponent systems as well as to limit the experimental effort for screening of microemulsion carriers.

3.4 EVALUATION OF POTENTIAL OF MICROEMULSION/ NANOEMULSION SYSTEMS FOR ORAL DELIVERY OF NSAIDS

The potential advantages of NSAIDs encapsulation by using microemulsion/ nanoemulsion carriers, including development of physically stable pharmaceutical dosage form with high drug-loading capacity, dispersibility, rate and extent of absorption, and thus increased BA, are illustrated by observations and conclusions derived from the extensive results of the relevant studies in this field (Table 3.2).

Examples of enhancement of in vitro release rate of NSAIDs by manipulation with the relative contents of the ingredients of the nanoemulsion/microemulsion carrier are already described (Djekic and Primorac, 2014). Ibuprofen-loaded SMEDDS comprising Labrasol/Cremophor RH40/medium-chain triglycerides, at surfactant-to-cosurfactant mass ratios ranged from 9.0 to 0.11, and with 10% of the oil phase, were filled into hard gelatin capsules. Investigation of the release profiles of ibuprofen from the designed SMEDDS was performed in

TABLE 3.2 The Review of In Vitro and In Vivo Studies on NSAIDs Oral Delivery Potential of the Nanoemulsion/Microemulsion-Based Systems

Active substance	Study	Carrier	Main results	References
Ibuprofen	In vitro drug release	SMEDDS	Formulation study with optimization of drug loading capacity, dispersibility in aqueous media and in vitro drug release	Djekic et al. (2013a)
Diclofenac	In vitro drug release	SNEDDS	Formulation study with optimization of dispersibility in aqueous media and in vitro drug release	Attama et al. (2003)
Etodolac	In vivo assessment (in rabbits) of oral BA	SNEDDS	Faster absorption of etodolac from the SNEDDS than that from the other formulations	Barakat (2010)
Celecoxib	In vivo assessment of BA in healthy male volunteers	SMEDDS	Increased relative BA (132%) of the SMEDDS formulation to the conventional capsule	Subramanian et al. (2004)
Ketoprofen	In vitro drug release and BA in healthy male volunteers	Gelled self-nanoemulsifying formulation	BA equivalent with the pure drug filled into hard gelatin capsules	Patil et al. (2005)

BA, Bioavailability.

accordance with the USP 30–NF 25 dissolution tests for ibuprofen oral suspensions and tablets. The ibuprofen release profiles were compared with the release profiles obtained for the referent drugs in the dosage form of soft gelatin capsules and coated tablets, with the same strength of the drug substance (200 mg of ibuprofen). The fulfillment of the USP 30–NF 25 request for at least 80% of ibuprofen released after 60 min was observed for the formulations at surfactant-to-cosurfactant mass ratio 9.0 (M1) and 0.11 (M5). In contrast, the release of ibuprofen from the other investigated samples (M2, M3, and M4), was considerably slower (i.e., near 70% of the drug for 60 min). Furthermore, the ibuprofen release profiles of the samples M1 and M5 were different from each other. The release of ibuprofen from the sample M1 was complete after the first 10 min, while at the same time the release from the sample M5 was near 30%. The physicochemical characterization revealed that M1 represented the SMEDDS which efficiently solubilized ibuprofen in acidic media, while upon introduction into alkaline medium, the drug rapidly released from the carrier. The results obtained during the characterization of self-microemulsification ability of the M1–M5 systems supported these assumptions. Although the microemulsion was formed in the acidic medium, in the alkaline medium the nanodispersed carrier formed from the samples M1 and M5 was disturbed, the capacity for solubilization of ibuprofen was reduced, and the drug was rapidly transferred onto the surrounding aqueous medium. Slower release from the carriers M2, M3, and M4 has been associated with the formation of oil-in-water microemulsion of which stability and structure in the alkaline medium were well preserved, due to the establishment of stronger synergy in stabilization of the interfacial film between the surfactant and the cosurfactant. Therefore, the release of the drug molecules from the surfactant/cosurfactant film was limited. The differences in the release profiles of ibuprofen from the samples M1 and M5 have been associated with different solubilization power of the surfactant/cosurfactant mixtures at different surfactant-to-cosurfactant mass ratios (Djekic and Primorac, 2008; Djekic et al., 2011b). The sample M5 contains a significantly higher amount of Cremophor RH 40, thus the risk of disturbance, if the carrier, is lower than for the sample M1. Interestingly, it was observed that the referent products released 55 and 65% of ibuprofen, for 10 min. In the first case (coated tablets) the release was limited by the dissolution rate of the drug substance, while in the second case (soft capsules), the disintegration rate of a capsule shell, the solubility of ibuprofen in the formulation and the partition between the formulation and the acceptor medium may also retard the drug release. From the in vitro release study was concluded that the formulated SMEDDS M1 can be considered as the promising system for achievement of the more rapid onset of action of ibuprofen (Djekic and Primorac, 2014). Attama et al. (2003) evaluated the in vitro dissolution profile of diclofenac from the solid self-emulsifying systems comprising goat fat and polysorbate 65 (Tween 65) in SGF without pepsin. The self-emulsifying systems were formulated as tablets containing 50 mg of diclofenac. The surfactant-to-oil mass ratios were 1:14 (batch 1), 2:13 (batch 2), 3:12 (batch 3), 4:11 (batch 4), and 5:10 (batch 5). Figs. 3.4 and 3.5 show the obtained diclofenac dissolution profiles. The overall percentage of the released drug was high for all samples (i.e., near 100%). The obtained results indicated that the drug release increased with increase in polysorbate 65 content or decrease in goat fat content, since a higher surfactant content ensures faster emulsification. The release of diclofenac from the tablets was further analyzed using Fickian diffusion model to determine the mechanism of release of diclofenac from the tablets. The analysis showed that release of diclofenac from the self-emulsifying tablets followed the non-Fickian diffusion model (anomalous behavior). However, batches 1 and 2 exhibited almost zero-order kinetics, while batches 4 and 5 demonstrated faster drug release. The latter observation was related with

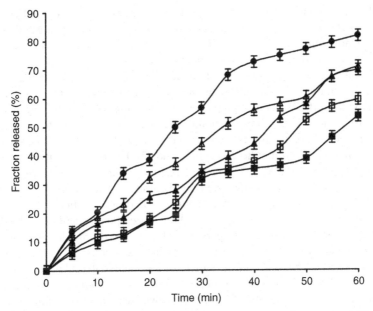

FIGURE 3.4 Dissolution profile of diclofenac from the tablets at agitation rate of 100 rpm B1 (■), B2 (□), B3 (▲), B4 (△), and B5 (●). *(Reprinted from Attama AA, Nzekwe IT, Nnamani PO, Adikwu MU, Onugu CO: The use of self-emulsifying systems in the delivery of diclofenac,* Int J Pharm *262(1–2):23–28, 2003, Copyright (2003), with permission from Elsevier)*

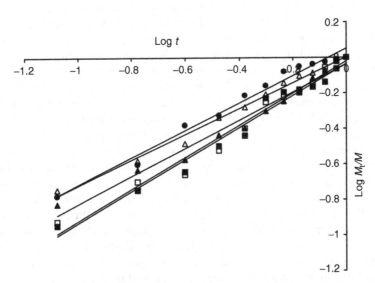

FIGURE 3.5 Log–log plot of the amount of diclofenac released B1 (■), B2 (□), B3 (▲), B4 (△), and B5 (●). *(Reprinted from Attama AA, Nzekwe IT, Nnamani PO, Adikwu MU, Onugu CO: The use of self-emulsifying systems in the delivery of diclofenac,* Int J Pharm *262(1–2):23–28, 2003, Copyright (2003), with permission from Elsevier)*

the higher content of polysorbate 65 in these samples, that is, the batches with higher polysorbate 65 to goat fat content ratios gave better diclofenac release rates. Under mild agitation as occurs under GI conditions, the release rates may be comparable to those of conventional tablets.

Comparative biopharmaceutical studies showed a significant potential for more superior biopharmaceutical and pharmacokinetic profile of poorly soluble drugs with SMEDDS compared to conventional oral solid dosage forms (tablets or capsules). There are two main aspects of the SMEDDS formulations: (1) the potential of the formulation to maintain the drug in the dissolved state in the GIT lumen during the absorption, and (2) the enhancement of the drug absorption (Pouton, 2000). The critical factors of the in vivo performance of SMEDDS that have been suggested are: solubility of the drug in SMEDDS, the location of the drug in the microemulsion, partition coefficient of the drug between oil and water phase (i.e., GIT fluids), specific interactions of the drug with excipients, the size, polydispersity, and charge of the droplets, site or path of absorption, the presence of components that can act as absorption enhancers as well as the influence of the variety of food materials and digestive fluids present in the GIT. Solubility of the drug in SMEDDS formulations is usually high, but the overall utility of each system will depend on its dilutability on use, and whether the risk of the loss of solvent capacity on dilution followed by precipitation of the drug in the GIT arises. The surfactants used in these formulations are known to improve drug dissolution, however, their concentrations can occasionally be insufficient to promote the self-emulsification process which will lead to drug precipitation upon dilution in vivo (Pouton, 2006). It was generally accepted that during the dilution of SMEDDS, the hydrophilic surfactant will partition into the continuous (water) phase and percolation or phase separation may occur, which may affect overall solubilization capacity for the drug. The extent of the precipitation will mainly depend on the log P of the drug, and to what extent the surfactant is involved to its solubilization within the formulation. In the cases where a water soluble cosolvent (such as PEG or alcohol) takes an important part in formulation, dilution with water will usually result in partition of cosolvent into the continuous phase, that may also lead to destruction of the microemulsion, and subsequently, to drug precipitation (Humberstone and Charman, 1997; Pouton, 2000). The results of numerous studies have shown that the rate and extent of the drug release from microemulsions depends on the physicochemical properties of the drug as well as on the microemulsions composition and microstructure (Bagwe et al., 2001; Kogan and Garti, 2006; Malmstein, 1999). Hydrophobic drugs are most likely dissolved in oil phase and/or are located at the interfacial film in the region of hydrophobic tails of amphiphile molecules. Therefore, the diffusion of drug molecules is hindered and drug release is slow and predominantly depends on partition coefficient of the drug. In some cases, the drug may interact with the other components of microemulsion and significantly modify the phase behavior of the system as well as the dilution kinetics and drug release. This issue particularly may arise if the drug possesses amphiphilic properties (Djordjevic et al., 2004, 2005). Several studies in this field demonstrated that NSAIDs formulated in the preconcentrates of nanoemulsions and microemulsions could be favorable with regard to a rapid onset of action, especially if an acute analgesic effect is required. Barakat (2010) performed in vitro drug release evaluation of the SEDDS containing 20% etodolac in soft gelatin capsules (comparing with 100 mg pure powder filled in hard gelatin capsules using lactose as the diluent) using USP 23 Apparatus II and SGF without pepsin (pH 1.2) and water as dissolution media. Pure etodolac shows pH-dependent and incomplete dissolution behavior. Etodolac is a weakly acidic drug, having a pK_a of 4.65, and its solubility is known to increase rapidly with pH values above the pK_a of the drug (Herzfeldi and Kummel, 1983). Etodolac dissolution at pH 1.2 was lower than the dissolution in water. After 60 min, cumulative etodolac released was 3 and 13% in SGF and water, respectively. On the other hand, the dissolution of etodolac from SEDDS formulations was not influenced by pH and it was completely and rapidly dissolved, regardless of the fluid condition (more than 90% of etodolac was released within 30 min in both of the dissolution media tested). The best formulation (small droplet and maximum in vitro dissolution) (composed of 20% etodolac, 30% oil Labrafac WL1349, 10% Lauroglycol 90, and 40% Labrasol) was selected for further in vivo assessment (in rabbits) of oral BA. The SNEDDS formulation of etodolac administered orally to rabbits was compared to the same dose of etodolac (50 mg/kg) in a suspension formulation containing 1% povidone as a suspending agent and also against pure etodolac powder. The peak plasma concentration of 16.4 ± 1.1 mg/mL appeared after 1.3 ± 0.2 h, whereas with powder drug and etodolac suspension the values were 7.5 ± 0.5 and 10.6 ± 0.7 mg/mL at 4.2 ± 0.4 and 2.4 ± 0.2 h, respectively, indicating a faster absorption of etodolac from the SNEDDS than that from the other formulations. The AUC_{0-8} of the etodolac SEDDS formulation was 2.3 times that of the pure drug and 1.4 times that of the suspension form. The obtained results were related with the fact that the lipophilic drug is present in solution or in small droplets of oil, leading to elimination of the dissolution step and the maintenance of the drug in a dissolved state during transport to the unstirred water layer of the intestinal membrane throughout its period in the GI tract (Shah, 2011). The presence of the surfactant (Labrasol, HLB = 14) may also affect the BA of the drug in the SEDDS (Ezrahi et al., 1999). Furthermore, the anti-inflammatory effect in carrageenan-induced paw edema was determined in vivo in male Wister rats, and compared with powder drug and etodolac suspension in water (50 mg/kg). SEDDS formulation exhibits a 21% increase in paw thickness compared with a 39% increase on oral administration of etodolac suspension after 4 h at the same dose of the drug (20 mg/kg). The pronounced anti-inflammatory effect of the etodolac SNEDDS was attributed to an increased availability due to enhanced GI absorption of the drug.

Patil et al. (2005) assessed in vitro drug release and BA of ketoprofen incorporated in gelled self-emulsifying formulation consisting diesters of caprylic/capric acids (Captex 200), C8/C10 mono/diglycerides (Capmul MCM), polyoxyethylene 20 sorbitan monooleate (Tween 80), and colloidal silicon oxide (A 200). They observed that the addition of colloidal silicon dioxide caused an increase in the viscosity of the liquid crystal phase, which in turn increased the average droplet size of the emulsion formed and slowed the drug release. Increasing the amount of cosurfactant was found to increase the drug release (Patil et al., 2004). The in vivo study was performed on the gelled self-emulsifying ketoprofen formulation filled into hard gelatin capsules and the pure drug filled into hard gelatin capsules, in healthy adult human volunteers under fasted conditions. Eight healthy, male volunteers between 22 and 28 years old (mean, 24.75; SD, 2.55 years) and weighing from 59 to 65 kg (mean, 61.5; SD, 2.00 kg) participated in the study. The study was conducted according to a single-dose, 2-way crossover design with four subjects in each of the two treatment groups and a washout period of 1 week between two phases of study. Overnight fasted subjects were randomly divided into two groups, and dose was administered with 200 mL of water in the morning. Food and drinks were withheld for at least 2 h after dosing. A low fat content breakfast and lunch were served at 2 h after sampling and 4 h after dosing, respectively. The volunteers were required to refrain from other food during the conduct of study. Water was allowed ad libitum. The time to reach maximum plasma concentration (t_{max}) in all the volunteers was 2 h for both the products tested. It was observed that C_{max} ratios (test/reference), as such and log transformed, indicating no significant difference between both the products in terms of C_{max}. Since t_{max} was also the same (2 h) for both the products, it can be concluded that there was no significant difference in the rate of absorption of ketoprofen from these products. $AUC_{(0-8\ h)}$ values for Test were not significantly different than those for Reference. These observations suggested that the Test and Reference were not significantly different in terms of BA. When used with lipids, A 200 retards the drug release. The surface of A 200 nanospheres is covered with hydroxyl groups that interact with each other via hydrogen bonding. The earlier observation indicated that with incorporation of A 200 in self-emulsifying systems, the average droplet size of the resultant (micro)emulsion increased and drug release from the droplets slowed. This effect of A 200 was attributed to its gelling in oils due to formation of hydrogen bonds between polar silanol (Si—OH) groups (Raghavan et al., 2000). Although lipids and surfactants have been shown to be the inhibitors of different efflux carriers, ketoprofen is a relatively polar drug and adequate oral BA and rapid absorption are indicative of its cellular uptake process that is not subject to efflux system. Cellular uptake of ketoprofen may perhaps be mediated primarily through the paracellular pathway. Probably the effect of the used system components on this uptake route is not prominent, hence no significant increase in BA was observed when ketoprofen was administered in self-emulsifying formulation by the oral route. However, gelling of self-emulsifying formulation with A 200, which has shown its effect on liquid crystal viscosity and the drug release in vitro, did not retard the rate and extent of ketoprofen absorption from such gelled system.

The optimized SMEDDS formulation developed by Subramanian et al. (2004) consisted of 49.5% PEG-8 caprylic/capric glycerides, 40.5% mixture of polysorbate 20 and propylene glycol monocaprylic ester (3:1) and 10% celecoxib, and its BA has been compared with conventional capsule. Six healthy male volunteers (three in each group) between the ages of 27 and 33 years were administered a single dose of celecoxib with 200 mL of water. Subjects were fasted for at least 8 h before their scheduled treatment regimen. Group A volunteers received hard gelatin capsule containing 200 mg of celecoxib (Celact, Celecoxib 200 mg) while group B volunteers were administered SMEDDS containing 200 mg celecoxib filled in hard gelatin capsules in fasted human male volunteers. The plasma profiles of celecoxib in human volunteers following oral administration of the conventional capsule and SMEDDS formulation were compared. Relative BA of SMEDDS formulation to the conventional capsule was significantly different ($p < 0.05$). The values of $AUC_{0-\infty}$ and C_{max} of SMEDDS formulation increased 1.32- and 1.21-fold and T_{max} decreased 2-fold compared with that of conventional capsule. The relative BA of SMEDDS formulation to the conventional capsule was 132%. The results indicate that, SMEDDS formulation increases the rate and extent of absorption of celecoxib in a considerable manner probably due to the enhanced solubilization as well as rapid and efficient dispersion of the drug in the GI tract. This formulation was stable and prevented precipitation of the celecoxib for the time period relevant for absorption. The developed SMEDDS consisted of less amount of oil making them less prone to gastric emptying delays and resulting in faster absorption. The developed SMEDDS formulations have the potential to minimize variability in absorption and to provide rapid onset of action of celecoxib. The mechanisms by which SMEDDS influence drug delivery are complex and not yet fully elucidated. Mechanisms of enhanced drug absorption mediated by lipid-based formulations include: (1) increased membrane fluidity facilitating transcellular absorption, (2) opening of tight-junctions to allow paracellular transport, (3) inhibition of P-glycoprotein-mediated drug efflux and/or metabolism by gut membrane–bound CYP450 enzymes, and (4) enhanced lymphatic drug transport occurring in conjunction with stimulation of lipoprotein/chylomicron production (O'Driscoll, 2002). Increased intestinal epithelial permeability, increased tight-junction permeability and/or decreased/inhibited P-glycoprotein drug efflux, are frequently ascribed to the surfactants and cosolvents (Pouton, 2000, 2006; Pouton and Porter, 2008). The presence of the excipients that have the potential to enhance the absorption is very important for the ability of the SMEDDS to improve BA of the drugs. Thus, the important challenge for formulators is to find the effective absorption enhancers which can also form SMEDDS over a wide range of water concentrations.

3.5 CONCLUSIONS

Improvement in oral delivery of poorly soluble NSAIDs in terms of reducing the time of onset of action and/or a reduction of variability in the absorption represents a current challenge. Encapsulation of NSAIDs in nanodispersions of microemulsion type and nanoemulsion type represents a novel approach with the potential for achieving the aforementioned objectives and thereby improving their biological availability. Generally, design of microemulsions and nanoemulsions is already established as a promising approach for improvement of oral delivery of poorly soluble drugs due to a significant potential for more superior biopharmaceutical and pharmacokinetic profile compared to conventional oral dosage forms. The focus of the published studies was on design of NSAIDs-loaded microemulsion carriers and nanoemulsion carriers that are formed in vitro and/or in situ in the GIT, from preconcentrates of self-micro/nanoemulsifying type (i.e., SMEDDS and SNEDDS, respectively). The published results demonstrated that active substances from the group of NSAIDs have a significant effect on the dispersibility and the thermodynamic stability of the carrier, which is formed in an aqueous medium. The studies showed that development of SMEDDS and SNEDDS with NSAIDs requires a complex strategy starting from the choice of excipients and their relative contents, assessment of solubility of the active substance in the carrier, evaluation of the drug solubilization capacity of the carrier and mechanism of the drug release from the carrier, as well as a review and assessment of a potential impact of the carrier and/or its components on absorption of the active substance. Recent studies pointed the need to develop novel biorelevant in vitro methods for characterization and evaluation of influence of GIT factors on dispersibility on release and absorption of the active substance from the carrier. At the same time, further considerations regarding the possibilities of modifying the composition of SMEDDS/SNEDDS with the aim to design pharmaceutical dosage forms which have better performances in terms of physicochemical stability and where the improvement of adherence, are already announced in the relevant literature. Further development of methods for in vitro and in vivo animal characterization and development and adoption of standard protocols will facilitate design of SMEDDS and SNEDDS for oral administration of NSAIDs and thus accelerate further progress in this area.

REFERENCES

Agrawal S, Giri TK, Tripathi DK, Ajazuddin, Alexander A: A review on novel therapeutic strategies for the enhancement of solubility for hydrophobic drugs through lipid and surfactant based self micro emulsifyng drug delivery system: a novel approach, *Am J Drug Discov Dev* 2:143–183, 2012.

Alany RG, El Maghraby GMM, Krauel-Goellner K, Graf A: Microemulsion systems and their potential as drug carriers. In Fanun M, editor: *Microemulsions: properties and applications*, Boca Raton, 2009, CRC Press Taylor & Francis Group, pp 247–291.

Alvarez C, Nunez I, Torrado JJ, Gordon J, Potthast H, Garcia-Arieta A: Investigation on the possibility of biowaivers for ibuprofen, *J Pharm Sci* 100:2343–2349, 2011.

Anton N, Vandamme TF: Nano-emulsions and micro-emulsions: clarifications of the critical differences, *Pharm Res* 28:978–985, 2011.

Aronson J: *Meylers side effects of drugs, The International Encyclopedia of Adverse Drug Reactions and Interactions,* ed 16, Amsterdam, 2016, Elsevier Science, pp 236–272.

Attama AA, Nzekwe IT, Nnamani PO, Adikwu MU, Onugu CO: The use of self-emulsifying systems in the delivery of diclofenac, *Int J Pharm* 262:23–28, 2003.

Bagwe RP, Kanicky JR, Palla BJ, Patanjali PK, Shah DO: Improved drug delivery using microemulsions: rationale, recent progress, and new horizons, *Crit Rev Ther Drug* 18:77–140, 2001.

Barakat NS: Etodolac-liquid-filled dispersion into hard gelatin capsules: an approach to improve dissolution and stability of etodolac formulation, *Lett Drug Des Discov* 32:865–876, 2009.

Barakat NS: Enhanced oral bioavailability of etodolac by self-emulsifying systems: in-vitro and in-vivo evaluation, *J Pharm Pharmacol* 62:173–180, 2010.

Chuasuwan B, Binjesoh V, Polli JE, Zhang H, Amidon GL, Junginger HE, Midha KK, Shah VP, Stavchansky S, Dressman JB, Barends DM: Biowaiver monographs for immediate release solid oral dosage forms: diclofenac sodium and diclofenac potassium, *J Pharm Sci* 98:1206–1219, 2009.

Djekic L: *Biocompatible nonionic microemulsions: formulation and characterization approach,* Saarbrücken, 2012, Lambert Academic Publishing.

Djekic L, Cirkovic V, Heleta M, Krajisnik D, Primorac M: Water-dilutable biocompatible microemulsion systems: design and characterisation, *Tenside Surfact Det* 50:409–413, 2013a.

Djekic L, Ibrić S, Primorac M: Application of artificial neural networks (ANNs) in development of pharmaceutical microemulsions. In Flores JA, editor: *Focus on artificial neural networks,* Hauppauge, 2011a, Nova Science Publishers, pp 1a–28a.

Djekic L, Primorac M: The influence of cosurfactants and oils on the formation of pharmaceutical microemulsions based on PEG-8 caprylic/capric glycerides, *Int J Pharm* 352:231–239, 2008.

Djekic L, Primorac M: Microemulsion systems—application in delivery of poorly soluble drugs. In Fanun M, editor: *Colloids in drug delivery,* Abingdon, 2010, Taylor & Francis Group, CRC Press, pp 245–270.

Djekic L, Primorac M: Formulation and characterization of self-microemulsifying drug delivery systems based on biocompatible nonionic surfactants, *Hem Ind* 68:565–573, 2014.

Djekic L, Primorac M, Filipic S, Agbaba D: Investigation of surfactant/cosurfactant synergism impact on ibuprofen solubilization capacity and drug release characteristics of nonionic microemulsions, *Int J Pharm* 433:25–33, 2012.

Djekic L, Primorac M, Jockovic J: Phase behaviour, microstructure and ibuprofen solubilization capacity of pseudo-ternary nonionic microemulsions, *J Mol Liq* 160:81–87, 2011b.

Djekic L, Vasiljevic D, Primorac M: Computer-aided formulation development. In Djuris J, editor: *Computer-aided applications in pharmaceutical technology,* Cambridge, 2013b, Woodhead Publishing, pp 17–29.

Djordjevic L, Primorac M, Stupar M: In vitro release of diclofenac diethylamine from caprylocaproyl macrogolglycerides based microemulsions, *Int J Pharm* 296:73–79, 2005.

Djordjevic L, Primorac M, Stupar M, Krajisnik D: Characterization of caprylocaproyl macrogolglycerides based microemulsion drug delivery vehicles for an amphiphilic drug, *Int J Pharm* 271:11–19, 2004.

DrugBank. Drug & Drug Target Database, 2015. Available from http://www.drugbank.ca/

Ezrahi S, Aserin A, Garti N: Aggregation behaviour in one-phase (Winsor IV) microemulsion systems. In Kumar P, Mittal KL, editors: *Handbook of microemulsion: science and technology,* New York, Basel, 1999, Marcel Dekker, pp 185–246.

Fanun M: Oil type effect on diclofenac solubilization in mixed nonionic surfactants microemulsions, *Colloids Surf A* 343:75–82, 2009a.

Fanun M: Microemulsions with mixed nonionic surfactants. In Fanun M, editor: *Microemulsions: properties and applications*, Boca Raton, 2009b, CRC Press Taylor & Francis Group, pp 87–142.

Fanun M: Biocompatible microemulsions. In Fanun M, editor: *Colloids in biotechnology*, Boca Raton, 2011, CRC Press Taylor & Francis Group, pp 417–436.

Fatouros DG, Karpf DM, Nielsen FS, Mullertz A: Clinical studies with oral lipid based formulations of poorly soluble compounds, *Ther Clin Risk Manag* 3:591–604, 2007.

FDA Center for Drug Evaluation and Research: Inactive ingredient search for approved drug products, 2015. Available from http://www.accessdata.fda.gov/scripts/cder/iig/index.cfm

Friberg SE, Aikens PA: A phase diagram approach to microemulsions. In Fanun M, editor: *Microemulsions: properties and applications*, Boca Raton, 2009, CRC Press Taylor & Francis Group, pp 1–15.

Gupta S, Kesarla R, Omri A: Formulation strategies to improve the bioavailability of poorly absorbed drugs with special emphasis on self-emulsifying systems. ISRN Pharmaceutics 2013 Article ID 848043, 16 pages, 2013.

Gursoy RN, Benita S: Self-emulsifying drug delivery systems (SEDDS) for improved oral delivery of lipophilic drugs, *Biomed Pharmacother* 58:173–182, 2004.

Hauss DJ: Oral lipid-based formulations, *Adv Drug Deliv Rev* 59:667–676, 2007.

Herzfeldi C, Kummel R: Dissociation constants, solubilities and dissolution rates of some selected nonsteroidal anti-inflammatories, *Drug Dev Ind Pharm* 9:767–793, 1983.

Huiling M, Rene H, Mullertza AB: Lipid-based formualtions for oral administration of poorly water-soluble drugs, *Int J Pharm* 453:215–224, 2013.

Humberstone A, Charman WN: Lipid-based vehicles for the oral delivery of poorly water soluble drugs, *Adv Drug Deliv Rev* 25:103–128, 1997.

Jankovic J, Djekic L, Dobricic V, Primorac M: Evaluation of critical formulation parameters in design and differentiation of self-microemulsifying drug delivery systems (SMEDDSs) for oral delivery of aciclovir, *Int J Pharm* 497:301–311, 2016.

Jannin V, Musakhanian J, Marchaud D: Approaches for the development of solid and semi-solid lipid-based formulations, *Adv Drug Deliv Rev* 60:734–746, 2008.

Kahlweit M: Microemulsions, *Annu Rep Prog Chem Sect C* 95:89–116, 1999.

Kang BK, Lee JS, Chon SK, Jeong SY, Yuk SH, Khang G, Lee HB, Cho SH: Development of self-microemulsifying drug delivery systems (SMEDDS) for oral bioavailability enhancement of simvastatin in beagle dogs, *Int J Pharm* 274:65–73, 2004.

Khamkar GS: Self micro-emulsifying drug delivery system (SMEDDS) o/w micro-emulsion for BCS Class II drugs: an approach to enhance an oral bioavailability, *Int J Pharm Pharm Sci* 3:1–3, 2011.

Kogan A, Garti N: Microemulsions as transdermal drug delivery vehicles, *Adv Colloid Interface Sci* 16:369–385, 2006.

Kommuru TR, Gurley B, Khan MA, Reddy IK: Self-emulsifying drug delivery systems (SEDDS) of coenzyme Q10: formulation development and bioavailability assessment, *Int J Pharm* 212:233–246, 2001.

Koushik Y, Preethi S, Satish P, Uma Shankar MS, Takur RS: Development of solid-self micron emulsifying drug delivery systems, *Int J Pharm Sci Nanotechnol* 6:2014–2021, 2013.

Krstić MZ, Ražić SS, Djekić LM, Dobričić VD, Momčilović MA, Vasiljević DD, Ibrić SR: Application of a mixture experimental design in the optimization of the formulation of solid self-emulsifying drug delivery systems containing carbamazepine, *Lat Am J Pharm* 34:885–894, 2015.

Kuentz M: Lipid-based formulations for oral delivery of lipophilic drugs, *Drug Discov Today* 9:97–104, 2012.

Lacy JE, Embleton JK: Delivery system for hydrophobic drugs. US Patent No. 5,645,856, 1997.

Levy MY, Benita S: Drug release from submicronized O/W emulsion: a new in vitro kinetic evaluation model, *Int J Pharm* 66:29–37, 1990.

Malmstein M: Microemulsion in pharmaceuticals. In Kumar P, Mittal KL, editors: *Handbook of microemulsion: science and technology*, New York, 1999, Marcel Dekker, pp 755–772.

Marciani L, Faulks R, Wickham M, Bush D, Wright J, Cox EF, Fillery-Travis A, Gowland P, Spiller RC: Effect of intragastric acid stability of fat emulsions on gastric emptying, plasma lipid profile and postprandial satiety, *Br J Nutr* 101:919–928, 2009.

Marciani L, Wickham M, Bush D, Faulks R, Wright J, Fillery-Travis A, Gowland P, Spiller RC: Magnetic resonance imaging of the behaviour of oil-in-water emulsions in the gastric lumen of man, *Br J Nutr* 95:331–339, 2006.

Marciani L, Wickham M, Wright J, Bush D, Faulks R, Fillery-Travis A, Gowland P, Spiller RC: Magnetic resonance imaging (MRI) insights into how fat emulsion stability alters gastric emptying, *Gastroenterology* 124:A581, 2003.

Mason TG, Wilking JN, Meleson K, Chang CB, Graves SM: Nanoemulsions: formation, structure, and physical properties, *J Phys* 18:R635–R666, 2006.

McClements DJ: Crystals and crystallization in oil-in-water emulsions: implications for emulsion-based delivery systems, *Adv Colloid Interface Sci* 15:1–30, 2012.

Mercuri A, Passalacqua A, Wickham MS, Faulks RM, Craig DQ, Barker SA: The effect of composition and gastric conditions on the self-emulsification process of ibuprofen-loaded self-emulsifying drug delivery systems: a microscopic and dynamic gastric model study, *Pharm Res* 28:1540–1551, 2011.

Mrsny RJ: Oral drug delivery research in Europe, *J Control Release* 161:247–253, 2012.

O'Driscoll CM: Lipid-based formulations for intestinal lymphatic delivery, *Eur J Pharm Sci* 15:405–415, 2002.

Patel D, Sawant KK: Oral bioavailability enhancement of acyclovir by self-microemulsifying drug delivery systems (SMEDDS), *Drug Dev Ind Pharm* 33:1318–1326, 2007.

Patil P, Joshi P, Paradkar A: Effect of formulation variables on preparation and evaluation of gelled self-emulsifying drug delivery system (SEDDS) of ketoprofen, *AAPS PharmSciTech* 5:E42, 2004.

Patil PR, Praveen S, Shobha Rani RH, Paradkar AR: Bioavailability assessment of ketoprofen incorporated in gelled self-emulsifying formulation: a technical note. AAPS PharmSciTech 6 Article 4, 2005.

Porter CJH, Pouton CW, Cuine JF, Charman WN: Enhancing intestinal drug solubilisation using lipid-based delivery systems, *Adv Drug Deliv Rev* 60:673–691, 2008.

Potthast H, Dressman JB, Junginger HE, Midha KK, Oeser H, Shah VP, Vogelpoel H, Barends DM: Biowaiver monographs for immediate release solid oral dosage forms: ibuprofen, *J Pharm Sci* 94:2121–2131, 2005.

Pouton CW: Lipid formulations for oral administration of drugs: non-emulsifying, self-emulsifying and "self-microemulsifying" drug delivery systems, *Eur J Pharm Sci* 2:S93–S98, 2000.

Pouton CW: Formulation of poorly water-soluble drugs for oral administration: physicochemical and physiological issues and the lipid formulation classification system, *Eur J Pharm Sci* 29:278–287, 2006.

Pouton CW, Porter CJ: Formulation of lipid-based delivery systems for oral administration: materials, methods and strategies, *Adv Drug Deliv Rev* 60:625–637, 2008.

Raghavan SR, Walls HJ, Khan SA: Rheology of silica dispersions in organic liquids: new evidence for salvation forces dictated by hydrogen bonding, *Langmuir* 16:7920–7930, 2000.

Raja Sekharan T, Muthumari M, Lanka G, Esakiyammal A: Dissolution Improvement of etodolac using mannitol by solid dispersion method, *WJPPS* 33:1206–1216, 2014.

Rane SS, Anderson BD: What determines drug solubility in lipid vehicles: is it predictable? *Adv Drug Deliv Rev* 60:638–656, 2008.

Sha X, Yan G, Wu Y, Li J, Fang X: Effect of self-microemulsifying drug delivery systems containing Labrasol on tight junctions in Caco-2 cells, *Eur J Pharm Sci* 24:477–486, 2005.

Shah I: Development and characterization of oil-in-water nanoemulsions from self-microemulsifying mixtures, The University of Toledo Digital Repository, theses and dissertations, 2011.

Shohin IE, Kulinich JI, Ramenskaya GV, Abrahamsson B, Kopp S, Langguth P, Polli JE, Shah VP, Groot DW, Barends DM, Dressman JB: Biowaiver monographs for immediate-release solid oral dosage forms: ketoprofen, *J Pharm Sci* 101:3593–3603, 2012.

Sjöblom J, Lindbergh R, Friberg SE: Microemulsions—phase equilibria characterization, structures, applications and chemical reactions, *Adv Colloid Interface* 65:125–287, 1996.

Sole I, Pey CM, Maestro A, Gonzalez C, Porras M, Solans C, Gutierrez JM: Nano-emulsions prepared by the phase inversion composition method: preparation variables and scale, *J Colloid Interface Sci* 344:417–423, 2010.

Sprunk A, Strachan CJ, Graf A: Rational formulation development and in vitro assessment of SMEDDS for oral delivery of poorly water soluble drugs, *Eur J Pharm Sci* 46:508–515, 2012.

Strey R: Microemulsion microstructure and interfacial curvature, *Colloid Polym Sci* 272:1005–1019, 1994.

Strickley RG: Solubilizing excipients in oral and injectable formulations, *Pharm Res* 21:201–230, 2004.

Subramanian N, Ray S, Ghosal SK, Bhadra R, Moulik SP: Formulation design of self-microemulsifying drug delivery systems for improved oral bioavailability of celecoxib, *Biol Pharm Bull* 27:1993–1999, 2004.

Sweetman SC: *Martindale: the complete drug reference*, ed 36, London, 2009, Pharmaceutical Press.

Wennerström H, Balogh J, Olsson U: Interfacial tensions in microemulsions, *Colloid Surf A* 291:69–77, 2006.

Wu CY, Benet LZ: Predicting drug disposition via application of BCS: transport/absorption/elimination interplay and development of a biopharmaceutics drug disposition classification system, *Pharm Res* 22:11–23, 2005.

Yazdanian M, Briggs K, Jankovsky C, Hawi A: The "high solubility" definition of the current FDA Guidance on Biopharmaceutical Classification System may be too strict for acidic drugs, *Pharm Res* 21:293–299, 2004.

Ying C, Gao L, Xianggen W, Zhiyu C, Jiangeng H, Bei Q, Song C, Ruihua W: Self-microemulsifying drug delivery system (SMEDDS) of vinpocetine: formulation development and in vivo assessment, *Biol Pharm Bull* 31:118–125, 2008.

Zhang Q, Jiang X, Jiang W, Lu W, Su L, Shi Z: Preparation of nimodipine-loaded microemulsion for intranasal delivery and evaluation on the targeting efficiency to the brain, *Int J Pharm* 275:85–96, 2004.

Chapter 4

Diversity and Functionality of Excipients for Micro/Nanosized Drug Carriers

Jela Milić, Bojan Čalija, Sanela M. Đorđević
Department of Pharmaceutical Technology and Cosmetology, Faculty of Pharmacy, University of Belgrade, Belgrade, Serbia

4.1 INTRODUCTION

Pharmaceutical preparations/products rarely consist only of active pharmaceutical ingredient(s) (APIs). More often, they are composed of one or more APIs and auxiliary substances, commonly known as excipients. Although traditionally defined as pharmacologically inactive substances, excipients cannot be considered as absolutely inert ingredients owing to their influence on the quality, safety, and efficacy of pharmaceutical preparations (Bhattacharyya et al., 2006).

The European Pharmacopoeia (2013) simply defines excipient as: "Any constituent of a medicinal product that is not an active substance." The United States Pharmacopeia (2016) defines excipients as: "Substances, other than the active drug substance(s) or finished dosage form, that have been appropriately evaluated for safety and are included in drug delivery systems 1) to aid in the processing of the drug delivery system during its manufacture; 2) to protect, support, or enhance stability, bioavailability, or patient acceptability; 3) to assist in product identification; or 4) to enhance any other attribute of the overall safety, effectiveness, or delivery of the drug during storage or use."

Excipients are a group of heterogeneous materials, ranging from simple, well-known inorganic substances to new, more complex, and functionally highly specific materials, such as biomacromolecules, which significantly differ in origin, physical, and chemical characteristics. More than 800 substances are currently used as excipients in marketed pharmaceutical preparations in the United States (Bhattacharyya, 2006). This number is continuously growing and according to the survey by MarketsandMarkets (2015) the global pharmaceutical excipients market is estimated at around $6 billion in 2014.

Microsized and Nanosized Carriers for NSAIDs. http://dx.doi.org/10.1016/B978-0-12-804017-1.00004-2

Being drug ingredients, all excipients have to meet strict safety requirements imposed by authorized regulatory bodies (Elder et al., 2015). The US Food and Drug Administration maintains a database of inactive ingredients in approved drug products as an aid in formulation of new drug products (FDA Center for Drug Evaluation and Research, 2015). The database is available on the FDA website and contains information on route of administration, dosage form, chemical abstracts service (CAS) number, unique ingredient identifier (UNI), and maximum potency (maximum amount of excipient contained in an approved drug).

Traditionally, pharmaceutical excipients are used to ease drug manufacturing process, assist in product identification, and improve patient compliance, bioavailability, and drug stability. Depending on their role in drug formulation, excipients may be classified into 40 functional categories recognized in The United States Pharmacopeia (2016) (e.g., diluent, binder, disintegrant, lubricant, coloring agent, plasticizer, antimicrobial preservative, antioxidant, sweetening agent, etc.). In the past few decades, continuous efforts to improve drug performance via incorporation in particulate and soft colloidal carriers have introduced new functional categories of excipients. These excipients are mostly used to modify drug release, protect API, and improve their bioavailability and selectivity for target tissues. Some of these substances are newly synthesized, while others are well known with a long tradition of use as excipients.

Variability in the properties of these excipients caused by differences in starting materials used for their production and/or in production conditions may affect their primary role in the final formulation. Hence, it is essential to identify and assess the physical or chemical characteristics of importance for the intended use of excipients, which are known as functionality-related characteristics.

This chapter gives an overview of the characteristics and variability of the three distinct groups of excipients frequently used for the preparation of particulate and soft colloidal carriers: polymeric materials, natural surfactants, and silica-based materials. Special attention is paid to functionality and functionality-related characteristics of these materials in relation to their use in the formulation of the aforementioned drug carriers.

4.2 FUNCTIONALITY AND PERFORMANCE OF EXCIPIENTS: DEFINITIONS AND COMPENDIAL STATUS

According to The European Pharmacopoeia (2013), the intended function of an excipient is to guarantee the required physical and biopharmaceutical properties of the pharmaceutical preparation. The way and degree to which an excipient meets the intended function in the formulation is referred to as excipient functionality. In the guide *Qualification of Excipients for Use in Pharmaceuticals*, published by International Pharmaceutical Excipients Council (IPEC, 2008), functionality has been defined as: "A desirable property of an excipient that aids and/or improves the manufacture, quality, or performance of the drug product." The functionality of the excipient depends on its physical and chemical properties, on the presence of by-products or additives, manufacturing conditions, and interactions with other formulation ingredients (The European Pharmacopoeia, 2013).

The most important issues related to the excipient functionality are its evaluation and control (Moreton, 2009a). Given that functionality depends on the final formulation and manufacturing process, it can be evaluated only in the context of a particular formulation and manufacturing process and it is virtually impossible to set standard for a specific functionality (Moreton, 2009b). Nevertheless, it is of great importance to identify the characteristics that can be associated with certain functionality. These characteristics of excipients are known as functionality-related characteristics. The European Pharmacopoeia (2013) defines functionality-related characteristic as: "controllable physical or chemical characteristic of an excipient that is shown to impact on its functionality." These characteristics can be used as surrogates for functionality, since they can be quantified and their limits can be set (Moreton, 2004). In that way, the functionality-related characteristics can be used to identify the right excipient quality for a specific purpose and assure consistent quality of drug products.

In the context of the Quality by Design (QbD) paradigm, functionality-related characteristics can be considered as critical quality attributes (CQAs) that should be within an appropriate limit, range, or distribution to ensure the desired and consistent drug quality (ICH, 2009). Changes in excipients performance caused by source-to-source and lot-by-lot variability are frequent and may have significant influence on the quality of the final product. Therefore, functionality-related characteristics of excipients are CQAs and have to be evaluated and controlled to ensure consistent performance throughout the drug life cycle.

The importance of functionality-related characteristics has been recognized by both formulation scientists and regulatory authorities. In 1995, the European Pharmacopoeia Commission decided to include functionality-related tests in the European Pharmacopoeia. Working Party on functionality-related characteristics established by the Commission in 2004, prepared general chapter for information on functionality-related characteristics of excipients. The chapter was adopted by the Commission in 2007 (Kristensen, 2007). Its purpose is to provide information about the functionality-related characteristics concept and to serve as a guidance for use of the functionality-related characteristics section of certain monographs. The first functionality-related section was introduced in the *Lactose Anhydrous* monograph in 2005. Since 2014, this nonmandatory section has become part of more than 60 monographs of The European Pharmacopoeia (2013). This section provides information to manufacturers and regulatory authorities on characteristics of excipients that may influence the manufacturing process and performance of the final preparation and, in some cases, methods suitable for their assessment and the typical values. As can be seen from Table 4.1, most of these methods are described in other chapters of the European Pharmacopoeia. The examples of functional categories and functionality-related characteristics from Ph. Eur. 8.0 (The European Pharmacopoeia, 2013) monographs are given in Table 4.2. As can be seen in

TABLE 4.1 Compendial Methods for Assessment of Functionality-Related Characteristics of Solid State Excipients (The European Pharmacopoeia, 2013)

Method	Chapter
Viscosity	2.2.8.
Capillary viscometer method	2.2.9.
Viscosity rotating viscometer method	2.2.10.
Melting point—open capillary method	2.2.15.
Size-exclusion chromatography	2.2.30.
Loss on drying	2.2.32.
Thermal analysis	2.2.34.
Density of solids	2.2.42.
Specific surface area by air permeability	2.9.14.
Flowability	2.9.16.
Specific surface area by gas adsorption	2.9.26.
Particle size analysis by laser light diffraction	2.9.31.
Porosity and pore-size distribution of solids by mercury porosimetry	2.9.32.
Characterization of crystalline and partially crystalline solids by X-ray powder diffraction	2.9.33.
Bulk density and tapped density of powders	2.9.34.
Powder fineness	2.9.35.
Powder flow	2.9.36.
Particle-size distribution estimation by analytical sieving	2.9.38.
Gas pycnometric density of solids	2.9.43.
Wettability of porous solids including powders	2.9.45.
Polymorphism	5.9.

Table 4.2, one excipient may have different roles in the final formulation and therefore can be classified in different functional categories. Depending on the excipient functional category, different characteristics are recognized as functionality-related. Future efforts will be focused on the introduction of new functionality-related characteristic chapters and revision of the general chapter in order to clarify the importance of the functionality-related characteristics in the context of QbD.

In parallel with the introduction of a general chapter on functionality-related characteristics in the European Pharmacopoeia, the United States Pharmacopeia Excipient Expert Committee conducted a survey at the Annual Science Meeting of excipient users and manufacturers on the need for performance testing in the

TABLE 4.2 Examples of Functional Categories and Functionality-Related Characteristics of Some Excipients (The European Pharmacopoeia, 2013)

Excipient	Functional category	Functionality-related characteristics
Alginic acid	Disintegrant and/or binder	Particle-size distribution Settling volume
	Gelling agent or viscosity-increasing agent	Apparent viscosity
Cellulose acetate	Film former	Apparent viscosity Acetyl groups
	Matrix former (in prolonged-release tablets)	Apparent viscosity Acetyl groups Molecular mass distribution Particle-size distribution Powder flow
Crospovidone	Disintegrant	Hydration capacity Particle-size distribution Powder flow
	Suspension stabilizer	Settling volume
Hypromellose	Binder, viscosity-increasing agent or film former	Viscosity Degree of substitution
	Matrix former (prolonged-release tablets)	Molecular mass distribution Particle-size distribution Powder flow
Povidone	Solubilizer and stabilizer (in liquid dosage forms)	Viscosity Molecular mass
	Binder (in tablets and granules)	Molecular mass
Magnesium stearate	Lubricant (in tablets and capsules)	Particle-size distribution Specific surface area Thermogavimetry (water content and polymorphic form)
Xanthan gum	Viscosity-increasing agent	Apparent viscosity
	Matrix former (in prolonged-release tablets)	Apparent viscosity Particle-size distribution Powder flow

United States Pharmacopeia. The survey results published in 2006 have shown the need for additional information in USP–NF regarding excipient testing and performance (Amidon, 2006). In 2007, stimuli article on the development of General Information Chapter, <1059> Excipient Performance was released (Amidon et al., 2007). Four years later this chapter was included in the second Supplement of USP 33–NF 28 (Sheehan and Amidon, 2011). This chapter

TABLE 4.3 Pharmaceutical Dosage Forms and Corresponding Functional Categories of Excipients According to the Chapter <1059> Excipient Performance (The United States Pharmacopeia, 2016)

Dosage form(s)	Functional category	Dosage form(s)	Functional category
Tablets and capsules	Diluent	Oral liquids	pH modifier
	Binder		Wetting and/or solubilizing agent
	Disintegrant		Antimicrobial preservative
	Lubricant		Chelating and/or complexing agents
	Glidant and/or anticaking agent		Antioxidant
	Coloring agent		Sweetening agent
	Capsule shell	Semisolids, topicals, and suppositories	Suppository base
	Coating agent		Suspending and/or viscosity-increasing agent
	Plasticizer		Ointment base
Parenterals	Pharmaceutical water		Stiffening agent
	Diluent		Emollient
	Tonicity agent	Aerosols	Propellant

gives an overview of the main functional categories of excipients organized by their typical use in common pharmaceutical dosage forms (Table 4.3), tests that may assess excipient performance, and test procedures that may not be presented in compendial monographs (The United States Pharmacopeia, 2016). Each functional category contains a general description, explanations of the mechanisms by which the excipients fulfill intended function, physical, and chemical properties common to these excipients and a list of general chapters that may be useful in the development of specific tests, procedures, and acceptance criteria. Their purpose is to ensure that the critical material attributes are adequately monitored and controlled (The United States Pharmacopeia, 2016).

4.3 BIODEGRADABLE POLYMERIC MATERIALS IN MICRO/NANOPARTICLES

Along with metals, minerals, ceramics, and lipids, biodegradable polymers are the most frequently used excipients for micro/nanoencapsulation of structurally different drugs, genes, and cells. Polymers are nowadays used for development of new generation of therapeutics due to controllable properties including degree of polymerization, architecture, and polydispersity (Dhal et al., 2009). Increasing interest for these encapsulating agents can be ascribed to their biocompatibility, versatility, and significant potential to deliver drugs to the desired site of action. Another important feature of these polymers is possibility of their functionalization, which is, in most cases, based on structural modifications or blending with other excipients (Freiberg and Zhu, 2004). That is, polymers can be tailored or mixed with other excipients to meet the specific needs such as stability, sensitivity to biological stimuli (e.g., pH, enzymes, temperature, ionic strength, etc.), acceptable encapsulation efficiency, and drug loading capacity. Recent progress in controlled polymerization has enabled synthesis of multifunctional polymeric encapsulating agents for preparation of micro/nanoparticles of desired characteristics in terms of size, morphology, stability, drug release, and toxicological properties (Elsabahy and Wooley, 2012).

4.3.1   Definition, Structure, and Characteristics of Polymers

Polymers are defined as systems of large dimension entities, obtained by the covalent linking of a large number of repeating units commonly known as monomers (Gnanou and Fontanille, 2008). Their multilevel structure comprises monomer structure and distribution, stereochemistry, and assembly of chains (Gnanou and Fontanille, 2008; Fried, 2014). Therefore, it is quite challenging to define and determine the structure of a polymer. The in vivo behavior of polymer is governed by various structure-related properties, such as monomer composition/distribution, molecular weight and molecular weight distribution, molecular architecture, tacticity, morphology, thermal properties, and ionization ability (Markland and Yang, 2002).

Monomer composition/distribution. Polymers consisting of two or more different monomers are known as copolymers (Fried, 2014). Monomers can be distributed randomly (A-B-A-A-A-B), alternately (A-B-A-B-A-B), or in blocks (AAA-BBB-AAA) (Fried, 2014). The molar ratio of monomers and their distribution along the polymer chain influence copolymer properties, such as morphology and bulk hydrophilicity (Labarre et al., 2011; Markland and Yang, 2002).

Molecular weight and molecular weight distribution. Polymers usually consist of chains of different lengths and can be characterized by a size distribution with an average value of the molecular weight. Average molecular weight of a polymer may be expressed as the number-average molecular weight (M_n) and weight-average molecular weight (M_w) (Fried, 2014; Visser et al., 2004). The first one is the most sensitive to the presence of a large number of low molecular weight molecules and the second one to the number of molecules with a high molecular weight (Labarre et al., 2011). The M_w/M_n ratio, known as polydispersity index (PDI), describes molecular weight distribution (Attwood and Florence, 2008; Labarre et al., 2011). Many polymer properties, such as viscosity, thermodynamic properties, and toughness, depend on the molecular weight and molecular-weight distribution (Fried, 2014; Labarre et al., 2011).

Tacticity. Tacticity refers to the spatial arrangement of substituent groups around the polymer chain. If all the substituents lie on the same side of the extended polymer chain, such polymer is referred to as isotactic. In the syndiotactic polymers, substituents are located alternately on both the sides of the polymer chain (Attwood and Florence, 2008). Substituent can be also placed randomly on both the sides and such arrangement is designated as atactic (Visser et al., 2004) Thermal, mechanical properties and crystallinity may be dependent on the tacticity. For instance, isotactic and syndiotactic polymers are usually partially crystalline and atactic polymers are amorphous (Fried, 2014).

Morphology and thermal properties. Polymers are either amorphous or semicrystalline. Degree of crystallinity affects both mechanical and thermal properties of polymers (Visser et al., 2004). The key thermal properties of polymers are melting temperature (T_m) and glass transition temperature (T_g). Semicrystalline polymers on heating exhibit melting of their crystalline fraction at temperature referred as T_m (Visser et al., 2004). At temperatures below T_g polymers are glassy solids. Upon heating above their T_g, polymers become soft and elastic (Visser et al., 2004; Widmann, 2009). Depending on their thermal properties, polymers can be classified as thermoplastics, elastomers, or thermosets. Heating of thermoplastics results in their melting or softening, allowing them to be molded and recycled. Below T_g they act as rigid glass-like solids (Widmann, 2009). In contrast, thermosets are heavily crosslinked and cannot be melted, but undergo decomposition at higher temperatures (Widmann, 2009). Elastomers are also crosslinked polymers, but their degree of crosslinking is significantly lower. Due to crosslinking, these polymers cannot melt on heating, hence cannot be molded and dissolved. They suffer significant reversible deformation under mechanical stress (Widmann, 2009). The thermal properties of polymers are important as they affect stability, mechanical and drug release properties of polymeric drug carriers (Labarre et al., 2011; Markland and Yang, 2002). For instance, polymeric drug carriers are more stable at temperatures below T_g of consisting polymers (Markland and Yang, 2002). Also, at temperatures below T_g mass transport through polymer is slower due to lower polymers chain mobility (Markland and Yang, 2002).

Ionization ability. Ionization ability of a polymer is determined by type, number, and distribution of ionizable groups along polymer chain. Polymers carrying a large number of ionizable groups are known as polyelectrolytes (Čalija et al., 2015). Depending on the nature of ionizable groups, these polymers may act as weak bases or weak acids. Their solubility in aqueous media and ability to interact with other polymers or drugs is affected by changes in pH values since their ionization degree depends on the pH value of the surrounding medium. Consequently, drug release rates from drug carriers consisting of such polymers are pH-dependent (Čalija et al., 2013a).

4.3.2   Classification of Biodegradable Encapsulating Polymers

There are several criteria for classification of polymers, such as origin, structure, processing characteristics, and types of polymerization mechanisms (Fried, 2014). Based on their origin, biodegradable encapsulating polymers can be classified into two major groups: synthetic polymers and naturally occurring polymers and their derivatives. The most commonly used synthetic biodegradable encapsulating polymers are polyesters, polyamides, polyanhydrides, and phosphorous-based polymers (Akagi et al., 2011; Bala et al., 2004; Gaucher et al., 2010; Goonoo et al., 2015; Soppimath et al., 2001). Among naturally occurring polymers the most important groups are polysaccharides and protein/peptide-based polymers (Liu et al., 2008; Nitta and Numata, 2013). Examples of commonly used biodegradable encapsulating polymers are given in Table 4.4

4.3.3   The Selection of Encapsulating Polymer

Selection of the optimal encapsulating polymer is a challenging task that depends on the drug properties and desired characteristics of the drug carrier in relation to its specific in vivo application and intended route of administration. Initially, several requirements have to be considered, such as biocompatibility, initial and later polymer compatibility with the drug, and other intended excipients.

Biocompatibility is one of the main requirements for safe use of excipients that refers to their compatibility with cells and tissues. It can be defined as the acceptance of a material by the surrounding tissues and by the body as a whole, and, therefore, it is closely related to the regulatory status of the polymer (Park, 1995). Many characteristics of polymers may affect their biocompatibility, such as presence of various functional groups, hydrophilicity/hydrophobicity balance, surface electric charge, molecular weight, conformational flexibility, surface topography, and roughness (Wang et al., 2004). Besides, biocompatibility depends on the route of administration, so the polymer has to be selected with respect to the desired route of administration (Angelova and Hunkeler, 1999).

Another critical factor to be considered is the reason for encapsulation. The reason for encapsulation is directly related to desired characteristics of the drug carries. The main reasons for encapsulation are to protect the drug from degradation during storage or upon administration, modify drug release rate, improve selectivity for tissues and cells and enable direct administration to the place of action. For instance, if the drug prone to acidic degradation has to be administered orally, the choice comes down to the gastroresistant polymers. Another interesting example is improvement of drug bioavailability by prolonging residence time at the absorption sites via mucoadhesion (Takeuchi et al., 2001). In such case, selected polymer should possess mucoadhesive properties.

Encapsulating/manufacturing feasibility is another factor of importance for potential use of a polymer as encapsulating agent (Zhang et al., 2013a). Some polymers are suitable for various encapsulation techniques, offering

TABLE 4.4 Commonly Used Biodegradable Encapsulating Polymers

Polymer class		Polymer	Functional group(s)	References
Natural polymers and their derivatives	Polysaccharides	Alginate	—COOH; —OH; —O—	Reis et al. (2006)
		Carrageenan	—OSO$_3^-$; —OH; —O—	Rodrigues et al. (2012)
		Chitosan	—NH$_2$; —NHCOCH$_3$—OH; —O—	Jayakumar et al. (2010)
		Dextran	—OH; —O—	Li et al. (2009)
		Hyaluronic acid	—COOH; —NHCOCH$_3$; —OH; —O—	Choi et al. (2010)
		Starch	—OH; —O—	Le Corre et al. (2010)
	Protein/peptide-based polymers	Albumin	—CO—NH— and functional groups of amino acid residues	Kratz (2008)
		Collagen		Lee et al. (2001)
		Gelatin		Lee et al. (2012)
Synthetic polymers	Polyesters	Poly(hydroxybutyrate)	—ROCO—	Chen et al. (2006)
		Poly(lactide)		Baier et al. (2014)
		PLGA		Bala et al. (2004)
		Poly(ε-caprolactone)		Chen et al. (2000)
	Polyamides	Polyamino acids	—CO—NH—	Akagi et al. (2011)
	Phosphorous-based polymers	Polyphosphate	—OR$_1$O—PO(OR$_2$)—	Alexandrino et al. (2014)
		Polyphosphazenes	—N = PR$_1$R$_2$—	Zheng et al. (2011)
		Polyphosphoesters	—O—PO(OR$_1$)—OR$_2$-	Mao and Leong (2005)
	Polyanhydrides	Poly(sebacic acid)	—CO—R—CO—O—	Fu et al. (2002)
		Poly(adipic acid)		Puri et al. (2008)

PLGA, Poly(lactide-co-glycolide).

the possibility to choose the best solution for encapsulation of certain active. For commercial application, simple encapsulation procedures, performed with minimal loss of the drug and without use of toxic solvents, are particularly preferred. The main limitations for selection of encapsulation procedure are polymer and drug solubility and stability (e.g., thermosensitivity and pH-sensitivity).

Another important issue that has to be considered is polymer stability. Selected polymer must be stable in a final formulation in order to ensure acceptable shelf-life. In addition, stability of particles upon administration is mainly driven by in vivo stability of encapsulating polymer. Besides, polymeric micro/nanoparticles intended for ophthalmic or parenteral route of administration have to be prepared under aseptic conditions and, if possible, sterilized before use. In such cases, it is important to consider the possibilities for sterilization of individual components and final formulation. Selected sterilization method should not cause structural changes, chain shortening, crosslinking, alteration in mechanical properties, or any other changes in polymer properties of importance for in vivo performance (Angelova and Hunkeler, 1999). Therefore, the use of thermosensitive polymers excludes the use of high temperature–sterilization techniques, which are generally considered as the most effective.

4.3.4   Functionality of Biodegradable Polymers as Excipients for Micro/Nanosized Drug Carriers

Encapsulating polymers are good examples of how characteristics of excipients affect their intended use. Molecular weight, composition of copolymers, and viscosity are among the most studied functionality-related characteristics of encapsulating polymers.

Molecular weight. Molecular weight of polymers ranges from few hundred to several million Daltons (Labarre et al., 2011) and it may have profound influence on both encapsulation procedure and properties of micro/nanoparticles. This can be further elucidated using chitosan or poly(lactide-*co*-glycolide) (PLGA) copolymers as example. Chitosan is linear binary heteropolysaccharide composed of β-(1 → 4) linked *N*-acetyl-D-glucosamine and D-glucosamine monomers (Souza et al., 2011). Its oligomers, known as oligochitosans, have molecular weight less than 10 kDa and are readily soluble in water. Their aqueous solutions are nonviscous even at high concentrations (Čalija et al., 2013b; Casettari et al., 2012; Xia et al., 2011). On the other hand, high molecular weight chitosans are insoluble in water under physiological conditions and viscosity of these solutions significantly increases by increasing molecular weight (Čalija et al., 2011; Jeon and Kim, 2000). Limited solubility of high molecular weight chitosans makes the preparation of their aqueous solutions prior encapsulation quite challenging and, in some cases, even impossible. In addition, high viscosity of these solutions may distort spherical shape of polyelectrolyte complex chitosan microparticles, if particles are obtained by dropping polyanion solution (e.g., sodium alginate solution) into highly viscous chitosan solution (González-Rodrıguez et al., 2002).

Degradation rate of polymeric microparticles may also be affected by molecular weight of consisting polymer (Freiberg and Zhu, 2004). Moreover, for some particulate drug carriers, such as PLGA micro/nanoparticles, degradation is one of the main drug release controlling mechanisms, especially from the particles consisting of low molecular weight PLGA polymers (Mittal et al., 2007; Park, 1994). This is in agreement with earlier findings that 10 kDa PLGA polymer degrades in vivo approximately twofold faster than 20 kDa PLGA polymer (Kamei et al., 1992). In that way, polymer molecular weight controls drug release from PLGA-based drug carriers.

Drug release from particulate carriers consisting of hydrophilic polymers, such as polysaccharides and their derivatives, may also be dependent on polymer molecular weight. In contact with water these carriers start to swell and form hydrogels. In general, polymers of higher molecular weight form stronger and thicker gels which are less prone to erosion (Čalija et al., 2011; Maderuelo et al., 2011; Ribeiro et al., 1999). Hence, drug release from these hydrogels is slower in comparison to the hydrogels consisting of low molecular weight polymers.

Several studies confirmed influence of polymer molecular weight on biocompatibility of polymers and polymeric drug carriers (Choksakulnimitr et al., 1995; Fischer et al., 2003; Huang et al., 2004). In most cases, it was found that low molecular weight polymers are less cytotoxic in comparison to the high molecular weight polymers at same concentrations (Choksakulnimitr et al., 1995; Wang et al., 2004).

Composition of copolymers. Molar ratio and distribution of monomers along polymer backbone may affect encapsulation process and properties of polymeric micro/nanoparticles, including their biocompatibility, size, morphology, structural, and drug release properties. Hence, it can be tailored with the aim to obtain particulate carriers of desired characteristics. Alginates and chitosans are good examples of how molar ratio of monomers influences characteristics of particulate carriers based on these polymers. Alginates are unbranched copolymers comprising $(1 \rightarrow 4)$-linked β-D-mannuronic acid and α-L-guluronic acid repeating units arranged in three types of sequences: homopolymeric mannuronic (M-blocks), homopolymeric guluronic (G-blocks), and heteropolymeric alternating sequences (M–G blocks) (Gombotz and Wee, 2012; Sankalia et al., 2007). The use of these encapsulating copolymers is based on the interaction of G-blocks with divalent cations (excluding Mg^{2+}) (Donati et al., 2005; Tønnesen and Karlsen, 2002). This rapid reaction, known as ionotropic gelation, results in the formation of tridimensional hydrogel network. Under certain conditions, these hydrogels can be shaped as micro/nanoparticles (Paques et al., 2014; Prüsse et al., 2008). Given that G-blocks are responsible for the hydrogel formation, strength, and mechanical stability of the resulting hydrogels are dependent on the copolymer composition. Hence, alginates with higher G/M ratio and longer G-blocks give stronger and stiffer particulate hydrogel carriers (Draget et al., 1997). Nevertheless, these particles are more porous when compared to particles consisting of alginates with low G content (Paques et al., 2014). In that way, alginate composition affects drug release and in vivo performance of alginate ionotropic hydrogel micro/nanoparticles.

The ability of chitosans to form micro/nanoparticles is based on polycationic nature which is related to the presence of free amino groups on the C-2 position of D-glucosamine residues. The presence of free amino groups in chitosans structure is usually expressed as D-glucosamine/N-acetyl D-glucosamine molar ratio, known as deacetylation degree. Deacetylation degree is one of the most important characteristics of chitosans affecting their solubility, viscosity of their solutions, and ability to interact with polyanions (Čalija et al., 2015; Hejazi and Amiji, 2003; Rinaudo, 2006). By increasing the number of free amino groups in chitosans structure, their solubility and viscosity increases (Hejazi and Amiji, 2003). The ability of chitosans to interact with low (e.g., tripolyphosphate) and high molecular weight anions (e.g., alginate, carrageenan, and pectin) is widely used to prepare micro/nanoparticles (Čalija et al., 2015). Given that interaction with (poly)anions is based on electrostatic interactions, highly deacetylated chitosans are commonly used for this purpose. Another frequently used approach for preparation of chitosan-based particulate carriers is crosslinking with glutaraldehyde (Milašinović et al., 2016; Mirzaei et al., 2013). It is based on covalent interaction of primary amine groups of chitosan with aldehyde group of glutaraldehyde (Monteiro and Airoldi, 1999). For that reason, certain properties of particulate carriers obtained by this approach depend on the deacetylation degree of chitosan. This is in line with the results of study performed by Gupta and Jabrail (2006) which confirmed the influence of deacetylation degree on surface properties, hydrophobicity, and drug release properties.

Biodegradability of chitosans is also affected by the number of D-glucosamine units. Several studies confirmed that low deacetylation degree favors enzymatic degradation of chitosans (Aiba, 1992; Aranaz et al., 2009; Yang et al., 2007). Besides, chitosans with lower deacetylation degree and nanoparticles obtained from these chitosans demonstrate lower cytotoxicity (Huang et al., 2004).

The influence of PLGA composition on particles properties was also confirmed. Fonseca et al. (2002) prepared paclitaxel-loaded nanoparticles from PLGA with different lactic acid/glycolic acid molar ratio. It was shown that molar ratio of monomers affects surface charge of the particles while the encapsulation efficiency was not dependent on the copolymer composition. In contrast, Mittal et al. (2007) reported significant influence of PLGA composition on encapsulation efficiency of estradiol into PLGA nanoparticles. PLGA with higher PLA content demonstrated higher efficiency of estradiol encapsulation.

Such influence of PLA content can be ascribed to its hydrophobic nature. That is, as PLA content was increased, overall hydrophobicity of PLGA increased along with its capacity for hydrophobic drugs, such as estradiol. Besides, high hydrophobicity of PLGA copolymers with high PLA content slows down in vitro degradation of nanoparticles and decreases release rate of encapsulated drug (Mittal et al., 2007).

Rheological properties. Rheological behavior and viscosity of a polymer in solution used for preparation of micro/nanoparticles may also be critical for both encapsulation procedure and properties of the resulting particles. These properties depend on the concentration and chemical structure of polymers, their molecular weight, and nature of solvent (Maderuelo et al. 2011). The influence of rheological properties on encapsulation procedure is particularly evident in case of viscosity–enhancing polymers, such as alginates, chitosans, cellulose derivatives, etc. Even at low concentrations, high viscosity of solutions of these polymers can make preparation procedure quite challenging. For example, if particulate carriers are produced by dropwise addition of polymer solution into medium with gelling ions (e.g., chitosan or alginate solution into solutions containing tripolyphosphate or Ca^{2+} ions, respectively), viscosity of polymer solution determines size and shape of droplets and subsequently size and shape of the particles. In general, high viscosity of these solutions leads to the formation of less spherical and larger particles. Additionally, highly viscous solutions of polymers in some cases cannot be used for preparation of particles by using this approach (Prüsse et al., 2008). High viscosity of these solutions makes preparation of uniform-sized particles difficult even if emulsification approach is used. In other words, as the viscosity increases it is more difficult to obtain emulsions with narrow size distribution of droplets from which the particles are obtained (Zhang et al., 2006). Similar influence of viscosity of a polymer in solution on particles size was observed for particles obtained by spray drying procedure (He et al., 1999).

High viscosity of polymers solution may also affect interaction between oppositely charged polymers during microparticles preparation. The results of several studies suggest that the high viscosity of chitosan solutions hinder interaction with alginate making the formation of alginate–chitosan polyelectrolyte complex more difficult (Čalija et al., 2011; Polk et al., 1994; Yu et al., 2008).

The influence of polymer molecular weight on drug release from particulate carriers consisting of hydrophilic polymers was already discussed previously. It is closely related with viscosity of these polymers and its dependence on the molecular weight. That is, high molecular weight polymers form more viscous gel layer around the beads upon their hydration, making the release of encapsulated drug more difficult. Besides, their resistance to erosion also contributes to slow release of the drug (Maderuelo et al., 2011). In vitro release studies performed from PLGA micro/nanoparticles prepared from PLGA of different viscosities revealed similar influence of PLGA inherent viscosity on drug release rates (Araújo et al., 2009; Zidan et al., 2006).

4.4   NATURAL AND SYNTHETIC SILICA-BASED MATERIALS AS MICRO/NANOSIZED DRUG CARRIERS

Traditionally, various inorganic substances have been used as both actives and excipients in pharmaceutical preparations and some of them have compendial status for decades (López-Galindo et al., 2007; Viseras et al., 2010). Excellent stability, high adsorption capacity, and large surface area, rheological and colloidal properties, as well as acceptable biocompatibility are the most common reasons for their use as excipients (Carretero and Pozo, 2009). This versatile group of materials includes oxides, hydroxides, carbonates, chlorides, sulfates, and silica-based materials. The latter comprise a number of inorganic materials of both natural and synthetic origin. The most commonly used silica-based clay minerals are smectites, palygorskite, bentonite, sepiolite, kaolinite, and talc. In addition, zeolites, microporous, aluminosilicate minerals, and diatomites, mesoporous, siliceous sedimentary minerals have also considerable potential as excipients due to their large specific surface area and high adsorption capacity (Aguzzi et al., 2007; Aw et al., 2012). In the last decade special attention has been paid to the synthetic mesoporous silica materials as carriers for both hydrophilic and lipophilic drugs. The possibility of tailoring the morphology, surface chemistry, and pore size of these materials makes them particularly interesting as drug carriers (Xu et al., 2013). For that reason, this section is focused on these silica-based materials as micro/nanosized drug carriers and possibility of their functionalization.

4.4.1   Structure and Functional Characteristics of Silica-Based Materials

Clay minerals are phyllosilicate minerals and minerals which impart plasticity to clay and harden upon drying or firing (Guggenheim and Martin, 1995). The use of phyllosilicates in drug delivery is mainly based on large surface area, cation exchange ability, chemical inertness availability, and low toxicity (Aguzzi et al., 2007; Choy et al., 2007). The most important functional properties of these minerals are adsorption and cation exchange capacity, swelling ability, solubility, and rheological properties (Carretero and Pozo, 2009). Among these minerals, smectites, such as montmorillonite and saponite, are especially known for their excellent cation exchange capacity. These minerals have been successfully used alone or in combination with different polymers to encapsulate various drugs to improve their stability, solubility, and/or achieve modified release (Chrzanowski et al., 2013; Dong and Feng, 2005; Ito et al., 2001; Park et al., 2008; Zheng et al., 2007).

In recent decades, mesoporous silica-based micro/nanosized materials have been extensively investigated as potential drug delivery systems (Yang et al., 2012). They are intended to improve therapeutic efficacy and/or reduce toxicity of existing drugs, usually by enhancing dissolution and permeation of low-soluble/permeable drugs or by modifying the rate, the time, and/or the site of drug release (Aw et al., 2012; Xu et al., 2013). The main advantages of these materials are well-defined surface properties, high porosity, large surface area, low density, diffusion-controlled drug release mechanism, excellent biocompatibility, thermal and chemical stability (Aw et al., 2012; Wang, 2009).

Morphology, pore volume, size, and surface chemistry are the key properties for drug delivery application of mesoporous silica-based materials (Wang, 2009; Xu et al., 2013). These properties can be tailored through careful adjustment of reaction conditions and by using various additives/chemical modifiers (Du et al., 2009; Linton and Alfredsson, 2008; Nooney et al., 2002; Yu et al., 2004). The properties affecting biocompatibility, drug loading and release are of particular importance. In general, drug loading increases, and drug release rate decreases by decreasing pore size and vice versa. Namely, the pores act as sieves, so the ratio of pore diameter and drug molecule size should be higher than 1 to allow drug loading (Xu et al., 2013). The nature (e.g., hydrophobic, electrostatic, and hydrogen bonding) and intensity of interactions between the drug and the host also affect drug loading, release rate and mechanism (Wang, 2009; Xu et al., 2013). It is expected that stronger interaction between the drug and the host results in higher drug loading and slower release. Depending on the drug nature, these properties can be optimized by introducing hydrophobic or hydrophilic groups, as discussed later.

The first family of mesoporous silica materials designated as M41S, was synthesized in the early 1990s by the calcination of aluminosilicate gels in presence of surfactants (Beck et al., 1992; Kresge et al., 1992). These highly porous materials possess regular arrays of uniform channels and tunable structure. Their use for drug delivery purpose was first introduced by Vallet-Regí et al. (2001), and from that moment rapid progress has been made in the application of these materials in this field.

The most extensively studied mesoporous silica material for drug delivery applications is Mobil Composition of Matter No. 41, known as MCM-41. MCM-41 is a member of M41S family, obtained by a liquid crystal templating mechanism from tetraethyl orthosilicate by using cetyltrimethylammonium bromide as a surfactant and alkali as catalyst (Beck et al., 1992). It can be synthesized in a form of nanoparticles of different shapes and sizes, usually from 20 to 500 nm (Slowing et al., 2007). Its chain-like pores are arranged in a hexagonal manner and surrounded by walls consisting of siloxane bridges and silanol groups (Wang, 2009). Such porous and highly ordered structure makes them promising carriers for both drug and genes (Balas et al., 2006; Radu et al., 2004; Vallet-Regí et al., 2001).

Another type of mesoporous silica material with potential for drug delivery is SBA-15. SBA-15 is highly ordered mesoporous material with two-dimensional hexagonal structure. It was first synthesized in the late 1990s by Zhao et al. (1998) in acidic conditions using amphiphilic block copolymers as organic structure-directing agents. SBA-15 possesses better hydrothermal stability than MCM-41 and its walls are thicker and pores are wider (Zhao et al., 1998). However, it is more difficult to produce small-sized SBA-15 nanoparticles, particularly with diameter below 200 nm (Tang et al., 2012).

In general, synthetic mesoporous silica materials can be prepared in acidic or basic conditions from silica precursors, such as organic silane, fumed silica, or inorganic silicate, through polymerization on a surfactant template. Surfactant template is removed by organic solvent extraction or calcination at high temperatures (Xu et al., 2013). Shape and size of the resulting material, as well as its pore sizes and geometry can be tailored by careful selection of reactants, additives, and reaction conditions (Vallet-Regí and Balas, 2008; Xu et al., 2013).

Nevertheless, synthesis of mesoporous materials is often complex, time- and energy-consuming process involving use of toxic substances (Aw et al., 2012; Bariana et al., 2013). For these reasons, researchers are exploring natural silica materials for drug delivery applications, such as diatomaceous earth. Diatomaceous earth (diatomite) is a soft, very fine-grained, siliceous sedimentary rock created by the deposition of cell walls of dead microscopic single-cell algae (diatoms) on the ocean and fresh water floors (Janićijević et al., 2014). It can be obtained in large quantities by simple, environmentally friendly, and low energy consumption process (Zhang et al., 2013b). Diatomite is chemically inert, biocompatible, highly permeable material with low density, high surface area, and modifiable surface chemistry (Fig. 4.1) (Aw et al., 2012; Janićijević et al., 2014). All of these properties impose this material as an excellent candidate for drug delivery applications. The results of recently published studies confirmed that low molecular drug molecules can be easily loaded on both internal and external diatomite surfaces, whereas the release of adsorbed drug was bimodal, rapid from the surface, and sustained from the inner structure

FIGURE 4.1   SEM image of diatomite from Kolubara Coal Basin (Serbia).

(Aw et al., 2012). Besides, it was shown that diatoms act as permeation enhancers for orally administered BCS III drugs (Zhang et al., 2013b).

4.4.2 Functionalization of Natural and Synthetic Silica-Based Materials as Micro/Nanosized Drug Carriers

Performance of silica micro/nanosized drug carriers can be significantly improved through various chemical modifications. The most widely used methods for immobilization of functional groups onto synthetic mesoporous silica via covalent bonding are cocondensation and postsynthesis grafting (Vinu et al., 2005). Cocondensation method is sometimes referred to as single-pot method since it is based on mixing of the organic functional species with the silica precursors in the same reaction pot (Vallet-Regí and Balas, 2008). This approach allows more homogenous distribution of the functionalized groups in comparison to the postsynthesis grafting. However, cocondensation method leads to a decrease in the degree of order within mesoporous structure and the pore size and the volume decrease along with overall surface area (Maria Chong and Zhao, 2003). This effect is more pronounced if higher concentrations of organic functional species are used. On the other hand, the postgrafting method does not alter ordered mesoporous structure since it takes place after formation of mesoporous matrix (Xu et al., 2013). This approach allows selective functionalization of the materials (Cheng and Landry, 2007). That is, grafting before removal of the surfactant template leads exclusively to the functionalization of exterior surface while grafting after the removal of the surfactant template takes place on both external and internal surface.

In general, chemical modification of mesoporous silica materials modifies their adsorption capacity, polarity, and drug release properties. In recent decades, numerous successful attempts were made to improve drug delivery performance of mesoporous materials by functionalization with different groups such as amino, carboxyl, and alkyl groups (Munoz et al., 2003; Ritter and Bruhwiler, 2009; Voicu et al., 2004; Yang et al., 2005). Munoz et al. (2003) successfully sustained ibuprofen release from MCM-41 matrices by its functionalization with aminopropyl groups. Due to the presence of one carboxylic group in its structure, ibuprofen can interact ionically with introduced amino groups. This is in complete agreement with the results of ^{13}C and ^1H solid state NMR spectroscopy of MCM-41 prior and after functionalization obtained by Babonneau et al. (2004). These results revealed that amino group functionalization caused decreased mobility of the entrapped drug molecules within the matrix. Similar results were obtained after postsynthesis grafting of MCM-41 with 3-aminopropyltriethoxysilane (Szegedi et al., 2011). Song et al. (2005) performed amino functionalization of SBA-15 through both single-pot and postgrafting methods. This functionalization resulted in increased loading and decreased release rates of ibuprofen in comparison to the nonmodified SBA-15. Another interesting approach used to sustain the release of entrapped drug from mesoporous silica materials is functionalization with long alkyl chains. Doadrio et al. (2006) performed successful functionalization of SBA-15 with long alkyl chains and showed that drug-release rate decreased as the population of hydrophobic —CH_2 moieties in the host increased. Functionalized mesoporous nanoparticles can be further encapsulated/coated by biodegradable polymers, such as alginate or polydimethyldiallylammonium chloride, to achieve sustained release of water-insoluble drugs (Hu et al. 2014; Zhang et al., 2014).

Performance of natural silica materials as drug carriers, such as diatomite, can also be altered through modification with various functional groups. Bariana et al. (2013) performed diatomite functionalization with various silanes and phosphonates by changing its hydrophilic and hydrophobic properties. For that purpose, 2-carboxyethyl-phosphonic acid, 16-phoshono-hexadecanoic acid, and 3-aminopropyltriethoxy silane were used as chemical modifiers, while gentamicin sulfate and indomethacin were used as hydrophilic and hydrophobic model drugs, respectively. The obtained results revealed biphasic drug release from the functionalized diatomite samples, comprising initial burst release, followed by near zero-order sustained release. The effect of functionalization was dependent on both the types of modification agent and hydrophilic/hydrophobic properties of the model drug.

Another successful attempt to improve performance of diatomite by its modification was reported by Janićijević et al. (2014, 2015). They proposed a simple, fast, and environmentally friendly procedure of diatomite modification with partially neutralized aluminum sulfate solution to improve its loading capacity for anionic drugs, such as diclofenac sodium. Modified diatomite had significantly higher adsorbent loading with diclofenac sodium in comparison to the starting material and exhibited prolonged drug release. Moreover, the results of in vivo toxicity testing on mice pointed on potential safety of both starting and functionalized diatomite.

4.5 NATURAL SURFACTANTS IN MICRO/NANOEMULSIONS

The success of micro/nanoemulsions as drug delivery vehicles is critically related to their composition (oil phase, aqueous phase, surfactant, and most frequently cosurfactant). Clearly, the choice of the appropriate excipients, particularly surfactants, in the right concentration, is one of the key factors determining formation, stability, physicochemical, interfacial, and sensorial properties, as well as functional performances of produced micro/nanoemulsions. Especially surfactants should be chosen thoughtfully, since they can alter interactions of the carrier with the target site and/or the applied drug, therefore influencing drug release, disposition, and therapeutic efficacy. Consequently, the careful selection of proper surfactant/cosurfactant mixtures (type, concentration, nature, and properties) is of paramount importance for efficient design of micro/nanoemulsions tailored for specific applications (Adjonu et al., 2014; Klang and Valenta, 2011; McClements, 2011).

4.5.1 Surfactant Role in Micro/Nanoemulsions

The practical application of surfactants as emulsifying/stabilizing agents in micro/nanoemulsion formulations lies within the intrinsic duality of their molecular characteristics, meaning that the surfactant molecules are composed of a polar, hydrophilic headgroup linked to a nonpolar, hydrophobic tail. Due to their amphiphilic nature, surfactants are able to adsorb onto interfaces (air–water, oil–water, solid–liquid), decrease surface and interfacial tensions between nonmiscible phases, and bring new surface behavior to the system (West and Harwell, 1992; Yunfei et al., 2012). It is now generally recognized that specific properties of surfactants, such as the critical micelle concentration, hydrophilic–lipophilic balance (HLB), spontaneous curvature, as well as the critical packing parameter (CPP) dictate the static and dynamic properties of micro/nanoemulsions. These include phase behavior, microstructure, stability, rheology, as well as solubilization and interfacial properties (McClements, 2011; Solans and García-Celma, 1997).

The ability of surfactants to locate at the oil–water interface allows them to play a major role in formation and stabilization of micro/nanoemulsions: by lowering the interfacial tension of the system and by forming the interfacial surfactant layer separating the oil and water domains. This interfacial surfactant film provides an effective structural–mechanical barrier as well as repulsive electrostatic, steric, or electrosteric forces to prevent the coalescence of newly created droplets, thereby stabilizing efficiently the formed emulsion systems (Adjonu et al., 2014; Hippalgaonkar et al., 2010; Tadros et al., 2004). Apart from the role of emulsifying/stabilizing agents, in micro/nanoemulsions surfactants may also serve to improve the solubilization of drug, reduce toxicity, and enhance drug penetration/absorption through biological barriers (Klang and Valenta, 2011).

Overall, nanoemulsions can be formulated with a wider range of surface-active substances than microemulsions, including low molecular weight surfactants, proteins, and polysaccharides. On the other hand, only small molecule surfactants can be used for microemulsion formation, since only they are capable of generating ultralow interfacial tension (at particular monolayer curvatures) characteristic of microemulsion systems (Adjonu et al., 2014; McClements, 2012). In addition, with microemulsions, higher surfactant concentrations (20–50%) are required to facilitate spontaneous formation of thermodynamically stable system, whereas kinetically stable nanoemulsions can be produced using a reasonable lower surfactant concentration (1.2–5%) (Klang and Valenta, 2011; Tadros et al., 2004).

4.5.2 Definition, Structure, and Classification of Natural Surfactants

Most studies on the formulation of micro/nanoemulsions have utilized traditional ionic or ethoxylated nonionic surfactants. Although these synthetic surfactants possess excellent interfacial diffusivity and high emulsifying/stabilizing potential, concerns about their safety, toxicity, and in vivo fate may limit their clinical applications. Furthermore, during the last decades, there has been a growing interest in formulating both conventional and advanced drug delivery systems using nature-derived ingredients to satisfy present patient/consumer as well as environmental, biological, and economic demands. Given these well-recognized issues, a great deal of recent research and development efforts have been focused on the identification, evaluation, and utilization of natural surfactants, with particular emphasis on the molecular features required for their functional performance (Savić et al., 2010; Solans and García-Celma, 1997).

From a strict point of view, the term "natural surfactants" relates to surface-active substances obtained directly from a natural source of either plant, animal, or microbial origin, by using some kind of separation procedure, such as extraction, precipitation, or distillation, and no organic synthesis should be involved at any stage of the preparation process (Holmberg, 2001). There are not many surfactants in use today that meet these criteria for truly natural surfactants; lecithin, isolated from soybean or egg, is probably the best example of surfactants belonging to this category. In general, the term "natural surfactants" is commonly used to indicate some natural origin of the compound—surfactants coming from natural raw materials. However, in the broadest sense of the word, this term means surfactants with one of the main building blocks, the hydrophilic headgroup or the hydrophobic tail, obtained from a natural source (Holmberg, 2001).

Generally, there are three categories of natural surfactants: (1) surfactants/biosurfactants produced by yeast or bacteria through fermentation (e.g., glycolipids, lipopeptides, polysaccharides, proteins, lipopolysaccharides, and lipoproteins); (2) surfactants based on a natural hydrophilic headgroup (e.g., surfactants containing either sugar or amino acid as natural polar headgroup); and (3) surfactants based on a natural hydrophobic tail (e.g., surfactants containing either fatty acid or sterol as natural hydrophobic tail). Nowadays, research is peculiarly intense in the field of sugar-based surfactants, including alkyl polyglucosides/alkyl glucosides (APGs) and sucrose fatty acid esters/sucrose esters (SEs), which are of special interest as prospective, regulatory accepted, pharmaceutical excipients (Holmberg, 2001; Savić et al., 2010; Stubenrauch, 2001).

4.5.3 Functionality of Natural Surfactants as Excipients in Micro/Nanoemulsions

A fundamental understanding of the structural as well as physical or chemical properties of surfactants related to their functionality in the final formulation (the so-called functionality-related characteristics) is of great importance and should aid in the rational selection of natural surfactants suitable for use in pharmaceutical preparations. In the following pages, we provide an overview of the characteristics and functionality of the most explored and, probably, the most promising natural surfactants for the preparation of biocompatible micro/nanoemulsions as drug delivery vehicles, highlighting the properties of these surfactants in relation to the performances of developed natural surfactant-based micro/nanoemulsion systems. Examples of natural surfactants commonly employed in the formulation of pharmaceutical micro/nanoemulsions are shown in Fig. 4.2.

4.5.3.1 Lecithin

Currently, lecithin is by far the most widely used natural surface-active agent in the food, cosmetic, and pharmaceutical industries, primarily owing to its excellent toxicity/tolerability/biocompatibility profile, but also due to the fact that it is produced from renewable sources with eco-friendly processes, and is available in large scale at relatively low costs (Klang and Valenta, 2011; Solans and García-Celma, 1997; van Hoogevest and Wendel, 2014). It is well established, generally recognized as safe (GRAS), pharmaceutical excipient, described in Pharmacopoeias (American, Chinese, Japanese) and well accepted by regulatory authorities (FDA, EMA) (van Hoogevest and Wendel, 2014). Pharmaceutically employed natural lecithin is usually derived from soybeans or egg yolk and may be further hydrogenated or treated with enzymes to generate saturated and enzyme-modified lecithin forms, which are also considered as natural and can be safely utilized in the development of pharmaceutical preparations (Klang and Valenta, 2011; van Hoogevest and Wendel, 2014). In pharmaceutical technology, lecithin is used as emulsifier/stabilizer, solubilizer, wetting agent, and liposome former, in many formulation types—lipid emulsions, mixed micelles, suspensions, liposomes—for any administration route (van Hoogevest and Wendel, 2014).

Actually, the term "lecithin" was originally assigned to pure phosphatidylcholine (PC) as the most abundant phospholipid and the main component of natural lecithin. However, today the name lecithin is typically used for a complex mixture of different phosphatides/phospholipids combined with various amounts of other substances such as triglycerides and fatty acids. Besides PC, other common phospholipids in lecithin mixtures are phosphatidylethanolamine (PE), phosphatidylinositol (PI), phosphatidylserine (PS), phosphatidic acid (PA), sphingomyelin, lysophospholipids, and other glycerol phospholipids of complex fatty acid composition (Klang and Valenta, 2011; van Hoogevest and Wendel, 2014).

Phospholipids are surface-active because of their amphiphilic character; the phospholipid molecule comprises a glycerol backbone, which is esterified in positions C-1 and C-2 with fatty acids (hydrophobic tail groups) and in position C-3 with phosphoric acid, which is further esterified with an additional alcohol (hydrophilic headgroup) (van Hoogevest and Wendel, 2014). Depending on the structure of the polar group and pH value of the system, PC and PE are zwitterionic and uncharged at neutral pH, whereas PA, PS, and PI are negatively charged and able to impart sufficiently high negative surface charge to the

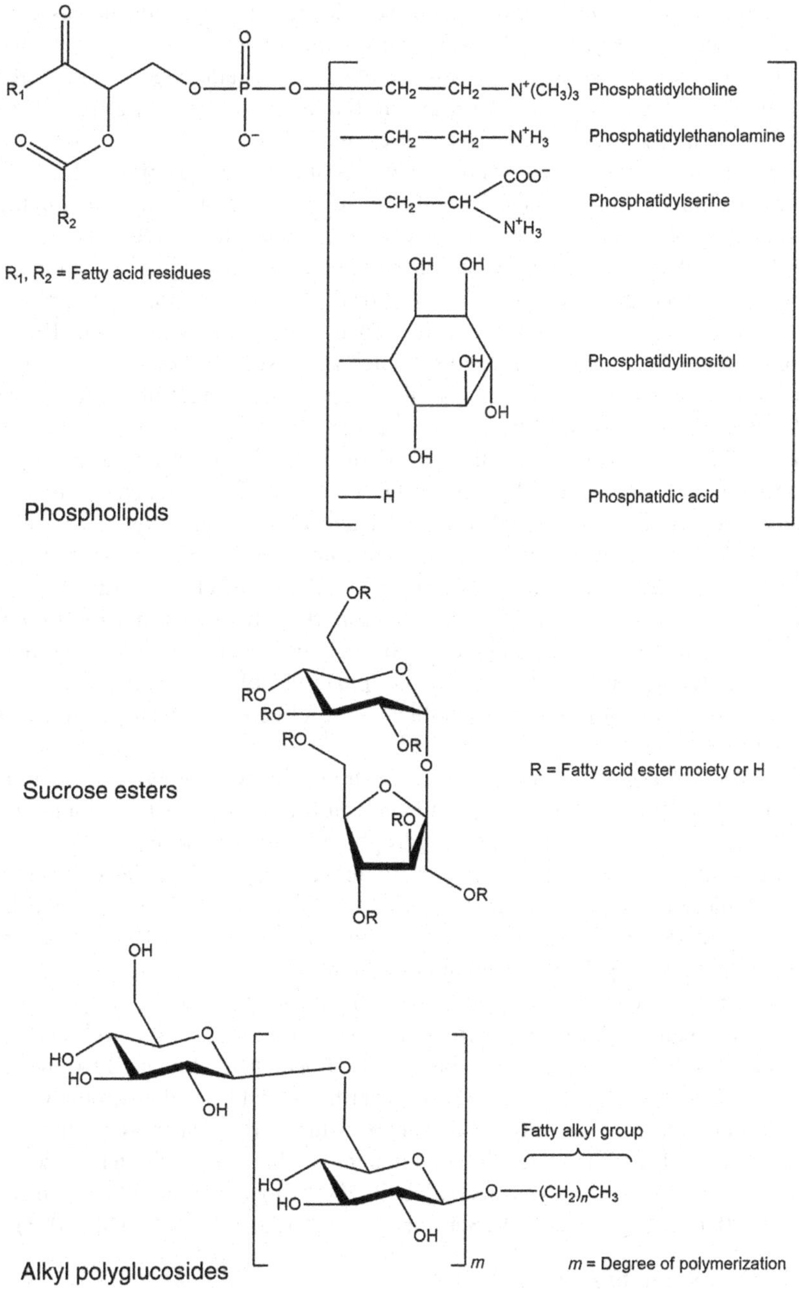

Phospholipids

R_1, R_2 = Fatty acid residues

$-CH_2-CH_2-N^+(CH_3)_3$ Phosphatidylcholine

$-CH_2-CH_2-N^+H_3$ Phosphatidylethanolamine

$-CH_2-CH\langle{COO^-}\atop{N^+H_3}$ Phosphatidylserine

Phosphatidylinositol

$-H$ Phosphatidic acid

Sucrose esters

R = Fatty acid ester moiety or H

Alkyl polyglucosides

Fatty alkyl group

$O-(CH_2)_nCH_3$

m = Degree of polymerization

FIGURE 4.2 **Molecular structures of natural surfactants commonly used in micro/ nanoemulsion drug-carrier systems.**

emulsion droplets, thus leading to increased electrostatic repulsion and, as a result, to increased stability of the emulsion system. Since pure PC does not have sufficient charge to produce emulsions stable enough, natural lecithin mixtures are preferred for formulation development (Hippalgaonkar et al., 2010; Klang and Valenta, 2011; van Hoogevest and Wendel, 2014).

Systematic studies investigating the effects of different phospholipid derivatives on emulsion formation and stability have suggested that differences in the structure of phospholipids, such as the carbon chain length, degree of saturation of the acyl chains, as well as nature of the headgroup, may significantly impact their physicochemical properties, and, consequently, the formation, properties, and stability of lecithin-based micro/nanoemulsions (Washington, 1996). For example, PCs with shorter and saturated acyl hydrocarbon chains are considered more potent emulsifiers than those containing longer and unsaturated chains, and, therefore, may be advantageous in preparing stable emulsions (Nii and Ishii, 2004). In line with this, Kawaguchi et al. (2008) found that lipid nanoemulsions prepared with saturated PC, containing long- and medium-chain fatty acids ester-linked to glycerol at C-1 and C-2, respectively, had smaller droplet size and greater stability than nanoemulsions formulated with purified egg yolk lecithin. In one study (Hoeller et al., 2008), the effect of various lecithin compositions was investigated with respect to the microemulsion formation: the observed difference in the size of monophasic area could be explained by the difference in PC, PE, and lysophosphatidylcholine contents, since each of the non-PC components may influence the effective CPP of lecithin in a different manner.

However, it has been reported that the emulsification properties of lecithin alone are not sufficient to form micro/nanoemulsions with satisfying long-term stability. Lecithin is in general too hydrophobic and its molecular geometry is not perfectly suited for the formation of curved surfaces. In order to produce stable micro/nanoemulsions, it is necessary to adjust the HLB and modify the packing characteristics of lecithin, thus providing the interfacial film sufficient flexibility to take up different curvatures required to form micro/nanoemulsions. To achieve this, different types of cosurfactants (e.g., polysorbate 80, poloxamer, short-chain alcohols), that form a close-packed, complex film with lecithin at the oil–water interface, can be employed (Hippalgaonkar et al., 2010; Klang and Valenta, 2011; Trotta et al., 2002). Nevertheless, additional incorporation of mild, nontoxic, skin-friendly surfactants of natural origin, such as sugar-based ones (SEs and APGs) in micro/nanoemulsions stabilized by lecithin has been of special interest in recent years (Graf et al., 2008; Hoeller et al., 2009; Isailović et al., 2016; Klang et al., 2010; Schwarz et al., 2012a; Takegami et al., 2008).

4.5.3.2 Sucrose Esters

In the search for environmentally safer surfactants from renewable sources, the SEs have drawn increasing attention due to their biocompatible, biodegradable, nontoxic, and nonirritant nature. In parallel, knowledge about the physicochemical properties and functional performances of this surfactant group has steadily grown in recent years. SEs, typically referred to as sugar esters, are widely used in the food and cosmetic industries, and have lately been recognized as promising excipients in the pharmaceutical field (Garti et al., 1999; Szűts and Szabó-Révész, 2012; Ullrich et al., 2008). Thanks to their surfactant and other versatile properties, SEs have many possible pharmaceutical applications including emulsification and stabilization, bioavailability modification, dissolution improvement, sustained/controlled drug release, as well as absorption and penetration enhancement (Szűts and Szabó-Révész, 2012). However, applicability of SEs in different areas of drug delivery depends, to a great extent, on their regulatory and toxicological status. They are already approved as food additives (E473) (Szűts and Szabó-Révész, 2012; Thevenin et al., 1996; Ullrich et al., 2008), and some SEs have a Drug Master File as well. Furthermore, sucrose stearate and sucrose palmitate have compendial status (Ph. Eur., USP-NF), certifying their safety and applicability in humans (Szűts and Szabó-Révész, 2012).

Yet, the most interesting feature of SEs arises from their chemical structure being amphiphilic (Garti et al., 1999). Namely, SEs are polyol nonionic surfactants consisting of sucrose as the hydrophilic headgroup and fatty acids as the hydrophobic tails. SEs are synthesized from nature-derived raw materials by an organic chemical route, that is, esterification of sucrose with fatty acids (Szűts and Szabó-Révész, 2012; Thevenin et al., 1996). As sucrose has eight free hydroxyl groups that can be esterified, compounds ranging from sucrose mono- to octafatty acid esters can be produced. The commercial SEs are complex mixtures with various degrees of esterification, that is, mono-, di-, tri-, and polyesters of different fatty acids (Szűts and Szabó-Révész, 2012). Depending on the type (lipophilic chain length) and number of the fatty acid groups, SEs with a wide range of HLB values (1–16), and with good surfactant functionality can be obtained. The composition of the mixture will also determine the physical state, solubility in water, melting temperature, gelling characteristics, self-aggregation behavior, solubilizing abilities, as well as the emulsification properties of SEs. For example, SEs with higher monoester content are more hydrophilic, with high HLB values and good water solubility; while a high esterification degree yields more lipophilic SEs, with low HLB values (Das et al., 2014; Garti et al., 1999; Szűts and Szabó-Révész, 2012).

The emulsification features of SEs are somehow unique since almost any HLB value can be obtained, providing various hydrophilic–lipophilic properties, and since SEs, unlike the ethoxylated derivatives, do not significantly change their HLB with changes in temperature (Garti et al., 1999; Glatter et al., 2001). Due to the strong hydration of the sucrose hydroxyl groups, which are mainly responsible for the affinity of SE for the aqueous phase, the heat stable emulsion systems based on SEs can be prepared (Das et al., 2014). Given the advantages of SEs, particularly large emulsifying capacity and good stabilizing ability against various stresses, it is not surprising that SEs are of great potential as emulsifiers and stabilizers in various (conventional and advanced) drug delivery systems (Szűts and Szabó-Révész, 2012). Although the number of articles on SEs is continuously increasing, only a few works dealing with the use of SEs in pharmaceutical micro/nanoemulsions have been reported so far (Bolzinger et al., 1998; Fanun, 2007, 2008; Garti et al., 1999; Glatter et al., 2001; Isailović et al., 2016; Klang et al., 2010, 2011; Thevenin et al., 1996; Todosijević et al., 2014, 2015; Takegami et al., 2008).

SE-based microemulsions for transdermal delivery consisting of cetearyl octanoate, different SEs, ethanol, and water have been investigated first by Thevenin et al. (1996). The authors concluded that SEs when used alone, without cosurfactant, are not able to form microemulsions under tested conditions. Furthermore, sucrose stearate and sucrose palmitate could not form microemulsion systems, even in the presence of ethanol as cosurfactant. On the other hand, the combinations of sucrose monodilaurate/ethanol, sucrose myristate/ethanol, and sucrose oleate/ethanol improved the extent of microemulsion domains, respectively, and these domains became longer with the increase in surfactant/cosurfactant mass ratio. Recently, Todosijević et al. (2014) have assessed the functionality of various SEs (sucrose laurate, myristate, palmitate, and stearate; HLB 16) in formulation of biocompatible microemulsions (isopropyl myristate/SE-isopropyl alcohol/water) as vehicles for skin delivery of aceclofenac. It was found that minor changes in the SE tail length strongly affect the phase behavior, water solubilization capacity, as well as the microstructure of investigated microemulsion systems, probably by influencing the packing and flexibility/fluidity of surfactant molecules at the oil–water interface.

As stated earlier (Klang et al., 2011), nanoemulsions intended for dermal drug delivery are usually stabilized by natural lecithins. In order to improve nanoemulsion stability and therapeutic efficacy, but retain high biocompatibility and excellent skin friendliness, naturally derived SEs have recently been employed as highly suitable coemulsifying agents in lecithin-based nanoemulsion systems (Hoeller et al., 2009; Isailović et al., 2016; Klang et al., 2010; Takegami et al., 2008). Accordingly, Isailović et al. (2016) have successfully developed biocompatible lecithin-based nanoemulsions for effective aceclofenac skin delivery utilizing SEs (sucrose palmitate, HLB 16 and/or sucrose stearate, HLB 9) as additional stabilizers and penetration enhancers. Formulation design approach, improved physicochemical characteristics and in vivo skin performances of developed aceclofenac-loaded lecithin and SE-based nanoemulsions are discussed in detail in Chapter 7.

With the aim of avoiding the shortcomings of lecithin molecules, such as pronounced tendency toward self-aggregation and susceptibility to oxidative and hydrolytical degradation, Klang et al. (2011) have developed highly stable and homogenous nanoemulsions for dermal drug delivery by employing natural sucrose stearate (~50% monoester, HLB 9) as sole emulsifier. In their study, a thorough comparison between the novel sucrose stearate-based nanoemulsions and the corresponding lecithin-based ones demonstrated the superiority of sucrose stearate in terms of emulsifying efficiency, droplet formation, morphology, and physical and chemical stability. Furthermore, it was observed that the in vitro skin permeation of the model lipophilic drugs incorporated in sucrose stearate nanoemulsions was similar to that obtained with lecithin-based systems.

4.5.3.3 Alkyl Polyglucosides

Among natural-origin, environment-friendly, and skin-friendly surfactants with sugar as a polar headgroup, the APGs have established themselves as prospective, multifunctional surface-active agents for several types of applications. Their promising use as pharmaceutical excipients in the formulation of both conventional and advanced drug delivery systems, in the possible roles of emulsifiers/stabilizers, solubilizers, and penetration/permeation enhancers, has been accentuated by their favorable ecological, toxicological, dermatological, as well as physicochemical properties. Indeed, APGs represent an old/new class of very mild, polyethylene glycol-free, nonionic surfactants produced from renewable raw materials (starch and plant oils) and having outstanding biodegradability, excellent skin compatibility, high surface activity, and interesting interfacial properties (Geetha and Tyagi, 2012; Hoffmann and Platz, 2001; Holmberg, 2001; Savić et al., 2010; von Rybinski and Hill, 1998).

APG molecules consist of a hydrophobic alkyl residue derived from fatty alcohol and a hydrophilic saccharide moiety derived from glucose, which are connected via an ether bond. Most of the commercially available APG products are complex mixtures of various compounds (homologs, anomers, and isomers) differing in the alkyl chain length (typically 6–18 carbon atoms), glucosidation/polymerization degree (usually 1.1–1.7), and stereochemistry (Balzer, 2000; Geetha and Tyagi, 2012). It was shown that the molecular structure, that is, the alkyl chain length as well as the average number of condensed glucose units in the headgroup, may influence the biodegradability, phase and aggregation behavior, surface activity, emulsifying power, solubilization capacity, as well as penetration-modifying ability of APG surfactants (Geetha and Tyagi, 2012; Hoffmann and Platz, 2001; Pantelic et al., 2015; Savić et al., 2010; von Rybinski and Hill, 1998). The hydroxyl groups in the polar part of APG molecules are highly lipophilic, whereas, at the same time, molecules with long enough hydrocarbon chain are highly hydrophobic; APG surfactants, therefore, have a high tendency to remain at the oil–water interface (Holmberg et al., 2003). In general, increasing the degree of polymerization increases the solubility of APGs in water, while extending the alkyl chain increases the hydrophobicity and, hence, the oil solubility of APG surfactants, forming highly stable emulsions (Balzer, 2000; Geetha and Tyagi, 2012). Similar to emulsification potential, the solubilization capacity of APGs has been shown to increase with increase in their chain length (Savić et al., 2010).

In addition, APG surfactants show also peculiar physicochemical behavior—temperature insensitivity, relatively good electrolyte and pH stability, liquid crystalline phase behavior, as well as specific aggregation, interfacial, and adsorption phenomena (Savić et al., 2010; Stubenrauch, 2001). One favorable property of APGs is certainly the potential to form transparent, thermodynamically stable microemulsions, almost independently of temperature. Namely, the phase behavior of APG/oil/water systems is only slightly influenced by temperature and, therefore, no temperature-dependent phase inversion is expected to occur in APG-containing emulsions. In this regard, APG-based microemulsions with very low interfacial tension, very largely electrolyte- and temperature-insensitive, can be formed by careful selection of appropriate APG surfactant/lipophilic cosurfactant combinations and ratios, as well as optimal oil and water contents, in a tailor-made formulation approach (Förster et al., 1996; Fukuda et al., 1993; Savic et al., 2014; von Rybinski and Hill, 1998).

Although there have been many basic studies regarding microemulsions with APG surfactants, only few reports of APG-stabilized microemulsions as innovative drug carriers have been published to date (Goebel et al., 2010, 2011; Graf et al., 2008; Pakpayat et al., 2009). An interesting study by Schwarz et al. (2012a) investigated and compared, for the first time, three different natural surfactants, namely APG (coco glucoside and coconut alcohol), lecithin, and sucrose laurate, in terms of their suitability to form microemulsions as topical drug delivery systems. Mixed surfactant films of APG/lecithin and sucrose laurate/lecithin (1:1, w/w) were also tested. Lecithin showed the largest isotropic area, followed by sucrose laurate, while only few isotropic microemulsions could be identified for APG as single surfactant. However, a considerable increase in the isotropic areas was achieved with APG/lecithin and, particularly, sucrose laurate/lecithin combinations. Moreover, excellent skin diffusion profiles for two model drugs, flufenamic acid and fluconazole, were obtained from lecithin and APG/lecithin microemulsion formulations.

After APGs proved to be suitable for stabilization of lipid nanocarriers intended for dermal drug delivery (Mitri et al., 2011; Schwarz et al., 2012b), a further study from the authors' laboratory (Đorđević et al., 2013) proceeded in evaluating the potential of eudermic surfactant of APG type (caprylyl/capryl glucoside) to form and stabilize nanoemulsions with increasing oil content (20, 30, and 40%), being important for higher solubilization capacity for poorly soluble actives. On the day of production, all APG nanoemulsions had satisfying physicochemical properties. However, during storage (6 months at 25°C, 1 month at 40°C), significant changes (size increases, phase separation) were noticed, possibly due to insufficient quantity of APG as single emulsifier in tested formulations.

4.6 CONCLUSIONS

Traditional understanding of excipients as simple and inert materials has undergone significant changes in the last few decades. Nowadays, it is generally accepted that excipients are indispensable ingredients of modern pharmaceutical preparations having significant influence on their quality, safety, and efficacy.

Growing need for improvement of therapeutic outcomes of existing drugs has introduced new functional categories of excipients, such as encapsulating agents in micro/nanoparticles or surfactants as emulsifying/stabilizing agents in micro/ nanoemulsions. These excipients comprise a variety of materials of natural and synthetic origin, whose functionality depends on various physicochemical properties known as functionality-related characteristics. These characteristics have to be identified and their influence on intended use should be carefully investigated. Thereafter, these properties can be modified by using various physical and chemical approaches in order to improve overall performance of the final formulation.

ACKNOWLEDGMENT

This work was realized within the framework of the project TR 34031 supported by the Ministry of Education, Science and Technological Development of Republic of Serbia.

REFERENCES

Adjonu R, Doran G, Torley P, Agboola S: Whey protein peptides as components of nanoemulsions: a review of emulsifying and biological functionalities, *J Food Eng* 122:15–27, 2014.

Aguzzi C, Cerezo P, Viseras C, Caramella C: Use of clays as drug delivery systems: possibilities and limitations, *Appl Clay Sci* 36:22–36, 2007.

Aiba SI: Studies on chitosan: 4. Lysozymic hydrolysis of partially *N*-acetylated chitosans, *Int J Biol Macromol* 31:225–228, 1992.

Akagi T, Shima F, Akashi M: Intracellular degradation and distribution of protein-encapsulated amphiphilic poly (amino acid) nanoparticles, *Biomaterials* 32:4959–4967, 2011.

Amidon GE: Performance related tests in excipients, USP Annual Science Meeting, Denver, CO, 2006.

Alexandrino EM, Ritz S, Marsico F, Baier G, Mailänder V, Landfester K, Wurm FR: Paclitaxel-loaded polyphosphate nanoparticles: a potential strategy for bone cancer treatment, *J Mater Chem B* 2:1298–1306, 2014.

Amidon GE, Peck GE, Block LH, Moreton RC, Katdare A, Lafaver R, Sheehan C: Proposed new USP general information chapter, excipient performance, *Pharmacopeial Forum* 33:1311–1323, 2007.

Angelova N, Hunkeler D: Rationalizing the design of polymeric biomaterials, *Trends Biotechnol* 17:409–421, 1999.

Aranaz I, Mengíbar M, Harris R, Paños I, Miralles B, Acosta N, Galed G, Heras Á: Functional characterization of chitin and chitosan, *Curr Chem Biol* 3:203–230, 2009.

Araújo J, Vega E, Lopes C, Egea MA, Garcia ML, Souto EB: Effect of polymer viscosity on physicochemical properties and ocular tolerance of FB-loaded PLGA nanospheres, *Colloid Surf B* 72:48–56, 2009.

Attwood D, Florence AT: *Physical pharmacy*, ed 1, London, 2008, Pharmaceutical Press.

Aw MS, Simovic S, Yu Y, Addai-Mensah J, Losic D: Porous silica microshells from diatoms as biocarrier for drug delivery applications, *Powder Technol* 30:52–58, 2012.

Babonneau F, Yeung L, Steunou N, Gervais C, Ramila A, Vallet-Regi M: Solid state NMR characterisation of encapsulated molecules in mesoporous silica, *J Sol Gel Sci Technol* 31:219–223, 2004.

Baier G, Cavallaro A, Friedemann K, Müller B, Glasser G, Vasilev K, Landfester K: Enzymatic degradation of poly (L-lactide) nanoparticles followed by the release of octenidine and their bactericidal effects, *Nanomedicine* 31:131–139, 2014.

Bala I, Hariharan S, Kumar MR: PLGA nanoparticles in drug delivery: the state of the art, *Crit Rev Ther Drug* 21:387–422, 2004.

Balas F, Manzano M, Horcajada P, Vallet-Regí M: Confinement and controlled release of bisphosphonates on ordered mesoporous silica-based materials, *J Am Chem Soc* 128:8116–8117, 2006.

Balzer D: Surfactant properties. In Balzer D, Lüders H, editors: *Nonionic surfactants: alkyl polyglucosides*, New York, 2000, Marcel Dekker, pp 85–278.

Bariana M, Aw MS, Losic D: Tailoring morphological and interfacial properties of diatom silica microparticles for drug delivery applications, *Adv Powder Technol* 24:757–763, 2013.

Beck JS, Vartuli JC, Roth WJ, Leonowicz ME, Kresge CT, Schmitt KD, Chu CT, Olson DH, Sheppard EW: A new family of mesoporous molecular sieves prepared with liquid crystal templates, *J Am Chem Soc* 114:10834–10843, 1992.

Bhattacharyya L: Excipient quality in pharmaceutical development, understanding their function benefits process control, *Contract Pharma*, 2006, http://www.contractpharma.com/issues/2006-06/view_features/excipient-quality-in-pharmaceutical-development.

Bhattacharyya L, Schuber S, Sheehan C, William R: Excipients: background/introduction. In Katdare A, Chaubal M, editors: *Excipient development for pharmaceutical, biotechnology, and drug delivery systems*, Boca Raton, 2006, CRC Press, pp 1–36.

Bolzinger MA, Carduner T, Poelman MC: Bicontinuous sucrose ester microemulsion: a new vehicle for topical delivery of niflumic acid, *Int J Pharm* 176:39–45, 1998.

Čalija B, Cekić N, Milić J: Chitosan-based polyelectrolyte complexes: characteristics and application in formulation of particulate drug carriers. In Tiwari A, Patra HK, Choi JW, editors: *Advanced theranostic materials*, Hoboken, 2015, John Wiley & Sons, pp 235–270.

Čalija B, Cekić N, Savić S, Daniels R, Marković B, Milić J: pH-sensitive microparticles for oral drug delivery based on alginate/oligochitosan/Eudragit® L100-55 "sandwich" polyelectrolyte complex, *Colloid Surf B* 110:395–402, 2013a.

Čalija B, Cekić N, Savić S, Krajišnik D, Daniels R, Milić J: An investigation of formulation factors affecting feasibility of alginate–chitosan microparticles for oral delivery of naproxen, *Arch Pharm Res* 34:919–929, 2011.

Čalija B, Milić J, Cekić N, Krajišnik D, Daniels R, Savić S: Chitosan oligosaccharide as prospective cross-linking agent for naproxen-loaded Ca-alginate microparticles with improved pH sensitivity, *Drug Dev Ind Pharm* 39:77–88, 2013b.

Carretero MI, Pozo M: Clay and non-clay minerals in the pharmaceutical industry: part I. Excipients and medical applications, *Appl Clay Sci* 46:73–80, 2009.

Casettari L, Vllasaliu D, Castagnino E, Stolnik S, Howdle S, Illum L: PEGylated chitosan derivatives: synthesis, characterizations and pharmaceutical applications, *Prog Polym Sci* 37:659–685, 2012.

Chen DR, Bei JZ, Wang SG: Polycaprolactone microparticles and their biodegradation, *Polym Degrad Stabil* 67:455–459, 2000.

Chen C, Yu CH, Cheng YC, Peter HF, Cheung MK: Biodegradable nanoparticles of amphiphilic triblock copolymers based on poly(3-hydroxybutyrate) and poly(ethylene glycol) as drug carriers, *Biomaterials* 30:4804–4814, 2006.

Cheng K, Landry CC: Diffusion-based deprotection in mesoporous materials: a strategy for differential functionalization of porous silica particles, *J Am Chem Soc* 129:9674–9685, 2007.

Choi KY, Chung H, Min KH, Yoon HY, Kim K, Park JH, Kwon IC, Jeong SY: Self-assembled hyaluronic acid nanoparticles for active tumor targeting, *Biomaterials* 31:106–114, 2010.

Choksakulnimitr S, Masuda S, Tokuda H, Takakura Y, Hashida M: In vitro cytotoxicity of macromolecules in different cell culture systems, *J Control Release* 34:233–241, 1995.

Choy JH, Choi SJ, Oh JM, Park T: Clay minerals and layered double hydroxides for novel biological applications, *Appl Clay Sci* 36:122–132, 2007.

Chrzanowski W, Kim SY, Neel EA: Biomedical applications of clay, *Aust J Chem* 66:1315–1322, 2013.

Das S, Ng WK, Tan RBH: Sucrose ester stabilized solid lipid nanoparticles and nanostructured lipid carriers: I. Effect of formulation variables on the physicochemical properties, drug release and stability of clotrimazole-loaded nanoparticles, *Nanotechnology* 25:105101, 2014.

Dhal PK, Polomoscanik SC, Avila LZ, Holmes-Farley SR, Miller RJ: Functional polymers as therapeutic agents: concept to market place, *Adv Drug Deliv Rev* 61:1121–1130, 2009.

Doadrio JC, Sousa EM, Izquierdo-Barba I, Doadrio AL, Perez-Pariente J, Vallet-Regí M: Functionalization of mesoporous materials with long alkyl chains as a strategy for controlling drug delivery pattern, *J Mater Chem* 16:462–466, 2006.

Donati I, Holtan S, Mørch YA, Borgogna M, Dentini M, Skjåk-Bræk G: New hypothesis on the role of alternating sequences in calcium-alginate gels, *Biomacromolecules* 6:1031–1040, 2005.

Dong Y, Feng SS: Poly (D, L-lactide-*co*-glycolide)/montmorillonite nanoparticles for oral delivery of anticancer drugs, *Biomaterials* 26:6068–6076, 2005.

Đorđević SM, Cekić ND, Isailović TM, Milić JR, Vuleta GM, Lazić ML, Savić SD: Nanoemulsions produced by varying the type of emulsifier and oil content: effect of formulation and process parameters on the characteristics and physical stability, *Hem Ind* 67:795–809, 2013.

Draget KI, Skjåk-Bræk G, Smidsrød O: Alginate based new materials, *Int J Biol Macromol* 21:47–55, 1997.

Du L, Song H, Liao S: Tuning the morphology of mesoporous silica by using various template combinations, *Appl Surf Sci* 255:9365–9370, 2009.

Elder DP, Kuentz M, Holm R: Pharmaceutical excipients—quality, regulatory and biopharmaceutical considerations, *Eur J Pharm Sci* 87:88–99, 2015.

Elsabahy M, Wooley KL: Design of polymeric nanoparticles for biomedical delivery applications, *Chem Soc Rev* 41:2545–2561, 2012.

Fanun M: Conductivity, viscosity, NMR and diclofenac solubilization capacity studies of mixed nonionic surfactants microemulsions, *J Mol Liq* 135:5–13, 2007.

Fanun M: Phase behavior, transport, diffusion and structural parameters of nonionic surfactants microemulsions, *J Mol Liq* 139:14–22, 2008.

FDA Center for Drug Evaluation and Research: Inactive ingredient search for approved drug products, 2015. Available from http://www.accessdata.fda.gov/scripts/cder/iig/index.cfm

Fischer D, Li Y, Ahlemeyer B, Krieglstein J, Kissel T: In vitro cytotoxicity testing of polycations: influence of polymer structure on cell viability and hemolysis, *Biomaterials* 24:1121–1131, 2003.

Fonseca C, Simoes S, Gaspar R: Paclitaxel-loaded PLGA nanoparticles: preparation, physicochemical characterization and in vitro anti-tumoral activity, *J Control Release* 83:273–286, 2002.

Förster T, Guchkenbiehl B, Hensen H, von Rybinski W: Physico-chemical basics of microemulsions with alkyl polyglycosides, *Prog Colloid Polym Sci* 101:105–112, 1996.

Freiberg S, Zhu XX: Polymer microspheres for controlled drug release, *Int J Pharm* 282:1–18, 2004.

Fried JR: *Polymer science and technology*, ed 3, Upper Saddle River, 2014, Prentice Hall.

Fu J, Li XY, Ng DK, Wu C: Encapsulation of phthalocyanines in biodegradable poly(sebacic anhydride) nanoparticles, *Langmuir* 18:3843–3847, 2002.

Fukuda K, Söderman O, Lindman B, Shinoda K: Microemulsions formed by alkyl polyglucosides and an alkyl glycerol ether, *Langmuir* 9:2921–2925, 1993.

Garti N, Clement V, Leser M, Aserin A, Fanun M: Sucrose ester microemulsions, *J Mol Liq* 80:253–296, 1999.

Gaucher G, Marchessault RH, Leroux JC: Polyester-based micelles and nanoparticles for the parenteral delivery of taxanes, *J Control Release* 143:2–12, 2010.

Geetha D, Tyagi R: Alkyl poly glucosides (APGs) surfactants and their properties: a review, *Tenside Surf Det* 49:417–427, 2012.

Glatter O, Orthaber D, Stradner A, Scherf G, Fanun M, Garti N, Clément V, Leser ME: Sugar-ester nonionic microemulsion: structural characterization, *J Colloid Interface Sci* 241:215–225, 2001.

Gnanou Y, Fontanille M: *Organic and physical chemistry of polymers*, ed 1, Hoboken, 2008, John Wiley & Sons.

Goebel AS, Knie U, Abels C, Wohlrab J, Neubert RH: Dermal targeting using colloidal carrier systems with linoleic acid, *Eur J Pharm Biopharm* 75:162–172, 2010.

Goebel AS, Neubert RH, Wohlrab J: Dermal targeting of tacrolimus using colloidal carrier systems, *Int J Pharm* 404:159–168, 2011.

Gombotz WR, Wee SF: Protein release from alginate matrices, *Adv Drug Deliv Rev* 64:194–205, 2012.

González-Rodríguez ML, Holgado MA, Sanchez-Lafuente C, Rabasco AM, Fini A: Alginate/chitosan particulate systems for sodium diclofenac release, *Int J Pharm* 232:225–234, 2002.

Goonoo N, Jeetah R, Bhaw-Luximon A, Jhurry D: Polydioxanone-based bio-materials for tissue engineering and drug/gene delivery applications, *Eur J Pharm Biopharm* 97:371–391, 2015.

Graf A, Ablinger E, Peters S, Zimmer A, Hook S, Rades T: Microemulsions containing lecithin and sugar-based surfactants: nanoparticle templates for delivery of proteins and peptides, *Int J Pharm* 350:351–360, 2008.

Guggenheim S, Martin RT: Definition of clay and clay mineral: joint report of the AIPEA nomenclature and CMS nomenclature committees, *Clay Clay Miner* 43:255–256, 1995.

Gupta KC, Jabrail FH: Effects of degree of deacetylation and cross-linking on physical characteristics, swelling and release behavior of chitosan microspheres, *Carbohydr Polym* 66:43–54, 2006.

He P, Davis SS, Illum L: Chitosan microspheres prepared by spray drying, *Int J Pharm* 187:53–65, 1999.

Hejazi R, Amiji M: Chitosan-based gastrointestinal delivery systems, *J Control Release* 89:151–165, 2003.

Hippalgaonkar K, Majumdar S, Kansara V: Injectable lipid emulsions—advancements, opportunities and challenges, *AAPS PharmSciTech* 11:1526–1540, 2010.

Hoeller S, Klang V, Valenta C: Skin-compatible lecithin drug delivery systems for fluconazole: effect of phosphatidylethanolamine and oleic acid on skin permeation, *J Pharm Pharmacol* 60:587–591, 2008.

Hoeller S, Sperger A, Valenta C: Lecithin based nanoemulsions: a comparative study of the influence of non-ionic surfactants and the cationic phytosphingosine on physicochemical behaviour and skin permeation, *Int J Pharm* 370:181–186, 2009.

Hoffmann B, Platz G: Phase and aggregation behaviour of alkylpolyglucosides, *Curr Opin Colloid Interface Sci* 6:171–177, 2001.

Holmberg K: Natural surfactants, *Curr Opin Colloid Interface Sci* 6:148–159, 2001.

Holmberg K, Jönsson B, Kronberg B, Lindman B: *Surfactants and polymers in aqueous solution*, ed 2, West Susex, 2003, John Wiley & Sons, Ltd, p 34.

Hu L, Sun C, Song A, Chang D, Zheng X, Gao Y, Jiang T, Wang S: Alginate encapsulated mesoporous silica nanospheres as a sustained drug delivery system for the poorly water-soluble drug indomethacin, *Asian J Pharm Sci* 9:183–190, 2014.

Huang M, Khor E, Lim LY: Uptake and cytotoxicity of chitosan molecules and nanoparticles: effects of molecular weight and degree of deacetylation, *Pharm Res* 21:344–353, 2004.

ICH: ICH Q8 (R2) pharmaceutical development, 2009. Available from http://www.ich.org/fileadmin/public_web_site/ICH_products/guidelines/quality/Q8_R1/step4/Q8_R2_guideline.pdf

IPEC: Qualification of excipients for use in pharmaceuticals, 2008. Available from http://ipecamericas.org/sites/default/files/ExcipientQualificationGuide.pdf

Isailović T, Đorđević S, Marković B, Ranđelović D, Cekić N, Lukić M, Pantelić I, Daniels R, Savić S: Biocompatible nanoemulsions for improved aceclofenac skin delivery: formulation approach using combined-mixture process experimental design, *J Pharm Sci* 105:308–323, 2016.

Ito T, Sugafuji T, Maruyama M, Ohwa Y, Takahashi T: Skin penetration by indomethacin is enhanced by use of an indomethacin/smectite complex, *J Supramol Chem* 1:217–219, 2001.

Janićijević J, Krajišnik D, Čalija B, Dobričić V, Daković A, Krstić J, Marković M, Milić J: Inorganically modified diatomite as a potential prolonged-release drug carrier, *Mat Sci Eng C* 42:412–420, 2014.

Janićijević J, Krajišnik D, Čalija B, Vasiljević BN, Dobričić V, Daković A, Antonijević MD, Milić J: Modified local diatomite as potential functional drug carrier—a model study for diclofenac sodium, *Int J Pharm* 496:466–474, 2015.

Jayakumar R, Menon D, Manzoor K, Nair SV, Tamura H: Biomedical applications of chitin and chitosan based nanomaterials—a short review, *Carbohydr Polym* 82:227–232, 2010.

Jeon YJ, Kim SK: Production of chitooligosaccharides using an ultrafiltration membrane reactor and their antibacterial activity, *Carbohydr Polym* 41:133–141, 2000.

Kamei S, Inoue Y, Okada H, Yamada M, Ogawa Y, Toguchi H: New method for analysis of biodegradable polyesters by high-performance liquid chromatography after alkali hydrolysis, *Biomaterials* 13:953–958, 1992.

Kawaguchi E, Shimokawa K, Ishii F: Physicochemical properties of structured phosphatidylcholine in drug carrier lipid emulsions for drug delivery systems, *Colloids Surf B* 62:130–135, 2008.

Klang V, Matsko N, Raupach K, El-Hagin N, Valenta C: Development of sucrose stearate-based nanoemulsions and optimization through γ-cyclodextrin, *Eur J Pharm Biopharm* 79:58–67, 2011.

Klang V, Matsko N, Zimmermann AM, Vojnikovic E, Valenta C: Enhancement of stability and skin permeation by sucrose stearate and cyclodextrins in progesterone nanoemulsions, *Int J Pharm* 393:152–160, 2010.

Klang V, Valenta C: Lecithin-based nanoemulsions, *J Drug Deliv Sci Technol* 21:55–76, 2011.

Kratz F: Albumin as a drug carrier: design of prodrugs, drug conjugates and nanoparticles, *J Control Release* 132:171–183, 2008.

Kresge CT, Leonowicz ME, Roth WJ, Vartuli JC, Beck JS: Ordered mesoporous molecular sieves synthesized by a liquid-crystal template mechanism, *Nature* 359:710–712, 1992.

Kristensen HG: Functionality-related characteristics of excipients, *Pharm Technol* 31:134, 2007.

Labarre DJ, Ponchel G, Vauthier C: *Biomedical and pharmaceutical polymers*, ed 1, London, 2011, Pharmaceutical Press.

Le Corre D, Bras J, Dufresne A: Starch nanoparticles: a review, *Biomacromolecules* 11:1139–1153, 2010.

Lee EJ, Khan SA, Park JK, Lim KH: Studies on the characteristics of drug-loaded gelatin nanoparticles prepared by nanoprecipitation, *Bioproc Biosyst Eng* 35:297–307, 2012.

Lee CH, Singla A, Lee Y: Biomedical applications of collagen, *Int J Pharm* 222:1–22, 2001.

Li YL, Zhu L, Liu Z, Cheng R, Meng F, Cui JH, Ji SJ, Zhong Z: Reversibly stabilized multifunctional dextran nanoparticles efficiently deliver doxorubicin into the nuclei of cancer cells, *Angew Chem Int Ed* 48:9914–9918, 2009.

Linton P, Alfredsson V: Growth and morphology of mesoporous SBA-15 particles, *Chem Mater* 20:2878–2880, 2008.

Liu Z, Jiao Y, Wang Y, Zhou C, Zhang Z: Polysaccharides-based nanoparticles as drug delivery systems, *Adv Drug Deliv Rev* 60:1650–1662, 2008.

López-Galindo A, Viseras C, Cerezo P: Compositional, technical and safety specifications of clays to be used as pharmaceutical and cosmetic products, *Appl Clay Sci* 36:51–63, 2007.

Maderuelo C, Zarzuelo A, Lanao JM: Critical factors in the release of drugs from sustained release hydrophilic matrices, *J Control Release* 154:2–19, 2011.

Mao HQ, Leong KW: Design of polyphosphoester-DNA nanoparticles for non-viral gene delivery, *Adv Genet* 53:275–306, 2005.

Maria Chong AS, Zhao XS: Functionalization of SBA-15 with APTES and characterization of functionalized materials, *J Phys Chem B* 107:12650–12657, 2003.

Marketsand Markets: The pharmaceutical excipients market by products, functionality, & by route of administration (oral, topical, parenteral, others)—global forecast to 2019, 2015. Available from http://www.marketsandmarkets.com/Market-Reports/pharma-excipients-market-956.html

Markland P, Yang VC: Biodegradable polymers as drug carriers. In Swarbrick J, Boylan JC, editors: *Encyclopedia of pharmaceutical technology*, New York, 2002, Marcel Dekker, pp 176–193.

McClements DJ: Edible nanoemulsions: fabrication, properties, and functional performance, *Soft Matter* 7:2297–2316, 2011.

McClements DJ: Nanoemulsions versus microemulsions: terminology, differences and similarities, *Soft Matter* 8:1719–1729, 2012.

Milašinović N, Čalija B, Vidović B, Sakač MC, Vujić Z, Knežević-Jugović Z: Sustained release of α-lipoic acid from chitosan microbeads synthetized by inverse emulsion method, *J Taiwan Inst Chem E* 60:106–112, 2016.

Mirzaei BE, Ramazani SAA, Shafiee M, Danaei M: Studies on glutaraldehyde crosslinked chitosan hydrogel properties for drug delivery systems, *Int J Polym Mater* 62:605–611, 2013.

Mitri K, Shegokar R, Gohla S, Anselmi C, Müller RH: Lipid nanocarriers for dermal delivery of lutein: preparation, characterization, stability and performance, *Int J Pharm* 414:267–275, 2011.

Mittal G, Sahana DK, Bhardwaj V, Kumar MR: Estradiol loaded PLGA nanoparticles for oral administration: effect of polymer molecular weight and copolymer composition on release behavior in vitro and in vivo, *J Control Release* 119:77–85, 2007.

Monteiro OA, Airoldi C: Some studies of crosslinking chitosan–glutaraldehyde interaction in a homogeneous system, *Int J Biol Macromol* 26:119–128, 1999.

Moreton C: Excipient functionality, *Pharm Technol* 28:98–119, 2004.

Moreton C: Functionality and performance of excipients in Quality-by-Design world part 1, *Am Pharm Rev* 12:6–9, 2009a.

Moreton C: Functionality and performance of excipients in Quality-by-Design world part 4: obtaining information on excipient variability, *Am Pharm Rev* 12:28–33, 2009b.

Munoz B, Ramila A, Perez-Pariente J, Diaz I, Vallet-Regi M: MCM-41 organic modification as drug delivery rate regulator, *Chem Mater* 15:500–503, 2003.

Nii T, Ishii F: Properties of various phosphatidylcholines as emulsifiers or dispersing agents in microparticle preparations for drug carriers, *Colloids Surf B* 39:57–63, 2004.

Nitta SK, Numata K: Biopolymer-based nanoparticles for drug/gene delivery and tissue engineering, *Int J Mol Sci* 14:1629–1654, 2013.

Nooney RI, Thirunavukkarasu D, Chen Y, Josephs R, Ostafin AE: Synthesis of nanoscale mesoporous silica spheres with controlled particle size, *Chem Mater* 14:4721–4728, 2002.

Pakpayat N, Nielloud F, Fortuné R, Tourne-Peteilh C, Villarreal A, Grillo I, Bataille B: Formulation of ascorbic acid microemulsions with alkyl polyglycosides, *Eur J Pharm Biopharm* 72:444–452, 2009.

Pantelic I, Milic J, Vuleta G, Dragicevic N, Savic S: Natural emulsifiers of the alkyl polyglucoside type and their influence on the permeation of drugs. In Dragicevic N, Maibach HI, editors: *Percutaneous penetration enhancers. Chemical methods in penetration enhancement*, Berlin, Heidelberg, 2015, Springer-Verlag, pp 231–250.

Paques JP, van der Linden E, van Rijn CJM, Sagis LMC: Preparation methods of alginate nanoparticles, *Adv Colloid Interface* 209:163–171, 2014.

Park TG: Degradation of poly(D, L-lactic acid) microspheres: effect of molecular weight, *J Control Release* 30:161–173, 1994.

Park JB: Biomaterials. In Bronzino JD, editor: *Biomedical engineering handbook*, Boca Raton, 1995, CRC Press, IEEE Press, pp 530–610.

Park JK, Choy YB, Oh JM, Kim JY, Hwang SJ, Choy JH: Controlled release of donepezil intercalated in smectite clays, *Int J Pharm* 359:198–204, 2008.

Polk A, Amsden B, De Yao K, Peng T, Goosen MF: Controlled release of albumin from chitosan—alginate microcapsules, *J Pharm Sci* 83:178–185, 1994.

Prüsse U, Bilancetti L, Bučko M, Bugarski B, Bukowski J, Gemeiner P, Lewińska D, Manojlovic V, Massart B, Nastruzzi C, Nedovic V: Comparison of different technologies for alginate beads production, *Chem Pap* 62:364–374, 2008.

Puri S, Kallinteri P, Higgins S, Hutcheon GA, Garnett MC: Drug incorporation and release of water soluble drugs from novel functionalised poly(glycerol adipate) nanoparticles, *J Control Release* 125:59–67, 2008.

Radu DR, Lai CY, Jeftinija K, Rowe EW, Jeftinija S, Lin VS: A polyamidoamine dendrimer-capped mesoporous silica nanosphere-based gene transfection reagent, *J Am Chem Soc* 126:13216–13217, 2004.

Reis CP, Neufeld RJ, Vilela S, Ribeiro AJ, Veiga F: Review and current status of emulsion/dispersion technology using an internal gelation process for the design of alginate particles, *J Microencapsul* 23:245–257, 2006.

Ribeiro AJ, Neufeld RJ, Arnaud P, Chaumeil JC: Microencapsulation of lipophilic drugs in chitosan-coated alginate microspheres, *Int J Pharm* 187:115–123, 1999.

Rinaudo M: Chitin and chitosan: properties and applications, *Prog Polym Sci* 31:603–632, 2006.

Ritter H, Bruhwiler D: Accessibility of amino groups in postsynthetically modified mesoporous silica, *J Phys Chem C* 113:10667–10674, 2009.

Rodrigues S, da Costa AM, Grenha A: Chitosan/carrageenan nanoparticles: effect of cross-linking with tripolyphosphate and charge ratios, *Carbohydr Polym* 89:282–289, 2012.

Sankalia MG, Mashru RC, Sankalia JM, Sutariya VB: Reversed chitosan–alginate polyelectrolyte complex for stability improvement of alpha-amylase: optimization and physicochemical characterization, *Eur J Pharm Biopharm* 65:215–232, 2007.

Savic S, Pantelic I, Lukic M, Markovic B, Milic J: Behind the alkyl polyglucoside-based structures: lamellar liquid crystalline and lamellar gel phases in different emulsion systems. In Pantelić I, editor: *Alkyl polyglucosides: from natural-origin surfactants to prospective delivery systems*, Cambridge, 2014, Woodhead Publishing, Elsevier, pp 21–52.

Savić S, Tamburić S, Savić M: From conventional towards new—natural surfactants in drug delivery systems design: current status and perspectives, *Expert Opin Drug Deliv* 7:353–369, 2010.

Schwarz JC, Klang V, Hoppel M, Mahrhauser D, Valenta C: Natural microemulsions: formulation design and skin interaction, *Eur J Pharm Biopharm* 81:557–562, 2012a.

Schwarz JC, Weixelbaum A, Pagitsch E, Löw M, Resch GP, Valenta C: Nanocarriers for dermal drug delivery: influence of preparation method, carrier type and rheological properties, *Int J Pharm* 437:83–88, 2012b.

Sheehan C, Amidon GE: Excipients-compendial standards and excipient performance in the QbD Era: USP Excipient Performance Chapter< 1059 >, *Am Pharm Rev* 14:10, 2011.

Slowing II, Trewyn BG, Giri S, Lin VY: Mesoporous silica nanoparticles for drug delivery and biosensing applications, *Adv Funct Mater* 17:1225–1236, 2007.

Solans C, García-Celma MJ: Surfactants for microemulsions, *Curr Opin Colloid Interface Sci* 2:464–471, 1997.

Song SW, Hidajat K, Kawi S: Functionalized SBA-15 materials as carriers for controlled drug delivery: influence of surface properties on matrix–drug interactions, *Langmuir* 21:9568–9575, 2005.

Soppimath KS, Aminabhavi TM, Kulkarni AR, Rudzinski WE: Biodegradable polymeric nanoparticles as drug delivery devices, *J Control Release* 70:1–20, 2001.

Souza CP, Almeida BC, Colwell RR, Rivera IN: The importance of chitin in the marine environment, *Mar Biotechnol* 13:823–830, 2011.

Stubenrauch C: Sugar surfactants—aggregation, interfacial, and adsorption phenomena, *Curr Opin Colloid Interface Sci* 6:160–170, 2001.

Szegedi A, Popova M, Goshev I, Mihály J: Effect of amine functionalization of spherical MCM-41 and SBA-15 on controlled drug release, *J Solid State Chem* 184:1201–1207, 2011.

Szűts A, Szabó-Révész P: Sucrose esters as natural surfactants in drug delivery systems—a mini-review, *Int J Pharm* 433:1–9, 2012.

Tadros T, Izquierdo P, Esquena J, Solans C: Formation and stability of nano-emulsions, *Adv Colloid Interface Sci* 108–109:303–318, 2004.

Takegami S, Kitamura K, Kawada H, Matsumoto Y, Kitade T, Ishida H, Nagata C: Preparation and characterization of a new lipid nano-emulsion containing two cosurfactants, sodium palmitate for droplet size reduction and sucrose palmitate for stability enhancement, *Chem Pharm Bull* 56:1097–1102, 2008.

Takeuchi H, Yamamoto H, Kawashima Y: Mucoadhesive nanoparticulate systems for peptide drug delivery, *Adv Drug Deliv Rev* 47:39–54, 2001.

Tang F, Li L, Chen D: Mesoporous silica nanoparticles: synthesis, biocompatibility and drug delivery, *Adv Mater* 24:1504–1534, 2012.

The European Pharmacopoeia: The European pharmacopoeia 8th edition (Ph. Eur. 8.0), Strasbourg, 2013, Council of Europe.

The United States Pharmacopeia: The United States pharmacopeia (USP 39–NF 34). Rockville, MD, 2016, United States Pharmacopeial Convention, Inc.

Thevenin MA, Grossiord JL, Poelman MC: Sucrose esters/cosurfactant microemulsion systems for transdermal delivery: assessment of bicontinuous structures, *Int J Pharm* 137:177–186, 1996.

Todosijević MN, Cekić ND, Savić MM, Gašperlin M, Ranđelović DV, Savić SD: Sucrose ester-based biocompatible microemulsions as vehicles for aceclofenac as a model drug: formulation approach using D-optimal mixture design, *Colloid Polym Sci* 292:3061–3076, 2014.

Todosijević MN, Savić MM, Batinić BB, Marković BD, Gašperlin M, Ranđelović DV, Lukić MŽ, Savić SD: Biocompatible microemulsions of a model NSAID for skin delivery: a decisive role of surfactants in skin penetration/irritation profiles and pharmacokinetic performance, *Int J Pharm* 496:931–941, 2015.

Tønnesen HH, Karlsen J: Alginate in drug delivery systems, *Drug Dev Ind Pharm* 28:621–630, 2002.

Trotta M, Pattarino F, Ignoni T: Stability of drug-carrier emulsions containing phosphatidylcholine mixtures, *Eur J Pharm Biopharm* 53:203–208, 2002.

Ullrich S, Metz H, Mäder K: Sucrose ester nanodispersions: microviscosity and viscoelastic properties, *Eur J Pharm Biopharm* 70:550–555, 2008.

Vallet-Regí M, Balas F: Silica materials for medical applications, *Open Biomed Eng J* 2:1–9, 2008.

Vallet-Regí M, Ramila A, Del Real RP, Pérez-Pariente J: A new property of MCM-41: drug delivery system, *Chem Mater* 13:308–311, 2001.

van Hoogevest P, Wendel A: The use of natural and synthetic phospholipids as pharmaceutical excipients, *Eur J Lipid Sci Technol* 116:1088–1107, 2014.

Vinu A, Hossain KZ, Ariga K: Recent advances in functionalization of mesoporous silica, *J Nanosci Nanotechnol* 5:347–371, 2005.

Viseras C, Cerezo P, Sanchez R, Salcedo I, Aguzzi C: Current challenges in clay minerals for drug delivery, *Appl Clay Sci* 48:291–295, 2010.

Visser SA, Hergenrother RW, Cooper SI, Lamba NMK: Polymers. In Ratner BD, Hoffman AS, Schoen FJ, Lemons JE, editors: *Biomaterials science: an introduction to materials in medicine*, Oxford, 2004, Elsevier Academic Press, pp 67–79.

Voicu R, Boukherroub R, Bartzoka V, Ward T, Wojtyk JT, Wayner DD: Formation, characterization, and chemistry of undecanoic acid-terminated silicon surfaces: patterning and immobilization of DNA, *Langmuir* 20:11713–11720, 2004.

von Rybinski W, Hill K: Alkyl polyglycosides—properties and applications of a new class of surfactants, *Angew Chem Int Ed* 37:1328–1345, 1998.

Wang S: Ordered mesoporous materials for drug delivery, *Micropor Mesopor Mater* 117:1–9, 2009.

Wang YX, Robertson JL, Spillman WB Jr, Claus RO: Effects of the chemical structure and the surface properties of polymeric biomaterials on their biocompatibility, *Pharm Res* 21:1362–1373, 2004.

Washington C: Stability of lipid emulsions for drug delivery, *Adv Drug Deliv Rev* 20:131–145, 1996.

West CC, Harwell JH: Surfactants and subsurface remediation, *Environ Sci Technol* 26:2324–2330, 1992.

Widmann G: Thermogravimetric analysis. In Wagner M, editor: *Thermal analysis in practice*, Schwerzenbach, 2009, Mettler Toledo.

Xia W, Liu P, Zhang J, Chen J: Biological activities of chitosan and chitooligosaccharides, *Food Hydrocoll* 25:170–179, 2011.

Xu W, Riikonen J, Lehto VP: Mesoporous systems for poorly soluble drugs, *Int J Pharm* 453:181–197, 2013.

Yang P, Gai S, Lin J: Functionalized mesoporous silica materials for controlled drug delivery, *Chem Soc Rev* 41:3679–3698, 2012.

Yang YM, Hu W, Wang XD, Gu XS: The controlling biodegradation of chitosan fibers by N-acetylation in vitro and in vivo, *J Mater Sci* 18:2117–2121, 2007.

Yang Q, Wang S, Fan P, Wang L, Di Y, Lin K, Xiao FS: pH-responsive carrier system based on carboxylic acid modified mesoporous silica and polyelectrolyte for drug delivery, *Chem Mater* 17:5999–6003, 2005.

Yu C, Fan J, Tian B, Zhao D: Morphology development of mesoporous materials a colloidal phase separation mechanism, *Chem Mater* 16:889–898, 2004.

Yu CY, Zhang XC, Zhou FZ, Zhang XZ, Cheng SX, Zhuo RX: Sustained release of antineoplastic drugs from chitosan-reinforced alginate microparticle drug delivery systems, *Int J Pharm* 357:15–21, 2008.

Yunfei H, Yazhuo S, Honglai L, Dominique L, Anniina S: Surfactant adsorption onto interfaces: measuring the surface excess in time, *Langmuir* 28:3146–3151, 2012.

Zhang FJ, Cheng GX, Gao Z, Li CP: Preparation of porous calcium alginate membranes/microspheres via an emulsion templating method, *Macromol Mater Eng* 291:485–492, 2006.

Zhang Z, Ortiz O, Goyal R, Kohn J: Biodegradable polymers. In Modjarrad K, Ebnesajjad S, editors: *Handbook of polymer applications in medicine and medical devices*, Philadelphia, 2013a, Elsevier, pp 303–335.

Zhang H, Shahbazi MA, Mäkilä EM, da Silva TH, Reis RL, Salonen JJ, Hirvonen JT, Santos HA: Diatom silica microparticles for sustained release and permeation enhancement following oral delivery of prednisone and mesalamine, *Biomaterials* 34:9210–9219, 2013b.

Zhang C, Zhao Q, Wan L, Wang T, Sun J, Gao Y, Jiang T, Wang S: Poly dimethyl diallyl ammonium coated CMK-5 for sustained oral drug release, *Int J Pharm* 461:171–180, 2014.

Zhao D, Feng J, Huo Q, Melosh N, Fredrickson GH, Chmelka BF, Stucky GD: Triblock copolymer syntheses of mesoporous silica with periodic 50 to 300 angstrom pores, *Science* 279:548–552, 1998.

Zheng JP, Luan L, Wang HY, Xi LF, Yao KD: Study on ibuprofen/montmorillonite intercalation composites as drug release system, *Appl Clay Sci* 36:297–301, 2007.

Zheng C, Xu J, Yao X, Xu J, Qiu L: Polyphosphazene nanoparticles for cytoplasmic release of doxorubicin with improved cytotoxicity against dox-resistant tumor cells, *J Colloid Interface Sci* 355:374–382, 2011.

Zidan AS, Sammour OA, Hammad MA, Megrab NA, Hussain MD, Khan MA, Habib MJ: Formulation of anastrozole microparticles as biodegradable anticancer drug carriers, *AAPS PharmSciTech* 7:E38–E46, 2006.

Chapter 5

Influence of Polycation Functional Properties on Polyanion Micro/Nanoparticles for NSAIDs Reinforced Via Polyelectrolyte Complexation: Alginate–Chitosan Case Study

Bojan Čalija*, Nebojša Cekić**, Jela Milić*

*Department of Pharmaceutical Technology and Cosmetology, Faculty of Pharmacy, University of Belgrade, Belgrade, Serbia; **Faculty of Technology, University of Niš; R&D Sector, DCP Hemigal, Leskovac, Serbia

5.1 INTRODUCTION

Nonsteroidal anti-inflammatory drugs (NSAIDs) are among the oldest and the most frequently used drugs (Naesdal and Brown, 2006; Vonkeman and van de Laar, 2010). Owing to their anti-inflammatory, analgesic, and antipyretic effects these drugs are used in treatment of rheumatoid arthritis, osteoarthritis, ankylosing spondylitis, psoriatic arthritis systemic lupus, posttraumatic pain, headache, and toothache (Suleyman et al., 2007). However, their use is associated with several upper gastrointestinal (GI) side effects, varying from mild dyspepsia to severe GI ulceration and bleeding (Naesdal and Brown, 2006; Vonkeman and van de Laar, 2010). The main mechanism of GI mucosal damage is related to the inhibition of synthesis of prostaglandins, endogenous molecules that play a vital role in protection of GI mucosa from harmful effects of aggressive substances and surrounding conditions (Wallace, 2008). The other mechanism is based on local irritation of GI mucosa (Bjorkman, 1996; Maghsoodi, 2009; Soll et al., 1989). For that reason, certain NSAIDs are more harmful after oral than parenteral administration (Beck et al., 1990; Cioli et al., 1979).

Microsized and Nanosized Carriers for NSAIDs. http://dx.doi.org/10.1016/B978-0-12-804017-1.00005-4

Severity of the upper GI side effects of orally administered NSAIDs can be reduced by the use of gastroresistant drug-delivery formulations. These formulations are usually protected with gastroresistant coatings to avoid direct contact between the drug and mucosa in the upper parts of GI tract. Once they reach the lower parts of GI tract, their coating dissolves releasing the drug. These formulations are commonly available as conventional monolithic dosage forms, such as tablets or capsules. Multiparticulate drug carriers such as micro- and nanoparticles have several advantages in comparison to these monolithic dosage forms. First, after they reach lower parts of GI tract, these carriers can spread over a larger area, minimizing the local irritant effect of the drug. Second, their GI transit time is less variable, since they can pass through the constricted pyloric sphincter (Eskilson, 1985; Iruin et al., 2005; Krämer and Blume, 1994; Maghsoodi, 2009). Besides, it was shown that size reduction of drug carriers might improve their accumulation in the inflamed regions of colon, which is of great importance in treatment of some localized disorders such as inflammatory bowel disease (Lamprecht et al., 2001a,b). Due to their small size, nanoparticles and smaller microparticles can be administered by injection directly to the inflamed region. Such administration improves efficacy and safety of NSAIDs in treatment of localized disorders. Finally, in most cases these carriers release encapsulated NSAIDs in sustained manner, which allows reduction of dosing frequency and improves patient convenience and compliance.

During the last two decades Ca-alginate micro- and nanoparticles have been developed and studied as prospective carriers for cells, genes, and structurally different drugs, including NSAIDs (Arica et al., 2005; Fathy, 2006; Hansen et al., 2002; Hwang et al., 1995; Kakkar, 1995; Varma and Rao, 2013; You and Peng, 2005). Despite their biocompatibility, rapid and simple preparation procedure, these carriers exhibit porosity and sensitivity on some cations and anions normally present in physiological fluids (Martinsen et al., 1989; Tønnesen and Karlsen, 2002; Trabelsi et al., 2014). These drawbacks can be overcome by reinforcement of the particles hydrogel network via polycations, such as chitosans (Calija et al., 2013b; Yu et al., 2008). This reinforcement is based on electrostatic interactions between deprotonated carboxylic groups of alginate and protonated amino groups of chitosans and subsequent formation of alginate–chitosan polyelectrolyte complex (PEC) (Sun et al., 1996; Takahashi et al., 1990). This PEC is biodegradable and its physicochemical properties differ considerably from those of the consisting polymers (Hamman, 2010). Numerous studies have shown that alginate–chitosan PEC significantly improves stability of Ca-alginate particulate carriers including their ability to sustain the release of encapsulated NSAIDs (Fernandez-Hervas et al., 1998; González-Rodrıguez et al., 2002; Iruin et al., 2005; Mladenovska et al., 2007b; Shah and Patel, 2015). The expected therapeutic benefits from encapsulation of NSAIDs into alginate–chitosan micro- and nanoparticles are: (1) reduction of side effects by preventing direct contact between the drug and the upper GI mucosa upon oral administration; (2) reduction of dosing frequency, especially for NSAIDs

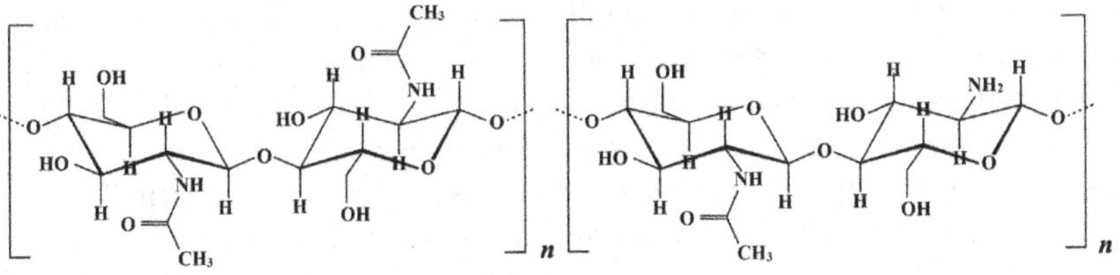

FIGURE 5.1   Chemical structure of chitin and chitosan (deacetylation degree = 0.5).

with short biological half-life, and (3) improved selectivity for target tissues, such as inflamed colonic mucosa (Calija et al., 2011; Fattahpour et al., 2015; González-Rodríguez et al., 2002; Iruin et al., 2005; Mladenovska et al., 2007b; Shah and Patel, 2015).

Characteristics of alginate-chitosan micro- and nanoparticles depend on the characteristics of the consisting polymers and the preparation conditions. Alginate and chitosan are versatile biopolymers, so their structure and physicochemical properties have to be carefully considered prior to encapsulation procedure (Calija et al., 2015a).

This chapter summarizes characteristics and basic principles of alginate–chitosan PEC formation along with the potential benefits of its use for delivery of NSAIDs in the form of micro- and nanoparticles. The special attention is paid to the influence of functionality-related characteristics of chitosan, such as molecular weight and viscosity, on feasibility of these particulate carriers for oral delivery of NSAIDs. Additionally, chitosan structure, safety, and overall characteristics are discussed in detail for better understanding.

5.2 CHITOSANS: AN OVERVIEW ON PROPERTIES, FUNCTIONALITY, AND SAFETY

5.2.1 Source and Structural Characteristics of Chitosans

Chitosan is a linear binary copolymer of (1R4)-2-amino-2-deoxy-β-D-glucan (D-glucosamine) and (1R4)-2-acetamido-2-deoxy- β-D-glucan (N-acetyl D-glucosamine) units linked by β(1→4)-glycosidic bonds (Fig. 5.1) (Dash et al., 2011; Thein-Han et al., 2009). Its history dates back to 1859, when French scientist Rouget derived a new substance from chitin by treating it with hot and concentrated potassium hydroxide and named it "modified chitin." The term chitosan was introduced for the first time in 1894 by F. Hoppe Seyler (Yeul and Rayalu, 2013). Nowadays, this term is commonly used to describe deacetylated form of chitin having D-glucosamine/N-acetyl D-glucosamine molar ratio > 0.5 (Rinaudo, 2006).

As the main component of the exoskeleton of crustaceans and arthropods, and the cell walls of certain fungi, chitin is the second most bountiful natural polysaccharide (Joseph et al., 2010; Suginta et al., 2013; Yeul and Rayalu, 2013).

On the other hand, chitosan is naturally occurring only in some fungi (*Mucoraceae*) (Aranaz et al., 2009). The role of chitin is similar to that of cellulose in plants and collagen in higher animals (Pillai et al., 2009). Chemically, chitin is a linear homopolymer comprised of $\beta(1 \rightarrow 4)$-linked N-acetyl D-glucosamine units (Fig. 5.1) (Hajji et al., 2014; Kamburov and Lalov, 2012). During the extraction of chitin deacetylation can occur, so this polymer may contain between 5 and 15% of free amino groups. Chitin can be further converted to chitosan by chemical or enzymatic deacetylation (Younes and Rinaudo, 2015). Chemical deacetylation can be performed by using either acids or alkalis. Still, in order to avoid breaking of glycosidic bonds between the N-acetyl D-glucosamine units and subsequent degradation of polymeric chains under acidic conditions, alkaline deacetylation is more frequently used (Rege and Block, 1999; Younes and Rinaudo, 2015). In general, chemical deacetylation is inexpensive procedure suitable for large-scale production. On the other hand, enzymatic deacetylation is considered as safe and allows better control of deacetylation degree and pattern, leading to the formation of chitosans with well-defined properties (Tsigos et al., 2000; Xia et al., 2011; Zhao et al., 2010).

The most important structural characteristics of chitosans affecting their performance are molecular weight, deacetylation degree, and distribution of free amino groups along the polymer chain. These properties depend on the mechanism and conditions of deacetylation procedure (Aranaz et al., 2009).

Molecular weight of chitosans usually ranges from 10 to 1000 kDa (Pillai et al., 2009). Depending on their molecular weight, chitosans can be classified into high (>700 kDa), medium, and low molecular weight chitosans (<150 kDa) (Wong, 2009). In recent years, there is growing interest in chitosans having molecular weight below 10 kDa. These oligomers are commonly known as oligochitosans or chitooligosaccharides (Kim and Rajapakse, 2005; Xia et al., 2011).

The deacetylation degree of chitosans represents the D-glucosamine/N-acetyl D-glucosamine molar ratio. Therefore, it is directly related to the number of free amino groups in chitosans' structure and is one of the most important structural characteristics that depend on the mechanism and conditions of deacetylation procedure. It usually varies in range between 0.5 and 0.95 (Pillai et al., 2009).

5.2.2 Physicochemical Properties and Reactivity of Chitosans

In the solid state chitosans are a semicrystalline polymers (Rinaudo, 2006). Their crystallinity depends on the origin and conditions of chitin extraction and deacetylation (Aranaz et al., 2009).

In contrast to chitins, chitosans are soluble in aqueous acidic media due to protonation of free amino groups on the C-2 position of the D-glucosamine units and subsequent formation of water-soluble polycationic form (Aranaz et al., 2009; Rinaudo, 2006; Singla and Chawla, 2001; Wong, 2009). As weak bases with pK_a values between 6.0 and 7.0, chitosans exhibit low solubility at pH values above 6.0 (Hejazi and Amiji, 2003; Pillai et al., 2009; Wong, 2009). Besides pH, ionic strength, the nature of the acid used for protonation, and the nonaqueous solvents also affect chitosans aqueous solubility (Aranaz et al., 2009; Rinaudo, 2006). Increase in ionic strength decreases their solubility as a consequence of reduction of repulsive forces between protonated amino groups. This leads to the transformation of extended conformation to the less soluble coil-like formation and eventually causes salting out and precipitation of chitosans (Errington et al., 1993; Singla and Chawla, 2001). Structural characteristics, particularly deacetylation degree and molecular weight have also significant influence on chitosans' aqueous solubility. The influence of deacetylation degree is directly related to the number of free amino groups available for the protonation. That is, as deacetylation degree increases, solubility in acidic media increases and vice versa. Therefore, chitosans having deacetylation degree 0.5 are soluble in pH-neutral solutions, while those having deacetylation degree 0.4 are soluble in aqueous solutions with pH up to 9.0 (Hejazi and Amiji, 2003; Singla and Chawla, 2001). Chitosans of lower molecular weight exhibit better solubility (Agnihotri et al., 2004). This is one of the most important advances of the chitooligomers in comparison to their high molecular weight precursors (Jeon and Kim, 2000). Another molecular characteristic of importance is distribution of N-acetyl groups along the linear backbone of the polymer due to its influence on the interchain interactions via hydrogen bonds and the hydrophobic character of this functional group (Kubota et al., 2000; Rinaudo, 2006).

Another characteristic of importance for biomedical use of chitosans is rheological behavior of their aqueous solutions. These solutions exhibit pseudoplastic behavior since their viscosity decreases by increasing shear rate (Singla and Chawla, 2001). Their viscosity largely depends on the concentration, molecular weight, and deacetylation degree of chitosan (Singla and Chawla, 2001; Wong, 2009). Chitosans of higher molecular weight, even at low concentrations, form viscous solutions and therefore can be used as viscosity enhancing agents (Singla and Chawla, 2001). On the other hand, aqueous solutions of oligochitosans are less viscous, event at high concentrations (Kim and Rajapakse, 2005). Deacetylation degree is directly proportional to the viscosity of chitosan solutions owing to its influence on the persistent length and conformation of chitosan molecules (Hejazi and Amiji, 2003; Rinaudo, 2006). That is, highly deacetylated molecules are more extended due to the more intensive repulsion between positively charged amino groups (Hejazi and Amiji, 2003). Rheological behavior of aqueous chitosan solutions also depends on the environmental conditions, such as pH and temperature. Both of these factors are inversely proportional to the viscosity of chitosan solutions (Hejazi and Amiji, 2003; Wong, 2009; Yeul and Rayalu, 2013).

Chitosans possess the four types of reactive functional groups: primary amino/acetamido at the C-2 position, primary and secondary hydroxyl groups at the C-6 and C-3 positions, respectively (Pillai et al., 2009; Xia et al., 2011). The chemical derivatization can be undertaken to improve physicochemical and biological properties of chitosans in terms of their potential use (Alves and Mano, 2008).

The most important chemical modifications involving amino groups are N-alkylation with alkyl halides, N-acylation with acid chlorides, and reductive alkylation with aldehydes or ketones to an N-alkylated derivative (Yeul and Rayalu, 2013). The hydroxyl groups are responsible for the etherification and esterification of chitosans (Pillai et al., 2009; Rinaudo, 2006; Yeul and Rayalu, 2013).

Owing to the presence of free amino groups chitosans also possess complexation ability. They can form complexes with divalent and trivalent cations and this interaction is dependent on chitosans' physical state, number and distribution of free amino groups, degree of polymerization, pH of the surrounding environment, and cation type (Rinaudo, 2006; Wong, 2009).

Being polycations, chitosans can interact with polyanions under suitable conditions forming complex structures which are known as PECs (Calija et al., 2015a; Hamman, 2010; Rinaudo, 2006; Wong, 2009). Complexation of polyelectrolytes is based on the electrostatic interaction between oppositely charged polyions and depends on numerous factors including polyelectrolyte structural properties and concentration, polycation/polyanion molar ratio, charge density, pH, ionic strength, order of mixing, and temperature of the starting solutions (Calija et al., 2015a). Polyelectrolyte complexation can be achieved under mild reaction conditions, without use of organic solvents, extreme temperatures, and pH values (Calija et al., 2013b, 2015b; Hamman, 2010). Furthermore, this reaction leads to the formation of reversible complexes that can be easily degraded in vivo, in contrast to the covalently modified chitosans, which is very important from the regulatory standpoint (Calija et al., 2015a; Hamman, 2010). A number of polyanions can form PECs with chitosans, including those of natural (alginate, pectin, xanthan gum, carboxymethyl cellulose, carrageenan, collagen, gelatin, albumin, and fibroin) and synthetic origin (polymethacrylate copolymers and polymers of acrylic acid crosslinked with alkenyl esters of sugars or polyalcohols) (Araujo et al., 2014; Bellini et al., 2012; Bhardwaj and Kundu, 2011; Bhattarai et al., 2010; Birch and Schiffman, 2014; Calija et al., 2015b; Deng et al., 2010; Dhar et al., 2012; Jana et al., 2014; Moustafine et al., 2008).

5.2.3 Safety and Regulatory Status of Chitosans

Numerous studies confirmed that chitosans are low-toxic, biocompatible, and biodegradable polymers. However, biodegradation and biodistribution of these polymers depend on their structural characteristics such as molecular weight/polymerization degree, deacetylation degree, and distribution of amino/acetamido groups along the polymer backbone (Aranaz et al., 2009; Wong, 2009). As for other polymers, renal clearance of chitosans depends on the molecular weight and suitable molecular weight for renal clearance ranges between 30 and 40 kDa. Therefore, larger chitosans have to be degraded first

(Dash et al., 2011). Several enzymes normally presented in different body fluids and tissues are involved in biodegradation of chitosans in mammals, including lysozyme, di-N-acetylchitobiase, N-acetyl-beta-D-glucosaminidase, and chitiotriosidase (Garcia-Fuentes and Alonso, 2012; Kean and Thanou, 2010; Ren et al., 2005). High deacetylation degree and homogenous distribution of acetyl groups also make enzymatic degradation of chitosans more difficult (Aiba, 1992; Aranaz et al., 2009; Yang et al., 2007).

Toxicity and biodegradation of chitosans depend on the administration pathways (Garcia-Fuentes and Alonso, 2012). For instance, the first signs of cytotoxicity in rabbits and dogs were observed upon subcutaneous administration of doses between 5 and 50 mg/kg per day (Carreno-Gomez and Duncan, 1997; Minami et al., 1996). On the other hand, daily doses between 4.5 and 6.75 g did not show any adverse effects when given orally to human volunteers (Gades and Stern, 2003; Tapola et al., 2008).

Chitosans are nowadays commonly used as dietary supplements for weight loss in many countries (Aranaz et al., 2009; Dash et al., 2011; Garcia-Fuentes and Alonso, 2012). Their salt, chitosan hydrochloride, has compendial status in the European Pharmacopoeia since 2002 (Ph. Eur. 4.0). Due to their hemostatic, antimicrobial, and mild analgesic properties chitosans are also used in wound dressings (Baldrick, 2010; Boateng et al., 2008). Some of these medicinal products have been approved by FDA (Calija et al., 2015a; Wedmore et al., 2006).

Despite the fact that chitosans have been widely investigated as pharmaceutical excipients in the last few decades, there are no approved drugs containing chitosan as an excipient (Baldrick, 2010). This could be explained by their structural diversity, meaning that chitosans may exhibit different distribution and degradation in vivo depending on their structural characteristics. Therefore, every study should include a detailed description of the chitosan used, including information regarding its toxicological profile, biodegradation, and biodistribution (Kean and Thanou, 2010).

5.3 ALGINATE–CHITOSAN MICRO/NANOPARTICLES AS DRUG CARRIERS

5.3.1 Ca-Alginate Hydrogels as Drug Carriers: Characteristics and Disadvantages

Alginates have been used for encapsulation of various materials, including cells and pharmaceutical actives since the early 1980s (Lim and Sun, 1980). Alginates are linear polysaccharides produced by brown algae and some bacteria, comprised of β-D-mannuronic acid and its C-5 epimer α-L-guluronic acid units linked by β(1→4)-glycosidic bonds (Pawar and Edgar, 2012) (Fig. 5.2). These monomers are distributed in blocks of repeating mannuronic acid residues (M-blocks), guluronic acid residues (G-blocks), and blocks of the alternating mannuronic and guluronic acid residues (MG-blocks) (Pawar and Edgar, 2012;

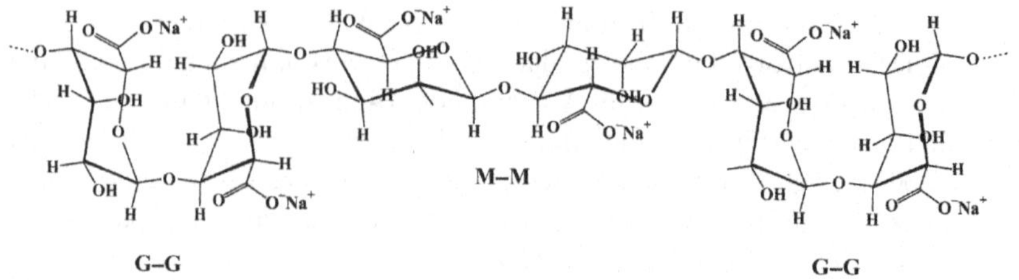

FIGURE 5.2 **Chemical structure of sodium alginate.**

Yang et al., 2011). Biocompatibility, biodegradability, excellent gelling proper-ties, natural origin, and low cost make them excellent candidates for encapsula-tion of different actives (Sosnik, 2014).

Gelation of alginates from their aqueous solutions can be induced by di-valent cations (except Mg^{2+}). This reaction, known as ionotropic gelation, is based on specific and strong interactions between G-blocks and divalent cations which associate to form tight junctions, whereas MG blocks also contribute to this process by forming weak junctions (Donati et al., 2005). As can be seen in Fig. 5.3, divalent ions are surrounded by the pair of G-blocks like eggs in card-board box and therefore this structure is usually referred as the "egg box struc-ture" (Grant et al., 1973). Given that G-blocks are of the great importance for the gel formation, strength of the resulting gel is proportional to the G/M ratio and length of the G-blocks (Draget et al., 1997). Hence, gels obtained from high G alginates are stronger, stiffer, more brittle but more porous in comparison to gels obtained from low G alginates (Paques et al., 2014).

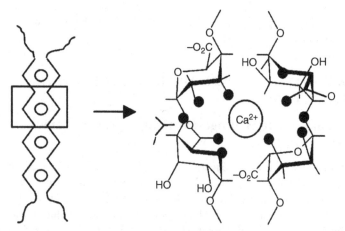

FIGURE 5.3 **Schematic drawing of the egg-box model.** *(Reprinted with permission from Braccini I, Pérez S: Molecular basis of Ca^{2+}-induced gelation in alginates and pectins: the egg-box model revisited,* Biomacromolecules *2:1089–1096, 2001, Copyright (2001) American Chemical Society)*

Due to their biocompatibility and ability to interact rapidly with alginates, Ca^{2+} ions are the most frequently used cations for alginates gelation. Depending on the experimental conditions these hydrogels can be produced in form of microparticles, nanoparticles, films, "block" gels, and fibers (Cuadros et al., 2012; Gombotz and Wee, 2012; Russo et al., 2007; You and Peng, 2005; You et al., 2000). However, their structure could be disrupted in the presence of Na^+, Mg^{2+} ions, and calcium chelators, such as lactate, citrate, and phosphate (Martinsen et al., 1989; Tønnesen and Karlsen, 2002; Trabelsi et al., 2014). These ions are present in physiological fluids and once they get in contact with Ca-alginate drug carriers, they can trigger unwanted and rapid release of encapsulated drug. Another important drawback that limits the use of Ca-alginate hydrogels as drug carries is their porosity, which depends on the structural characteristics of the alginate, but also on the preparation procedure (Fundueanu et al., 1999).

5.3.2   Chitosans as Cationic Modifiers of Ca-Alginate Micro/Nanoparticles

As it has already been pointed out, porosity and sensitivity on sequestering ions may limit the use of Ca-alginate micro/nanoparticles as drug carriers. These limitations can be overcome by using polycations, such as chitosans and poly-L-lysine (Calija et al., 2013b; De and Robinson, 2003; Sun et al., 1996; Yu et al., 2008). Under suitable conditions these polycations can interact ionically with alginate forming PECs. Owing to their biocompatibility and ability to form strong and stable PECs under mild conditions, chitosans are frequently used for reinforcement of Ca-alginate micro/nanoparticles. Basically, formation of alginate–chitosan PEC is based on electrostatic attraction of deprotonated carboxylic groups of alginate with protonated amino groups of chitosan (Takahashi et al., 1990). Schematic representation of this process is presented in Fig. 5.4.

A number of formulation and process factors affect characteristics and stability of alginate–chitosan PECs. The most important are molecular weight, chemical composition, concentration, and molar ratio of the polymers, order of mixing of the polymers solutions, reaction time, pH, and ionic strength of the reaction medium (Baruch and Machluf, 2006; Li et al., 2009; Sankalia et al., 2007; Sæther et al., 2008).

One of the key features of the alginate–chitosan PECs is pH-sensitivity. Alginate and chitosan are the weak acid and weak base, respectively, whose ionization degrees depend on the pH value of the surrounding medium (Sankalia et al., 2007). Under extremely acidic or alkaline conditions, only one of these polymers is completely ionized, while the other is practically in nonionized form. Hence, the electrostatic interaction between alginate and chitosan is weak at low or high pH values, and strong in pH range between the pK_a values of these two polymers, which is roughly between 3.0 and 7.0 (Simsek-Ege et al., 2003). For that reason, pH value of the surrounding medium is one of the

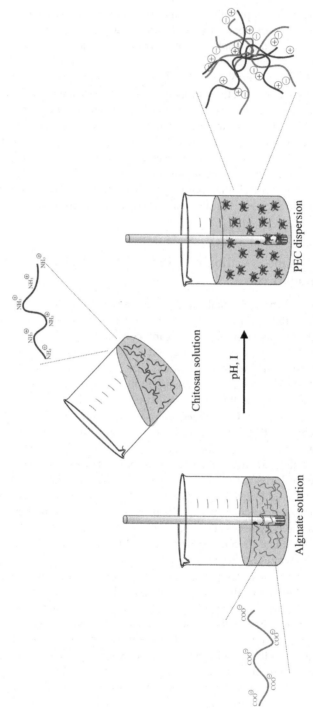

FIGURE 5.4 Schematic representation of alginate–chitosan PEC formation.

key factors for the formation and stability of this PEC and therefore affects drug release from the carriers reinforced with this PEC. Several studies conducted by different research groups have shown that pH-sensitivity of alginate–chitosan microparticles could be used to avoid direct contact between gastric mucosa and NSAIDs, such as diclofenac salts and naproxen, and deliver them to the lower parts of GI tract (Fernandez-Hervas et al., 1998; González-Rodríguez et al., 2002; Calija et al., 2011).

5.3.3   Preparation Methods of Alginate–Chitosan Micro/Nanoparticles

Selection of micro/nanoencapsulation procedure generally depends on the nature of drug, encapsulating polymers, and desired properties of the particles, including their size and size distribution, morphology, stability, drug loading, release kinetics, and residual toxicity (Agnihotri et al., 2004). Besides, it is of great importance to achieve the highest possible encapsulation efficiency, meaning that loss of drug during encapsulation procedure has to be minimized by careful choice of experimental conditions. The most important characteristics of the drug and the encapsulating polymers that have to be considered are solubility, mutual compatibility, and stability under proposed experimental conditions. Therefore, it is important to verify that proposed encapsulation procedure does not affect pharmacological activity of encapsulated active.

One of the most significant advantages of alginate–chitosan particulate carriers is the possibility of their preparation under mild pH values, at room temperature, and without use of organic solvents. This makes them suitable for encapsulation of various actives, including those sensitive to the environmental conditions, such as peptides, genes, and cells (Douglas and Tabrizian, 2005; Haque et al., 2005; Sarmento et al., 2007). Another important advantage is rapid reaction of polyelectrolyte complexation between alginate and chitosan, which starts immediately when the two polymers get in contact (Jeong et al., 2010). This makes encapsulation procedure rapid and reduces the loss of the drug during encapsulation procedure.

The term alginate–chitosan particles is usually used to describe hydrogel particles consisting of alginate crosslinked with Ca^{2+} ions and reinforced with chitosan via polyelectrolyte complexation. Basically, two approaches are used for production of these particles: a one-stage and a two-stage procedure (Fig. 5.5) (Gåserød et al., 1999). In the first one, the crosslinking of alginate with Ca^{2+} ions occurs simultaneously with the polyelectrolyte complexation with chitosan. This can be achieved by dropwise addition of alginate solution into reaction medium containing Ca^{2+} ions and chitosan. In the second procedure, crosslinking of alginate with Ca^{2+} ions is followed by polyelectrolyte complexation with chitosan. More precisely, alginate solution is first added in aqueous solution of Ca^{2+} ions to obtain Ca-alginate particles. Thereafter, the particles are transferred to the chitosan solution where polyelectrolyte

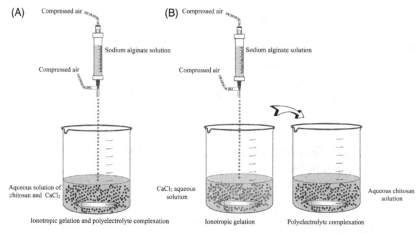

FIGURE 5.5   Schematic representation of (A) one-stage and (B) two-stage procedure for production of alginate–chitosan particles.

complexation takes place. In the aforementioned procedures, Ca^{2+} ions diffuse from the external solution into droplets of alginate solution and this method is known as "diffusion method" or "external gelation" (Paques et al., 2014; Pawar and Edgar, 2012).

Both the procedures are usually based on the extrusion of drug-containing alginate solution through a needle in the reaction medium under constant stirring to prevent coalescence of the droplets. Given that alginate solutions are generally viscous, the droplets detached from the tip of the needle under the influence of the gravity force would be quite large, with a diameter larger than 500 μm (Paques et al., 2014). In order to obtain smaller particles, external gelation method has to be combined with some other techniques, such as coaxial air-flow extrusion, electrostatic extrusion, vibration extrusion, and spray-drying technique (Belščak-Cvitanović et al., 2011; Cekić et al., 2007; Crcarevska et al., 2008; De Prisco et al., 2015).

In the coaxial air-flow technique small droplets of alginate solution are created by directing pressurized air at the needle tip in an outer concentric cylinder (Fig. 5.6A) (Prüsse et al., 2008). Diameter of the droplets is determined by viscosity and flow rate of the alginate solution, needle diameter and the flow rate of the pressurized air (Paques et al., 2014). Electrostatic extrusion is based on application of electric field to detach droplets from the needle tip (Fig. 5.6B) (Bugarski et al., 1994). Viscosity and flow rate of the alginate solution, needle diameter and applied voltage affect the size of generated droplets (Bugarski et al., 1994). In the vibrating extrusion micrometric droplets are formed by vibrations applied on a laminar flowing liquid jet (Fig. 5.6C) (Heinzen et al., 2002). Diameter of the droplets depends on the viscosity and flow rate of the alginate solution, needle diameter, and frequency of applied vibrations (Heinzen et al., 2002).

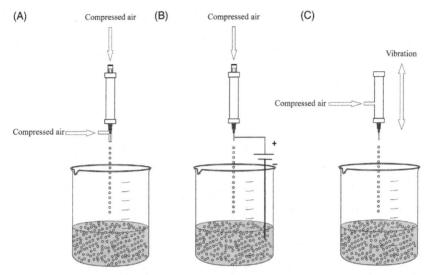

FIGURE 5.6   The most common extrusion techniques for production of alginate–chitosan microparticles. (A) Coaxial-air flow extrusion, (B) electrostatic extrusion, and (C) vibration extrusion.

Spray drying is rapid and reproducible technique suitable for scale-up to mass production of microparticles in pharmaceutical industry (Estevinho et al., 2013). In this method drug-containing alginate solution is infused into a spray dryer nozzle and sprayed in a drying chamber filled with hot gas (usually air) (Fig. 5.7). At high temperatures, water from droplets evaporates instantaneously leaving behind fine, micrometric drug-containing alginate particles. The particles can be directly sprayed into reaction medium containing chitosan (with or without Ca^{2+} ions) placed in the apparatus collector or collected first and then transferred into reaction medium (Coppi et al., 2001; Mladenovska et al., 2007a). The main parameters affecting properties of the particles are viscosity and flow rate of alginate solution, gas flow rate, and air inlet and outlet temperatures (Estevinho et al., 2013).

Crosslinking of alginate with Ca^{2+} ions can be also achieved by the addition of insoluble calcium salt, such as calcium carbonate, in the alginate solution (Fig. 5.8A). Thereafter, obtained dispersion is emulsified in oil phase to form a w/o emulsion (Fig. 5.8B). Once the emulsion is formed, Ca^{2+} ions can be released from the insoluble salt by addition of an oil-soluble acid (Fig. 5.8C). Released Ca^{2+} ions react immediately with alginate chains creating Ca-alginate particles from emulsion droplets. The composition of the emulsion and the power consumed for emulsification regulate the size the particles (Paques et al., 2014). This method is referred as "emulsification method" or "internal gelation" (Paques et al., 2014; Pawar and Edgar, 2012; Silva et al., 2005). Ca-alginate micro/nanoparticles obtained by internal gelation are less dense, more porous, and less capable of sustaining the release of encapsulated drug in

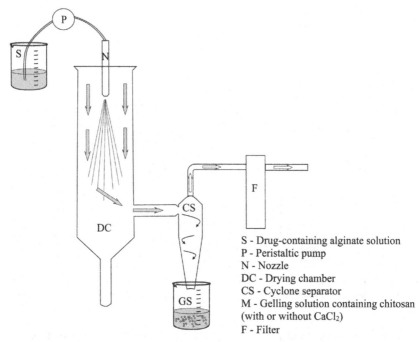

S - Drug-containing alginate solution
P - Peristaltic pump
N - Nozzle
DC - Drying chamber
CS - Cyclone separator
M - Gelling solution containing chitosan
(with or without CaCl₂)
F - Filter

FIGURE 5.7   **Schematic representation of spray-drying technique for alginate–chitosan microparticles production.**

comparison to the particles obtained by external gelation (Chan et al., 2006). Reinforcement with chitosan can be performed by using two different approaches (Ribeiro et al., 2005). In the first, o/w emulsion of chitosan is added to the oily dispersed Ca-alginate particles after calcium solubilization (Fig. 5.8D-E). In the second, Ca-alginate particles are removed from the emulsion, transferred into aqueous chitosan solution and stirred for a while to allow polyelectrolyte complexation.

The most widely used procedure for preparation of alginate/chitosan nanoparticles is a two-stage procedure based on the method for production of alginate–poly-L-lysine nanoparticles developed by Rajaonarivony et al. (1993) (Li et al., 2008; Sarmento et al., 2007). Basically, this procedure is similar to the aforementioned two-stage procedure used for preparation of alginate–chitosan microparticles. In the first stage calcium chloride solution is added in sodium alginate solution under constant stirring. Thereafter, solution of polycation is added to obtain alginate nanoparticles reinforced with polycation (poly-L-lysine or chitosan) via polyelectrolyte complexation. The key difference lies in concentrations of sodium alginate and calcium chloride which are lower than of those that lead to the gel formation (Rajaonarivony et al., 1993). At low concentrations, alginate and crosslinking agent form Ca-alginate nanoparticles with a diameter between 250 and 850 nm (depending on the alginate concentration)

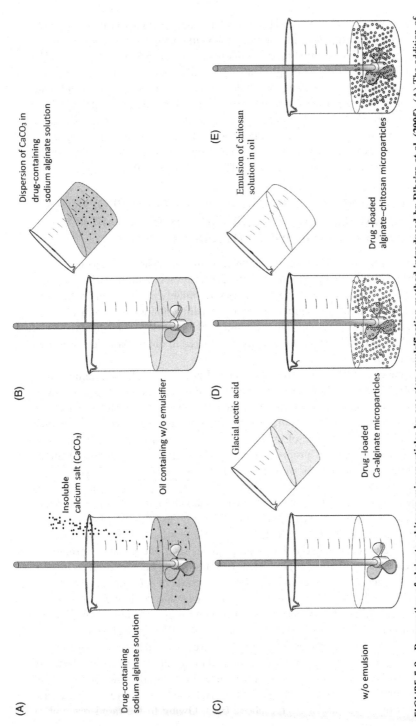

FIGURE 5.8 **Preparation of alginate–chitosan microparticles by one-step emulsification method introduced by Ribeiro et al. (2005).** (A) The addition of insoluble calcium salt in the alginate solution. (B) The resulting dispersion is emulsified in oil phase to form a w/o emulsion. (C) Ca^{2+} ions are released from the insoluble salt by addition of an oil-soluble acid to react with alginate chains creating Ca-alginate particles from emulsion droplets. (D) o/w emulsion of chitosan is added to the oily dispersed Ca-alginate particles to start interaction between alginate and chitosan. (E) The resulting alginate–chitosan microparticles.

Labels within figure:

(A) Insoluble calcium salt ($CaCO_3$)
Drug-containing sodium alginate solution
Oil containing w/o emulsifier

(B) Dispersion of $CaCO_3$ in drug-containing sodium alginate solution

(C) w/o emulsion

(D) Glacial acetic acid
Drug-loaded Ca-alginate microparticles

(E) Emulsion of chitosan solution in oil
Drug-loaded alginate–chitosan microparticles

(Rajaonarivony et al., 1993). The size of the nanoparticles is predominantly controlled by the alginate/chitosan ratio, molecular weight of the both polymers, and the pH value of reaction medium (Douglas and Tabrizian, 2005). Instead of Ca^{2+} ions, sodium tripolyphosphate (TPP) could be used as crosslinking agent to obtain alginate–chitosan nanoparticles. TPP ions can interact ionically with chitosans and nanoparticles can be formed by rapid mixing of the alginate–TPP solution with chitosan solution (Goycoolea et al., 2009). Moreover, alginate–chitosan nanoparticles can be produced without the use of crosslinking agent, by a simple dropwise addition of the one polymer solution to the other under suitable conditions (Nagarwal et al., 2012; Sæther et al., 2008).

5.4 INFLUENCE OF CHITOSANS FUNCTIONAL PROPERTIES ON CHARACTERISTICS OF ALGINATE–CHITOSAN MICRO/NANOPARTICLES LOADED WITH NSAIDs

Characteristics of alginate–chitosan micro- and nanoparticles depend on the properties of included polymers and the preparation conditions. The most important properties of consisting polymers refer mainly to structural characteristics, such as chain length, molar ratio of consisting monomers, and distribution of functional groups along the polymers backbone. Hence, characteristics of the both polymers have to be carefully considered to obtain particles of desired characteristics.

In practice, a number of formulation and process variables simultaneously control properties of these carriers. Therefore, it is very difficult to assess the influence of individual characteristics of the polymers on the particles properties. This is aggravated by the fact that these variables may interact with one another, meaning that the influence of one variable may depend on the other variables. Several research groups proposed the use of experimental design to evaluate the influence of different formulation and process variables on NSAID-loaded alginate–chitosan micro- and nanoparticles and/or to optimize their properties (Calija et al., 2011; Fattahpour et al., 2015; Shah and Patel, 2015). Experimental design is a powerful statistical tool that can be used to calculate factor effects of different variables, which demonstrate to what extent these variables affect certain dependent variable (e.g., particles size, encapsulation efficiency, drug release rate) (Djuris et al., 2013). Besides, it can be employed to investigate combined effect of several variables on certain dependent variable. Calija et al. (2011) used a 2^4 full factorial design to evaluate the influence of several process and formulation variables, including chitosan molecular weight, on encapsulation efficiency and release profiles of NSAID naproxen from the alginate–chitosan microparticles. The particles were prepared by a two-stage procedure using the coaxial air-flow extrusion technique similar to that presented in Fig. 5.5B. The two types of chitosan were used in this study: low (50–190 kDa) and high molecular weight (310–375 kDa). Both chitosans were highly deacetylated with deacetylation degree above 0.75. Owing to the rapid reaction of encapsulation and low solubility of naproxen in reaction media, encapsulation efficiencies were relatively high, ranging from $75.19 \pm 2.11\%$ to $84.45 \pm 2.16\%$, depending on the formulation. Statistical analysis showed no influence of chitosan molecular weight on encapsulation efficiencies. On the other hand, this functional characteristic of chitosan had the most pronounced effect on the release rates of encapsulated naproxen and the corresponding factor effect had positive value, suggesting that PECs consisting of high molecular weight chitosans are able to sustain naproxen release from the particles more efficiently. Similar results were found for alginate–chitosan microparticles obtained by a modified emulsification procedure (Ribeiro et al., 1999). This could be ascribed to the formation of thicker and less permeable PEC (Polk et al., 1994).

However, the use of high molecular weight chitosans, especially at high concentrations, make encapsulation procedure quite difficult, and in some cases even impossible. Namely, these chitosans are less soluble in water and preparation of concentrated solutions could be quite challenging even at low pH. Furthermore, if the one-stage procedure is used, highly viscous gelling medium consisting of high molecular weight chitosans may cause shape deformation or coalescence of alginate droplets leading to the formation of irregular shaped particles or PEC surface hydrogel layer instead of the particles, respectively (González-Rodríguez et al., 2002; Calija, 2013). The results of several studies imply that high viscosity of chitosan solutions can hinder formation of alginate–chitosan PEC (Cekić et al., 2009; Fernandez-Hervas et al., 1998; Polk et al., 1994; Yu et al., 2008). This effect is related to the molecular weight of chitosan and its concentration in gelling medium. Calija et al. (2011) have studied the influence of chitosan molecular weight and its concentration in hardening medium on the release of naproxen from the particles. It was shown that effect of chitosan concentration on the drug release depends on the molecular weight. More precisely, increase in chitosan concentration led to a more significant increase in drug release rate when high molecular weight chitosan was used and vice versa. Having in mind that high molecular weight chitosans in the same concentration form more viscous solution in comparison to the low molecular weight chitosans, these results support the assertion that the viscosity of the chitosan solution affects the formation of alginate–chitosan PEC (Calija et al., 2011).

These drawbacks could be overcome by using oligochitosans instead of their high molecular weight precursors (Bartkowiak and Hunkeler, 1999). Owing to shorter chain length and presence of free amino groups in their structure, oligochitosans can be easily dissolved in water forming nonviscous aqueous solutions even at high concentrations (Kim and Rajapakse, 2005). Bartkowiak and Hunkeler (1999) have shown that alginate–oligochitosan microparticles can be prepared by a simple one-stage procedure without use of crosslinking ions, under physiological conditions, in contrast to the alginate–chitosan microparticles, which can be prepared under acidic conditions at pH < 6.5. Calija et al. (2013b) investigated the influence of oligochitosan as a reinforcing agent on

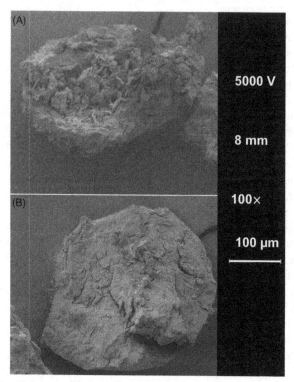

FIGURE 5.9 Cross-sectional SEM images of naproxen-loaded Ca-alginate microparticle (A) before and (B) after treatment with oligochitosan. *(Reprinted from Čalija B, Milić J, Cekić N, Krajišnik D, Daniels R, Savić S: Chitosan oligosaccharide as prospective cross-linking agent for naproxen-loaded Ca-alginate microparticles with improved pH sensitivity,* Drug Dev Ind Pharm, *39:86, 2013, with permission from Taylor & Francis Ltd. http://www.tandfonline.com/toc/iddi20/current)*

the pH sensitivity of Ca-alginate microparticles and their feasibility for oral delivery of naproxen. The microparticles prepared by the two-stage procedure were spherical in shape with a mean diameter below 350 μm. The formation of alginate-oligochitosan PEC was confirmed by FT-IR and thermal analysis (Calija et al., 2013b). Cross-sectional SEM images of the particles revealed the presence of hollow core filled with the drug crystals in the inner structure of Ca-alginate microparticles, whereas the core of the oligochitosan–alginate particles was compact and nonporous. The observed difference could be ascribed to the PEC formation, implying that oligochitosan intensively diffused through the porous Ca-alginate hydrogel network during the second stage of preparation procedure (Fig. 5.9). This confirmed the assumption that small-sized molecules of oligochitosan can form PEC with alginate in the particles core, and not just on the surface. In contrast, high molecular weight chitosans interact with alginates predominantly on the particles surface. This is in line with the findings reported by Mladenovska et al. (2007a) who used confocal laser scanning

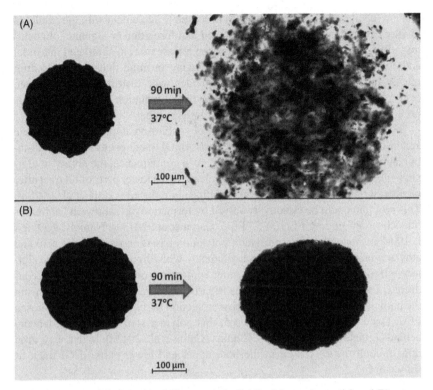

FIGURE 5.10   Swelling behavior of (A) naproxen-loaded Ca-alginate microparticle and (B) naprox-en-loaded alginate–oligochitosan microparticle in simulated intestinal fluid. *(Reprinted from Calija B, Cekic N, Milic J: Chitosan-based polyelectrolyte complexes: characteristics and application in formulation of particulate drug carriers. In Tiwari A, Patra HK, Choi JW, editors:* Advanced Theranostic Materials, *Hoboken, 2015, John Wliey & Sons, p 246, with permission from John Wiley and Sons)*

microscopy and fluoresceine 5(6)-isothiocyanate to investigate distribution of chitosan (MW = 150 kDa, deacetylation degree > 0.85) in the alginate–chitosan microparticles loaded with 5-aminosalicylic acid, which is anti-inflammatory drug. Obtained results confirmed the presence of chitosan mostly in the particles wall, implying that polyelectrolyte complexation took place predominantly on the particles surface.

Swelling studies performed on naproxen-loaded alginate–oligochitosan microparticles have shown that formation of alginate–oligochitosan PEC significantly improves mechanic strength of the particles and decreases naproxen release rates in simulated intestinal and colonic fluid (Calija et al., 2013b). As shown in Fig. 5.10, the Ca-alginate particles exhibited rapid and intensive swelling in simulated intestinal fluid (USP phosphate buffer at pH 6.8) followed by complete erosion for less than 90 min. On the other hand, Ca-alginate particles reinforced with oligochitosan swelled less intensively showing no signs of erosion (Calija et al., 2015a). This was in complete agreement with the results of in vitro drug release studies which showed that formation of alginate–oligochitosan PEC significantly decreased naproxen release rates in simulated intestinal and colonic fluid (Calija et al., 2013a). Having in mind that prolonged drug release in the lower parts of GI tract provides wide distribution of naproxen over a large area, minimizing in that way topical irritation of GI mucosa, this improvement might be important from a clinical aspect.

Nevertheless, intensive protonation of oligochitosan amino groups in acidic conditions, similar to those in the upper parts of GI tract, results in partial destabilization of alginate–oligochitosan PEC. As a consequence, the ability of alginate–oligochitosan PEC to sustain drug release in the lower parts of GI tract after incubation in acidic environment is significantly reduced (Calija et al., 2013a). This problem could be effectively solved by formation of "sandwich" alginate–oligochitosan–Eudragit L 100-55 PEC (Calija et al., 2013a). Namely, Eudragit L 100-55 is synthetic gastroresistant polyanion based on methacrylic acid and ethylacrylate that can interact electrostatically with oligochitosan from the alginate–oligochitosan microparticles under appropriate conditions. In acidic conditions, Eudragit L 100-55 from this tripartite PEC reduces drug release from the particles but also provides effective protection to the alginate–oligochitosan PEC. Once the pH value exceeds 5.5, this polymer starts to dissolve leaving behind alginate-oligochitosan PEC intact (Calija et al., 2013a). In that way, drug release could be decreased in the both upper and lower parts of GI tract, as shown in Fig. 5.11.

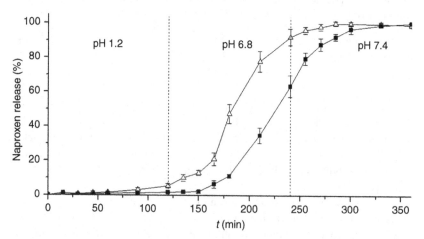

FIGURE 5.11 Naproxen release profiles from naproxen-loaded alginate–oligochitosan micropar-ticles *(Δ)* and naproxen-loaded alginate–oligochitosan–Eudragit L 100-55 microparticles *(■)* in conditions mimicking GI tract. *(Reprinted from Calija B, Cekić N, Savić S, Daniels R, Marković B, Milić J: pH-sensitive microparticles for oral drug delivery based on alginate/oligochitosan/Eudragit® L100-55 "sandwich" polyelectrolyte complex, Colloids Surf B 110:401, 2013, with per-mission from Elsevier)*

In recent years, research interest has been shifted to nanosized drug carriers, such as nanoparticles. Despite the fact that numerous studies have been carried out to investigate the properties and potential use of alginate–chitosan nanoparticles as drug carriers, only a few refer to NSAIDs. These studies were mainly designed with aim to achieve sustained release of certain NSAIDs from these carriers (Fattahpour et al., 2015; Shah and Patel, 2015). Their submicron size makes them suitable for different routes of administration, which is especially important in treatment of localized inflammatory processes.

Fattahpour et al. (2015) synthetized alginate–chitosan–pluronic nanoparticles for intraarticular delivery of NSAID meloxicam. The nanoparticles were prepared from medium molecular weight chitosan by varying alginate/chitosan mass ratio, pluronic and meloxicam concentration, according to the previously described procedure introduced by Rajaonarivony et al. (1993). The nanoparticles optimized by Box–Behnken design had the following characteristics: average hydrodynamic radius of 283 nm, zeta potential -16.9 mV, encapsulation efficiency 55%, and mean dissolution time in phosphate-buffered saline at pH 7.4 was 8.9 h. Shah and Patel (2015) successfully encapsulated another NSAID—zaltoprofen in alginate–chitosan nanoparticles—and studied the influence of alginate/chitosan mass ratio and several process parameters on the particles properties. The particles optimized by using Box–Behnken design were stable and spherical with average hydrodynamic radius 156 nm, zeta potential +25.3 mV, and zaltoprofen entrapment efficiency 88.67%. Both the studies confirmed importance of the alginate/chitosan mass ratio for particles properties. However, there is no information on chitosan functionality-related characteristics and their influence on the particles properties.

The influence of chitosan functional characteristics on blank alginate–chitosan submicron particles was investigated in detail by Sæther et al. (2008). The particles were prepared at room temperature by dropwise addition of 0.1% w/v alginate solution (pH ≈ 6.5) in 0.1% w/v chitosan solution (pH ≈ 4.0) under vigorous stirring. To investigate molecular-based structure–function relationship for the formation of alginate–chitosan PEC particles, authors used seven chitosan samples with different molecular weight (47–400 kDa) and deacetylation degree (0.02–0.61). Dynamic light scattering analysis confirmed the influence of chitosan molecular weight on the particles' hydrodynamic radius. Namely, low molecular weight chitosans formed smaller particles in comparison to high molecular weight chitosans. It is likely that higher molecular weight supports interactions with those polymer fragments that are not involved in other interactions to a larger extent, and hence promotes formation of the larger particles. The observed influence of molecular weight was more evident when chitosan was used in excess. On the other hand, chitosan molecular weight showed no influence on zeta potential of the particles (Sæther et al., 2008). Despite the fact that chitosan samples had broad range of deacetylation degree there was no significant difference between the resulting particles. The possible explanation is that not all of the protonated groups were available for interaction with the carboxylate moieties of alginate due to conformational features (Sæther et al., 2008).

5.5 CONCLUSIONS

Porosity and sensitivity on sequestering ions are the main weaknesses of Ca-alginate micro/nanoparticles as carriers of different actives, including NSAIDs. A number of studies have demonstrated that reinforcement with polycations, such as chitosans, provides effective solution for these drawbacks. The reinforcement is based on the rapid reaction of polyelectrolyte complexation between alginate and chitosan and subsequent formation of alginate–chitosan PEC under mild conditions.

Among various factors influencing properties of this PEC, molecular characteristics of the included polymers are of particular relevance. Published results designate molecular weight of chitosans and their viscosity as the most important features affecting properties of NSAID-loaded alginate–chitosan particulate carriers, such as size, shape, encapsulation efficiencies, swelling and drug release properties. Besides, the influence of chitosans' functional characteristics depends on the encapsulation technique and conditions. Therefore, chitosans' molecular characteristics have to be carefully balanced with formulation factors and preparation conditions in order to obtain alginate–chitosan particulate carriers with desired characteristics.

ACKNOWLEDGMENT

This work was realized within the framework of the project TR 34031 supported by the Ministry of Education, Science and Technological Development of Republic of Serbia.

REFERENCES

Agnihotri SA, Mallikarjuna NN, Aminabhavi TM: Recent advances on chitosan-based micro-and nanoparticles in drug delivery, *J Control Release* 100:5–28, 2004.
Aiba SI: Studies on chitosan: 4. Lysozymic hydrolysis of partially N-acetylated chitosans, *Int J Biol Macromol* 14:225–228, 1992.
Alves NM, Mano JF: Chitosan derivatives obtained by chemical modifications for biomedical and environmental applications, *Int J Biol Macromol* 43:401–414, 2008.
Aranaz I, Mengíbar M, Harris R, Paños I, Miralles B, Acosta N, Galed G, Heras Á: Functional characterization of chitin and chitosan, *Curr Chem Biol* 3:203–230, 2009.
Araujo JV, Davidenko N, Danner M, Cameron RE, Best SM: Novel porous scaffolds of pH responsive chitosan/carrageenan-based polyelectrolyte complexes for tissue engineering, *J Biomed Mater Res A* 102:4415–4426, 2014.
Arica B, Calis S, Atilla P, Durlu NT, Cakar N, Kas HS, Hincal AA: In vitro and in vivo studies of ibuprofen-loaded biodegradable alginate beads, *J Microencapsul* 22:153–165, 2005.
Baldrick P: The safety of chitosan as a pharmaceutical excipient, *Regul Toxicol Pharm* 56:290–299, 2010.

Bartkowiak A, Hunkeler D: Alginate-oligochitosan microcapsules: a mechanistic study relating membrane and capsule properties to reaction conditions, *Chem Mater* 11:2486–2492, 1999.

Baruch L, Machluf M: Alginate–chitosan complex coacervation for cell encapsulation: effect on mechanical properties and on long-term viability, *Biopolymers* 82:570–579, 2006.

Beck WS, Schneider HT, Dietzel K, Nuernberg B, Brune K: Gastrointestinal ulcerations induced by anti-inflammatory drugs in rats, *Arch Toxicol* 64:210–217, 1990.

Bellini MZ, Pires ALR, Vasconcelos MO, Moraes AM: Comparison of the properties of compacted and porous lamellar chitosan–xanthan membranes as dressings and scaffolds for the treatment of skin lesions, *J Appl Polym Sci* 125:E421–E431, 2012.

Belščak-Cvitanović A, Stojanović R, Manojlović V, Komes D, Juranović Cindrić I, Nedović V, Bugarski B: Encapsulation of polyphenolic antioxidants from medicinal plant extracts in alginate–chitosan system enhanced with ascorbic acid by electrostatic extrusion, *Food Res Int* 44:1094–1101, 2011.

Bhardwaj N, Kundu SC: Silk fibroin protein and chitosan polyelectrolyte complex porous scaffolds for tissue engineering applications, *Carbohydr Polym* 85:325–333, 2011.

Bhattarai N, Gunn J, Zhang M: Chitosan-based hydrogels for controlled, localized drug delivery, *Adv Drug Deliv Rev* 62:83–99, 2010.

Birch NP, Schiffman JD: Characterization of self-assembled polyelectrolyte complex nanoparticles formed from chitosan and pectin, *Langmuir* 30:3441–3447, 2014.

Bjorkman DJ: Nonsteroidal anti-inflammatory drug-induced gastrointestinal injury, *Am J Med* 101:S25–S32, 1996.

Boateng JS, Matthews KH, Stevens HNE, Eccleston GM: Wound healing dressings and drug delivery systems: a review, *J Pharm Sci* 97:2892–2923, 2008.

Bugarski B, Li Q, Goosen MFA, Poncelet D, Neufeld RJ, Vunjak G: Electrostatic droplet generation: mechanism of polymer droplet formation, *AIChE J* 40:1026–1031, 1994.

Calija B: *Functionality of chitosans in formulation of alginate-chitosan microparticles as drug carriers for nonsteroidal anti-inflammatory drugs*. Ph.D. thesis, Belgrade, 2013, University of Belgrade—Faculty of Pharmacy. Available from: 10.2298/BG20130607CALIJA

Calija B, Cekic N, Savic S, Krajisnik D, Daniels R, Milic J: An investigation of formulation factors affecting feasibility of alginate-chitosan microparticles for oral delivery of naproxen, *Arch Pharm Res* 34:919–929, 2011.

Calija B, Cekic N, Savic S, Daniels R, Markovic B, Milic J: pH-sensitive microparticles for oral drug delivery based on alginate/oligochitosan/Eudragit® L100-55 "sandwich" polyelectrolyte complex, *Colloid Surf B* 110:395–402, 2013a.

Calija B, Milic J, Cekic N, Krajisnik D, Daniels R, Savic S: Chitosan oligosaccharide as prospective cross-linking agent for naproxen-loaded Ca-alginate microparticles with improved pH sensitivity, *Drug Dev Ind Pharm* 39:77–88, 2013b.

Calija B, Cekic N, Milic J: Chitosan-based polyelectrolyte complexes: characteristics and application in formulation of particulate drug carriers. In Tiwari A, Patra HK, Choi JW, editors: *Advanced theranostic materials*, Hoboken, 2015a, John Wiley & Sons, pp 235–270.

Calija B, Savic S, Krajisnik D, Daniels R, Vucen S, Markovic B, Milic J: pH-sensitive polyelectrolyte films derived from submicron chitosan/Eudragit® L 100-55 complexes: physicochemical characterization and in vitro drug release, *J Appl Polym Sci* 132:42583, 2015b.

Carreno-Gomez B, Duncan R: Evaluation of the biological properties of soluble chitosan and chitosan microspheres, *Int J Pharm* 148:231–240, 1997.

Cekić ND, Savić SD, Milić JR, Savić MM, Jović Z, Malesević M: Preparation and characterisation of phenytoin-loaded alginate and alginate-chitosan microparticles, *Drug Deliv* 14:483–490, 2007.

Cekić ND, Milić JR, Savić SD, Savić MM, Jović Z, Daniels R: Influence of the preparation procedure and chitosan type on physicochemical properties and release behavior of alginate–chitosan microparticles, *Drug Dev Ind Pharm* 35:1092–1102, 2009.

Chan LW, Lee HY, Heng PWS: Mechanisms of external and internal gelation and their impact on the functions of alginate as a coat and delivery system, *Carbohydr Polym* 63:176–187, 2006.

Cioli V, Putzolu S, Rossi V, Barcellona PS, Corradino C: The role of direct tissue contact in the production of gastrointestinal ulcers by anti-inflammatory drugs in rats, *Toxicol Appl Pharm* 50:283–289, 1979.

Coppi G, Iannuccelli V, Leo E, Bernabei MT, Cameroni R: Chitosan-alginate microparticles as a protein carrier, *Drug Dev Ind Pharm* 27:393–400, 2001.

Crcarevska MS, Dodov MG, Goracinova K: Chitosan coated Ca–alginate microparticles loaded with budesonide for delivery to the inflamed colonic mucosa, *Eur J Pharm Biopharm* 68:565–578, 2008.

Cuadros TR, Skurtys O, Aguilera JM: Mechanical properties of calcium alginate fibers produced with a microfluidic device, *Carbohydr Polym* 89:1198–1206, 2012.

Dash M, Chiellini F, Ottenbrite RM, Chiellini E: Chitosan—a versatile semi-synthetic polymer in biomedical applications, *Prog Polym Sci* 36:981–1014, 2011.

De S, Robinson D: Polymer relationships during preparation of chitosan–alginate and poly-L-lysine–alginate nanospheres, *J Control Release* 89:101–112, 2003.

De Prisco A, Maresca D, Ongeng D, Mauriello G: Microencapsulation by vibrating technology of the probiotic strain *Lactobacillus reuteri* DSM 17938 to enhance its survival in foods and in gastrointestinal environment, *LWT Food Sci Technol* 61:452–462, 2015.

Deng C, Zhang P, Vulesevic B, Kuraitis D, Li F, Yang AF, Griffith M, Ruel M, Suuronen EJ: A collagen–chitosan hydrogel for endothelial differentiation and angiogenesis, *Tissue Eng A* 16:3099–3109, 2010.

Dhar N, Akhlaghi SP, Tam KC: Biodegradable and biocompatible polyampholyte microgels derived from chitosan, carboxymethyl cellulose and modified methyl cellulose, *Carbohydr Polym* 87:101–109, 2012.

Djuris J, Ibric S, Djuric Z: Experimental design application and interpretation in pharmaceutical technology. In Djuris J, editor: *Computer-aided applications in pharmaceutical technology*, Cambridge, 2013, Woodhead Publishing Limited, pp 31–56.

Donati I, Holtan S, Mørch YA, Borgogna M, Dentini M, Skjåk-Bræk G: New hypothesis on the role of alternating sequences in calcium-alginate gels, *Biomacromolecules* 6:1031–1040, 2005.

Douglas KL, Tabrizian M: Effect of experimental parameters on the formation of alginate–chitosan nanoparticles and evaluation of their potential application as DNA carrier, *J Biomater Sci Polym Ed* 16:43–56, 2005.

Draget KI, Skjåk-Bræk G, Smidsrød O: Alginate based new materials, *Int J Biol Macromol* 21:47–55, 1997.

Errington N, Harding SE, Vårum KM, Illum L: Hydrodynamic characterization of chitosans varying in degree of acetylation, *Int J Biol Macromol* 15:113–117, 1993.

Eskilson C: Controlled release by microencapsulation, *Manuf Chem* 56:33–39, 1985.

Estevinho BN, Rocha F, Santos L, Alves A: Microencapsulation with chitosan by spray drying for industry applications—a review, *Trends Food Sci Technol* 31:138–155, 2013.

European Pharmacopeia fourth edition. Strasbourg, 2002, Council of Europe.

Fathy M: Ca-alginate beads loaded with meloxicam: effect of alginate chemical composition on the properties of the beads and ulcerogenicity of the drug, *J Drug Deliv Sci Technol* 16:183–189, 2006.

Fattahpour S, Shamanian M, Tavakoli N, Fathi M, Sheykhi SR, Fattahpour S: Design and optimization of alginate–chitosan–pluronic nanoparticles as a novel meloxicam drug delivery system, *J Appl Polym Sci* 132:42241, 2015.

Fernandez-Hervas MJ, Holgado MA, Fini A, Fell JT: In vitro evaluation of alginate beads of a diclofenac salt, *Int J Pharm* 163:23–34, 1998.

Fundueanu G, Nastruzzi C, Carpov A, Desbrieres J, Rinaudo M: Physico-chemical characterization of Ca-alginate microparticles produced with different methods, *Biomaterials* 20:1427–1435, 1999.

Gades MD, Stern JS: Chitosan supplementation and fecal fat excretion in men, *Obes Res* 11: 683–688, 2003.

Garcia-Fuentes M, Alonso MJ: Chitosan-based drug nanocarriers: where do we stand? *J Control Release* 161:496–504, 2012.

Gåserød O, Sannes A, Skjåk-Bræk G: Microcapsules of alginate–chitosan II. A study of capsule stability and permeability, *Biomaterials* 20:773–783, 1999.

Gombotz WR, Wee SF: Protein release from alginate matrices, *Adv Drug Deliv Rev* 64:194–205, 2012.

González-Rodríguez ML, Holgado MA, Sanchez-Lafuente C, Rabasco AM, Fini A: Alginate/chitosan particulate systems for sodium diclofenac release, *Int J Pharm* 232:225–234, 2002.

Goycoolea FM, Lollo G, Remunán-López C, Quaglia F, Alonso MJ: Chitosan-alginate blended nanoparticles as carriers for the transmucosal delivery of macromolecules, *Biomacromolecules* 10:1736–1743, 2009.

Grant GT, Morris ER, Rees DA, Smith PJC, Thom D: Biological interactions between polysaccharides and divalent cations: the egg-box model, *FEBS Lett* 32:195–198, 1973.

Hajji S, Younes I, Ghorbel-Bellaaj O, Hajji R, Rinaudo M, Nasri M, Jellouli K: Structural differences between chitin and chitosan extracted from three different marine sources, *Int J Biol Macromol* 65:298–306, 2014.

Hamman JH: Chitosan based polyelectrolyte complexes as potential carrier materials in drug delivery systems, *Mar Drugs* 8:1305–1322, 2010.

Hansen LT, Allan-Wojtas PM, Jin YL, Paulson AT: Survival of Ca-alginate microencapsulated *Bifidobacterium* spp. in milk and simulated gastrointestinal conditions, *Food Microbiol* 19:35–45, 2002.

Haque T, Chen H, Ouyang W, Martoni C, Lawuyi B, Urbanska AM, Prakash S: In vitro study of alginate–chitosan microcapsules: an alternative to liver cell transplants for the treatment of liver failure, *Biotechnol Lett* 27:317–322, 2005.

Heinzen C, Marison I, Berger A, von Stockar U: Use of vibration technology for jet break-up for encapsulation of cells, microbes and liquids in monodisperse microcapsules, *Landbauforschung Völkenrode* 241:19–25, 2002.

Hejazi R, Amiji M: Chitosan-based gastrointestinal delivery systems, *J Control Release* 89: 151–165, 2003.

Hwang SJ, Rhee GJ, Lee KM, Oh KH, Kim CK: Release characteristics of ibuprofen from excipient-loaded alginate gel beads, *Int J Pharm* 116:125–128, 1995.

Iruin A, Fernandez-Arevalo M, Alvarez-Fuentes J, Fini A, Holgado MA: Elaboration and "in vitro" characterization of 5-ASA beads, *Drug Dev Ind Pharm* 31:231–239, 2005.

Jana S, Manna S, Nayak AK, Sen KK, Basu SK: Carbopol gel containing chitosan-egg albumin nanoparticles for transdermal aceclofenac delivery, *Colloid Surf B* 114:36–44, 2014.

Jeon YJ, Kim SK: Continuous production of chitooligosaccharides using a dual reactor system, *Process Biochem* 35:623–632, 2000.

Jeong SI, Krebs MD, Bonino CA, Samorezov JE, Khan SA, Alsberg E: Electrospun chitosan–alginate nanofibers with in situ polyelectrolyte complexation for use as tissue engineering scaffolds, *Tissue Eng A* 17:59–70, 2010.

Joseph S, John MJ, Pothen LA, Thomas S: Raw and renewable polymers. In Eyerer P, Weller M, Hübner C, editors: *Polymers—opportunities and risks II*, Berlin, Heidelberg, 2010, Springer, pp 55–80.

Kakkar A: Characterization of ibuprofen loaded microcapsules prepared by ionotropic gelation, *Indian J Pharm Sci* 57:56–60, 1995.

Kamburov M, Lalov I: Preparation of chitosan beads for trypsin immobilization, *Biotechnol Biotechnol Equip* 26:156–163, 2012.

Kean T, Thanou M: Biodegradation, biodistribution and toxicity of chitosan, *Adv Drug Deliv Rev* 62:3–11, 2010.

Kim SK, Rajapakse N: Enzymatic production and biological activities of chitosan oligosaccharides (COS): a review, *Carbohydr Polym* 62:357–368, 2005.

Krämer J, Blume H: Biopharmaceutical aspects of multiparticulates, *Drugs Pharm Sci* 65:307–332, 1994.

Kubota N, Tatsumoto N, Sano T, Toya K: A simple preparation of half N-acetylated chitosan highly soluble in water and aqueous organic solvents, *Carbohydr Res* 324:268–274, 2000.

Lamprecht A, Schäfer U, Lehr CM: Size-dependent bioadhesion of micro-and nanoparticulate carriers to the inflamed colonic mucosa, *Pharm Res* 18:788–793, 2001a.

Lamprecht A, Ubrich N, Yamamoto H, Schäfer U, Takeuchi H, Maincent P, Kawashima Y, Lehr CM: Biodegradable nanoparticles for targeted drug delivery in treatment of inflammatory bowel disease, *J Pharmacol Exp Ther* 299:775–781, 2001b.

Li P, Dai YN, Zhang JP, Wang AQ, Wei Q: Chitosan-alginate nanoparticles as a novel drug delivery system for nifedipine, *Int J Biomed Sci* 4:221–228, 2008.

Li X, Xie H, Lin J, Xie W, Ma X: Characterization and biodegradation of chitosan–alginate polyelectrolyte complexes, *Polym Degrad Stabil* 94:1–6, 2009.

Lim F, Sun AM: Microencapsulated islets as bioartificial endocrine pancreas, *Science* 210:908–910, 1980.

Maghsoodi M: Physicomechanical properties of naproxen-loaded microparticles prepared from Eudragit l100, *AAPS PharmSciTech* 10:120–128, 2009.

Martinsen A, Skjåk-Bræk G, Smidsrød O: Alginate as immobilization material: I. Correlation between chemical and physical properties of alginate gel beads, *Biotechnol Bioeng* 33:79–89, 1989.

Minami S, Oh-Oka M, Okamoto Y, Miyatake K, Matsuhashi A, Shigemasa Y, Fukumoto Y: Chitosan-inducing hemorrhagic pneumonia in dogs, *Carbohydr Polym* 29:241–246, 1996.

Mladenovska K, Cruaud O, Richomme P, Belamie E, Raicki RS, Venier-Julienne MC, Popovski E, Benoit JP, Goracinova K: 5-ASA loaded chitosan–Ca–alginate microparticles: preparation and physicochemical characterization, *Int J Pharm* 345:59–69, 2007a.

Mladenovska K, Raicki RS, Janevik EI, Ristoski T, Pavlova MJ, Kavrakovski Z, Dodov MG, Goracinova K: Colon-specific delivery of 5-aminosalicylic acid from chitosan-Ca-alginate microparticles, *Int J Pharm* 342:124–136, 2007b.

Moustafine RI, Margulis EB, Sibgatullina LF, Kemenova VA, Van den Mooter G: Comparative evaluation of interpolyelectrolyte complexes of chitosan with Eudragit® L100 and Eudragit® L100-55 as potential carriers for oral controlled drug delivery, *Eur J Pharm Biopharm* 70:215–225, 2008.

Naesdal J, Brown K: NSAID-associated adverse effects and acid control aids to prevent them, *Drug Saf* 29:119–132, 2006.

Nagarwal RC, Kumar R, Pandit JK: Chitosan coated sodium alginate–chitosan nanoparticles loaded with 5-FU for ocular delivery: in vitro characterization and in vivo study in rabbit eye, *Eur J Pharm Sci* 47:678–685, 2012.

Paques JP, van der Linden E, van Rijn CJM, Sagis LMC: Preparation methods of alginate nanoparticles, *Adv Colloid Interface* 209:163–171, 2014.

Pawar SN, Edgar KJ: Alginate derivatization: a review of chemistry, properties and applications, *Biomaterials* 33:3279–3305, 2012.

Pillai CKS, Paul W, Sharma CP: Chitin and chitosan polymers: chemistry, solubility and fiber formation, *Prog Polym Sci* 34:641–678, 2009.

Polk A, Amsden B, Yao KD, Peng T, Goosen MFA: Controlled release of albumin from chitosan—alginate microcapsules, *J Pharm Sci* 83:178–185, 1994.

Prüsse U, Bilancetti L, Bučko M, Bugarski B, Bukowski J, Gemeiner P, Lewińska D, Manojlovic V, Massart B, Nastruzzi C, Nedovic V, Poncelet D, Siebenhaar S, Tobler L, Tosi A, Vikartovska A, Vorlop KD: Comparison of different technologies for alginate beads production, *Chem Pap* 62:364–374, 2008.

Rajaonarivony M, Vauthier C, Couarraze G, Puisieux F, Couvreur P: Development of a new drug carrier made from alginate, *J Pharm Sci* 82:912–917, 1993.

Rege PR, Block LH: Chitosan processing: influence of process parameters during acidic and alkaline hydrolysis and effect of the processing sequence on the resultant chitosan's properties, *Carbohydr Res* 321:235–245, 1999.

Ren D, Yi H, Wang W, Ma X: The enzymatic degradation and swelling properties of chitosan matrices with different degrees of N-acetylation, *Carbohydr Res* 340:2403–2410, 2005.

Ribeiro AJ, Neufeld RJ, Arnaud P, Chaumeil JC: Microencapsulation of lipophilic drugs in chitosan-coated alginate microspheres, *Int J Pharm* 187:115–123, 1999.

Ribeiro AJ, Silva C, Ferreira D, Veiga F: Chitosan-reinforced alginate microspheres obtained through the emulsification/internal gelation technique, *Eur J Pharm Sci* 25:31–40, 2005.

Rinaudo M: Chitin and chitosan: properties and applications, *Prog Polym Sci* 31:603–632, 2006.

Russo R, Malinconico M, Santagata G: Effect of cross-linking with calcium ions on the physical properties of alginate films, *Biomacromolecules* 8:3193–3197, 2007.

Sæther HV, Holme HK, Maurstad G, Smidsrød O, Stokke BJ: Polyelectrolyte complex formation using alginate and chitosan, *Crabohydr Polym* 74:813–821, 2008.

Sankalia MG, Mashru RC, Sankalia JM, Sutariya VB: Reversed chitosan–alginate polyelectrolyte complex for stability improvement of alpha-amylase: optimization and physicochemical characterization, *Eur J Pharm Biopharm* 65:215–232, 2007.

Sarmento B, Ribeiro AJ, Veiga F, Ferreira DC, Neufeld RJ: Insulin-loaded nanoparticles are prepared by alginate ionotropic pre-gelation followed by chitosan polyelectrolyte complexation, *J Nanosci Nanotechnol* 7:2833–2841, 2007.

Shah HA, Patel RP: Statistical modeling of zaltoprofen loaded biopolymeric nanoparticles: characterization and anti-inflammatory activity of nanoparticles loaded gel, *Int J Pharm Investig* 5:20–27, 2015.

Silva CM, Ribeiro AJ, Figueiredo M, Ferreira D, Veiga F: Microencapsulation of hemoglobin in chitosan-coated alginate microspheres prepared by emulsification/internal gelation, *AAPS J* 7:E903–E913, 2005.

Simsek-Ege FA, Bond GM, Stringer J: Polyelectrolyte complex formation between alginate and chitosan as a function of pH, *J Appl Polym Sci* 88:346–351, 2003.

Singla AK, Chawla M: Chitosan: some pharmaceutical and biological aspects—an update, *J Pharm Pharmacol* 53:1047–1067, 2001.

Soll AH, Kurata J, McGuigan JE: Ulcers, nonsteroidal anti-inflammatory drugs, and related matters, *Gastroenterology* 96:561–568, 1989.

Sosnik A: Alginate particles as platform for drug delivery by the oral route: State-of-the-Art. ISRN pharmaceutics, 2014.

Suginta W, Khunkaewla P, Schulte A: Electrochemical biosensor applications of polysaccharides chitin and chitosan, *Chem Rev* 113:5458–5479, 2013.

Suleyman H, Demircan B, Karagoz Y: Anti-inflammatory and side effects of cyclooxygenase inhibitors, *Pharmacol Rep* 59:247–258, 2007.

Sun Y, Ma X, Zhou D, Vacek I, Sun AM: Normalization of diabetes in spontaneously diabetic cynomologus monkeys by xenografts of microencapsulated porcine islets without immunosuppression, *J Clin Invest* 98:1417–1422, 1996.

Takahashi T, Takayama K, Machida Y, Nagai T: Characteristics of polyion complexes of chitosan with sodium alginate and sodium polyacrylate, *Int J Pharm* 61:35–41, 1990.

Tapola NS, Lyyra ML, Kolehmainen RM, Sarkkinen ES, Schauss AG: Safety aspects and cholesterol-lowering efficacy of chitosan tablets, *J Am Coll Nutr* 27:22–30, 2008.

Thein-Han WW, Saikhun J, Pholpramoo C, Misra RDK, Kitiyanant Y: Chitosan–gelatin scaffolds for tissue engineering: physico-chemical properties and biological response of buffalo embryonic stem cells and transfectant of GFP–buffalo embryonic stem cells, *Acta Biomater* 5:3453–3466, 2009.

Tønnesen HH, Karlsen J: Alginate in drug delivery systems, *Drug Dev Ind Pharm* 28:621–630, 2002.

Trabelsi I, Ayadi D, Bejar W, Bejar S, Chouayekh H, Salah RB: Effects of *Lactobacillus plantarum* immobilization in alginate coated with chitosan and gelatin on antibacterial activity, *Int J Biol Macromol* 31:84–89, 2014.

Tsigos I, Martinou A, Kafetzopoulos D, Bouriotis V: Chitin deacetylases: new, versatile tools in biotechnology, *Trends Biotechnol* 18:305–312, 2000.

Varma MM, Rao CHLN: Evaluation of aceclofenac loaded alginate mucoadhesive spheres prepared by ionic gelation, *Int J Pharm Sci Nanotechnol* 5:1847–1857, 2013.

Vonkeman HE, van de Laar MAFJ: Nonsteroidal anti-inflammatory drugs: adverse effects and their prevention, *Semin Arthritis Rheum* 39:294–312, 2010.

Wallace JL: Prostaglandins, NSAIDs, and gastric mucosal protection: why doesn't the stomach digest itself? *Physiol Rev* 88:1547–1565, 2008.

Wedmore I, McManus JG, Pusateri AE, Holcomb JB: A special report on the chitosan-based hemostatic dressing: experience in current combat operations, *J Trauma* 60:655–658, 2006.

Wong TW: Chitosan and its use in design of insulin delivery system, *Recent Pat Drug Deliv Formul* 3:8–25, 2009.

Xia W, Liu P, Zhang J, Chen J: Biological activities of chitosan and chitooligosaccharides, *Food Hydrocoll* 25:170–179, 2011.

Yang YM, Hu W, Wang XD, Gu XS: The controlling biodegradation of chitosan fibers by N-acetylation in vitro and in vivo, *J Mater Sci* 18:2117–2121, 2007.

Yang JS, Xie YJ, He W: Research progress on chemical modification of alginate: a review, *Carbohydr Polym* 84:33–39, 2011.

Yeul VS, Rayalu SS: Unprecedented chitin and chitosan: a chemical overview, *J Polym Environ* 21:606–614, 2013.

You JO, Peng CA: Calcium-alginate nanoparticles formed by reverse microemulsion as gene carriers, *Macromol Symp* 219:147–153, 2005.

You JO, Park SB, Park HY, Haam S, Chung CH, Kim WS: Preparation of regular sized Ca-alginate microspheres using membrane emulsification method, *J Microencapsul* 18:521–532, 2000.

Younes I, Rinaudo M: Chitin and chitosan preparation from marine sources. structure, properties and applications, *Mar Drugs* 13:1133–1174, 2015.

Yu CY, Zhang XC, Zhou FZ, Zhang XZ, Cheng SX, Zhuo RX: Sustained release of antineoplastic drugs from chitosan-reinforced alginate microparticle drug delivery systems, *Int J Pharm* 357:15–21, 2008.

Zhao Y, Park RD, Muzzarelli RAA: Chitin deacetylases: properties and applications, *Mar Drugs* 8:24–46, 2010.

Chapter 6

PLA-Based Nanoparticulate Drug Carriers as a Percutaneous Delivery System for Ketoprofen

Sonja Vučen*, Caroline O'Sullivan**

*School of Pharmacy, University College Cork, Cork, Ireland; **Department of Process, Energy & Transport Engineering, Cork Institute of Technology, Cork, Ireland

6.1 INTRODUCTION

Nanotechnology is an emerging therapeutic platform which involves the use, modeling, and manipulation of structures and materials at the nanoscale in order to improve pharmacological and therapeutic properties of drugs. Unique physicochemical properties of the nanoscale materials are of great scientific interest because they link the bulk materials and their molecular or atomic structure allowing for the novel applications (Roco, 2007). Owing to their distinctive properties, nanoscale drug carriers possess the potential to enhance pharmacodynamic and pharmacokinetic profiles of drug molecules (Veerapandian and Yuna, 2009). Moreover, these delivery vehicles have the ability to improve the therapeutic efficacy of pharmaceutical agents, as they can regulate their release, improve their stability and prolong circulation time by protecting the drug from elimination by phagocytic cells or premature degradation in the biological environment (Veerapandian and Yuna, 2009). The major research interest in the nanoranged world has particularly focused on wide spectrum of novel biomedical nanomaterials developed for formulation of carriers for diagnostics and drug delivery (Vučen, 2013).

In the field of polymeric biomaterials, the research interest is primarily focused on synthetic biodegradable polymers due to their fast degradation through the natural pathways, as well as exceptional control over polymer composition, architecture, and physical properties which is not fully accessible with natural polymers (Tamariz and Rios-Ramírez, 2013). However, biodegradability does not imply biocompatibility. Biocompatibility refers to several characteristics of the biomaterial which leads to the acceptance of the material in the body, such

Microsized and Nanosized Carriers for NSAIDs. http://dx.doi.org/10.1016/B978-0-12-804017-1.00006-6
161

as being nontoxic, noncarcinogenic, nonallergenic, nonimmunogenic (Tamariz and Rios-Ramírez, 2013). Hence, the biodegradable polymers that are degrading into small, nontoxic molecules are considered to be the ideal candidates for the preparation of polymeric nanocarriers for drug delivery.

After many years of research in this field numerous polymers have been developed, namely, polyesters, polyurethanes, polyanhydrides, polyacrylates, polyphosphoesters, and polydioxanone (Tamariz and Rios-Ramírez, 2013). However, only a few of them meet the criteria for biodegradability and biocompatibility. Examples of synthetic biodegradable polymers approved by US Food and Drug Administration (FDA) and the European Medicines Agency (EMA), which are able to assure complete biodegradation and high biocompatibility include cellulose acetate phthalate copolymers of methacrylic acid and methacrylate (Eudragit), poly(ε-caprolactone), polylactic (PLA) and polyglycolic (PGA) acids, and their copolymer poly(D,L-lactide-*co*-glycolide) (PLGA) (Maestrelli et al., 2015). Hence, these polymers appear as the preferred substrates to fabricate nanoparticles for controlled drug-delivery systems. PLA is a linear, lipophilic polymer approved for clinical use since its degradation products are biocompatible, metabolizable, and simply removed from the body via the citric acid cycle (Vučen, 2013). Colloidal drug carriers based on this polymer type are extensively investigated as delivery systems for systemic and topical applications. This is due to the fact that lactic acid, the constituting monomer, is easily derived from renewable resources, such as corn starch or sugarcane and is the sole resultant degradation product following polymer hydrolysis (Rancan et al., 2009). Their small particle size facilitates permeation through biological barriers and drug delivery over prolonged periods of time in the body (Xiao et al., 2012). In addition to their ability to control drug release, polymer nanoparticles are also capable to improve the delivery of water-insoluble drugs (Barichello et al., 1999), reduce the drug-associated side effects (Bernardi et al., 2009), protect the compounds from inactivation (Singh and Lillard, 2009), increase the intracellular penetration and enhance a higher drug-target accumulation (Rancan et al., 2009). Although these nanocarriers offer advantage of controlled drug release with improved stability, they have not been explored to a greater extent for percutaneous delivery. This route of drug administration is advantageous for skin diseases where the target site is present in the deep epidermis (Shah et al., 2012b). Moreover, skin delivery offers several advantages over the conventional oral and intravenous dosage forms, such as prevention of first-pass metabolism, minimization of pain, safe application, and improved patient compliance. However, one important feature of the skin as an organ is its function as a potent barrier to the external environment which is accomplished by the *stratum corneum* (SC) (Papakostas et al., 2011). For both the topical and transdermal application, the drug needs to cross this tough outer barrier layer. In the case of topical delivery, the flux through the skin into general circulation needs to be minimized with maximum retention, and vice versa for transdermal applications (Abdel-Mottaleb and Lamprecht, 2016). In order to enhance the drug penetration through the skin, various efforts have been made by different methods. These methods rely on either chemical enhancement including permeation enhancers and prodrug, physical enhancement methods (e.g., iontophoresis, microneedle pretreatment, ultrasound, and electroporation), or the use of novel vehicle systems (McGrath et al., 2014; Shah et al., 2012b; Vučen et al., 2013).

Several studies have been reported on a wide range of polymeric biodegradable nanocarriers for skin application offering increased efficacy, reduced enzymatic degradation, controlled drug release, enhanced stability, and reduced skin irritation (Naik et al., 2004; Papakostas et al., 2011). The composition, size, and surface charge of polymeric nanoparticles are significant characteristics which appear to be responsible for higher reactivity and unique interactions with biological systems leading to better pharmacokinetics of the encapsulated drugs (Abdel-Mottaleb and Lamprecht, 2016). Although such systems are undoubtedly able to enhance skin penetration and distribution, the mechanism by which this enhancement is achieved is not completely understood and as a result, is currently being intensively investigated. Rancan et al. investigated the PLA nanoparticles for local dermatotherapy. The research showed that the PLA accumulate in skin furrows and hair follicles and create high local concentrations of loaded drugs which can further diffuse into the viable layers of the skin (Rancan et al., 2009).

The diffusion through the lipid layers of the SC has long been observed as the exclusive penetration pathway for substances applied on the skin. Since the physicochemical properties and the size of topically applied substances are critical parameters that influence the degree of penetration within the skin, alternate penetration pathways or shunts have gained importance. Such is the case of hydrophilic compounds like proteins or carrier systems (Papakostas et al., 2011). There is evidence that the hair follicle can act as a shunt increasing the penetration and absorption of applied drug (Blume-Peytavi et al., 2010; Knorr et al., 2009; Lademann et al., 2001; Meidan, 2010). Hair follicles also act as a drug depot, thus multiplying the storage capabilities of the SC which promotes high concentrations within the reservoir of the follicular infundibulum (Otberg et al., 2004). This reservoir enables a sustained drug release which is the standard goal of pharmacotherapy (Lademann et al., 2001; Papakostas et al., 2011). In case of lipophilic dyes delivered to hair follicles by means of polymer particles, it was shown that the constant dye diffusion from the follicular canal to the perifollicular epidermis and sebaceous gland took place via a transcellular diffusion route (Rancan et al., 2009). Active and selective targeting of specific cells in the dermis are considered to be a major advantage of particulate formulations but still remain to be challenges for nanotechnology for dermatological application (Papakostas et al., 2011).

Topical formulations of macromolecules for the treatment of various skin diseases are still under development. Currently, these diseases are principally treated with topical corticosteroids that target a variety of pathways of the inflammation cascade (Shah et al., 2012a). However, severe and partially irreversible adverse effects including skin atrophy, secondary infections, and contact dermatitis are often accompanied with the clinical use of corticosteroid therapy limiting its application (Hengge et al., 2006). Hence, administration of potent nonsteroidal anti-inflammatory drug (NSAID), such as ketoprofen, is considered to have a great impact on the treatment of certain skin disorders with minimal adverse effects (Shah et al., 2012a). Ketoprofen is found to be a good candidate for topical and transdermal formulations since it has many desirable characteristics, a low molecular weight, a low melting point, and high lipophilicity. Moreover, pharmacokinetic properties of this drug, such as short half-life and numerous side effects following oral administration are also in favor to alternative routes of its administration.

6.2 KETOPROFEN-LOADED PLA NANOPARTICLES: PREPARATION AND CHARACTERIZATION ASPECTS

Transdermal delivery of ketoprofen delivery via skin is considered a promising alternative route for its administration. Complications exist following its oral administration as a result of its limited absorption and bioavailability. Severe adverse effects have been noted in about 10–30% of patients receiving the drug (Banga, 2011; Heyneman et al., 2000). In addition, important parameters, such as partition and diffusion coefficient need to be manipulated in order to enhance the drug penetration into the skin followed by the subsequent permeation across the skin layers. The most significant physicochemical and pharmacokinetic parameters which need to be considered in the selection of drug candidate for transdermal administration are presented in Table 6.1. With a wide therapeutic window and a high bioavailability after oral administration, ketoprofen is still classified as an ideal candidate for percutaneous delivery due to the stated parameters, as well as the numerous side effects associated with this drug. This is supported by a number of theoretical considerations and experimental studies (Halpern, 1994). However, the barrier function of the skin limits ketoprofen

TABLE 6.1 Parameters Considered in the Selection of Drug Candidate for Transdermal Drug Delivery (Vučen, 2013)

Parameter	Ideal properties	Ketoprofen
Molecular weight	<400 g/mol	254.3 g/mol
Partition coefficient (Log P)	1.0–4.0	3.2
Skin permeability coefficient	>0.5 × 10^{-3} cm/h	5.01 × 10^{-3} cm/h
Half-life	≤10 h	2 h
Oral bioavailability	Low	High
Therapeutic index	Low	High

delivery to deeper skin layers and disables its pharmacological action at the inflammation site (Hadgraft et al., 2000; Kim et al., 2008). Hence, extensive research has been done to develop both topical and transdermal ketoprofen formulations (Valenta and Almasi-Szabo, 1995; Vučen et al., 2013; McGrath et al., 2014; Shah et al., 2012b). One approach is designing polymeric nanoparticles as an enhancement aid for ketoprofen delivery to deeper skin layers, thus enabling it to exert its therapeutic effects at the inflammation site.

Polymeric nanoparticulate delivery systems can be designed to have therapeutic agents entrapped inside the nanocarrier, dissolved within its matrix, or adsorbed/chemically coupled onto the particle surface. As a result, drugs can be protected from a critical environment or their unfavorable biopharmaceutical properties can be masked and substituted by the properties of nanomaterials (Bamrungsap et al., 2012). Many methods are reported in literature for the synthesis of polymeric nanoparticles with defined dimensions, structure, and composition. In general, encapsulation techniques will depend on the nature of the encapsulated drug, type and physical properties of the nanocarrier, type of application, and anticipated retention time inside the body (Kumari et al., 2014). The selected encapsulation technique should give high encapsulation efficiency and loading capacity of drug (Vladisavljevic, 2012). Moreover, nanoparticles should not manifest aggregation or adherence, they should have a narrow particle size distribution and the process should be suitable for industrial scale production (Vladisavljevic, 2012). As discussed in the previous section, the bulk composition of the synthesized nanoparticle must be carefully chosen based on its biocompatibility (Thevenot et al., 2008; Wang et al., 2004), its immunotoxicity (Dobrovolskaia and McNeil, 2007), and its ability to solubilize or capture the drug of interest (Petros and DeSimone, 2010). Various methods of preparation of polymeric nanoparticles can be categorized into two major classes: the first involves polymerization of the monomers (e.g., emulsion and dispersion polymerization), whereas the second class is based on dispersion of the performed polymers (e.g., solvent displacement/evaporation, spontaneous emulsification, salting out/emulsification diffusion, nanoprecipitation) (Bamrungsap et al., 2012). This chapter focuses on the second class of methods used for laboratory-scale production of biodegradable PLA-based particles. The most common methods for the large-scale pilot production of drug-loaded nanoparticles, using spray drying and supercritical fluid spraying techniques are discussed elsewhere (Pathak and Thassu, 2009).

The applicability of the emulsion solvent evaporation process for loading the poorly soluble drug, ketoprofen, into PLA nanospheres was reported by Vučen et al. (2013). The nanoparticle preparation method described in this study was reproducible, consistent, and repeatable resulting in spherical, nonporous particles of about 145 nm and ketoprofen encapsulation efficiency of 75% (Fig. 6.1). Considering that the encapsulation efficiency of the drug depends on its solubility in both solvent and continuous phase, this result correlates well with the intermediate lipophilicity of ketoprofen (Vučen et al., 2013). A similar observation was

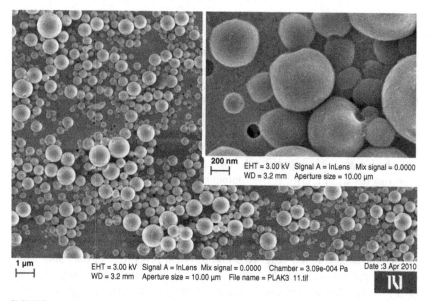

FIGURE 6.1 Scanning electron microphotograph of ketoprofen-loaded poly(D, L-lactic acid) nanoparticles. *(Reprinted from Vučen SR, Vuleta G, Crean AM, Moore AC, Ignjatović N, Uskokovic* D: Improved percutaneous delivery of ketoprofen using combined application of nanocarriers and silicon microneedles,* J Pharm Pharmacol 65:1451–1462, 2013, with permission from John Wiley and Sons)

also reported by Shah et al. (2012b), who used the same method for fabrication of PLGA nanoparticles and achieved a particle size of 150 nm and ketoprofen encapsulation with the efficiency of 80%. The emulsion-based method was again used in another study which showed a high percentage of ketoprofen-loaded into PLA microparticles (Ricci et al., 2005). These systems had an average size of 5 μm, and ketoprofen encapsulation efficiency of about 74%. The high percentage of drug entrapped into PLA/PLGA nanoparticles can be explained by the poor aqueous solubility of ketoprofen which resulted in minimal leakage of the drug into the external aqueous phase of the dispersion (Vučen et al., 2013). Although the solvent evaporation method employed by Vučen et al. resulted in a high degree of encapsulation of ketoprofen even better results can be achieved by increasing the drug/polymer ratio (Del Gaudio et al., 2009). In addition, it was found that particle sizes were directly proportional to the viscosities related to different drug/polymer ratios (Vučen et al., 2013). Hence, the ability to obtain the spherical particles in the nanosized range with a drug loading above 70% indicates a high degree of encapsulation. The selected method for nanoparticle fabrication determines the resultant size and size distribution of the spheres, which greatly affects the administration mode. Therefore, an extensive knowledge of the experimental parameters involved in each method is crucial as well as the effect that can alter the characteristics of the resulting particles (Lassalle and

Ferreira, 2007). Experimental parameters investigation included polarity of the solvent, concentration of polymer in the organic phase, internal/external phase ratio, drug/polymer ratio, and type and concentration of the surfactant in the aqueous phase (Quintanar-Guerrero et al., 1996; Vučen et al., 2013). Another method for fabrication of ketoprofen-loaded PLGA nanoparticles reported in the literature is nanoprecipitation (Barichello et al., 1999). This study focused primarily on the preparation and characterization of PLGA nanoparticles although the route of administration was not specified. Nevertheless, the application of nanoprecipitation technique revealed lower ketoprofen-entrapment efficiency (46%) for comparable particle with size (167 nm) produced by the emulsion solvent-evaporation method. According to the literature data, emulsion-based and nanoprecipitation methods appear as the most widely used techniques in the fabrication of PLA and PLGA nanoparticles designed for drug entrapment (Lassalle and Ferreira, 2007). However, the differences between both techniques are not evidently shown. Therefore, thorough considerations must be given to the selection of the most suitable method. Both processes begin with an organic polymer solution and finish with solvent evaporation. The contact between the polymer organic and aqueous solution is different when comparing the two methods. In emulsion-based method, the organic and aqueous phases are mixed together followed by a homogenization step, whereas in nanoprecipitation the organic solution is added dropwise into the aqueous solution while being stirred. Although it was shown that the nanoprecipitation technique leads to smaller size particles, the adjustment of experimental variables associated with each method is important as it may influence the properties of the generated particles. Other points to consider include the identity of the drug to be encapsulated and the route of administration, as both may affect the choice of the method used to produce the nanoparticles (Lassalle and Ferreira, 2007). Both emulsion-based and nanoprecipitation methods appear to be suitable techniques for ketoprofen encapsulation into PLA nanoparticles. Another important parameter for characterization of polymeric nanoparticles is surface charge (i.e., ζ-potential). Polyester-based nanoparticles are expected to have a negative charge due to hydrolyzed groups present on the particle surface (Teixeira et al., 2010). In general, ζ-potential is considered as an index of the nanoparticle physical stability. A higher absolute value of ζ-potential (>30 mV) represents a larger charge on the nanoparticle surface leading to higher stability with more uniform size of dispersed nanoparticles due to the electric repulsion between particles which is observed under most conditions (Vučen et al., 2013). Nevertheless, Vučen et al. showed that the absolute values of ζ-potential less than 30 mV (i.e., -27 mV) resulted in good short-term stability of ketoprofen-loaded PLA nanoparticles at room temperature. The surface charge results reported by Shah et al. (2012b) revealed positive ζ-potential of ketoprofen-loaded PLGA nanoparticles (11.17 mV) due to their cationic chitosan outer coat (free amino groups). However, the PLGA nanoparticles without a chitosan coat had a negative ζ-potential which was in agreement with other studies in the field.

Although the skin penetration depends on particle properties, such as size and surface charge, only a few studies have investigated the size-dependent penetration of polymeric nanoparticles into the skin. Alvarez-Román et al. (2004) studied the skin penetration and distribution of fluorescent-labeled 20- and 200-nm polystyrene nanoparticles through porcine skin and found no particles in the corneocytes or intercorneocyte spaces. Moreover, a size- and time-dependent accumulation of particles was observed in the follicular regions, where 20-nm particles accumulated more than the 200-nm particles. Similar skin penetration behavior was also observed in excised human skin (Vogt et al., 2006). The 40-nm particles were found to perforate deeper in the follicles and also further penetrate into the epidermal Langerhans cells present at the infundibulum of hair follicles. On the other hand, the larger particles (750 and 1500 nm) did not penetrate into the follicles. In this regard, hair follicles can be used as a reservoir for drug delivery to localize the drug to the hair follicles or deliver the drug to the surrounding epidermal cells, as discussed previously (Pathak and Thassu, 2009). This was found through tape-stripping studies in human volunteers by using fluorescent-labeled PLGA nanoparticles (300–400 nm). The nanoparticles were detected in hair follicles even 10 days after application, while the particles on the SC were cleared after 24 h. Nanoparticles were slowly cleared from the hair follicles by sebum secretions, the migration of particles to the nearby cells, and through the lymphatic system (Lademann et al., 2006; Pathak and Thassu, 2009). The surface charge on the polymeric nanoparticles also influences their permeation through the skin. In a comparative study using positive, negative, and neutral latex nanoparticles (50–500 nm), it was found that only the negatively charged nanoparticles were able to penetrate the SC and reach the viable epidermis (Kohli and Alpar, 2004). The higher penetration was attributed to the charge repulsion between the negatively charged skin lipids and the carboxylate groups in the negatively charged nanoparticles (Kohli and Alpar, 2004; Pathak and Thassu, 2009).

The effect of the drug encapsulation process on the thermal properties of the polymer was also investigated by the differential scanning calorimetry (DSC) and the thermogravimetric analysis (TGA) (Vučen et al., 2013). A very slight increase of glass transition temperature (T_g) from 49 to 53°C was observed indicating the structural relaxation of polymer chains as a result of the presence of ketoprofen (Zhou and Xanthos, 2009). Furthermore, TGA analyses revealed a rather similar trend of mass loss. It can be assumed that the drug probably had a minor thermal impact on PLA nanoparticles obtained in their work (Vučen et al., 2013).

Polymer-based nanoparticles offer the advantage of controlled and sustained drug release, enabling the encapsulated drug to be delivered in a controlled manner into the skin layers. However, achieving tailored activated release still represents a hurdle for nanoparticulate drug carriers. The predominant strategies so far incorporate biomaterials that are enzymatically degradable, pH-sensitive, or reductively labile, as well as materials which facilitate bond breaking between drug and carrier or destabilization of the carrier on reaching the intended site of action (Petros and DeSimone, 2010). Methods for quantifying drug release in vitro include the following: diffusion cells with artificial or biological membranes, equilibrium dialysis technique, reverse dialysis sac technique, ultracentrifugation, ultrafiltration, or centrifugal ultrafiltration technique (Soppimath et al., 2001). Diffusion and dialysis techniques have many advantages, such as noninvasive separation, rapid and simple sampling methods. However, it must be noted that the membrane used as a part of these processes can attenuate drug release (Cho et al., 2013). Moreover, in order to maintain a sink condition for drug release, these methods typically employ a large volume of release medium making the drug detection and analyses more difficult due to its low concentration. If separation techniques are used (i.e., filtration, centrifugation, or centrifugal filtration), the released drug is quantified by various analytical techniques. These methods are slow and often employ centrifugal forces or shear stresses which can alter the nanoparticles themselves and affect the resultant release kinetics (Cho et al., 2013). It should also be mentioned that the drug release is affected by particle size (Jahanshahi and Babaei, 2008). Smaller particles possess larger surface areas, thus, most of the drug associated would be at or near the particle surface, leading to fast drug release. While, larger particles have large cores which allow more drug to be encapsulated with slow drug diffusion (Redhead et al., 2001).

There are at least three possible mechanisms for drug release: desorption of the surface bound/adsorbed drug, diffusion from the polymer matrix, and release due to polymer erosion or degradation. In many cases, some of these processes may coexist, which should prove differentiation between the mechanisms complicated however, this is not the case (Jahanshahi and Babaei, 2008). For example, in matrix-type polymer nanoparticles the drug is uniformly distributed in the matrix, so the release occurs by diffusion and/ or erosion of the matrix. Rapid initial burst release is usually attributed to the fraction of the drug adsorbed or weakly bound to the surface of the nanoparticles (Hoffman, 2008). These findings are confirmed by several studies of ketoprofen release form PLA and PLGA nanoparticles (Shah et al., 2012a; Vučen et al., 2013). In both studies initial burst release of ketoprofen from nanoparticles was observed. Shah et al. (2012a) associated this burst ketoprofen release to unentrapped drug available in the nanoparticle dispersion. However, if the existing unentrapped drug is removed during the nanoparticle preparation process, as reported by Vučen et al., rapid initial release could not be attributed to free drug present on the surface of nanoparticles. It is more likely that the high percentage of burst release is due to drug molecules present in the outer layer of PLA nanoparticles (Mello and Ricci-Júnior, 2011). Nevertheless, the encapsulating process employed in these works led to sustained drug release corresponding to approximately 60% rate of ketoprofen release after 7 days (Vučen et al., 2013). Similar results were previously reported by Corrigan and Li (2009) for ketoprofen-loaded PLGA nanoparticles at a mean particle size and encapsulation efficiency around 540 nm and 40%, respectively. Generally, zero order, first order, Korsmeyer–Peppas, Hixson–Crowell, and Higuchi equations are used in determining the release kinetics of polymeric nanoparticles (Costa and Lobo, 2001). Korsmeyer–Peppas kinetics was found to be the most suitable model to describe the release pattern of ketoprofen from PLA and PLGA nanoparticles, demonstrating that the drug was released in a controlled manner by a combination of both diffusion and erosion mechanisms (Shah et al., 2012a; Vučen et al., 2013).

6.3 IN VITRO EVALUATION OF KETOPROFEN-LOADED PLA NANOPARTICLES AS COLLOIDAL SYSTEMS FOR PERCUTANEOUS DRUG DELIVERY

In vitro techniques to assess skin penetration and permeation are extensively used in a developing transdermal and topical drug delivery studies, as well as in a dermal toxicology screening settings (Ehrhardt and Kim, 2007; Ng et al., 2010; Valenta and Almasi-Szabo, 1995; Walters, 2002). Most common methods for evaluation of in vitro skin penetration/permeation use diffusion cells. The experimental conditions can be precisely controlled indicating the skin membrane and the test material as the only variable parameters. However, in vitro techniques provide limited information on the metabolism, distribution, and blood-flow effects on permeation. In order to achieve the best possible in vitro–in vivo correlation, following assumptions need to be applied as well as careful experimental design: the receptor phase is a perfect sink, depletion of the donor phase is negligible, and the skin membrane is homogeneous (Walters, 2002). There are two main types of diffusion cells; static (upright Franz cell or side-by-side type) and flow-through cell. Some general rules apply to both types of diffusion cells, such as that the excised skin is always mounted between a donor and receptor compartment, efficient mixing of receptor phase is crucial and neither of the processes should interfere with the drug diffusion (Gibson, 2009; Ng et al., 2010). Advantages and disadvantages of each cell type are extensively explained in literature (Ehrhardt and Kim, 2007). Standard upright static diffusion cells, such as Franz cells provide a simple, cost effective, and versatile system optimal for simulation in vivo performance and adopted to meet requirements of a wide range of studies. In general, the following parameters are important for designing and performing in vitro skin penetration/permeation studies (Walters, 2002):

- receptor chamber and medium;
- selection and preparation of skin membrane including intra- and intersubject variability, age, sex, and racial differences, storage conditions, anatomical site variation, membrane preparation (i.e., full-thickness vs. dermatomed skin) and skin integrity;
- application method, that is, infinite- and finite-dose techniques;

- permeant dose level; and
- experimental conditions, that is, duration of the experiment, sample interval, number of replicates, temperature, analytical method for permeant analysis.

There are also other in vitro methods used for studying percutaneous drug delivery, such as tape-stripping (Lademann et al., 2009; Escobar-Chavez et al., 2008), attenuated total reflectance—Fourier transform infrared spectroscopy (ATR-FTIR) (Yokomizo, 1996; Ge et al., 2014), confocal laser scanning microscopy (CLSM) (Shah et al., 2012b), Raman confocal spectroscopy (Bernard et al., 2007), isolated perfused tissue methods, artificial skin and model synthetic membranes. Commonly, these techniques are performed along with Franz diffusion cell method. For example, in the work presented by Ge et al. (2014) several different methods were employed to study percutaneous delivery of econazole including diffusion cell, tape striping, ATR-FTIR, and CLSM technique. The tape stripping method is well-suited to determine the dermatopharmacokinetics of topically applied substances. The tape strips contain the amount of corneocytes and the corresponding amount of the penetrated drug, which can be determined by analytical chemical methods (Lademann et al., 2009). The ATR-FTIR technique is used for the investigation of morphological differences between upper and lower layers of the SC in order to predict the interdiffusional path lengths (Walters, 2002). Moreover, both ATR-FTIR and Raman confocal spectroscopy are used for measurement of percutaneous penetration enhancement in vivo (Mak et al., 1990; Bernard et al., 2007).

The skin penetration of polymeric nanoparticles is restricted to the SC, whereas the follicular penetration appears to be the major transport pathway for particles that penetrate deeper in the skin (Pathak and Thassu, 2009).

In order to develop optimized nanoparticle formulation for topical and transdermal application, there is a need to understand the interactions of nanoparticles with the skin as well as their inherent transport mechanisms. Following topical application of nanoparticle formulations, absorption of active compounds can follow a transcellular, intercellular, or transappendageal route (Desai et al., 2010). Depending on their physicochemical properties, nanocarrier systems can penetrate intact into the skin without degradation or alternatively, they can be degraded near the skin surface with the loaded drug penetrating into skin layers. The same physicochemical properties of nanoparticles, such as size, surface charge, properties of nanomaterial used, drug-loading efficiency and mode of application are also responsible for the interaction of nanoparticles with the skin. However, irrespective of nanomaterial used, SC is impenetrable barrier for most nanoparticles and the dominant pathway for their entry into skin is transappendageal route (Desai et al., 2010). The same observation was found for the polyester-based nanoparticles. Stracke et al. (2006) observed that intact PLGA nanoparticles do not permeate the SC using multiphoton laser scanning microscopy. Similar findings were reported by Luengo Contreras (2007), who showed that flufenamic acid-loaded PLGA nanoparticles were unable to permeate into viable skin layers. As discussed previously, PLA nanoparticles can penetrate into 50% of the hair follicles and create high local concentrations of loaded drugs which can further be released into the skin (Rancan et al., 2009). The released dye can diffuse into sebum and penetrate into viable epidermis and dermis (Desai et al., 2010). A recent study on the application of PLGA nanoparticles to the intact skin showed that encapsulated drug was detectable in the recipient compartment after 24 h of exposure (Shah et al., 2012b). However, these nanoparticles were coated with chitosan and their surface was modified with polyethylene glycol (PEG)ylated oleic acid which is known as a potent chemical permeation enhancer (Vučen, 2013).

Another solution for overcoming the skin permeation barrier and enhance the drug penetration through the skin is to combine two or more different skin penetration enhancement approaches, such as microneedle pretreatment and the use of nanoparticulate systems. Vučen et al. investigated the ability of Immu-Patch silicon microneedles to enhance skin permeability of ketoprofen-loaded PLA nanoparticles by in vitro skin permeation studies. This work was based on the study previously designed by McGrath et al. (2014), who showed that ketoprofen-loaded into the structure of dissolvable microneedles prepared from aqueous solution of polyvinyl alcohol (PVA) was successfully released and deposited in ex vivo porcine skin. After 24 h of exposure, significant difference was observed between untreated and ImmuPatch-treated skin, with respect to drug permeation profile (Fig. 6.2). The silicon microneedles created micropores that permit the drug to breach the SC. As a result, an enhanced drug flux was

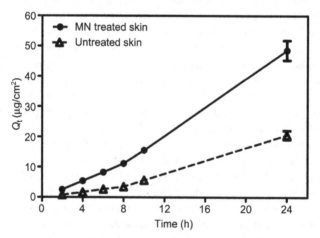

FIGURE 6.2 Cumulative amount (Q_t) of ketoprofen permeated per surface area of microneedle-treated and untreated porcine skin [means ± standard deviation (SD), $n \geq 3$; $P < 0.05$]. MN, Microneedle. (*Reprinted from Vučen SR, Vuleta G, Crean AM, Moore AC, Ignjatović N, Uskoković D: Improved percutaneous delivery of ketoprofen using combined application of nanocarriers and silicon microneedles,* J Pharm Pharmacol *65:1451–1462, 2013, with permission from John Wiley and Sons*)

observed, indicating that ImmuPatch silicon microneedles enabled the biodegradable PLA nanoparticles to supply the skin with drug over a prolonged period of time (Vučen et al., 2013). Hence, nanoparticle delivery via conduits created by microneedles is a more effective approach for delivery to a target site compared with their delivery via passive transport. Finally, when reporting on nanoparticle drug delivery systems, it should also be considered that in most cases, the aim is to exhibit sustained release in the skin and to administer a known amount of "free substance" into the body. In order to reduce the disposition of plasma proteins and the recognition by phagocytes, sterically stabilized carriers could be designed by changing the surface properties of the nanoparticles, or the size of the particle can be adapted to reduce cellular uptake (Nair et al., 2010). Limited penetration of polymeric nanoparticles into the intact skin was attributed to penetration via the open hair follicles, as observed by a number of researches to date (Alvarez-Román et al., 2004; Patlolla et al., 2010; Vučen et al., 2013). However, microneedles enhance the penetration of the applied nanoparticles due to the creation of channels of much higher density compared to that of the hair follicles over the applied area (Zhang et al., 2010).

In summary, PLA can be successfully used to produce dosage forms for topical and transdermal drug delivery owing to its excellent biocompatibility, biodegradability, mechanical strength, heat processability, and solubility in organic solvents (Xiao et al., 2012). As FDA-approved and clinically available material, this polymer has a great potential for sustained release of the drug from nanoparticulate systems. On the other hand, the lack of test results for these delivery systems using animal models or in clinical trials is of fundamental importance for real applications in biomedical therapy.

6.4 CONCLUSIONS

The recent emergence of nanotechnology has offered new opportunities to develop nanosystems for topical and transdermal applications. Uniform ketoprofen-loaded PLA and PLGA nanosized spheres can be successfully prepared with high drug encapsulation efficiency with capability to sustain and control the drug release over time. A major obstacle to topical and transdermal ketoprofen delivery can be overcome by combining different skin penetration enhancement methods. This delivery strategy demonstrates potential for enhanced and controlled delivery of ketoprofen in deeper skin layers. Unique qualities and performance of nanoparticles as drug-delivery systems depend directly on their physicochemical properties. Hence, physicochemical approach is required in order to explain some fundamental attributes that differentiate nanoparticles from conventional drug vehicles (De Villiers et al., 2008). In vitro and in vivo distribution of polymeric nanoparticles is influenced by their various properties, such as the particle size and size distribution, surface morphology, porosity, surface chemistry, surface adhesion, ζ-potential, drug stability, drug-encapsulation efficiency, surface/bulk erosion/degradation, diffusion of the drug and kinetics of drug release. Therefore, these particle characteristics should be used to guide future design efforts. Addressing the challenges of nanoparticulate drug-delivery systems will significantly accelerate their translation from the laboratory to the general public and bring the undoubted promise of the nanorevolution to reality.

REFERENCES

Abdel-Mottaleb MM, Lamprecht A: Polymeric nano (and micro) particles as carriers for enhanced skin penetration. In Dragicevic N, Maibach HI, editors: *Percutaneous penetration enhancers chemical methods in penetration enhancement*, Berlin, Heidelberg, 2016, Springer, pp 187–199.

Alvarez-Román R, Naik A, Kalia Y, Guy RH, Fessi H: Skin penetration and distribution of polymeric nanoparticles, *J Control Release* 99:53–62, 2004.

Bamrungsap S, Zhao Z, Chen T, Wang L, Li C, Fu T, Tan W: Nanotechnology in therapeutics: a focus on nanoparticles as a drug delivery system, *Nanomedicine* 7:1253–1271, 2012.

Banga AK: *Transdermal and intradermal delivery of therapeutic agents: application of physical technologies*, New York, 2011, CRC Press.

Barichello JM, Morishita M, Takayama K, Nagai T: Encapsulation of hydrophilic and lipophilic drugs in PLGA nanoparticles by the nanoprecipitation method, *Drug Dev Ind Pharm* 25:471–476, 1999.

Bernard G, Auger M, Soucy J, Pouliot R: Physical characterization of the stratum corneum of an in vitro psoriatic skin model by ATR-FTIR and Raman spectroscopies, *BBA Gen Subjects* 1770:1317–1323, 2007.

Bernardi A, Braganhol E, Jäger E, Figueiró F, Edelweiss MI, Pohlmann AR, Guterres SS, Battastini AM: Indomethacin-loaded nanocapsules treatment reduces in vivo glioblastoma growth in a rat glioma model, *Cancer Lett* 281:53–63, 2009.

Blume-Peytavi U, Massoudy L, Patzelt A, Lademann J, Dietz E, Rasulev U, Bartels NG: Follicular and percutaneous penetration pathways of topically applied minoxidil foam, *Eur J Pharm Biopharm* 76:450–453, 2010.

Cho EJ, Holback H, Liu KC, Abouelmagd SA, Park J, Yeo Y: Nanoparticle characterization: state of the art, challenges, and emerging technologies, *Mol Pharm* 10:2093–2110, 2013.

Corrigan OI, Li X: Quantifying drug release from PLGA nanoparticulates, *Eur J Pharm Sci* 37:477–485, 2009.

Costa P, Lobo JMS: Modeling and comparison of dissolution profiles, *Eur J Pharm Sci* 13:123–133, 2001.

De Villiers MM, Aramwit P, Kwon GS: *Nanotechnology in drug delivery*, New York, 2008, Springer Science & Business Media.

Del Gaudio P, Russo P, Lauro MR, Colombo P, Aquino RP: Encapsulation of ketoprofen and ketoprofen lysinate by prilling for controlled drug release, *AAPS PharmSciTech* 10:1178–1185, 2009.

Desai P, Patlolla RR, Singh M: Interaction of nanoparticles and cell-penetrating peptides with skin for transdermal drug delivery, *Mol Membr Biol* 27:247–259, 2010.

Dobrovolskaia MA, McNeil SE: Immunological properties of engineered nanomaterials, *Nat Nanotechnol* 2:469–478, 2007.

Ehrhardt C, Kim KJ: *Drug absorption studies: in situ, in vitro and in silico models*, New York, 2007, Springer Science & Business Media.

Escobar-Chavez JJ, Merino-Sanjuán V, López-Cervantes M, Urban-Morlan Z, Pinon-Segundo E, Quintanar-Guerrero D, Ganem-Quintanar A: The tape-stripping technique as a method for drug quantification in skin, *J Pharm Pharm Sci* 11:104–130, 2008.

Ge S, Lin Y, Lu H, Li Q, He J, Chen B, Wu C, Xu Y: Percutaneous delivery of econazole using microemulsion as vehicle: formulation, evaluation and vesicle–skin interaction, *Int J Pharm* 465:120–131, 2014.

Gibson M: *Pharmaceutical preformulation and formulation: a practical guide from candidate drug selection to commercial dosage form*, ed 2, New York, 2009, CRC Press.

Hadgraft J, Du Plessis J, Goosen C: The selection of non-steroidal anti-inflammatory agents for dermal delivery, *Int J Pharm* 207:31–37, 2000.

Halpern S: Topical non-steroidal anti-inflammatory drugs: a review of their use and toxicity, *J Dermatol Treat* 5:103–107, 1994.

Hengge UR, Ruzicka T, Schwartz RA, Cork MJ: Adverse effects of topical glucocorticosteroids, *J Am Acad Dermatol* 54:1–15, 2006.

Heyneman CA, Lawless-Liday C, Wall GC: Oral versus topical NSAIDs in rheumatic diseases, *Drugs* 60:555–574, 2000.

Hoffman AS: The origins and evolution of "controlled" drug delivery systems, *J Control Release* 132:153–163, 2008.

Jahanshahi M, Babaei Z: Protein nanoparticle: a unique system as drug delivery vehicles, *Afr J Biotechnol* 7:4926–4934, 2008.

Kim BS, Won M, Yang Lee KM, Kim CS: In vitro permeation studies of nanoemulsions containing ketoprofen as a model drug, *Drug Deliv* 15:465–469, 2008.

Knorr F, Lademann J, Patzelt A, Sterry W, Blume-Peytavi U, Vogt A: Follicular transport route–research progress and future perspectives, *Eur J Pharm Biopharm* 71:173–180, 2009.

Kohli A, Alpar H: Potential use of nanoparticles for transcutaneous vaccine delivery: effect of particle size and charge, *Int J Pharm* 275:13–17, 2004.

Kumari A, Singla R, Guliani A, Yadav SK: Nanoencapsulation for drug delivery, *EXCLI J* 13:265–286, 2014.

Lademann J, Jacobi U, Surber C, Weigmann H-J, Fluhr J: The tape stripping procedure–evaluation of some critical parameters, *Eur J Pharm Biopharm* 72:317–323, 2009.

Lademann J, Otberg N, Richter H, Weigmann HJ, Lindemann U, Schaefer H, Sterry W: Investigation of follicular penetration of topically applied substances, *Skin Pharmacol Physiol* 14:17–22, 2001.

Lademann J, Richter H, Schaefer U, Blume-Peytavi U, Teichmann A, Otberg N, Sterry W: Hair follicles–a long-term reservoir for drug delivery, *Skin Pharmacol Physiol* 19:232–236, 2006.

Lassalle V, Ferreira ML: PLA nano and microparticles for drug delivery: an overview of the methods of preparation, *Macromol Biosci* 7:767–783, 2007.

Luengo Contreras JE: *Human skin drug delivery using biodegradable plga-nanoparticles*, PhD thesis, 2007. Available from: http://scidok.sulb.unisaarland.de/volltexte/2007/1118/pdf/Luengo_Contreras.pdf

Maestrelli F, Bragagni M, Mura P: Advanced formulations for improving therapies with anti-inflammatory or anaesthetic drugs: a review, *J Drug Deliv Sci Technol* 32:192–205, 2015.

Mak VH, Potts RO, Guy RH: Percutaneous penetration enhancement in vivo measured by attenuated total reflectance infrared spectroscopy, *Pharm Res* 7:835–841, 1990.

McGrath MG, Vucen S, Vrdoljak A, Kelly A, O'Mahony C, Crean AM, Moore A: Production of dissolvable microneedles using an atomised spray process: effect of microneedle composition on skin penetration, *Eur J Pharm Biopharm* 86:200–211, 2014.

Meidan VM: Methods for quantifying intrafollicular drug delivery: a critical appraisal, *Expert Opin Drug Deliv* 7:1095–1108, 2010.

Mello VD, Ricci-Júnior E: Encapsulation of naproxen in nanostructured system: structural characterization and in vitro release studies, *Quim Nova* 34:933–939, 2011.

Naik A, Kalia YN, Guy RH, Fessi H: Enhancement of topical delivery from biodegradable nanoparticles, *Pharm Res* 21:1818–1825, 2004.

Nair HB, Sung B, Yadav VR, Kannappan R, Chaturvedi MM, Aggarwal BB: Delivery of anti-inflammatory nutraceuticals by nanoparticles for the prevention and treatment of cancer, *Biochem Pharmacol* 80:1833–1843, 2010.

Ng S-F, Rouse JJ, Sanderson FD, Meidan V, Eccleston GM: Validation of a static franz diffusion cell system for in vitro permeation studies, *AAPS PharmSciTech* 11:1432–1441, 2010.

Otberg N, Richter H, Schaefer H, Blume-Peytavi U, Sterry W, Lademann J: Variations of hair follicle size and distribution in different body sites, *J Invest Dermatol* 122:14–19, 2004.

Papakostas D, Rancan F, Sterry W, Blume-Peytavi U, Vogt A: Nanoparticles in dermatology, *Arch Dermatol Res* 303:533–550, 2011.

Pathak Y, Thassu D: *Drug delivery nanoparticles formulation and characterization*, New York, 2009, CRC Press.

Patlolla RR, Desai PR, Belay K, Singh MS: Translocation of cell penetrating peptide engrafted nanoparticles across skin layers, *Biomaterials* 31:5598–5607, 2010.

Petros RA, DeSimone JM: Strategies in the design of nanoparticles for therapeutic applications, *Nat Rev Drug Discov* 9:615–627, 2010.

Quintanar-Guerrero D, Fessi H, Allémann E, Doelker E: Influence of stabilizing agents and preparative variables on the formation of poly(D, L-lactic acid) nanoparticles by an emulsification-diffusion technique, *Int J Pharm* 143:133–141, 1996.

Rancan F, Papakostas D, Hadam S, Hackbarth S, Delair T, Primard C, Verrier B, Sterry W, Blume-Peytavi U, Vogt A: Investigation of polylactic acid (PLA) nanoparticles as drug delivery systems for local dermatotherapy, *Pharm Res* 26:2027–2036, 2009.

Redhead H, Davis S, Illum L: Drug delivery in poly(lactide-*co*-glycolide) nanoparticles surface modified with poloxamer 407 and poloxamine 908: in vitro characterisation and in vivo evaluation, *J Control Release* 70:353–363, 2001.

Ricci M, Blasi P, Giovagnoli S, Rossi C, Macchiarulo G, Luca G, Basta G, Calafiore R: Ketoprofen controlled release from composite microcapsules for cell encapsulation: effect on post-transplant acute inflammation, *J Control Release* 107:395–407, 2005.

Roco MC: National nanotechnology initiative-past, present, future. In Goddard WA III, Brenner D, Lyshevski SE, Iafrate GJ, editors: *Handbook on nanoscience, engineering and technology*, ed 2, New York, 2007, CRC Press.

Shah PP, Desai PR, Patel AR, Singh MS: Skin permeating nanogel for the cutaneous co-delivery of two anti-inflammatory drugs, *Biomaterials* 33:1607–1617, 2012a.

Shah PP, Desai PR, Singh M: Effect of oleic acid modified polymeric bilayered nanoparticles on percutaneous delivery of spantide II and ketoprofen, *J Control Release* 158:336–345, 2012b.

Singh R, Lillard JW: Nanoparticle-based targeted drug delivery, *Exp Mol Pathol* 86:215–223, 2009.

Soppimath KS, Aminabhavi TM, Kulkarni AR, Rudzinski WE: Biodegradable polymeric nanoparticles as drug delivery devices, *J Control Release* 70:1–20, 2001.

Stracke F, Weiss B, Lehr CM, König K, Schaefer UF, Schneider M: Multiphoton microscopy for the investigation of dermal penetration of nanoparticle-borne drugs, *J Invest Dermatol* 126:2224–2233, 2006.

Tamariz E, Rios-Ramírez A: Biodegradation of medical purpose polymeric materials and their impact on biocompatibility, Biodegradation-Life of Science. Croatia, 2013, InTech, 1–29.

Teixeira Z, Zanchetta B, Melo BA, Oliveira LL, Santana MH, Paredes-Gamero EJ, Justo GZ, Nader HB, Guterres SS, Durán N: Retinyl palmitate flexible polymeric nanocapsules: characterization and permeation studies, *Colloid Surf B* 81:374–380, 2010.

Thevenot P, Hu W, Tang L: Surface chemistry influence implant biocompatibility, *Curr Top Med Chem* 8:270–280, 2008.

Valenta C, Almasi-Szabo I: In vitro diffusion studies of ketoprofen transdermal therapeutic systems, *Drug Dev Ind Pharm* 21:1799–1805, 1995.

Veerapandian M, Yuna K: The state of the art in biomaterials as nanobiopharmaceuticals, *Dig J Nanomater Biostruct* 4:243–262, 2009.

Vladisavljevic GT: Encapsulation techniques. In Drioli E, Giorno L, editors: *Encyclopedia of membranes*, Heidelberg, 2012, Springer.

Vogt A, Combadiere B, Hadam S, Stieler KM, Lademann J, Schaefer H, Autran B, Sterry W, Blume-Peytavi U: 40 nm, but not 750 or 1,500 nm, nanoparticles enter epidermal cd1a+ cells after transcutaneous application on human skin, *J Invest Dermatol* 126:1316–1322, 2006.

Vučen SR: *Formulation and characterization of dissolvable microneedles for controlled transdermal delivery of ketoprofen encapsulated in polymeric nanoparticles*, Ph.D. thesis, 2013. Available from: http://nardus.mpn.gov.rs/handle/123456789/3140

Vučen SR, Vuleta G, Crean AM, Moore AC, Ignjatović N, Uskoković D: Improved percutaneous delivery of ketoprofen using combined application of nanocarriers and silicon microneedles, *J Pharm Pharmacol* 65:1451–1462, 2013.

Walters KA: *Dermatological and transdermal formulations*, New York, 2002, CRC Press.

Wang YX, Robertson JL, Spillman WB Jr, Claus RO: Effects of the chemical structure and the surface properties of polymeric biomaterials on their biocompatibility, *Pharm Res* 21:1362–1373, 2004.

Xiao L, Wang B, Yang G, Gauthier M: Poly(lactic acid)-based biomaterials: synthesis, modification and applications. In: Ghista DN, editor: *Biomedical science, engineering and technology*, 2012, InTech, pp 247–282. Available from: http://www.intechopen.com/books/biomedicalscience-engineering-and-technology/poly-lactic-acid-based-biomaterials-synthesis-modification-an-dapplications

Yokomizo Y: Effect of phosphatidylcholine on the percutaneous penetration of drugs through the dorsal skin of guinea pigs in vitro; and analysis of the molecular mechanism, using attenuated total reflectance-Fourier transform infrared (ATR-FTIR) spectroscopy, *J Control Release* 42:249–262, 1996.

Zhang W, Gao J, Zhu Q, Zhang M, Ding X, Wang X, Hou X, Fan W, Ding B, Wu X: Penetration and distribution of PLGA nanoparticles in the human skin treated with microneedles, *Int J Pharm* 402:205–212, 2010.

Zhou Q, Xanthos M: Nanosize and microsize clay effects on the kinetics of the thermal degradation of polylactides, *Polym Degrad Stabil* 94:327–338, 2009.

Chapter 7

Natural Surfactants-Based Micro/Nanoemulsion Systems for NSAIDs— Practical Formulation Approach, Physicochemical and Biopharmaceutical Characteristics/Performances

Tanja M. Isailović,* Marija N. Todosijević,* Sanela M. Đorđević, Snežana D. Savić
Department of Pharmaceutical Technology and Cosmetology, Faculty of Pharmacy, University of Belgrade, Belgrade, Serbia

7.1 INTRODUCTION

Over the past decades, the extensive use of prescribed as well as over-the-counter nonsteroidal anti-inflammatory drugs (NSAIDs) associated with a high incidence of serious gastrointestinal adverse events has promoted the development of different topical drug-delivery systems for the treatment of various musculoskeletal disorders (Vaile and Davis, 1998). The use of NSAIDs in the topical formulations may be beneficial not only in reducing the likelihood of a patient experiencing side effects related to systemic therapy, but also in avoiding the first-pass metabolism and drug–drug interactions, maintaining the relatively consistent plasma drug levels for long-term therapy and enhancing patient compliance (McPherson and Cimino, 2013).

Although there are a relatively large number of topical NSAID products in the market, an effective long-term treatment of peripheral pain and soreness is a still unmet medical need (Cevc and Vierl, 2010). Considering that the success of any topical NSAID therapy depends on the drug's ability to penetrate the

---

* The first two authors contributed equally to this work.

Microsized and Nanosized Carriers for NSAIDs. http://dx.doi.org/10.1016/B978-0-12-804017-1.00007-8

179

formidable barrier imposed by skin's outer *stratum corneum* (SC) layer in sufficiently high amount to exert its clinical effect, major research efforts have been focused toward different percutaneous penetration enhancement technologies. Hence, among the strategies reported to overcome the SC barrier properties and to reach therapeutic drug concentrations in the local target tissue or in the systemic circulation, colloidal drug delivery systems based on micro/nanoemulsions have gained increased attention during the last decades. Micro/nanoemulsions represent very attractive carriers, offering the superior advantages over conventional carriers for dermal/transdermal drug delivery, such as immense interfacial area with high solubilization capacity for lipophilic drugs, penetration enhancement through the skin, enhanced bioavailability, and controlled drug release (Lawrence and Rees, 2000; Sainsbury et al., 2014). Although fairly similar ingredients are required to fabricate them (oil phase, aqueous phase, surfactant, and possibly cosurfactant), these are distinctly different types of colloidal dispersions (McClements, 2012). Microemulsions are clear, transparent or translucent, optically isotropic, and thermodynamically stable surfactant-stabilized dispersions of water and oil (Bardhan et al., 2013). On the other hand, the term nanoemulsion is used to refer the thermodynamically unstable colloidal dispersion consisting of oil and water, with one of the liquids being dispersed as small spherical droplets in the other with the aid of surfactant and, most frequently, cosurfactant (McClements, 2012).

Apart from the crucial role in a formation and stability of both micro/nanoemulsions, surfactants can perturb skin barrier function thereby contributing to the penetration enhancing effect of these systems. However, this behavior can be related to the skin irritation (especially in case of microemulsions, which usually contain the high amount of surfactants/cosurfactants), and therefore, a major point of interest in the formulation of these systems is the question of skin tolerability. Most of studies on topical micro/nanoemulsions have been made with conventional polyethoxylated nonionic surfactants (Baspinar et al., 2010; Solans and Garcia-Celma, 1997). Although these molecules generally exhibit satisfying functionality in the stabilization of these systems, they are frequently accompanied by cutaneous adverse reactions which can limit their wide clinical application (Williams and Barry, 2004). As a result, over the past decades, sugar-based natural surfactants, popularly labeled as skin- and environmental-friendly, have emerged as an appropriate alternative for potentially harmful nonionic surfactants in the development of micro/nanoemulsions. In addition to the favorable safety and environmental profiles, these surfactants possess a wide range of desirable physicochemical properties, such as temperature insensitivity, relatively good stability in the presence of electrolytes and in different pH environments, and favorable phase behavior (Savić et al., 2010).

Among the sugar-based surfactants being studied, there has been increasing interest in exploiting the sucrose fatty acid esters (commonly abbreviated as sucrose esters, SEs), since it was shown that apart from the high ecological acceptability, low toxicity, biocompatibility, and biodegradability, they show the potential for skin penetration enhancement (Csóka et al., 2007; Savić et al., 2010). In this context, the present chapter aims to provide an overview of the application of SEs in the formulation development of biocompatible micro/nanoemulsions intended for topical administration of NSAIDs (Table 7.1), as well as their impact on percutaneous penetration of NSAIDs from these systems.

7.2 SUCROSE ESTER–BASED MICROEMULSIONS: PHASE BEHAVIOR, PHYSICOCHEMICAL CHARACTERIZATION, AND IMAGING PROPERTIES

Microemulsions are colloidal systems that are currently of pharmaceutical interest as promising vehicles for deep dermal and transdermal drug delivery (Naoui et al., 2011; Sahle et al., 2012). Immense interfacial area with high solubilization capacity, penetration enhancement through the skin, high stability, and ease of preparation are all key benefits of microemulsions over traditional formulation approaches (Bardhan et al., 2013; Changez et al., 2006; Lawrence and Rees, 2000; Sahle et al., 2012). Microemulsions, which are isotropic and macroscopically monophasic mixtures of water, surfactant, cosolvent/cosurfactant, and oil, may show various microstructures depending on the amount, nature and the ratio of components, spontaneous curvature, and flexibility of the surfactant film (Bolzinger-Thevenin et al., 1999; Podlogar et al., 2005). Hence, they can be characterized as water in oil (W/O)—water globules are dispersed in an oil phase, oil in water (O/W)—oil globules are dispersed in a water phase, or bicontinuous systems, where domains of water and oil coexist together, as illustrated in Fig. 7.1. For the purpose of potential pharmaceutical application of these colloidal systems, it is important to fully investigate their structure as it might have deep influence on the solubilization, release of a drug, as well as on the percutaneous drug penetration (Fanun, 2009a; Fanun et al., 2011; Podlogar et al., 2004). Despite the easy preparation, microemulsion characterization is a difficult task as it requires a multitechnique approach, which includes combination of several different direct and indirect techniques. Therefore, in order to understand relation between the composition and microstructure of these systems a group of various experimental techniques have been successfully used, including measurement of electrical conductivity (Alany et al., 2001; Chakraborty and Moulik, 2005; Fanun, 2007a,b, 2008b, 2009b, 2010a,b,c; Fanun and Al-Diyn, 2006; Fanun et al., 2011; Feldman et al., 1995; Mehta et al., 1994; Todosijević et al., 2014), viscosity measurements (Alany et al., 2001; Fanun, 2007b, 2008b, 2009b, 2010a,b; Mehta et al., 1994; Todosijević et al., 2014), differential scanning calorimetry (Garti et al., 1996, 2000; Todosijević et al., 2014; Yaghmur et al., 2002), electron paramagnetic resonance (Fanun et al., 2011; Kristl et al., 2003), dynamic light scattering (Fanun, 2009b, 2010a,c; Fanun et al., 2011; Glatter et al., 2001; Shukla and Neubert, 2006), nuclear magnetic resonance spectroscopy (Fanun, 2007a,b, 2010a; Fanun and Al-Diyn, 2006;

TABLE 7.1 Overview of the Sucrose Ester-Based Micro/Nanoemulsions as Vehicles for Dermal/Transdermal Delivery of NSAIDs

Composition of the system	Sucrose ester	Colloidal carrier system	NSAID	References
Medium chain alcohol/sucrose ester–octyl octanoate/water	Sucrose monolaurate + sucrose dilaurate	Microemulsion	Niflumic acid	Bolzinger et al. (1998)
Isopropyl myristate/sucrose ester–ethoxylated mono-di-glyceride/water	Sucrose laurate L-1695	Microemulsion	Sodium diclofenac	Fanun (2007b)
Isopropyl myristate + ethanol/sucrose ester–ethoxylated mono-di-glyceride/water	Sucrose laurate L-1695	Microemulsion	Sodium diclofenac	Fanun (2007b, 2009a, 2010d)
R(+)-limonene + ethanol/sucrose ester–ethoxylated mono-di-glyceride/water	Sucrose laurate L-1695	Microemulsion	Sodium diclofenac	Fanun (2009a, 2010d)
R(+)-limonene/sucrose ester–ethoxylated mono-di-glyceride/water	Sucrose laurate L-1695	Microemulsion	Sodium diclofenac	Fanun (2010d)
PCL-liquid/sucrose ester/water–potassium sorbate	Sucrose stearate S-970	Nanoemulsion	Flufenamic acid	Klang et al. (2011a,b)
PCL-liquid/sucrose ester/water–potassium sorbate	Sucrose stearate S-970	Nanoemulsion	Diclofenac acid	Klang et al. (2011b)
Isopropyl myristate/sucrose ester–isopropyl alcohol/water	Sucrose laurate L-1695	Microemulsion	Flufenamic acid	Schwarz et al. (2012)
Isopropyl myristate/sucrose ester–soybean lecithin–isopropyl alcohol/water	Sucrose laurate L-1695	Microemulsion	Flufenamic acid	Schwarz et al. (2012)
Isopropyl myristate/sucrose ester–isopropyl alcohol/water	Sucrose laurate D-1214/ Sucrose myristate C-1416	Microemulsion	Aceclofenac	Todosijević et al. (2014, 2015)
Medium chain triglycerides–castor oil–butylhydroxytoluene/egg lecithin–sucrose ester/water	Sucrose palmitate P-1670 –/+ sucrose stearate S-970	Nanoemulsion	Aceclofenac	Isailović et al. (2016)

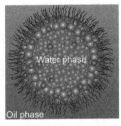
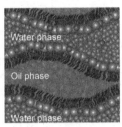
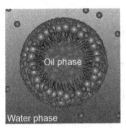

Suggested cross-section of water droplet   Suggested structure of bicontinuous   Suggested cross-section of oil droplet
in W/O microemulsions   microemulsions   in O/W microemulsions

FIGURE 7.1 Schematic representation of different types of microemulsions composed of iso-propyl myristate/sucrose ester–isopropyl alcohol/water.

Fanun et al., 2001; Söderman and Nyden, 1999), small-angle X-ray scattering (Fanun, 2008b, 2009b, 2010a,b,c; Fanun et al., 2001; Glatter et al., 2001), etc.

7.2.1 Phase Behavior of Sucrose Ester–Based Systems

Interfacial tension between otherwise immiscible oil and water phases in microemulsions is reduced to a very low value by the presence of amphiphile(s). Among nonionic tensides, SEs are currently of high interest in microemulsion formulation due to low skin sensitization potential, skin penetration enhancement, and high environmental compatibility, as potential advantages over conventionally used synthetic ethoxylated surfactants, such as polysorbates (Ayala-Bravo et al., 2003; Schwarz et al., 2012; Szűts and Szabó-Révész, 2012; Tadros, 2005). Namely, SEs are nonionic surfactants that have some unique properties—without addition of cosurfactant they cannot reduce the interfacial tension to the required low values, as necessary for the spontaneous formation of microemulsions (Glatter et al., 2001; Thevenin et al., 1996), and SEs do not significantly change their hydrophilic–lipophilic balance (HLB) value with increasing temperature (Glatter et al., 2001). Hence, the SE-based microemulsions are at least four-component systems, whereby interfacial film consists of surfactant(s) and cosurfactant(s), whereas the weak temperature dependence of the head group hydration makes adjustment of the spontaneous curvature of the surfactant film by changing the temperature difficult (Fanun, 2008a,c). However, as opposed to sucrose laurate– and sucrose myristate–based systems (Fanun, 2008a, 2010c), microemulsions formulated with SEs with a longer chain length (SE with palmitic and stearic acid) were found to be temperature sensitive in the range of 25–45°C (Fanun, 2008a). Particularly, the observed increase of the total monophasic area in pseudoternary phase diagrams was related to a disordering temperature effect on liquid crystals, structures which are closely related to microemulsions regarding the type and ratio of components. Namely, thermal motion of surfactant may be responsible for an increase of the monophasic area by destabilization of liquid crystals in favor of an isotropic phase (Fanun, 2008a). In addition, the spontaneous formation and phase behavior of SE-based microemulsions is governed by factors which should be carefully considered such as (1) chain length and monoester content of the SEs, (2) nature and concentration of the oil, cosolvent/cosurfactant, and aqueous phase, (3) SE/cosurfactant and oil/surfactant blend weight ratio, and (4) physicochemical characteristics of drug.

7.2.1.1 Effect of the Tail Length of SEs

Thevenin et al. (1996) highlighted that small differences in the structure of the hydrophobic part of SEs may lead to a significant change in layer curvature and hence in the amount of solubilized water. Since then, the investigation of a tail length effect on the SEs phase behavior has become a topic of a large number of studies. Fanun (2008c) demonstrated that the chain length directly affects the packing of surfactant (sucrose laurate L-1695, sucrose myristate M-1695, sucrose palmitate P-1670, sucrose oleate O-1570, and sucrose stearate S-1570) in the droplets, having a direct influence on the aggregation number, the core radius, and thereby on the interfacial area per surfactant molecule. Additionally, Todosijević et al. (2014) investigated the effect of the chain length of three SEs: sucrose laurate D-1216, sucrose myristate C-1416, and sucrose palmitate D-1616, on phase behavior of a microemulsion system isopropyl myristate/SE–isopropyl alcohol/water, keeping the SE–isopropyl alcohol weight ratio (K_m ratio) constant (Fig. 7.2). Considering the same HLB value and monoester content of the selected SEs as well as the same type of other components in the system, an evident difference among the presented phase diagrams was a proof that chemical structure of surfactant and consequently chain stiffness profoundly affected the phase behavior of the investigated system. In case of sucrose palmitate, the monophasic region existed in an extremely narrow area, while the observed water solubilization capacity in the presence of sucrose laurate and myristate was much higher. This noticeable increase of microemulsion area in the case of sucrose laurate and sucrose myristate may be ascribed to the formation of an interfacial film that is less sensitive to water dilution, when compared to a rigid surfactant film made of sucrose palmitate. A long chain sucrose palmitate limits the flexibility of the interfacial film, and hence a surfactant with shorter lipophilic tail is able to bind more water. This might suggest that increasing carbon number of the chain leads to the disruption of the packing of the surfactant molecules at the oil–water interface. Therefore, this study confirmed that an emulsion capacity of the SEs decreases as the hydrocarbon chain length increases. Moreover, the same study highlighted the importance of the oil structure and chain length compatibility between surfactant and oil molecules—the highest water solubilization capacity was observed in the case of the system containing sucrose myristate, as surfactant, when isopropyl myristate was used as oil phase. Indeed, these results were in line with the fact that tendency of oil molecules to penetrate in the interfacial film may significantly

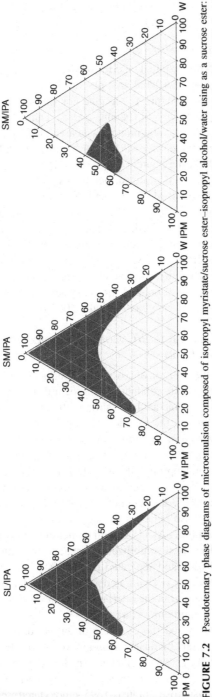

FIGURE 7.2 Pseudoternary phase diagrams of microemulsion composed of isopropyl myristate/sucrose ester–isopropyl alcohol/water using as a sucrose ester: sucrose laurate, sucrose myristate, and sucrose palmitate, respectively, at K_m ratio 1:1. *(Todosijević MN, Cekić ND, Savić MM, Gašperlin M, Ranđelović DV, Savić SD: Sucrose ester-based biocompatible microemulsions as vehicles for aceclofenac as a model drug: formulation approach using D-optimal mixture design, Colloid Polym Sci 292:3064, 2014, with permission of Springer)*

affect the surfactant layer curvature, influencing the total microemulsion area (Fanun, 2008c; Mehta et al., 2009).

7.2.1.2 Effect of Monoester Content of SEs

Variation in the monoester content of SEs with a given chain length, causes a significant effect on the interfacial area per surfactant head group, and consequently on the phase behavior, as reported for the system benzaldehyde–ethanol/SE/water–propylene glycol (Fanun, 2008a). Due to the known impact of surfactant tail length on the total monophasic area, the comparison was done independently between three sucrose laurate samples (L-595, L-1695, and SM-1200), with the monoester content of 30, 80, and 95%, respectively, and between three selected sucrose stearate surfactants (S-770, S-1170, and S-1570), having the monoester content of 30, 50, and 70%, respectively. The increase in the monoester content caused the expansion in the total area of the one-phase microemulsion region. Indeed, surfactants with high monoester content are more hydrophilic, and hence, solubilize more water when compared to less hydrophilic surfactants. Interestingly, this behavior was independent on the surfactant chain length, and also irrespective of the choice of oil phase, taking into account the same conclusions obtained for the system peppermint oil–ethanol/sucrose laurate/water–propylene glycol (Fanun, 2009b).

7.2.1.3 Effect of Cosurfactant/Cosolvent Choice and Surfactant/Cosurfactant Weight Ratio

As already mentioned, the addition of cosolvent/cosurfactant to SE-based system is necessary in order to obtain satisfactory microemulsion area. Moreover, the nature of the cosolvent/cosurfactant has a strong influence on the size and shape of the microemulsion area in the pseudoternary phase diagrams. The addition of cosurfactant improves the microemulsion stability by increasing the fluidity as well as by disordering effect on the surfactant film. Moreover, the addition of cosolvent (i.e., ethanol, isopropyl alcohol, etc.) suppresses the occurrence of liquid crystalline phases, having a significant effect on the size of microemulsion droplets (Fanun, 2009b). Thevenin et al. (1996) investigated the influence of alcohol type on the phase behavior of sucrose oleate–based system, using cetearyl octanoate as oil phase. Alcohols with higher molecular weights, such as pentanol or hexanol, decreased solubilization capacity for water, whereas heptanol and octanol decreased and separated monophasic area into two separate zones. On the other hand, short chain alcohols such as ethanol, propanol, and isopropanol increased disorder in the interfacial film, leading to the formation of a large one-phase single microemulsion region.

Fanun (2009e) investigated the effect of different surfactant–cosurfactant weight ratios in the surfactant blend consisting of SE, as a surfactant, and ethoxylated mono-di-glyceride, as a cosurfactant. In the same work, authors also investigated influence of cosolvent (ethanol) addition on the phase behavior of the same system oil phase/sucrose laurate L-1695–ethoxylated mono-di-glyceride/

water. It was observed that addition of ethoxylated cosurfactant to SE, as well as addition of ethanol to the oil phase [R(+)-limonene or isopropyl myristate] significantly expanded the total microemulsion area, which can be explained as a consequence of the changes in the spontaneous film curvature and fluidity of the surfactant film. Indeed, short chain alcohols increased the flexibility of the interfacial film, whereas the addition of ethoxylated mono-di-glyceride enhanced a partitioning of SE molecules at the water–oil interface. Moreover, the addition of cosurfactant to the ternary system is supposed to enhance the mutual solubilization of surfactant blend in both oil and water, resulting in the expansion of total monophasic area (Fanun, 2007b, 2008b, 2009e). Likewise, the addition of ethoxylated-mono-di-glyceride significantly enhanced the formation of the one-phase microemulsion region in the systems peppermint oil–isopropyl myristate/sucrose laurate–ethoxylated mono-di-glyceride/water (Fanun, 2009c), R(+)-limonene-isopropyl myristate/sucrose laurate/ethoxylated mono-di-glyceride/water (Fanun, 2009d), peppermint oil–ethanol/sucrose laurate–ethoxylated mono-di-glyceride/water (Fanun, 2010a), and R(+)-limonene/sucrose laurate–ethoxylated mono-di-glyceride/water-propylene glycol (Fanun, 2010c), reaching the maximum value at the equal amounts of ethoxylated-mono-di-glyceride and sucrose laurate in the surfactant blend (when surfactant–cosurfactant weight ratio equals unity). By further increase in the amount of ethoxylated-mono-di-glyceride the total one-phase area decreased. Indeed, in all systems a synergism in nonionic amphiphile mixtures enhanced the partitioning of surfactant molecules at the interface allowing larger interfacial area. When the mixture of nonionic amphiphiles was composed of an equal amount of surfactant and cosurfactant, the synergistic effect was found to be more pronounced. Therefore, the optimum amphiphiles arrangement at the interface led to an increase in stability of the interfacial film and consequently improved solubilization of water, as discussed elsewhere (Fanun, 2008b, 2009c,e, 2010a).

7.2.1.4   Effect of HLB Values of SE

In order to explore the influence of HLB values of SEs, Bolzinger-Thevenin et al. (1999) used the mixtures of two SEs—sucrose monolaurate and dilaurate, in the ratios corresponding to HLB values of 5, 7, 9, 11, 13, and 16. Cetyl 2-(hexylethyl)-2-hexanoate was used as an oil phase and diethyleneglycol monoethyl ether as a cosurfactant (surfactant–cosurfactant weight ratio was kept constant). It is well known that mixture of nonionic amphiphiles is more beneficial due to decrease in the surfactant monomer concentrations, they are not susceptible to precipitate, and the mixture provides an additional degree of freedom, enabling the adjustment of phase behavior (Fanun, 2008b). The use of two SEs resulted in the improved microemulsion area in comparison to the phase diagrams constructed using each surfactant alone, reaching optimal monophasic region at sucrose dilaurate:sucrose monolaurate weight ratio 82:18 (investigated sucrose dilaurate:sucrose monolaurate weight ratio were 100:0, 82:18, 64:36, 46:54, 28:72, and 0:100). Indeed, an increase in the HLB value of the surfactant mixture, leads to a shift of microemulsion monophasic area from the water-rich region over center, toward the oil-rich part of the phase diagram (Bolzinger-Thevenin et al., 1999).

7.2.2 Physicochemical Properties of Sucrose Ester–Based Microemulsions

Microemulsions are macroscopically homogenous systems, however, they are structured microscopically (Mehta and Kaur, 2011). In fact, knowing microemulsion macroscopic phase behavior makes possible the indirect investigation of the corresponding microstructures. Conductivity and viscosity, as well as thermal behavior are structure-sensitive properties, and differences in such transport and thermal physicochemical parameters, can be used for detection of microemulsion inner structures.

7.2.2.1 Electrical Conductivity

In the case of nonionic microemulsions, the substitution of the water with dilute aqueous solution of electrolyte may be necessary for electrical conduction, as nonionic surfactants do not provide charges to be easily transported through clusters and water channels (Fanun, 2007a,b, 2008b, 2009b,c, 2010a,c; Todosijević et al., 2014). However, the addition of electrolyte may cause variation in the internal microstructure of different regions of the phase diagram (Fanun 2008a; Podlogar et al., 2004). Although SEs are nonionic surfactants, the presence of impurities may contribute to the electrical conductance of the systems, and in some SE-based systems, measurements were performed without addition of aqueous electrolyte (Fanun, 2010b; Fanun et al., 2011).

Conductivity measurements are especially sensitive to the variations in water content in the system (Mehta and Kaur, 2011). For this reason, the investigation of relation between water volume fraction (ϕ_w) and electrical conductivity (σ) is the topic of a large number of researches focusing on structure investigation of SE-based microemulsions (Fanun, 2007a,b, 2008a,b, 2009b,c, 2010a,b,c; Fanun and Al-Diyn, 2006; Todosijević et al., 2014). The existence of three different slopes in the plot of σ versus ϕ_w is usually associated with three regions that differ in the inner microstructure. Practically negligible σ values obtained for systems with low ϕ_w indicate dispersions of noninteracted water droplets dispersed in nonconducting oil phase (W/O microemulsion) and separated by an interfacial monolayer that prevents water from conducting (Alany et al., 2001; Bardhan et al., 2013; Bhattachary et al., 1985; Fisher et al., 2013; Mehta et al., 1994). Initial increase of σ occurs perhaps due to the progressive hydration of the hydrophilic head group of SEs. With increasing ϕ_w, attraction among water droplets becomes stronger, leading to their collision, further leading to the formation of clusters and water channels which are responsible for a sharp linear enhancement of conductivity (Bardhan et al., 2013; Chakraborty and Moulik, 2005; Podlogar et al., 2004). In fact, σ increases slightly up to critical ϕ_w known as percolation threshold volume fraction (ϕ_p), followed by steep increase due to partial water drift to the outer phase and therefore transition from an oil-continuous to bicontinuous microemulsions (Alany et al., 2001; Bardhan et al. 2013; Chakraborty and Moulik, 2005; Fanun et al., 2011; Feldman et al., 1995). This behavior might be best discussed with the aid of the percolation theory, which assumes that the interactions between water globules and their clustering play a crucial rule (Bardhan et al. 2013; Bhattachary et al., 1985; Chakraborty and Moulik, 2005; Mehta et al., 1994). In most cases, the percolation theory was recommended for the explanation of this phenomenon; however, the mechanism leading to the percolation is controversial. Static model attributes percolation to the appearance of bicontinuous structure, that is, connected water paths responsible for an electrical conduction. On the other hand, dynamic percolation model considers the attractive interaction between water droplets as responsible for the formation of dynamic clusters, which are mobile and also rearrange in time due to the Brownian motion. In this model, water channels are formed after breaking down of the surfactant monolayer during collision or through droplets merging (Bhattachary et al., 1985; Feldman et al., 1995; Mehta and Kaur, 2011).

Power scaling approach was used to explain variations in conductivity profiles in SE-based systems (Fanun, 2008b, 2009b,c,e, 2010a). Two separate asymptotic scaling power laws can be used for interpretation of these changes, as given in the following:.

$$\sigma = A(\Phi_p - \Phi_w)^{-s}; (\Phi_w < \Phi_p) \tag{7.1}$$

$$\sigma = B(\Phi_w - \Phi_p)^t; (\Phi_p < \Phi_w) \tag{7.2}$$

In the Eqs. (7.1) and (7.2) A and B are free parameters, while s and t are constants, which depend on the dimensionality of the percolating system (i.e., number of variables) and does not depend on the details of the geometric structures or interactions (Alany et al., 2001; Mehta et al., 1994; Song et al., 1986). Indeed, when the value of s is smaller than 1 the percolation regime is classified as a static, while the value greater than 1 indicates dynamic percolation regime (Fanun, 2009e; Mehta et al., 2009). When ϕ_w is greater than ϕ_p, σ obeys Eq. (7.2). The plot of $\sigma^{1/t}$ versus ϕ_w must behave linearly, and ϕ_p can be estimated by arbitrarily selecting values for t within the specified range until a linear relationship is found (Alany et al., 2001). Alternatively, the first derivative $d\log(\sigma)/d\phi_w$ as a function of ϕ_w is sharply peaked, and was successfully used for estimation of ϕ_p, due to a distinct difference in the curve above and below the percolation threshold (Fanun, 2008a; Todosijević et al., 2014). Namely, the maximum of curve $d\log(\sigma)/d\phi_w$ versus ϕ_w confirms the presence of percolative behavior and coincides well with the percolation threshold (Fanun, 2008a,b, 2009e; Todosijević et al., 2014).

Conductivity behavior of the system isopropyl myristate/SE–isopropyl alcohol/water, using sucrose laurate D-1216 and sucrose myristate C-1416 as surfactants, was described in our work (Todosijević et al., 2014). After solubilization of aceclofenac in the microemulsions with ϕ_w of 35%, the σ increased only slightly in comparison to the drug-free formulations, indicating the absence of significant influence of drug on the inner structure, suggesting that aceclofenac persisted mostly in its unionized form (Todosijević et al., 2015).

On the other hand, Fanun (2010d) showed that addition of diclofenac to microemulsions increases the σ of the systems compared to the unloaded microemulsions, whereas the rate of changes varies depending on the water amount. When the water content in the system is low, the effect of drug solubilization on the σ is small. However, with increasing water content, the effect becomes more pronounced, implying stronger electrical conductivity effects that are derived from the drug. Actually, the first structural transition from the W/O to the bicontinuous microemulsions was not strongly affected after drug addition, whereas it affected the curvature of the bicontinuous domains, postponing their transition into O/W systems.

7.2.2.2 Viscosity

In concordance with conductivity profiles of SE-based microemulsions, viscosity values (η) strongly depend on ϕ_w (Fanun, 2007b, 2008a,b, 2009b,c,e, 2010b; Todosijević et al., 2014). The changes in η with increase in ϕ_w can also be ascribed to the structural changes and consequently the occurrence of microemulsion phase inversion. Like σ, viscosity may also follow scaling type equations:

$$\eta = A(\Phi_p - \Phi_w)^{-s}; (\Phi_w < \Phi_p) \tag{7.3}$$

$$\eta = B(\Phi_w - \Phi_p)^{-\mu}; (\Phi_p < \Phi_w) \tag{7.4}$$

where A and B are free variables, and μ and s are scaling exponents. It was proven that these values are similar to the values of the exponents t and s obtained for conductivity percolation (Fanun, 2008b, 2009b,e).

The viscosity plots for some SE-based microemulsions have curves usually called bell-shaped. In this case (Fanun, 2009c, 2010a), transition from W/O to bicontinuous microemulsions is associated with a drastic increase in η values. The attractive interaction and aggregation of droplets lead to the formation of water clusters causing an increase in η values. The sharp decrease in dynamic viscosity for microemulsions with high water contents can be ascribed to the structural transition into O/W microemulsions, where the water, as the lowest viscous component, is the continuous phase. On the other hand, in the case of isopropyl myristate/SE-isopropyl alcohol/water system, a different trend in the viscosity plots is observed (Todosijević et al., 2014), whereas the same trend was noted for the systems benzaldehyde–ethanol/SE/water–propylene glycol (Fanun, 2008a) and peppermint oil–ethanol/SE/water–propylene glycol–sodium chloride (Fanun, 2009b). In these systems, depending on the composition, η values decrease as water content in microemulsions increases.

First addition of water to the mixture of oil phase/surfactant blend caused sharp decrease in η, perhaps because of dilution of continuous phase which led to the weakening of interaction and the reduction of micellar aggregation phenomena. After that, slight decrease in η suggested transition from oil-continuous to water-continuous passing through intermediate bicontinuous phase. Again, with high water content relatively low values of η were observed, indicating an occurrence of individual spherical droplets of inner oil phase dispersed in the continuous water phase with lower viscosity.

7.2.2.3 Thermal Behavior

Determination of the state of water in SE-based colloidal carrier systems can be of great importance for their characterization, since water molecules are highly sensitive to the presence of adjacent interfaces which may alter thermodynamic properties of water (Garti et al., 1996). Thus, freezing temperature, as well as respective enthalpies, obtained by exploring position and size of the peaks on DSC cooling curves can serve as a useful tool in the differentiation of bulk (free) and bound (interfacial) water. It should be noted that bound water represents strongly bound water molecules to the surfactant head groups, whereas bulk water is weakly bound and has properties not much different than water itself (Garti et al., 1996, 2000; Yaghmur et al., 2002). Indeed, with stronger interactions of water molecules with other components, freezing temperatures of water shift toward the lower values (Podlogar et al., 2005). Thermal behavior of SE-based microemulsions was firstly investigated by Garti et al. (2000). Our group has made a detailed study on the investigation of thermal behavior of the system isopropyl myristate/SE–isopropyl alcohol/water, using sucrose laurate D-1216 and sucrose myristate C-1416 (Todosijević et al., 2014). For samples with low water content (below 20%) it was evident that water molecules interact strongly with sucrose head groups of SEs via hydrogen bonds. In addition, we assumed that isopropyl alcohol competitively forms hydrogen bonds with water. Both interactions alter thermodynamic properties of water, leading to its freezing point decrease to very low temperatures, indicating nonfreezable water dispersed in the oil-continuous phase. In the curves of samples which contain at least 20% water, a broad peak appeared, whereas the low freezing temperatures (between −60°C and −30°C) indicated bound water in the systems. The increase in water content in microemulsions leads to weakening of the interactions, resulting in a higher area under the peak with freezing point at higher temperatures. Additionally, the plots of temperature at which freezing of water phase occurs at different ϕ_w suggest the same freezing pattern, for both SEs, in spite of the appreciable scattering of the data (Fig. 7.3). In fact, with gradual addition of water, concentration of isopropyl alcohol and SEs decreases, thus water molecules become progressively less bound, as it is also reflected by increasing freezing temperature. Further addition of water causes saturation in hydration of surfactant head groups and isopropyl alcohol, leading to an appearance of sharp peak on DSC cooling curves, indicating freezing of bulk

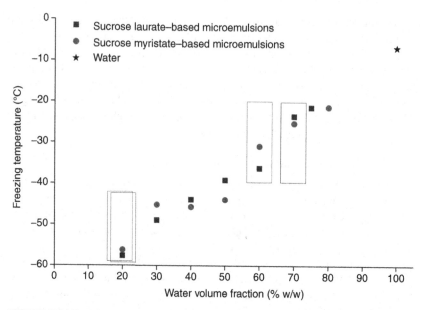

FIGURE 7.3 Freezing temperature of water versus water volume fraction for microemulsions with increasing amount of water at surfactant blend/oil weight ratio 9/1 composed of isopropyl myristate/sucrose ester–isopropyl alcohol/water, using as a sucrose ester: sucrose laurate and sucrose myristate. The *squares* indicate points of phase inversion.

water. Isopropyl alcohol (either in continuous phase or incorporated into the interfacial layer) along with surfactant head groups (which are exposed to water continuous phase) bind some of the water molecules, causing slight deviation in the water freezing behavior. Therefore, the large, sharp peak of loosely bound water indicates water drift to the outer phase, as inversion from bicontinuous to O/W microemulsion occurs.

7.2.3 Imaging Properties of Sucrose Ester–Based Microemulsions

One of the major tasks in characterization of colloidal carrier systems is to provide a direct confirmation of the phase inversion, which occurs from W/O to O/W via bicontinuous microemulsions, which are microstructurally disordered but optically isotropic systems. Additionally, it is of a great importance to prove that solubilization of a drug in the microemulsion does not significantly change the colloidal structure of the system, as might be expected due to its effect on the surfactant film and hence on the interaction between surfactant and other components (Liu and Chang, 2011). Several microscopic techniques have been successfully used as direct examination methods for the demonstration of the inner structure of SE-based microemulsions and for the assessment of alteration in the colloidal structure after incorporation of NSAIDs.

7.2.3.1   Cryo-Transmission Electron Microscopy

Fanun (2009e, 2010a) used cryo-transmission electron microscopy (Cryo-TEM) for imaging the structures of microemulsion samples along selected water dilution line in the phase diagrams of the systems R(+)-limonene/sucrose laurate–ethoxylated mono-di-glyceride/water and peppermint oil–ethanol/ sucrose laurate–ethoxylated mono-di-glyceride/water. However, author reported some difficulties in obtaining clear images for concentrated samples with low water content in both systems. On the other hand, the images for diluted samples with high water content revealed the presence of spheroidal droplets of up to 10 nm diameter.

7.2.3.2   Freeze Fracture–Transmission Electron Microscopy

Freeze fracture–transmission electron microscopy (FF-TEM) technique was successfully employed as an effective tool to reveal the microemulsion morphological diversity in SE-based systems (Bolzinger et al. 1998). This technique allowed a detection of intertwined domains of water and oil in bicontinuous structure of blank SE-based microemulsions. In the same work Bolzinger et al. (1998) confirmed the absence of structural changes in irregular bicontinuous structure after incorporation of niflumic acid, using the same microscopic technique.

In another work of the same research group (Bolzinger-Thevenin et al., 1999), FF-TEM allowed observation of a specific bicontinuous structure of selected microemulsion. It should be noted that authors verified that differentiation between water and oil domains was not possible with the selected shadow material. Moreover, some microemulsion samples could not have been easily classified and their type could not have been determined based on the obtained micrographs.

7.2.3.3   Atomic Force Microscopy

Transmission electron microscopy (TEM) is a valuable tool in visualization of inner microemulsion structuration, however, besides the mentioned problem (Bolzinger-Thevenin et al., 1999), several more drawbacks of this technique have been reported which might interfere with microemulsion characterization. By employing atomic force microscopy (AFM), some of the artifacts and disadvantages, such as ice contamination, phase separation, and structural transition, might be avoided (Alany et al., 2001; Klang et al., 2012a, 2013; Krauel et al., 2007). This was proven in the work of Todosijević et al. (2014, 2015) and Fanun et al. (2010a,b), where intermittent contact AFM mode, also known as tapping mode, was used to investigate the structure and to detect a type of SE-based microemulsions.

Bearing in mind that sample preparation can potentially introduce artifacts, AFM images of the microemulsions after vacuum drying and drying in desiccator were compared. No significant dissimilarities between the two sets of images were obtained (Todosijević et al., 2014). In our work (Todosijević et al., 2014), AFM was successfully used as a microscopic technique for determination of the inner structure of isopropyl myristate/sucrose laurate–isopropyl alcohol/water system, including the differentiation between bicontinuous and droplet-like structures. As shown in Fig. 7.4, we have proven that this technique allows direct visualization of the W/O (FL10), O/W (FL70) as well as bicontinuous structure (FL40) of sucrose laurate–based microemulsions. In case of W/O microemulsion, isolated globular structures were observed, whereas the structure of bicontinuous microemulsion was evidently different from the ones noted for droplet microemulsions. This micrograph showed characteristic intertwined domains of oil and water, giving the same information about inner structuration of those samples as FF-TEM. Regarding the globular type of microemulsions, average diameter of droplets was successfully calculated. All these results were convincing proof that AFM yields direct imaging of the structural system transition from oil-continuous over bicontinuous to water-continuous. The same technique was also used to investigate potential changes in the inner structure of microemulsion after incorporation of aceclofenac (Todosijević et al., 2015). Addition of aceclofenac did not have a significant influence on the vehicle's nanostructure, as can be seen in the atomic force micrographs in which water clusters and channels, which coexist together with oil domains, could be observed.

On the other hand, in the work of Fanun et al. (2010a,b), micrographs were obtained in tapping mode in air in order to avoid deformation of the microemulsions. Again, the use of AFM-enabled direct visualization of the inner structure of samples along selected dilution line in the system isopropyl myristate–ethanol/sucrose laurate–ethoxylated mono-di-glyceride/water. Finally, comparing those results we can conclude that the sample preparation set does not introduce major artifacts, when AFM is used to detect inner structure of SE-based microemulsions.

7.3 LECITHIN- AND SUCROSE ESTER–BASED NANOEMULSIONS—FORMULATION DESIGN ASPECTS, PHYSICOCHEMICAL CHARACTERIZATION, AND STABILITY

Over the past 10 years, due to the numerous attractive advantages over liposomal, nanoparticulate, and microemulsion formulations, such as small and controllable droplet size, high drug loading capacity, powerful penetrability, low surfactant concentration, and consequently low skin irritation potential, as well as relatively easy manufacture and scale-up (Sainsbury et al., 2014; Zhou et al., 2010), nanoemulsions have been recognized as promising carriers worth exploring for improving dermal uptake of NSAIDs. Although there is generally an increasing number in publications dealing with nanoemulsions intended for topical administration of NSAIDs, the readers should be aware that some of the developed systems, described as thermodynamically stable, spontaneously

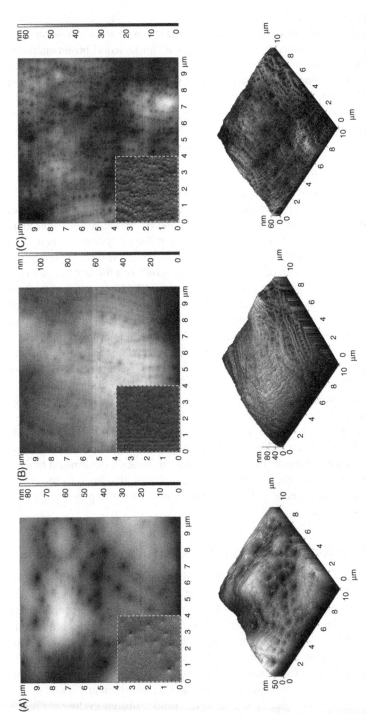

FIGURE 7.4   AFM images showing the structures of droplet and bicontinuous microemulsions. 2D and 3D topography images of the samples: (A) FL10, (B) FL40, and (C) FL70, are shown with smaller 2D error signal images inserted into 2D topography images. (*(Todosijević MN, Cekić ND, Savić MM, Gašperlin M, Ranđelović DV, Savić SD: Sucrose ester-based biocompatible microemulsions as vehicles for aceclofenac as a model drug: formulation approach using D-optimal mixture design, Colloid Polym Sci 292:3073, 2014, with permission of Springer)*)

formed mixtures of oil, water, and large amount of surfactants (20–50%), in fact, represent microemulsions. To avoid any confusion with microemulsions, we follow the well-established term "nanoemulsion" for nonequilibrium emulsion systems with droplets in lower submicron range and with spontaneous tendency to break down into the constituent phases over the time (Gutiérrez et al., 2008; Klang and Valenta, 2011). However, due to a small droplet size, gravitationally driven sedimentation and creaming are largely prevented by Brownian motion, and therefore, nanoemulsion systems possess a relatively high kinetic stability (even for years) which makes them well suited for practical application (Klang and Valenta, 2011; Tadros et al., 2004).

When the lipophilic drugs, such as NSAIDs, are incorporated into the nanoemulsions, it should be kept in mind that the transport rate across the skin is determined not only by the properties of the drug, such as molecular size, charge, lipophilicity, and hydrogen-bonding ability, but also, to a considerable extent, by the properties of nanoemulsion delivery system (Roberts and Cross, 1999). It has been accepted that nanoemulsion droplet size is the key parameter affecting the drug percutaneous permeation, with the surfactant/emulsifier composition playing the most important role. The high total surface area and low surface tension of nanoemulsion droplets ensure close and prolonged contact with the skin, thus enabling high concentration gradient for drug skin uptake (Kong et al., 2011). Additionally, surfactants can interfere with the skin lipid structures, change the barrier properties of the skin, and thereby contribute to the penetration enhancing effect of nanoemulsions (Nam et al., 2012; Puglia et al., 2010). Therefore, the selection of surfactant(s) is of crucial importance for nanoemulsion formation and stability as well as for efficient dermal drug delivery. Besides, the safety is an important determining factor in choosing the appropriate surfactant(s)—the use of well-tolerated and skin-friendly surfactants is highly desirable. Although the physicochemical properties, stability, and functional performances of nanoemulsions are strongly determined by employed emulsifying agents, it is important to emphasize that the type of oil and aqueous phase, and especially the fabrication conditions, also play critical role in this regard.

7.3.1 The Selection of Emulsifiers—Lecithin and Sucrose Esters

Natural lecithins are the most frequently used emulsifying agents in nanoemulsions aimed at dermal drug delivery (Klang et al., 2011a). The numerous studies have confirmed the high skin compatibility of topically applied phospholipids and there are generally no restrictions concerning their use in pharmaceutical and cosmetic products (Daniels, 2001; Fiume, 2001; Hoeller et al., 2009). Moreover, the lecithin compounds are able to diffuse into the SC and enhance the skin lipid fluidity, thus enabling the drug molecules, incorporated in the nanoemulsions, to penetrate through the skin more efficiently (Klang and Valenta, 2011; Paolino et al., 2002). However, nanoemulsions exclusively based on lecithin are very sensitive to any modification in their content and only several drugs have been successfully marketed in these systems (Sznitowska et al., 2001). The stability of lecithin-based nanoemulsions is derived from the formation of multilamellar shell around each droplet which acts as an effective mechanical barrier for droplet coalescence and, importantly, from electrostatic repulsive forces which exist between adjacent, negatively charged droplets, thus impeding droplet coalescence upon random collisions (Klang and Valenta, 2011). Hence, incorporation of certain drugs capable of interacting with the emulsifier layer and/or droplet surface charge can reduce stability of nanoemulsions based on natural lecithins as sole emulsifiers and cause their phase separation (Trotta et al., 2002). This destabilization effects, inter alia, could be expected from the weak acidic drugs, such as NSAIDs, which are usually negatively charged at the formulation pH value. The charge on this type of drugs leads to their surface activity and therefore, they will be located, at least partly, at the oil–water interface, contributing to the surface charge of oil droplets and thus influencing the nanoemulsion stability (Washington, 1996).

To achieve the satisfying long-term stability of lecithin-based nanoemulsions in the presence of NSAIDs, the inclusion of additional coemulsifying agent has proven to be a useful approach. Generally, the coemulsifiers can improve the nanoemulsion stability by increasing the mechanical strength of interfacial film formed around oil droplets, by steric stabilization effects or by providing efficient electrostatic barrier for droplet coalescence (Buszello et al., 2000). For example, in one of the earliest studies dealing with nanoemulsions intended for topical administration of different NSAIDs (diclofenac, naproxen, indomethacin, and piroxicam), reported by Friedman et al. (1995), polyethoxylated nonionic surfactants (Tween 80/Tyloxapol/Cremophor EL) were incorporated as additional stabilizers of lecithin-based nanoemulsions. The addition of these surfactants can ensure the formation of complex close-packed interfacial film at the droplet surface as well as additional steric stabilization of dispersed nanodroplets, thus favoring a long-term stability of nanoemulsions (Baspinar et al., 2010; Klang and Valenta, 2011; Trotta et al., 2002).

However, in recent years, as a result of powerful influence of on-going "green" trends in the cosmetic industry, increased awareness for environmental issues, and growing consumer interest in health issues, such as allergies, the focus during nanoemulsion formulation design has shifted toward the application of biodegradable and skin-friendly coemulsifiers made from renewable, inexpensive, and inexhaustible natural resources (Hoeller et al., 2009; Isailović et al., 2016; Klang et al., 2011a; Savić et al., 2010). In this context, among the various carbohydrates being studied, SEs have gained an increasing attention due to the numerous beneficial properties in terms of stabilizing multiphase systems as well as dermal drug delivery. As previously discussed, the properties of SEs (solubility, HLB value, and interfacial behavior) are strongly determined by the nature of the esterified fatty acid and by the esterification degree of the sucrose moiety (Szűts and Szabó-Révész, 2012). SEs with medium to high HLB values, especially those with the longer acyl chain (12 or more carbon atoms) tend to efficiently cover the droplet surfaces, due to tighter molecular packing at the oil–water interface (Cruces et al., 2001; Das et al., 2014), and therefore, they are more frequently used as emulsifiers in emulsion formulations. Additionally, although exact mechanism of the percutaneous penetration enhancement of SEs is still not completely known, it is presumed that SEs can insert their hydrocarbon chains between the lipophilic tails of SC lipid bilayer, allowing the sucrose ring to interact with the polar head groups of SC lipids, thus disturbing their packing, increasing their fluidity, and consequently, leading to an easier diffusion of drug through the skin (Ayala-Bravo et al., 2003; Calderilla-Fajardo et al., 2006; Hoeller et al., 2009). However, it should be noted that the application of SEs in pharmaceutical nanoemulsions is relatively new, and only a few studies have dealt with their use as (co)emulsifiers in nanoemulsions intended for topical administration of NSAIDS (Table 7.1).

In one of the first studies, Hoeller et al. (2009) successfully developed the positively and negatively charged lecithin-based nanoemulsions containing either sucrose laurate or polysorbate 80 as coemulsifiers. Interestingly, polysorbate 80 significantly improved the physicochemical stability of nanoemulsions in comparison with the sucrose laurate, probably due to its capability to provide stronger steric hindrance for droplet coalescence. Later, Klang et al. (2010) reported that among the three tested SEs, sucrose laurate L-595 (HLB ~ 5), sucrose laurate L-1695 (HLB ~ 16) and sucrose stearate S-970 (HLB ~ 9), it was possible to develop physically stable nanoemulsions using only the sucrose stearate as a coemulsifier. As opposed to these two studies focused on the steroidal anti-inflammatory drugs as model drugs, the first study dealing with the application of SEs in lecithin-based nanoemulsions intended for topical delivery of aceclofenac, as a model NSAID, has been recently reported by Isailović et al. (2016). Two SEs differing in the fatty acid chain length and esterification degree (sucrose palmitate P-1670 ~ 16, sucrose stearate S-970 ~ 9) were chosen in order to evaluate possibility of usage of not only each of them, but also their combinations for development of physically stable nanoemulsions. We assumed that synergistic effect between sucrose palmitate and sucrose stearate on emulsion stability, which was previously postulated by Soultani et al. (2003), might contribute to the formation of lecithin-based nanoemulsions with improved stability. Indeed, depending on emulsifier mixture composition and process conditions it was possible to develop physically stable nanoemulsions in the presence of weak acidic and unstable drug, such as aceclofenac.

Although lecithin possesses a good functionality in nanoemulsion formulation, it should not be forgotten that there are also some drawbacks which can limit its widespread use. Namely, phospholipids are susceptible to hydrolytical and oxidative degradation (Baspinar et al., 2010), which leads to the changes in visual and olfactory appearance of nanoemulsion after a certain storage period (Klang et al., 2011a). Additionally, lecithin molecules exhibit high potential for self-aggregation, resulting in the formation of vesicular or multilamellar structures during nanoemulsion production (Klang et al., 2011a; Shchipunov, 1997). To avoid limitations of natural lecithin mixtures, an attempt was made to produce nanoemulsions by employing a natural sucrose stearate mixture (HLB value comparable to that of lecithin) as sole surfactant (Klang et al., 2011a). Throughout the comparison of lecithin and sucrose stearate–based nanoemulsions it was observed that the sucrose stearate is superior in terms of emulsifying efficiency, droplet formation, as well as nanoemulsion physicochemical stability.

7.3.2   The Selection of Oil and Aqueous Phase

When designing nanoemulsions as carriers for poorly water soluble drugs, such as NSAIDs, determination of drug solubility in different oils is essential in order to successfully exploit advantages of nanoemulsions in topical drug delivery, since drug loading per formulation is directly dependent on the drug solubility in the internal oil phase (Đorđević et al., 2015). Although most of the NSAIDs are more soluble in the oil than in aqueous phase, the amount of drug that can be dissolved in the oil core during conventional de novo preparation procedure is often insufficient to achieve desired product concentration with a certain amount (usually 20%) of oil phase. Although the temperature elevated method is the simplest way to enhance the oil solubility of drug, the drug might precipitate upon emulsification to reduce the supersaturation of the internal oil phase (Wang and Cory, 1999). Additionally, in case of aceclofenac, the sole heating of the oil phase at 50°C (production temperature) was useless, since dissolution of desired drug amount could not be obtained (Isailović et al., 2016). Therefore, the addition of lecithin, as the most frequently used solubilizer in nanoemulsion formulations (Sznitowska et al., 2001), has proven to be a feasible approach. It was shown that addition of egg lecithin in appropriate concentration (minimum 1%) significantly improved aceclofenac solubility in the selected oil phase, thus enabling the incorporation of targeted concentration and avoidance of drug precipitation during the storage (Isailović et al., 2016).

For weak acidic drugs, such as NSAIDs, the selection of appropriate nanoemulsion aqueous phase is also a quite challenging task. Generally, it is highly recommended to adjust the pH of the nanoemulsions stabilized with lecithin and SEs to values close to neutral ones (pH 6–7) in order to achieve the optimum charge at the droplet surfaces and minimum hydrolysis rate of oils, phospholipids, and SEs (Hippalgaonkar et al., 2010; Okumura et al., 2011). However, pK_a values of the most NSAIDs are in the range of 3.5–5.5, so the neutral pH values will induce their ionization and increase of aqueous solubility which in turn could result in the drug precipitation during the storage. Indeed, Isailović et al. (2016) observed that incorporation of aceclofenac (pK_a = 4.7) in lecithin and SEs-based nanoemulsions prepared using the ultrapure water as aqueous phase caused the significant pH drop (for approximately 1.5 pH units). This was attributed to ionization of aceclofenac at the oil–water interface, but also to the small amount of free aceclofenac present in the aqueous phase. To prevent ionization of indomethacin and to promote its localization in the oil phase, Muchtar et al. (1997) adjusted pH of lecithin-based nanoemulsions to 3.8 using HCl solution (0.1 N). However, this low pH value is generally unfavorable for nanoemulsion long-term stability. It is obvious that there is a need for more experimental work to identify the appropriate aqueous phase which can ensure localization of NSAIDs within the oil core, but also the satisfying stability of natural surfactant–based nanoemulsions.

7.3.3 Nanoemulsion Formulation and Preparation—QbD Approach

Among the various methods employed for nanoemulsion production, uptil now, the classical nanoemulsions stabilized with lecithin and SEs have been exclusively prepared using the high pressure homogenization (HPH). The main advantages of this fabrication method lie in the relative simplicity, the flexible control of droplet size distribution, and ability to produce fine emulsions from a large variety of materials (Jafari et al., 2008; Puglia et al., 2010). In a standard procedure, the coarse emulsion (usually prepared using a high-shear rotor–stator device, such as an Ultra-Turrax) passes through the narrow gap of a homogenizer at high pressure which generates the powerful disruptive forces, thus enabling the large droplets to be fragmented into the smaller ones. Although the mean droplet diameter tends to decrease with increasing homogenization pressure and number of passes (Klang and Valenta, 2011), it should be kept in mind that the homogenization outcome depends on competing processes within the homogenizer including: (1) droplet break up which increases the specific surface area of droplets, (2) stabilization of created interfaces by emulsifiers, and (3) (re)coalescence of newly formed droplets (Jafari et al., 2008; Sainsbury et al., 2014). Although small molecule surfactants, such as lecithin and SEs, exhibit rapid interfacial absorption kinetics and can provide effective barrier for droplet coalescence, in case of their insufficient concentration, the fresh interfaces will not be completely covered and this will result in droplet size increase despite the increasing energy input (Jafari et al., 2008; Sainsbury et al., 2014). Similarly, the type, volume, and viscosity of an oil phase may exert significant influence on efficacy of homogenization process and subsequently on the droplet size (Klang and Valenta, 2011). For example, oil phases with higher viscosities, such as the castor oil, require the higher homogenization pressures to achieve the smaller particle size distributions (Isailović et al., 2016; Jumaa and Müller, 1998). On the other hand, the heating during the homogenization generally reduces the viscosity of emulsion oil and aqueous phases, and the interfacial tension between them, thus facilitating the formation of smaller droplets (Floury et al., 2000; Jafari et al., 2008).

Therefore, it is obvious that the both formulation variables and processing conditions should be well integrated in the formulation development strategies in order to obtain the product with desired properties (quality by design—QbD approach) (Hafner et al., 2014; Hippalgaonkar et al., 2010). In this regard, design of experiments methodology has been recognized as a suitable tool which allows the investigation of the impact of several variables (formulation composition and/or processing conditions) and their interactions on desired system properties with a limited number of experiments (Gutiérrez et al., 2008). Hence, starting from an assumption that the operating conditions, when changed, may change the influence of formulation/mixture component proportions on the product properties, Isailović et al. (2016) utilized combined/crossed mixture–process experimental design to simultaneously analyze the effects of emulsifier mixture composition (egg lecithin, sucrose stearate, and sucrose palmitate), process variables (homogenization pressure and number of cycles) and the presence of a model drug (aceclofenac) on the critical quality attributes of nanoemulsions—droplet size and size distribution. This comprehensive design allowed to optimize formulation and manufacturing procedure at the same time, and thereby to identify drug-loaded nanoemulsions that meet the set requirements—the smallest droplet size and narrow size distribution.

7.3.4   Physicochemical Characterization and Stability Testing

Apart from the inherent skin-friendliness, physicochemical stability of nanoemulsions is a crucial prerequisite for their application in dermal drug delivery. In this context, the most important techniques utilized for evaluation of physicochemical properties and stability of SEs-based nanoemulsions are summarized here, together with the most important results, in order to obtain a deeper insight into relationship between the properties of SEs and overall NSAID-loaded nanoemulsion performances.

7.3.4.1   Droplet Size Analysis and Microstructure Evaluation

The first and most important step in characterization of any developed nanoemulsion is the determination of droplet size. Increase in droplet size is considered as a first indicator of formulation stability issues (Hippalgaonkar et al., 2010); therefore, initial and regular measurements of droplet size during the prolonged period of storage are required for an exact stability assessment (Klang et al., 2012a). Dynamic light scattering is the most commonly used technique for this purpose, which provides intensity weighted mean hydrodynamic diameter of nanoemulsion droplets as well as the polydispersity index (PDI) as a measure for the width of the particle size distribution (Klang and Valenta, 2011). Isailović et al. (2016) found that the droplet size (178–280 nm) and PDI (0.104–0.184) of nanoemulsions containing egg lecithin, sucrose palmitate, and/or sucrose stearate as emulsifiers were strongly defined by the ratio of surfactants (sum of all their proportions was restricted to 4%), presence of aceclofenac, as well as homogenization pressure (500/800 bar), and number of cycles (15/20). Interestingly, droplet size of optimal aceclofenac-loaded nanoemulsions (selected through combined mixture–process design) was slightly lower than of corresponding blanks, indicating that aceclofenac, due to established amphiphilic properties, was predominantly located at the oil–water interface. Additionally, droplet size and PDI remained almost unchanged during 3 months of storage for all optimal formulations except one containing 2% of sucrose stearate in the blend with egg lecithin (1%) and sucrose palmitate (1%), probably due to the weakening of electrostatic repulsion forces between droplets caused by low pH values. In another study, analyzing the particle size of nanoemulsions exclusively based on egg lecithin or sucrose stearate, Klang et al. (2011a) observed that with increasing surfactant-to-oil ratios, the emulsifying efficacy of both surfactants increased, thus resulting in smaller droplet sizes, whereby the sucrose stearate–based nanoemulsions exhibited significantly smaller droplets than their lecithin-based counterparts. Irrespective of the presence of drugs with different physicochemical properties (including flufenamic acid), formulations containing 2.5% of egg lecithin or sucrose stearate retained the droplet size around 180 or 140 nm, respectively, and PDI <0.2 during 6 months of storage, thus disclosing the high quality of dispersions.

To extend the measuring range and thus to detect the possible presence of larger emulsion droplets within the novel SE-based nanoemulsions, laser diffractometry (LD) was also employed, yielding volume-weighted diameters $d(0.5)$, $d(0.9)$, $D[4,3]$ and D_{max} as additional critical quality parameters (Isailović et al., 2016; Klang et al., 2011b). Considering the sensitivity limitations of LD to detect a small number of larger droplets (>1 μm) besides the large bulk population of nanosized ones (Keck and Müller, 2008), as well as its inability to differentiate between droplets and drug crystals (Müller et al., 2004), light microscopy is usually employed as an additional quality control tool to ensure the absence of larger structures (droplets and aggregates) and drug crystals over extended period of storage. Besides, Klang et al. (2011b) also observed the gelling behavior of nanoemulsions containing 5% of sucrose stearate as sole emulsifier, immediately after placing the sample on the object plate. Structured dispersed film, which remained at the edges of the droplet after the covering of sample, indicated the presence of a weak liquid crystalline network.

Similarly, Isailović et al. (2016) detected the gelling of nanoemulsions costabilized with sucrose palmitate and/or sucrose stearate during the preparation of samples for AFM imaging, and hence, dilution of samples (1:500) was necessary to obtain images of individual nanodroplets. The captured AFM images illustrated the homogenous distribution of spherical droplets with mean diameter around 180–200 nm (Fig. 7.5). In addition, TEM with cryogenic techniques for sample preparation can provide detailed information about the internal structure of nanoemulsions in their native state (Klang et al., 2012a). Therefore, Klang et al. (2011a) employed the Cryo-TEM to visualize the blank nanoemulsions stabilized with lecithin (2.5%) or sucrose stearate (2.5%). Images obtained

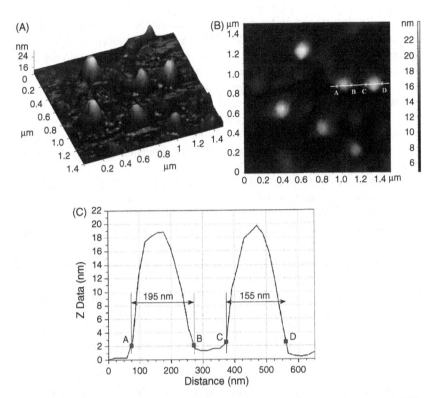

FIGURE 7.5 AFM images of aceclofenac-loaded nanoemulsions containing egg lecithin (1.5%), sucrose stearate (0.5%), and sucrose palmitate (2%) as emulsifiers. (A) 3D topography (1.4 × 1.4 μm² scan area), (B) 2D topography, and (C) height profiles of two selected nanoemulsion droplets. *(Reprinted from Isailović T, Đorđević S, Marković B, Ranđelović D, Cekić N, Lukić M, Pantelić I, Daniels R, Savić S: Biocompatible nanoemulsions for improved aceclofenac skin delivery: formulation approach using combined-mixture process experimental design, J Pharm Sci 105:318, 2016, Copyright Elsevier (2016))*

for lecithin-based nanoemulsions revealed the presence of irregularly shaped oil droplets and large number of vesicular structures such as liposomes and multilamellar-phospholipid layers. Contrarily, sucrose stearate nanoemulsions showed the spherical oil droplets, probably due to the better packing geometry of sucrose stearate at the O/W interface, which is, therefore, more suitable for the formation of curved surfaces.

7.3.4.2 Zeta Potential and pH Value Determination

Assessment of zeta potential (ZP) is a part of standard procedure frequently employed for thorough characterization of developed nanoemulsion systems. The ZP characterizes the droplet surface charge within the aqueous bulk phase, and it is usually determined by laser Doppler electrophoresis/anemometry (Klang and Valenta, 2011). The absolute ZP of 30 mV is usually taken as the arbitrary value to separate the systems with high and low droplet surface charge, that is, high and low electrochemical stability (Silva et al., 2012). It should be kept in mind that ZP of nanoemulsions, especially those stabilized with natural lecithin mixtures, may be influenced by many factors such as the system pH value, presence of electrolytes as well as the cationic molecules (Silva et al., 2012). For example, the lower system pH value results in the lower ZP due to decreased ionization of some functional groups of phospholipids on the droplets surface and vice versa (Benita and Levy, 1993).

However, Isailović et al. (2016) reported that despite a low pH value, aceclofenac-loaded nanoemulsions containing 2% of sucrose palmitate in the blends with egg lecithin (1–2%) and sucrose stearate (0.5–1%) exhibited the sufficiently high ZP values (around −40 mV), which remained almost unchanged during 3 months of storage. This phenomenon was explained by the presence of the higher content of hydrophilic sucrose monoesters in these samples and its ability to shield the negative droplet surface charge. On the contrary, ZP of formulation containing 2% of more lipophilic sucrose stearate in the blend with egg lecithin (1%) and sucrose palmitate (1%) was significantly reduced during storage, due to greater amount of lipophilic di- and higher esters of sucrose, which were probably deeply embedded in the phospholipid layer, resulting in more pronounced negative influence of low pH values on the droplet surface charge. Unexpectedly, the ZP values of blank sucrose stearate–based nanoemulsions (Klang et al., 2011a) were significantly higher than those of their lecithin-based counterparts at all tested concentrations (1, 2.5, and 5%) and increased concomitantly with increasing surfactant concentration (from −48.36 up to −70.81 mV). Although the sucrose stearate is a nonionic surfactant, the high ZP values clearly indicate that there are some negatively charged molecules that are located at the particle surface. Indeed, sucrose stearate contains the larger amount of nonesterified fatty acids as impurities in comparison with selected lecithin, which are negatively charged at formulation pH values, contributing to the improved electrochemical stability of these systems (Klang et al., 2011a). As opposed to lecithin (2.5%)-based nanoemulsions that showed a marked increase in absolute ZP in course of 6 months (from –20 to –40 mV), the mean ZP of sucrose stearate (2.5%)-based nanoemulsion systems did not change appreciably. The increase of ZP in case of lecithin-based nanoemulsions is usually attributed to the hydrolysis of lecithin molecules which results in the formation of lysolecithin and free fatty acids, which further confer more negative charge to the droplet surface (Baspinar et al., 2010; Klang and Valenta, 2011). This was supported by the more pronounced decrease of pH value of these systems when compared to sucrose stearate–based ones, implying that lecithin is more susceptible to hydrolysis than SEs (Klang et al., 2011a). Therefore, determination of the nanoemulsion pH value over the entire storage period provides the useful data about the chemical stability of developed systems.

7.3.4.3 Viscosity Measurements

The rheological studies are also required in order to estimate nanoemulsion physical stability since the flocculation and coalescence of oil droplets are generally accompanied with the increase of viscosity (Hippalgaonkar et al., 2010). Although sucrose palmitate and stearate tend to form gels in aqueous environment (Szűts et al., 2010), the corresponding nanoemulsions (blank and aceclofenac-loaded) exhibited Newtonian flow behavior and stable low viscosity (2.6–4.4 mPa s) during 3 months of storage, clearly indicating that employed SEs were mainly located at the oil–water interface, and therefore, were less available to participate in the formation of gel phase (Isailović et al., 2016). As opposed to this study, a minor shear-thinning flow behavior was observed for blank nanoemulsion prepared only with 5% of sucrose stearate (Klang et al., 2011b). Since the incorporation of flufenamic or diclofenac acid in this system led to significantly lower viscosity values as well as Newtonian flow behavior, it was reasonable to assume that these drugs could interact with the surplus of sucrose stearate present in these samples, thus reducing the nanoemulsion viscosity.

7.3.4.4 Assessment of Drug Chemical Stability

Generally, it is considered that the incorporation of drugs susceptible to hydrolysis into not only the nanoemulsion oil core, but also into the interfacial phospholipid layer can improve their stability (Baspinar et al., 2010; Hippalgaonkar et al., 2010). Hence, since it was previously shown that aceclofenac undergoes to substantial hydrolytic degradation under acidic, alkaline, and neutral conditions, as well as under exposure to light (Bhinge et al., 2008), Isailović et al. (2016) monitored the content of aceclofenac and its main degradation product — diclofenac in lecithin and SEs-based nanoemulsions during 3 months of storage at 25°C. The average content of aceclofenac remained around 97% for all tested nanoemulsions (diclofenac content was lower than 3%), confirming that the incorporation of drug into the interfacial phospholipid layer can maintain the chemical integrity of unstable drugs, such as aceclofenac.

7.4 NSAID-LOADED MICRO/NANOEMULSIONS: IN VITRO/EX VIVO/IN VIVO DERMAL AND TRANSDERMAL AVAILABILITY

Apart from the extensive physicochemical characterization, an assessment of drug percutaneous absorption is of crucial importance for design and optimization of any dermal or transdermal drug-delivery systems. This section will provide an overview of diverse experimental methods used for the investigation of in vitro release, as well as evaluation of dermal and systemic availability of NSAIDs from the newly formulated micro/nanoemulsions based on SEs.

7.4.1 In Vitro Release/Permeation Studies

Knowing that the drug release is a prerequisite for drug skin absorption and resulting pharmacological activity, it is of a great importance to establish in vitro model for investigation of drug release rate from topical colloidal carrier systems. Although there are no compendial or standard release methods/apparatus for the assessment of in vitro drug release from topical micro/nanoemulsions, various techniques can be employed using dialysis bag, Franz cell (vertical diffusion cell) or its modifications, flow-through diffusion cell, VanKel enhancer cell. Additionally, different synthetic membranes (e.g., cellulose, polysulfone, politetrafluoroetilen, polyamide, etc.), with low diffusion resistance, can be used for this type of studies (Morais and Burgess, 2014; Pantelic et al., 2014). For example, preliminary screening of aceclofenac release profiles from SE-based microemulsions, through previously rehydrated cellulose membrane, was performed using two different methods, first Franz diffusion cells, and second VanKel enhancer cells placed in standard apparatus for dissolution testing with minipaddles, at the temperature of 32°C. The obtained release profiles from SE-based microemulsions were compared with those which have the same weight ratio of all ingredients, but differ in the type of surfactant—traditional ethoxylated surfactant, polysorbate 80, was used instead of SEs. As demonstrated by the one-way analysis of variance (ANOVA), total amount of aceclofenac released was significantly higher from sucrose laurate– and sucrose myristate–based systems in comparison to polysorbate-based microemulsions. Since all the microemulsions have the same bicontinuous structure and uphold equal quantity of drug and the same total concentration of tensides (Todosijević et al., 2015), this difference can only be explained as a consequence of surfactant structure and its influence on drug release. Furthermore, the comparable tendencies between aceclofenac release profiles obtained with Franz and Van-Kel enhancer cells imply that both methods can be used for the assessment of in vitro aceclofenac release from colloidal carrier systems.

Apart from the synthetic membranes, rational approach for designing and optimizing skin formulations aimed for either regional or systemic drug actions requires the use of well-defined skin model, which can enable the assessment of drug permeation through the skin barrier (Flaten et al., 2015). The skin permeation studies are usually conducted using vertical diffusion cells where donor and receptor chamber are separated by excised skin or by one or more of its composing layers (e.g., SC sheets, epidermal sheets, dermatomed skin) (Selzer et al., 2013). Although human skin is considered as a "gold standard" for in vitro permeation studies, due to its limited availability, different animal skin models, including primate, porcine, rodent (mice, rats, guinea pigs), and snake skin may be utilized for this purpose (Flaten et al., 2015; Russell and Guy, 2009). Among them, porcine (abdominal or ear) skin, due to numerous anatomical, histopatological, and physiological similarities with the human skin (Flaten et al., 2015), has been most frequently used to assess the permeation of NSAIDs from SE-based micro/nanoemulsions.

For instance, Klang et al. (2011a) performed in vitro permeation study using porcine abdominal skin mounted on Franz diffusion cells in order to assess the suitability of novel sucrose stearate–based nanoemulsions for dermal delivery of four model drugs with different physicochemical properties. As opposed to investigated hydrophilic model drugs, almost the same skin permeation rates of lipophilic NSAID, flufenamic acid, from sucrose stearate nanoemulsions and corresponding egg lecithin-based ones, were achieved. Comparable efficacy of sucrose stearate- and lecithin-based nanoemulsions in terms of the skin permeation of lipophilic drugs as well as the superior properties of sucrose stearate mixture regarding nanoemulsion physicochemical stability, make these novel nanoemulsions the promising carriers worth exploring further for dermal drug delivery. In another study, Klang et al. (2011b) utilized the similar experimental procedure to evaluate the influence of the different formulation properties of viscous macroemulsions and fluid nanoemulsions prepared using the same chemical composition including the same concentration of sucrose stearate S-970 as emulsifier on the skin permeation of the three model drugs (flufenamic acid, diclofenac acid, and curcumin). Although it was frequently reported in the literature that nanoemulsions, due to small droplet size, can significantly improve drug permeation through the skin, in this study no statistically significant difference was observed between macroemulsions and nanoemulsions in terms of skin permeation of investigated drugs. Therefore, the authors assumed that the skin permeation of model drugs was mainly determined by employed excipients, that is, by sucrose stearate mixture.

7.4.2 In Vivo/Ex Vivo Tape Stripping Studies

Although it is generally considered that in vitro models can provide a relatively good approximation of the drug penetration/permeation in vivo, an ultimate estimation of topical drug delivery into/through the skin has to be always performed in vivo (Russell and Guy, 2009). Among the various in vivo methods, which are either invasive (e.g., skin biopsy) or require the application of sophisticated equipment (e.g., dermal microdialysis, confocal Raman spectroscopy), tape stripping stands out as a simple, minimally invasive (skin barrier properties are completely repaired within a few days), and economical technique for the assessment of drug dermal availability (Narkar, 2010; Pantelic et al., 2014). Briefly, the tape stripping involves the sequential removal of superficial skin layers using adhesive tapes, which are further analyzed with respect to drug content and amount/thickness of the removed SC, thus enabling an estimation of penetrated drug amount as well as its penetration depth (Klang et al., 2012b; Lademann et al., 2009; Narkar, 2010; Pantelic et al., 2014; Russell and Guy, 2009). Although the tape stripping is particularly useful to assess the local bioavailability of drugs whose site of action is the SC itself, this technique can be also used for drugs whose target is viable underlying tissues (Herkenne et al., 2008). Having in mind that the SC is a major obstacle for penetration of topically applied therapeutic agents into/through the skin, the drug levels within this membrane should be directly related to those attained in the viable skin components (Herkenne et al., 2008). Hence, Isailović et al. (2016) conducted the in vivo tape stripping study for an assessment of aceclofenac dermal availability from nanoemulsions containing different proportions of egg lecithin (1–2%), sucrose stearate (0.5–1%), and sucrose palmitate (2%) as stabilizers. As all selected nanoemulsions exhibited the similar droplet size and had the same concentration of aceclofenac (1%), the authors were interested to ascertain whether and to which extent the emulsifier mixture composition affects aceclofenac penetration into the human skin, by comparing them mutually and related to the reference nanoemulsion stabilized with conventional egg lecithin (2%)/polysorbate 80 (2%) combination. Penetration profiles obtained after 2-h application of the investigated samples unambiguously revealed that nanoemulsions costabilized with SEs were more effective in terms of aceclofenac penetration through the human skin than reference nanoemulsion with polysorbate 80 as coemulsifier (Fig. 7.6a). Among the various SEs-based nanoemulsions, significantly higher skin uptake of aceclofenac was observed from nanoemulsion containing 1.5% of egg lecithin, 0.5% of sucrose stearate, and 2% of sucrose palmitate (Fig. 7.6a), which appeared to interact synergistically in modification of skin barrier function, thus enabling drug to diffuse into the

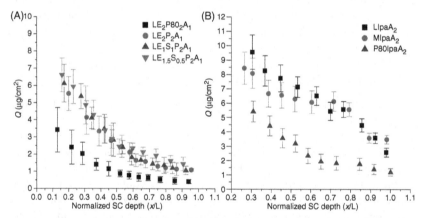

FIGURE 7.6 Aceclofenac penetration profiles from SEs- versus polysorbate 80-stabilized (A) nanoemulsions and (B) microemulsions, assessed in vivo via tape stripping technique. Formulation codes indicate the qualitative and quantitative composition of surfactant/cosurfactant mixtures and aceclofenac content (*LE*, egg lecithin; *S*, sucrose stearate; *P*, sucrose palmitate; *L*, sucrose laurate; *M*, sucrose myristate; *Ipa*, isopropyl alcohol; *P80*, polysorbate 80, and *A*, aceclofenac). *(Part A, reprinted from Isailović T, Đorđević S, Marković B, Ranđelović D, Cekić N, Lukić M, Pantelić I, Daniels R, Savić S: Biocompatible nanoemulsions for improved aceclofenac skin delivery: formulation approach using combined-mixture process experimental design, J Pharm Sci 105:321, 2016, Copyright Elsevier (2016); part B, reprinted from Todosijević MN, Savić MM, Batinić BB, Marković BD, Gašperlin M, Ranđelović DV, Lukić MŽ, Savić SD: Biocompatible microemulsions of a model NSAID for skin delivery: a decisive role of surfactants in skin penetration/irritation profiles and pharmacokinetic performance, Int J Pharm 496:939, 2015, Copyright (2016), with permission from Elsevier)*

skin more efficiently. Likewise, Todosijević et al. (2015) demonstrated that the penetrated amount of aceclofenac in SC after 1-h application period was significantly higher in case of sucrose laurate– and sucrose myristate–based microemulsions than from microemulsion formulated with polysorbate 80 (Fig. 7.6b). Due to the same aceclofenac concentration (2%) in vehicles, enhancing effect of the individual ingredients has to be considered: since all formulations contained equal amount of isopropyl alcohol and isopropyl myristate, components known to act as penetration enhancers (Teichmann et al., 2007), the presence of SEs in the microemulsions apparently increased the quantity of drug penetrated into SC. Moreover, some authors have previously observed that differences in the extent of penetration enhancement may be related to the hydrophobic chain length of SEs (Cázares-Delgadillo et al., 2005; Ganem-Quintanar et al., 1998). Our results are not concurrent with earlier study (Ganem-Quintanar et al., 1998) regarding the higher penetration efficacy of surfactant with lauryl hydrophobic chain, due to the lack of statistical significance between the total amount of aceclofenac penetrated from sucrose laurate– and sucrose myristate–based microemulsions. However, it is important to emphasize that the effects of SEs may depend on the various factors, such as concentration, characteristics of drug being studied, type of vehicle, the site of application, as well as experimental conditions (in vitro vs. in vivo studies) (Ganem-Quintanar et al., 1998), making the comparison of results from different studies somewhat challenging.

Additionally, in the past few years, in order to overcome the organizational and legislative issues frequently associated with in vivo tape stripping studies (e.g., the need for complex documentation when applying for ethical committee approval), the research efforts have been directed toward the validation of porcine ear skin as an ex vivo model for human skin (Klang et al., 2012b; Herkenne et al., 2006). As opposed to excised human skin, porcine ear skin remains on the cartilage, which prevents skin contraction as well as decelerates inevitable skin dehydration making it highly suitable in the assessment of drug dermal availability by tape stripping technique (Klang et al., 2012b). Hence, apart from the previously described in vitro permeation studies, Klang et al. (2011b) performed ex vivo tape stripping experiments to avoid the potential negative influence of receptor medium on the skin barrier properties and thereby to obtain more realistic data about the penetration of flufenamic acid, diclofenac acid, and curcumin from macro- and nanoemulsions based on sucrose stearate under the short finite-dose application conditions. Again, no statistically significant difference between macro- and nanoemulsions was observed regarding the skin penetration of model drugs, confirming that neither droplet size nor viscosity exerted any influence on penetration behavior of selected drugs. Later, the same authors conducted the in vivo tape stripping study on human volunteers to confirm results obtained using porcine ear skin and thus to evaluate the usefulness of this model for the penetration studies. The results obtained ex vivo were in satisfying agreement with in vivo results, proving that the porcine ear skin is an excellent surrogate for human skin in tape stripping experiments (Klang et al., 2012b).

7.4.3 In Vivo Pharmacokinetic Studies in Rats

During recent decades numerous studies have been conducted implying that microemulsions possessed improved transdermal delivery compared to the conventional carriers. Moreover, there is a certain amount of research investigating nanoemulsions as vehicles for transdermal drug delivery (Cevc and Vierl, 2010). However, it should be noted that investigated vehicles corresponded to thermodynamically stable (i.e., microemulsions) and not kinetically stable colloidal systems (i.e., nanoemulsions). Highly dynamic character of bicontinuous microemulsions may enhance transport of a drug through skin. Additionally, very low interfacial tension of bicontinuous microemulsions may improve wetting of SC which may also facilitate drug transport and consequently increase penetration through epithelial tissues (Bolzinger et al., 1998). Thus pharmacokinetic study in animal models has to be performed in order to evaluate the effectiveness of transdermal drug delivery and to calculate an amount of drug that is absorbed. Undeniably, the pharmacokinetic data (Todosijević et al., 2015) obtained after topical application of investigated microemulsions with proven bicontinuous structure on male Wistar rats during 24 h, highly supported the tape stripping results (Fig. 7.6b). Following the topical application of SE-based microemulsions, the peak plasma concentrations (c_{max}) of aceclofenac from sucrose laurate– and myristate–based microemulsions were 275.57 ± 109.49 and 281.31 ± 76.76 ng/mL, which were reached at 0.44 ± 0.19 and 0.74 ± 0.32 h, respectively. Due to its mesogenic structure, the solubilized aceclofenac could act as a cosurfactant, raising the probability of incorporation into the interfacial film of bicontinuous microemulsions (Todosijević et al., 2014). Apart from that, bicontinuous structure and close contact with the skin might contribute to the direct release of drug (no transfer between inner and outer phases), which may explain short time necessary for reaching c_{max}. However, in the case of bicontinuous polysorbate 80-based microemulsion the absorption was delayed (2.41 ± 2.70 h), which further indicates that the dermal/transdermal delivery of aceclofenac is dependent on the surfactant structure.

Kienzler et al. (2010) assumed that intraarticular tissues, may act as reservoirs for topically applied NSAID, from which it is slowly released into the systemic circulation. Additionally, reported low systemic concentrations after percutaneous delivery of few NSAIDs (Brunner et al., 2005, 2011; Heyneman et al., 2000; Kienzler et al., 2010; Rhee et al., 2013; Rolf et al., 1999; Toshiaki et al., 1988), led to the hypothesis that NSAIDs might accumulate in the skin and/or underlying periarticular and articular tissues, without significant concentration of drug in the bloodstream. In this way, topical application of NSAID-loaded SE-based microemulsions may bring larger benefits: systemic side effects should be negligible, while high localized concentrations in the inflamed subcutaneous tissues may maximize efficacy. Our results are concurrent with these assumptions: absolute bioavailability (F_{abs}) of aceclofenac after topical application of all microemulsions was less than 5%, suggesting that aceclofenac diffuses and accumulates into deeper tissues. However, the obtained value of F_{abs} after subcutaneous application of aceclofenac solution was also low. The values of relative bioavailability

(F_{rel}) of SE-based microemulsions (transdermal in comparison to subcutaneous administration) were greater than 30% (Todosijević et al., 2015), leading us to the conclusion that aceclofenac penetrates the SC and passes epidermis and dermis. Hence, our study is consistent with other researches regarding the low F_{abs} of NSAIDs, however, making any final conclusion about the fate of aceclofenac following penetration through SC is not possible without direct measurement of aceclofenac concentration in the local tissue. To confirm this hypothesis, future testing on animal models is required in order to determine whether the achieved concentration of aceclofenac, after topical application of microemulsions, is high enough to have a therapeutic effect in the inflamed tissues.

7.5 CONCLUSIONS

Driven by demand for environmental protection and similarity with natural molecules, progressive replacement of synthetic materials with "green" alternatives has distinguished a group of nonionic SE surfactants. This chapter provided a brief overview of the influence of chain length, HLB value, and monoester content of SEs, nature, and concentration of the cosurfactant, oil, and aqueous phase, as well as the components' weight ratio on the formation, performances, and stability of developed SE-based micro/nanoemulsion systems. In addition, the techniques most commonly used in the characterization of the phase behavior, inner structure, and physicochemical properties of submicron systems formulated with SEs, were presented. Additionally, we gave a short theoretical background on the in vitro/ex vivo/in vivo methods for the assessment of dermal and systemic availability concomitant with their practical application regarding different types of NSAID-loaded SE-based micro/nanosized colloidal carriers. Research conducted so far has suggested that presence of SEs significantly improved percutaneous delivery of a model NSAID, irrespectively of the carrier type, over conventionally used synthetic ethoxylated surfactants, such as polysorbate 80. Finally, micro/nanoemulsions based on natural surfactants proved to be promising carriers for effective dermal and/or transdermal NSAID delivery.

ACKNOWLEDGMENT

The authors would like to acknowledge the financial support from the Ministry of Education, Science and Technological Development, Republic of Serbia through the Project TR34031.

REFERENCES

Alany RG, Tucker IG, Davies NM, Rades T: Characterizing colloidal structures of pseudoternary phase diagrams formed by oil/water/amphiphile systems, *Drug Dev Ind Pharm* 27:31–38, 2001.

Ayala-Bravo HA, Quintanar-Guerrero D, Naik A, Kalia YN, Cornejo-Bravo JM, Ganem-Quintanar A: Effects of sucrose oleate and sucrose laureate on in vivo human stratum corneum permeability, *Pharm Res* 20:1267–1273, 2003.

Bardhan S, Kundu K, Saha SK, Paul BK: Physicochemical studies of mixed surfactant microemulsions with isopropyl myristate as oil, *J Colloid Interface Sci* 402:180–189, 2013.

Baspinar Y, Keck CM, Borchert HH: Development of a positively charged prednicarbate nano-emulsion, *Int J Pharm* 383:201–208, 2010.

Benita S, Levy MY: Submicron emulsions as colloidal drug carriers for intravenous administration: comprehensive physicochemical characterization, *J Pharm Sci* 82:1069–1079, 1993.

Bhattachary S, Stokes JP, Kim MW, Huang JS: Percolation in an oil-continuous microemulsion, *Phys Rev Lett* 55:1884–1887, 1985.

Bhinge JR, Kumar RV, Sinha VR: A simple and sensitive stability-indicating RP-HPLC assay method for the determination of aceclofenac, *J Chromatogr Sci* 46:440–444, 2008.

Bolzinger MA, Thevenin CC, Poelman MC: Bicontinuous sucrose ester microemulsion: a new vehicle for topical delivery of niflumic acid, *Int J Pharm* 176:39–45, 1998.

Bolzinger-Thevenin MA, Grossiord JL, Poelman MC: Characterization of a sucrose ester micro-emulsion by freeze fracture electron micrograph and small angle neutron scattering experi-ments, *Langmuir* 15:2307–2315, 1999.

Brunner M, Davies D, Martin W, Leuratti C, Lackner E, Müller M: A new topical formulation enhances relative diclofenac bioavailability in healthy male subjects, *Br J Clin Pharmacol* 71:852–859, 2011.

Brunner M, Dehghanyar P, Seigfried B, Martin W, Menke G, Müller M: Favourable dermal pen-etration of diclofenac after administration to the skin using a novel pray gel formulation, *Br J Clin Pharmacol* 60:573–577, 2005.

Buszello K, Harnisch S, Müller RH, Müller BW: The influence of alkali fatty acids on the proper-ties and the stability of parenteral O/W emulsions modified with Solutol HS15®, *Eur J Pharm Biopharm* 49:143–149, 2000.

Calderilla-Fajardo SB, Cázares-Delgadillo J, Villalobos-García R, Quintanar-Guerrero D, Ganem-Quintanar A, Robles R: Influence of sucrose esters on the in vivo percutaneous penetration of octyl methoxycinnamate formulated in nanocapsules, nanoemulsion, and emulsion, *Drug Dev Ind Pharm* 32:107–113, 2006.

Cázares-Delgadillo J, Naik A, Kalia YN, Quintanar-Guerrero D, Ganem-Quintanar A: Skin permeation enhancement by sucrose esters: a pH-dependent phenomenon, *Int J Pharm* 297:204–212, 2005.

Cevc G, Vierl U: Nanotechnology and the transdermal route: a state of the art review and critical appraisal, *J Control Release* 141:277–299, 2010.

Chakraborty I, Moulik SP: Physicochemical studies on microemulsions 9. Conductance percolation of AOT-derived W/O microemulsion with aliphatic and aromatic hydrocarbon oils, *J Colloid Interface Sci* 289:530–541, 2005.

Changez M, Varshney M, Chander J, Dinda AK: Effect of the composition of lecithin/*n*-propanol/isopropyl myristate/water microemulsions on barrier properties of mice skin for transdermal permeation of tetracaine hydrochloride: in vitro, *Colloids Surf B* 50:18–25, 2006.

Cruces MA, Plou FJ, Ferrer M, Bernabé M, Ballesteros A: Improved synthesis of sucrose fatty acid monoesters, *J Am Oil Chem Soc* 78:541–546, 2001.

Csóka G, Marton S, Zelko R, Otomo N, Antal I: Application of sucrose fatty acid esters in transder-mal therapeutic systems, *Eur J Pharm Biopharm* 65:233–237, 2007.

Daniels R: Galenic principles of modern skin care products. In: Skin Care Forum 2001, Society for Dermopharmacy, p. 25.

Das S, Ng WK, Tan RBH: Sucrose ester stabilized solid lipid nanoparticles and nanostructured lipid carriers: I. Effect of formulation variables on the physicochemical properties, drug release and stability of clotrimazole-loaded nanoparticles, *Nanotechnology* 25:105101, 2014.

Đorđević SM, Cekić ND, Savić MM, Isailović TM, Ranđelović DV, Marković BD, Savić SR, Timić Stamenić T, Daniels R, Savić SD: Parenteral nanoemulsions as promising carriers for brain delivery of risperidone: design, characterization and in vivo pharmacokinetic evaluation, *Int J Pharm* 493:40–54, 2015.

Fanun M: Structure probing of water/mixed nonionic surfactants/caprylic-capric triglyceride system using conductivity and NMR, *J Mol Liq* 133:22–27, 2007a.

Fanun M: Conductivity, viscosity, NMR and diclofenac solubilization capacity studies of mixed nonionic surfactants microemulsions, *J Mol Liq* 135:5–13, 2007b.

Fanun M: Phase behavior, transport, diffusion and structural parameters of nonionic surfactants microemulsions, *J Mol Liq* 139:14–22, 2008a.

Fanun M: A study of the properties of mixed nonionic surfactants microemulsions by NMR, SAXS, viscosity and conductivity, *J Mol Liq* 142:103–110, 2008b.

Fanun M: Surfactant chain length effect on the structural parameters of nonionic microemulsions, *J Dispers Sci Technol* 29:289–296, 2008c.

Fanun M: Oil type effect on diclofenac solubilization in mixed nonionic surfactants microemulsions, *Colloids Surf A* 343:75–82, 2009a.

Fanun M: Properties of microemulsions with sugar surfactants and peppermint oil, *Colloid Polym Sci* 287:899–910, 2009b.

Fanun M: Properties of microemulsions based on mixed nonionic surfactants and mixed oils, *J Mol Liq* 150:25–32, 2009c.

Fanun M: Microemulsions with nonionic surfactants and mixed oils, *Soft Mater* 7:258–276, 2009d.

Fanun M: Microemulsions with mixed nonionic surfactants. In Fanun M, editor: *Microemulsions: properties and applications*, Boca Raton, FL, 2009e, CRC Press, pp 87–142.

Fanun M: Formulation and characterization of microemulsions based on mixed nonionic surfactants and peppermint oil, *J Colloid Interface Sci* 343:496–503, 2010a.

Fanun M: Microemulsions with nonionic surfactants and mint oil, *Open Colloid Sci J* 3:9–14, 2010b.

Fanun M: Properties of microemulsions with mixed nonionic surfactants and citrus oil, *Colloids Surf A* 369:246–252, 2010c.

Fanun M: Diclofenac solubilization in mixed nonionic surfactants microemulsions. In Fanun M, editor: *Colloids in drug delivery*, Boca Raton, FL, 2010d, CRC Press, pp 271–298.

Fanun M, Al-Diyn WS: Electrical conductivity and self diffusion-NMR studies of the system: water/sucrose laurate/ethoxylated mono-di-glyceride/isopropylmyristate, *Colloids Surf A* 277:83–89, 2006.

Fanun M, Makharza S, Sowwan M: UV-visible and AFM studies of nonionic microemulsions, *J Dispers Sci Technol* 31:501–511, 2010a.

Fanun M, Makharza S, Sowwan M: Transition from micelles to microemulsions in sugar-based surfactant systems probed by fluorescence spectroscopy and atomic force microscopy, *J Dispers Sci Technol* 31:1212–1219, 2010b.

Fanun M, Papadimitriou V, Xenakis A: Characterization of cephalexin loaded nonionic microemulsions, *J Colloid Interface Sci* 361:115–121, 2011.

Fanun M, Wachtel E, Antalek B, Aserin A, Garti N: A study of the microstructure of four-component sucrose ester microemulsions by SAXS and NMR, *Colloids Surf A* 180:173–186, 2001.

Feldman Y, Kozlovich N, Nir I, Garti N: Dielectric relaxation in sodium bis (2-ethylhexyl) sulfosuccinate–water–decane microemulsions near the percolation temperature threshold, *Phys Rev E* 51:478–491, 1995.

Fisher S, Wachtel EJ, Aserin A, Garti N: Solubilization of simvastatin and phytosterols in a dilutable microemulsion system, *Colloids Surf B* 107:35–42, 2013.

Fiume Z: Final report on the safety assessment of lecithin and hydrogenated lecithin, *Int J Toxicol* 20:21–45, 2001.

Flaten GE, Palac Z, Engesland A, Filipović-Grčić J, Vanić Ž, Škalko-Basnet N: In vitro skin models as a tool in optimization of drug formulation, *Eur J Pharm Sci* 75:10–24, 2015.

Floury J, Desrumaux A, Lardières J: Effect of high pressure homogenization on droplet size distributions and rheological properties of model oil-in-water emulsions, *Innov Food Sci Emerg Technol* 1:127–134, 2000.

Friedman DI, Schwarz JS, Weisspapir M: Submicron emulsion vehicle for enhanced transdermal delivery of steroidal and nonsteroidal anti-inflammatory drugs, *J Pharm Sci* 84:324–329, 1995.

Ganem-Quintanar A, Quintanar-Guerrero D, Falson-Rieg F, Buri P: Ex vivo oral mucosal permeation of lidocaine hydrochloride with sucrose fatty acid esters as absorption enhancers, *Int J Pharm* 173:203–210, 1998.

Garti N, Aserin A, Ezrahi S, Tiunova I, Berkovic G: Water behavior in nonionic surfactant systems I: subzero temperature behavior of water in nonionic microemulsions studied by DSC, *J Colloid Interface Sci* 178:60–68, 1996.

Garti N, Aserin A, Tiunova I, Fanun M: A DSC study of water behavior in water-in-oil microemulsions stabilized by sucrose esters and butanol, *Colloids Surf A* 170:1–18, 2000.

Glatter O, Orthaber D, Stradner A, Scherf G, Fanun M, Garti N, Clement V, Leser ME: Sugarester nonionic microemulsion: structural characterization, *J Colloid Interface Sci* 241:215–225, 2001.

Gutiérrez JM, González C, Maestro A, Solè I, Pey CM, Nolla J: Nano-emulsions: new application and optimization of their preparation, *Curr Opin Colloid Interface Sci* 13:245–251, 2008.

Hafner A, Lovrić J, Lakoš GP, Pepić I: Nanotherapeutics in the EU: an overview on current state and future directions, *Int J Nanomed* 9:1005–1023, 2014.

Herkenne C, Alberti I, Naik A, Kalia YN, Mathy FX, Préat V, Guy RH: In vivo methods for the assessment of topical drug bioavailability, *Pharm Res* 25:87–103, 2008.

Herkenne C, Naik A, Kalia YN, Hadgraft J, Guy RH: Pig ear skin ex vivo as a model for in vivo dermatopharmacokinetic studies in man, *Pharm Res* 23:1850–1856, 2006.

Heyneman CA, Lawless-Liday C, Wall GC: Oral versus topical NSAIDs in rheumatic diseases: a comparison, *Drugs* 60:555–574, 2000.

Hippalgaonkar K, Majumdar S, Kansara V: Injectable lipid emulsions—advancements, opportunities and challenges, *AAPS PharmSciTech* 11:1526–1540, 2010.

Hoeller S, Sperger A, Valenta C: Lecithin based nanoemulsions: a comparative study of the influence of non-ionic surfactants and the cationic phytosphingosine on physicochemical behaviour and skin permeation, *Int J Pharm* 370:181–186, 2009.

Isailović T, Đorđević S, Marković B, Ranđelović D, Cekić N, Lukić M, Pantelić I, Daniels R, Savić S: Biocompatible nanoemulsions for improved aceclofenac skin delivery: formulation approach using combined-mixture process experimental design, *J Pharm Sci* 105:308–323, 2016.

Jafari SM, Assadpoor E, He Y, Bhandari B: Re-coalescence of emulsion droplets during high energy emulsification, *Food Hydrocoll* 22:1191–1202, 2008.

Jumaa M, Müller BW: The effect of oil components and homogenization conditions on the physicochemical properties and stability of parenteral fat emulsions, *Int J Pharm* 163:81–89, 1998.

Keck CM, Müller RH: Size analysis of submicron particles by laser diffractometry—90% of the published measurements are false, *Int J Pharm* 355:150–163, 2008.

Kienzler JL, Gold M, Nollevaux F: Systemic bioavailability of topical diclofenac sodium gel 1% versus oral diclofenac sodium in healthy volunteers, *J Clin Pharmacol* 50:50–61, 2010.

Klang V, Matsko N, Raupach K, El-Hagin N, Valenta C: Development of sucrose stearate-based nanoemulsions and optimization through γ-cyclodextrin, *Eur J Pharm Biopharm* 79:58–67, 2011a.

Klang V, Matsko NB, Valenta C, Hofer F: Electron microscopy of nanoemulsions: an essential tool for characterisation and stability assessment, *Micron* 43:85–103, 2012a.

Klang V, Matsko N, Zimmermann AM, Vojnikovic E, Valenta C: Enhancement of stability and skin permeation by sucrose stearate and cyclodextrins in progesterone nanoemulsions, *Int J Pharm* 393:152–160, 2010.

Klang V, Schwarz JC, Lenobel B, Nadj M, Auböck J, Wolzt M, Valenta C: Validation of the porcine ear skin and penetration assessment of novel sucrose stearate emulsions, *Eur J Pharm Biopharm* 80:604–614, 2012b.

Klang V, Schwarz JC, Matsko N, Rezvani E, El-Hagin N, Wirth M, Valenta C: Semi-solid sucrose stearate-based emulsions as dermal drug delivery systems, *Pharmaceutics* 3:275–306, 2011b.

Klang V, Valenta C: Lecithin-based nanoemulsions, *J Drug Deliv Sci Technol* 21:55–76, 2011.

Klang V, Valenta C, Matsko NB: Electron microscopy of pharmaceutical systems, *Micron* 44:45–74, 2013.

Kong M, Chen XG, Kweon DK, Park HJ: Investigations on skin permeation of hyaluronic acid based nanoemulsion as transdermal carrier, *Carbohydr Polym* 86:837–843, 2011.

Krauel K, Girvan L, Hook S, Rades T: Characterisation of colloidal drug delivery systems from the naked eye to Cryo-FESEM, *Micron* 38:796–803, 2007.

Kristl J, Volk B, Gasperlin M, Sentjurc M, Jurkovic P: Effect of colloidal carriers on ascorbyl palmitate stability, *Eur J Pharm Sci* 19:181–189, 2003.

Lademann J, Jacobi U, Surber C, Weigmann HJ, Fluhr JW: The tape stripping procedure—evaluation of some critical parameters, *Eur J Pharm Biopharm* 72:317–323, 2009.

Lawrence MJ, Rees GD: Microemulsion-based media as novel drug delivery systems, *Adv Drug Deliv Rev* 45:89–121, 2000.

Liu CH, Chang FY: Development and characterization of eucalyptol microemulsions for topic delivery of curcumin, *Chem Pharm Bull* 59:172–178, 2011.

McClements DJ: Nanoemulsions versus microemulsions: terminology, differences and similarities, *Soft Matter* 8:1719–1729, 2012.

McPherson LM, Cimino NM: Topical NSAID formulations, *Pain Med* 14:35–39, 2013.

Mehta SK, Dewan RK, Bala K: Percolation phenomenon and the study of conductivity, viscosity, and ultrasonic velocity in microemulsions, *Phys Rev E* 50:4759–4762, 1994.

Mehta SK, Kaur G: Microemulsions: thermodynamic and dynamic properties. In Tadashi M, editor: *Thermodynamics*, Rijeka, 2011, In Tech, pp 381–406.

Mehta SK, Kaur G, Mutneja R, Bhasin KK: Solubilization, microstructure, and thermodynamics of fully dilutable U-type Brij microemulsion, *J Colloid Interface Sci* 338:542–549, 2009.

Morais JM, Burgess DJ: In vitro release testing methods for vitamin E nanoemulsions, *Int J Pharm* 475:393–400, 2014.

Muchtar S, Abdulrazik M, Frucht-Perv J, Benita S: Ex vivo permeation study of indomethacin from a submicron emulsion through albino rabbit cornea, *J Control Release* 44:55–64, 1997.

Müller RH, Schmidt S, Buttle I, Akkar A, Schmitt J, Brömer S: SolEmuls®—novel technology for the formulation of i.v. emulsions with poorly soluble drugs, *Int J Pharm* 269:293–302, 2004.

Nam YS, Kim JW, Park JY, Shim J, Lee JS, Han SH: Tocopheryl acetate nanoemulsions stabilized with lipid–polymer hybrid emulsifiers for effective skin delivery, *Colloids Surf B* 94:51–57, 2012.

Naoui W, Bolzinger MA, Fenet B, Pelletier J, Valour JP, Kalfat R, Chevalier Y: Microemulsion microstructure influences the skin delivery of an hydrophilic drug, *Pharm Res* 28:1683–1695, 2011.

Narkar Y: Bioequivalence for topical products—an update, *Pharm Res* 27:2590–2601, 2010.

Okumura H, Kitazawa N, Wada S, Hotta H: Stability of sucrose fatty acid esters under acidic and basic conditions, *J Oleo Sci* 60:313–320, 2011.

Pantelic I, Lukic M, Daniels R, Savic S: Alkyl polyglucoside-based delivery systems: in vitro/in vivo skin absorption assessment. In Pantelić I, editor: *Alkyl polyglucosides: from natural-origin surfactants to prospective delivery systems*, Cambridge, 2014, Woodhead Publishing, Elsevier, pp 107–134.

Paolino D, Ventura CA, Nistico S, Puglisi G, Fresta M: Lecithin microemulsions for the topical administration of ketoprofen: percutaneous adsorption through human skin and in vivo human skin tolerability, *Int J Pharm* 244:21–31, 2002.

Podlogar F, Bester Rogac M, Gasperlin M: The effect of internal structure of selected water-Tween 40-Imwitor 308-IPM microemulsions on ketoprofene release, *Int J Pharm* 302:68–77, 2005.

Podlogar F, Gasperlin M, Tomsic M, Jamnik A, Rogac MB: Structural characterisation of water-Tween 40/Imwitor 308-isopropyl myristate microemulsions using different experimental methods, *Int J Pharm* 276:115–128, 2004.

Puglia C, Rizza L, Drechsler M, Bonina F: Nanoemulsions as vehicles for topical administration of glycyrrhetic acid: characterization and in vitro and in vivo evaluation, *Drug Deliv* 17:123–129, 2010.

Rhee YS, Nguyen T, Park ES, Chi SC: Formulation and biopharmaceutical evaluation of a transdermal patch containing aceclofenac, *Arch Pharm Res* 36(5):602–607, 2013.

Roberts MS, Cross SE: Percutaneous absorption of topically applied NSAIDs and other compounds: role of solute properties, skin physiology and delivery systems, *Inflammopharmacology* 7:339–350, 1999.

Rolf C, Engström B, Beauchard C, Jacobs LD, Le Liboux A: Intra-articular absorption and distribution of ketoprofen after topical plaster application and oral intake in 100 patients undergoing knee arthroscopy, *Rheumatology* 38:564–567, 1999.

Russell LM, Guy RH: Measurements and prediction of the rate and extent of drug delivery into and through the skin, *Expert Opin Drug Deliv* 6:355–369, 2009.

Sahle FF, Metz H, Wohlrab J, Neubert RH: Polyglycerol fatty acid ester surfactant-based microemulsions for targeted delivery of ceramide AP into the stratum corneum: formulation, characterisation, in vitro release and penetration investigation, *Eur J Pharm Biopharm* 82:139–150, 2012.

Sainsbury F, Zeng B, Middelberg APJ: Towards designer nanoemulsions for precision delivery of therapeutics, *Curr Opin Chem Eng* 4:11–17, 2014.

Savić S, Tamburić S, Savić M: From conventional towards new—natural surfactants in drug delivery systems design: current status and perspectives, *Expert Opin Drug Deliv* 7:353–369, 2010.

Schwarz JC, Klang V, Hoppel M, Mahrhauser D, Valenta C: Natural microemulsions: formulation design and skin interaction, *Eur J Pharm Biopharm* 81:557–562, 2012.

Selzer D, Abdel-Mottaleb MMA, Hahn T, Schaefer UF, Neumann D: Finite and infinite dosing: difficulties in measurements, evaluations and predictions, *Adv Drug Deliv Rev* 65:278–294, 2013.

Shchipunov YA: Self-organising structures of lecithin, *Russ Chem Rev* 66:301–322, 1997.

Shukla A, Neubert RHH: Diffusion behavior of pharmaceutical o/w microemulsions studied by dynamic light scattering, *Colloid Polym Sci* 284:568–573, 2006.

Silva HD, Cerqueira MA, Vicente AA: Nanoemulsions for food applications: development and characterization, *Food Bioprocess Technol* 5:854–867, 2012.

Söderman O, Nyden M: NMR in microemulsions. NMR translational diffusion studies of a model microemulsion, *Colloids Surf A* 158:273–280, 1999.

Solans C, Garcia-Celma MJ: Surfactants for microemulsions, *Curr Opin Colloid Interface Sci* 2:464–471, 1997.

Song Y, Noh TW, Lee SI, Gaines JR: Experimental study of the three-dimensional ac conductivity and dielectric constant of a conductor-insulator composite near the percolation threshold, *Phys Rev B* 33:904–908, 1986.

Soultani S, Ognier S, Engasser JM, Ghoul M: Comparative study of some surface active properties of fructose esters and commercial sucrose esters, *Colloids Surf A* 227:35–44, 2003.

Sznitowska M, Janicki S, Dabrowska E, Zurowska-Pryczkowska K: Submicron emulsions as drug carriers: studies on destabilization potential of various drugs, *Eur J Pharm Sci* 12:175–179, 2001.

Szűts A, Budai-Szűcs M, Erős I, Otomo N, Szabó-Révész P: Study of gel-forming properties of sucrose esters for thermosensitive drug delivery systems, *Int J Pharm* 383:132–137, 2010.

Szűts A, Szabó-Révész P: Sucrose esters as natural surfactants in drug delivery systems—a mini-review, *Int J Pharm* 433:1–9, 2012.

Tadros TF: *Applied surfactants—principles and applications*, Wiley VHC, 2005, Weinheim.

Tadros T, Izquierdo P, Esquena J, Solans C: Formation and stability of nano-emulsions, *Adv Colloid Interface Sci* 108–109:303–318, 2004.

Teichmann A, Heuschkel S, Jacobi U, Presse G, Neubert RH, Sterry W, Lademann J: Comparison of stratum corneum penetration and localization of a lipophilic model drug applied in an o/w microemulsion and an amphiphilic cream, *Eur J Pharm Biopharm* 67:699–706, 2007.

Thevenin MA, Grossiord JL, Poelman MC: Sucrose esters/cosurfactant microemulsion systems for transdermal delivery: assessment of bicontinuous structures, *Int J Pharm* 137:177–186, 1996.

Todosijević MN, Cekić ND, Savić MM, Gašperlin M, Ranđelović DV, Savić SD: Sucrose ester-based biocompatible microemulsions as vehicles for aceclofenac as a model drug: formulation approach using D-optimal mixture design, *Colloid Polym Sci* 292:3061–3076, 2014.

Todosijević MN, Savić MM, Batinić BB, Marković BD, Gašperlin M, Ranđelović DV, Lukić MŽ, Savić SD: Biocompatible microemulsions of a model NSAID for skin delivery: a decisive role of surfactants in skin penetration/irritation profiles and pharmacokinetic performance, *Int J Pharm* 496:931–941, 2015.

Toshiaki N, Akira K, Kiyoshi S, Koichi T, Koichi M, Kazuhiko S, Yujin T, Masaharu K, Tateo M, Nobuo T: Percutaneous absorption of diclofenac in rats and humans: aqueous gel formulation, *Int J Pharm* 46:1–7, 1988.

Trotta M, Pattarino F, Ignoni T: Stability of drug-carrier emulsions containing phosphatidylcholine mixtures, *Eur J Pharm Biopharm* 53:203–208, 2002.

Vaile JH, Davis P: Topical NSAIDs for musculoskeletal conditions: a review of the literature, *Drugs* 56:783–799, 1998.

Wang Y, Cory AL: A novel stable supersaturated submicron lipid emulsion of tirilazad, *Pharm Dev Technol* 4:333–345, 1999.

Washington C: Stability of lipid emulsions for drug delivery, *Adv Drug Deliv Rev* 20:131–145, 1996.

Williams AC, Barry BB: Penetration enhancers, *Adv Drug Deliv Rev* 56:603–618, 2004.

Yaghmur A, Aserin A, Tiunova I, Garti N: Sub-zero temperature behaviour of non-ionic microemulsions in the presence of propylene glycol by DSC, *J Therm Anal Calorim* 69:163–177, 2002.

Zhou H, Yue Y, Liu G, Li Y, Zhang J, Gong Q, Yan Z, Duan M: Preparation and characterization of a lecithin nanoemulsion as a topical delivery system, *Nanoscale Res Lett* 5:224–230, 2010.

Chapter 8

Natural and Modified Silica-Based Materials as Carriers for NSAIDs

Danina Krajišnik*, Aleksandra Daković**, Jelena Janićijević*, Jela Milić*
*Department of Pharmaceutical Technology and Cosmetology, Faculty of Pharmacy, University of Belgrade, Belgrade, Serbia; **Institute for the Technology of Nuclear and Other Mineral Raw Materials, Belgrade, Serbia

8.1 INTRODUCTION

Minerals are used in pharmaceutical preparations/products as either active ingredients or excipients. When used as active ingredients (i.e., having therapeutic properties), they can be administered either orally (by ingestion) or topically (by application on the skin). Traditionally, a variety of minerals have been used as excipients due to certain desirable physical and physicochemical properties, such as high adsorption capacity, high specific surface area, good swelling capacity, thixotropy, plasticity, opacity, and color. Clearly, such minerals must not be toxic to humans. Naturally occurring clay minerals, defined as the layered magnesium or aluminum silicates composed of tetrahedrally coordinated silicate sheets and octahedrally coordinated magnesium or aluminum hydroxide sheets, are fairly abundant on earth and so far the most commonly used in the aforementioned purposes as adsorbents, diluents, binders, suspending agents, or viscosity increasing agents (Carretero and Pozo, 2009, 2010; Rowe et al., 2009; Yang et al., 2016).

In the 1960s it was observed that oral absorption of several drugs was reduced by coadministration of clay-based intestinal adsorbents or by the presence of clay stabilizers (e.g., suspending or emulsifying agents) in liquid formulations. It was soon realized that the effects of such interactions in the concomitant administration of clay minerals with active substances might not be purely negative, but could also be used to achieve technological and biopharmaceutical benefits. This was the starting point in the use of clays in modified drug delivery (Aguzzi et al., 2007).

Microsized and Nanosized Carriers for NSAIDs. http://dx.doi.org/10.1016/B978-0-12-804017-1.00008-X

More recently, natural zeolites (NZs) have emerged as potential materials in pharmaceutical preparations. Zeolites are hydrated microporous tektoaluminosilicates consisting of three-dimensional frameworks of SiO_4^{4-} and AlO_4^{5-} tetrahedra linked through shared oxygen atoms. Clinoptilolite (CLI), mineral from the heulandite group of zeolites, $((Na,K)_6(Al_6Si_3O)O_{72} \cdot nH_2O)$, is the most abundant sedimentary zeolite in nature. The use of CLI in biomedicine has been demonstrated for the purpose of the external skin treatment, as antidiarrheal remedies, or as an active ingredient in antacid drugs. The main zeolite properties involved in reactions and/or processes relevant for its biomedical applications are its alkaline nature, cation exchange, physical sorption, and possibility to alter external surface properties with organic molecules, that is, long chain cationic surfactants (Cerri et al., 2016; Colella, 2011; Milić et al., 2014).

Both natural and modified clays and zeolites have been investigated as potential carriers for various drugs (Aguzzi et al., 2007; Chrzanowski et al., 2013; Colella, 2011; Milić et al., 2014; Rodrigues et al., 2013; Yang et al., 2016). Researches related to their application as carrier for nonsteroidal anti-inflammatory drugs (NSAIDs) are particularly interesting, since they are typically used chronically to reduce pain, decrease stiffness, improve function in patients with osteoarthritis, rheumatoid arthritis, and other forms of arthritis. Additionally, NSAIDs are also used for the more acute treatment of pain including headache, dysmenorrheal, and postoperative pain (Brooks and Day, 1991; Simon, 1996). However, since NSAIDs use can induce severe side effects, advances in NSAIDs pharmaceutics have recently been focused on the development of options to address serious dose-dependent gastrointestinal, cardiovascular, and renal adverse effects. One of the approaches to address these concerns is the development of drug carrier for modified (prolonged) NSAIDs release, enabling reduction of dose frequency, and thus reducing side effects along with the improvement of patience compliance (Altman et al., 2015).

In addition to the aforementioned natural porous mineral materials, diatomaceous earth (diatomite), natural and biogenic material has been intensively investigated as a potential excipient for various pharmaceutical applications (Aw et al., 2012; Todd et al., 2014; Vasani et al., 2015). Due to their unique properties, which include low density, high porosity, large surface area, high absorptive capacity, low thermal conductivity, and chemical inertness, on the basis of which this material so far has found wide application in industry, interest in diatomite as a potential drug carrier is increasing (Aw et al., 2011; Bariana et al., 2013; Janićijević et al., 2014; Losic et al., 2010; Zhang et al., 2013).

In this chapter an overview of physicochemical and functionality-related characteristics of natural silica–based materials (clays, zeolites, and diatomites), which have been investigated in the drug delivery of NSAIDs is presented, along with various possibilities of surface modification performed in order to improve their properties as potential drug carriers.

8.2 NATURAL AND MODIFIED ALUMINOSILICATES: CHARACTERIZATION AND APPLICATION IN DRUG DELIVERY

8.2.1 Physicochemical and Functionality-Related Characteristics of Natural and Modified Aluminosilicates: An Overview

Clay minerals are fairly abundant on earth, and they are defined as the layered magnesium or aluminum silicates composed of tetrahedrally coordinated silicate sheets and octahedrally coordinated magnesium or aluminum hydroxide sheets as shown in Fig. 8.1. Depending upon the way of combination between those octahedral and tetrahedral sheets, various clay minerals can be formed, such as 1:1 type in kaolinite or 2:1 in montmorillonite (MMT), saponite, and hectorite (Yang et al., 2016). Clays that are commonly used in pharmaceutical preparations are kaolinite, talc, smectites (MMT, saponite, and hectorite), palygorskite (Pal), and sepiolite. They are used as active ingredients (having therapeutic properties) in oral dosage forms as antacids, gastrointestinal protectors, antidiarrhetics as well as in topical preparations as dermatological protectors, anti-inflammatories and local anesthetics (Carretero and Pozo, 2009; Carretero et al., 2013; Cervini-Silva et al., 2015; Rodrigues et al., 2013; Viseras et al., 2010; Viseras and Lopez-Galindo, 1999).

In addition to application as active pharmaceutical ingredients, clay minerals have been used as excipients in various pharmaceutical products as lubricants,

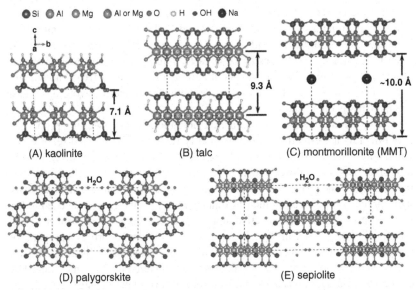

FIGURE 8.1 Crystal structures of the pharmaceutical used clays. (A) Kaolinite, (B) talc, (C) montmorillonite *(MMT)*, (D) palygorskite, and (E) sepiolite, where *dashed lines* represent the unit cell. *(Reprinted from Yang JH, Lee JH, Ryu HJ, Elzatahry AA, Alothman ZA, Choy JH: Drug–clay nanohybrids as sustained delivery systems, Appl Clay Sci n/a:n/a, 2016, with permission from Elsevier)*

adsorbents, disintegrants, diluents, binders, stabilizing agents, suspending agents, viscosity increasing agents, and flavor correctors due to their advantageous physicochemical and functional properties, such as high specific surface area, adsorption, and ion exchange, thixotropy, swelling property, chemical inertness, and low toxicity for oral administration. Additionally, their application in drug delivery has been intensively investigated in the last two decades due to its composition which can be easily modified to serve different purposes (Aguzzi et al., 2007; Carretero and Pozo, 2009; Chrzanowski et al., 2013; Yang et al., 2016).

MMT is a phyllosilicate clay of the smectite group which has been used traditionally as a pharmaceutical excipient. In MMT, which is composed of silica tetrahedral sheets layered between alumina octahedral sheets, trivalent Al replaces some of quadrivalent Si that induces a net negative charge that leads to the adsorption of alkaline earth metal ions in the interlayer space. Such imperfection is responsible for the activity and exchange reactions with inorganic compounds (Bhattacharyya and Gupta, 2008). MMT is unique in its structure; it has a platy structure with ≤1 nm unit thickness (Lee and Fu, 2003) with particle length of 100–150 nm, a high surface area, and adsorption capacity in addition to high cation exchange capacity (CEC) (up to 110 mEq/100 g) (Sinha Ray and Okamoto, 2003).

During consideration of clay minerals' application in drug delivery, several mechanisms (hydrophobic interactions, hydrogen bonding, protonation, ligand exchange, cation exchange, cation bridging, and water bridging) may be involved in the interaction between clay minerals and organic (drug) molecules (Aguzzi et al., 2007). Since clay minerals are naturally occurring inorganic cationic exchangers which may undergo ion exchange with basic drugs in solution, clay minerals, such as smectites, especially MMT and saponite, have been the most commonly studied because of their higher CEC compared to other pharmaceutical silicates (such as talc, kaolin, and fibrous clay minerals) (Aguzzi et al., 2007; Chrzanowski et al., 2013; Yang et al., 2016). An idealized ion exchange process during clay–drug complexation and in vivo drug-release mechanisms is presented in Fig. 8.2.

On the basis of clay–drug interactions and their special swelling properties, clay minerals are effectively used to modify (extended or delayed-release systems) and/or target (site-specific release systems) drug release or even improve drug solubility. In the development of clay-based modified-release formulations, modulation of the properties of the clay mineral (specific surface area, porosity, hydrophilic character, and kind of exchangeable cations) may be needed to improve its affinity with the bioactive molecules. According to the European Pharmacopoeia (2013, Ph. Eur. 8.0), a *modified-release* dosage form is a preparation where the rate and/or place of release of the active substance(s) is different from that of a conventional-release dosage form administered by the same route. This deliberate modification is achieved by a special formulation design and/or manufacturing method. Modified-release dosage forms include *prolonged-release* [showing a slower release of the active substance(s) than that of a conventional-release dosage form administered by the same route; equivalent

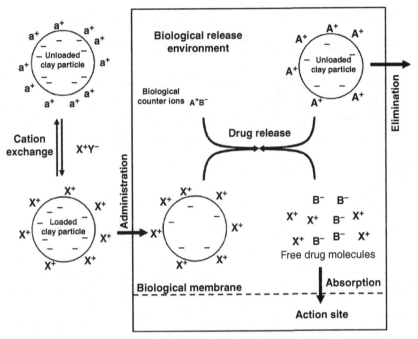

FIGURE 8.2 Idealization of clay–drug complexation and in vivo drug release mechanisms [clay mineral surface charge $(-)$; compensating cations (a^+); cationic drug (X^+); drug associated anions (Y^-); in vivo counter ions (A^+); anions associated with the counter ions (B^-)]. *(Reprinted from Aguzzi A, Cerezo P, Viseras C, Caramella C: Use of clays as drug delivery systems: possibilities and limitations, Appl Clay Sci 36:22–36, 2007, with permission from Elsevier)*

term: *extended-release* dosage form], *delayed-release* and *pulsatile-release* [showing a sequential release of the active substance(s)] dosage forms. Both thermal and chemical (mineral acid dissolutions, intercalation with inorganic or organic compounds) treatments have been reported to be useful for this purpose (Aguzzi et al., 2007; Chrzanowski et al., 2013; Rodrigues et al., 2013; Yang et al., 2016).

The hybridization between clays (specifically smectites, such as MMT, saponite, and hectorite) and drug molecules, to improve the sustained drug release, could be achieved by intercalative ion exchange reaction based on electrostatic or hydrogen bonding or ion-dipole interactions (Fig. 8.3A). Modification of the outer clay–drug nanohybrid's surface by coating with some biocompatible polymers, such as chitosan (CS), PVA (polyvinylalcohol), or polysaccharides (Joshi et al., 2012; Lee and Chen, 2004; Takahashi et al., 2005; Wang et al., 2008) was also investigated to realize the controlled or sustained release of drug molecules. As shown in Fig. 8.3B, the anionic drugs, such as flurbiprofen (FB) (Yang et al., 2013) and telmisartan (Yang et al., 2014) can be more strongly incorporated into clay layers grafted with aminopropyl silane, since

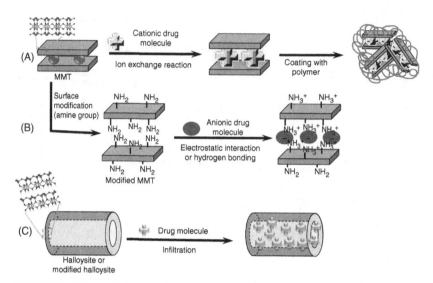

FIGURE 8.3 Schematic diagram for encapsulation method of drugs into clays for controlled and sustained release of drugs. *(Reprinted from Yang JH, Lee JH, Ryu HJ, Elzatahry AA, Alothman ZA, Choy JH: Drug–clay nanohybrids as sustained delivery systems, Appl Clay Sci n/a:n/a, 2016, with permission from Elsevier)*

the amine groups exposed on the clay layers can easily interact with anionic group of drugs via electrostatic interaction. Different from smectite, the tubular clay like halloysite could incorporate drug molecules not in interlayer space, but in a tubular pore via capillary condensation (Fig. 8.3C) (Yang et al., 2016). The number of studies related to halloysite application as microtubular drug delivery system has increased during the last two decades (Levis and Deasy, 2002; Lvov et al., 2008; Rawtani and Agrawal, 2012).

More recently, in addition to clays, some tectosilicates (zeolites) also feature in pharmaceutical preparations (Bonferoni et al., 2007; Carretero and Pozo 2009, 2010; Cerri et al., 2004; Colella, 2011). Zeolites and clays share some properties (e.g., CEC, reversible dehydration) although their structures are clearly different, being respectively tectosilicates and phyllosilicates (Cerri et al., 2016). In brief, zeolites are tectosilicates having crystalline, porous three-dimensional aluminosilicate frameworks with the loosely bound alkali (mainly Na^+ and K^+), alkaline earth (mainly Ca^{2+} and Mg^{2+}) cations, and water molecules occupying extraframework positions (Mumpton, 1999). The crystal structure of zeolites is based on a three-dimensional framework of $(SiAl)O_4$ tetrahedra wherein all four oxygen are shared with adjacent tetrahedra. Therefore, they possess a channel structure with molecular dimensions of 3–10 Å (Wang and Nguyen, 2016). Due to the isomorphic substitution of some of the quadrivalent Si with trivalent Al, the whole framework is negatively charged and normally neutralized by extraframework mono and/or divalent cations that are commonly

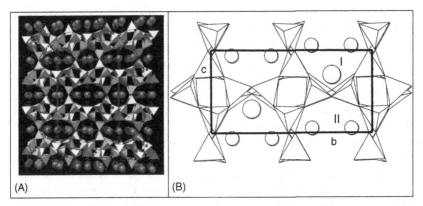

FIGURE 8.4   (A) Polyhedral model of the HEU-type framework projected parallel to the c-axis. *Large light gray spheres* represent extraframework cations in the 10-membered A and 8-membered B channels. *Small dark gray spheres* are H_2O molecules. In addition, unit cell outlines are displayed. (B) Projection of the structure of phillipsite on the b–c plane showing the position of sites I and II. Site I is located in a peripheral position displaced along one of the larger channels in the type I octagonal prism; site II is located in the cage formed by a type II octagonal prism and an adjacent type I octagonal prism, near an intersection of the two sets of channels running along a and b. *(Part A, Reprinted from Godelitsas A, Armbruster T: HEU-type zeolites modified by transition elements and lead,* Micropor Mesopor Mater *61:3–24, 2003, with permission from Elsevier; part B, Reprinted from Gualtieri A, Passaglia E, Galli E, Viani A: Rietveld structure refinement of Sr-exchanged phillipsites,* Micropor Mesopor Mater *31:33–43, 1999, with permission from Elsevier)*

exchangeable. Water molecules are also present in the structure cavities forming hydration spheres around exchangeable cations.

A wide variety of zeolites have been identified in sedimentary deposits, with the most common being CLI, analcime, heulandite, laumontite, and phillipsite. Due to their geographically widespread abundance, as well as their physical and chemical properties, NZs have generated a worldwide interest for their use in a broad range of biomedical applications as antacids for people and animals, hemostatic, or wound-healing accelerators (Cerri et al., 2016; Colella, 2011; Mumpton, 1999). Most of zeolite applications, concern CLI, that is, the most widespread and marketed zeolite in the world. Other NZs, such as phillipsite and chabazite, showed a behavior similar to that of CLI in the industrial field where they have been used as cation exchangers (Caputo and Pepe, 2007).

CLI has the same framework topology of heulandite. They share the same tetrahedral framework and monoclinic C2/m symmetry. HEU-type zeolites (Fig. 8.4A) consist of two different systems of micropores interconnected within the lattice, the first developed along the c-axis with both eight- and ten-membered rings forming A- and B-type channels (0.33 × 0.46 and 0.30 × 0.76 nm, respectively), and the second developed along the [1 0 2] and the a-axis with eight-membered rings forming C-type channels (0.26 × 0.47 nm) (Godelitsas and Armbruster, 2003).

Phillipsite is a monoclinic zeolite with a framework built up by layers of tetrahedra with eight- and four-rings roughly perpendicular to the a-axis

(Fig. 8.4B). The layers are vertically linked by four rings forming double crank-shafts with the four rings of the layer (Gualtieri et al., 1999).

Modification of minerals with long chain organic cations—surfactants is a very promising approach for designing materials with novel surface properties. The presence of surfactants at minerals' surfaces can induce or enhance the coadsorption of different organic molecules, due to the variation of the hydrophilic character of surface. The commonly used surfactants suitable for the modification of the minerals surfaces are quaternary alkyl ammonium salts. In zeolites, surfactant molecules are too large to enter zeolite channels or to access internal cation-exchange positions; their sorption is therefore limited to external surfaces of the zeolite particles. The external cation exchange capacity (ECEC) characterizes the exchange capacity of the zeolitic surfaces for surfactants. Adsorption of cationic surfactants, such as hexadecyltrimethylammonium bromide or cetylpyridinium chloride onto a negatively charged zeolitic surface involves both cation exchange and hydrophobic binding. When the amount of surfactant is below ECEC of the zeolite, surfactant cations are adsorbed at the zeolitic surface via ion exchange mechanism resulting in formation of the monolayer of the surfactants at the zeolitic surface. At surfactant concentrations greater than the critical micelle concentration (CMC) and in the presence of sufficient amounts of surfactant molecules, the adsorbed surfactants form a bilayer on the external surface of zeolites. The possible arrangement of surfactants at the zeolitic surface is presented in Fig. 8.5.

Formation of surfactant bilayer causes a charge reversal on the external zeolitic surface, providing sites where anions can be retained and cations repelled, while neutral species can partition into the hydrophobic phase. In addition, CEC remains on the internal zeolitic surfaces. Therefore, surfactant-modified NZs have properties to adsorb organic compounds and exchange inorganic cations and anions, while retaining favorable hydraulic properties.

Studies of using surfactant-modified minerals in environmental remediation were focused on removal of hydrophobic organic contaminants from water due to

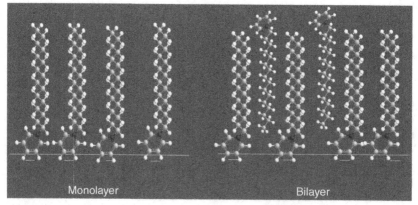

FIGURE 8.5 Surfactants monolayer and bilayer at the zeolitic surface.

the increase of hydrophobicity of the mineral surface. These modified materials showed excellent adsorption properties for organic pollutants like benzene, toluene, and xylene. Conversion of the negative surface charge by modification with surfactants increased adsorption of inorganic anions including chromate, selenate, sulfate, arsenate, antimonate, and nitrate from contaminated water (Bowman et al., 1995; de Gennaro et al., 2014; Sullivan et al., 2003; Wingenfelder et al., 2006). Surfactant-modified minerals have recently been investigated as adsorbents for mycotoxins, metabolites, and pollutants (Benkli et al., 2005; Daković et al., 2005, 2007a,b, 2010; Hrenovic et al., 2008; Rožić et al., 2009). Interactions of cationic surfactants with NZs have been extensively studied since surfactant-modified zeolites (SMZs) proved to be excellent adsorbents for various drug molecules contributing the possibility of their application in drug delivery (Milić et al., 2014).

Numerous techniques are involved in characterization of physicochemical aspects of drug–aluminosilicate complexes/composites and determination of the interaction-type between drug and carrier. X-ray diffraction (XRD), Fourier transform infrared (FTIR) spectroscopy, SEM and TEM microscopy, zeta potential measurement, surface area measurements (BET analysis), drug adsorption studies along with swelling behavior analysis are frequently used, along with pharmaceutical–technical characterization according to pharmacopoeial requirements. Biopharmaceutical evaluation is performed by in vitro (generally) drug release testing accompanied with analysis of drug release profiles while biocompatibility and safety are investigated via acute, subacute, and chronical toxicity studies.

8.2.2   Natural and Modified Aluminosilicates: Application as Carriers for NSAIDs

According to the literature, natural and modified clays can encapsulate various kinds of drugs including antibiotics, anticancer, and antifungal drugs, antihypertensives, analgesics, anti-inflammatory drugs, antipsychotics, antiarrythmics, antioxidants, etc., depending upon the interactions between host clays and guest drugs. In the aforementioned researches, MMT (natural and modified with, e.g., CS, PEG, PGLA, poloxamer, or polypropylenimine) was most frequently investigated, followed by other natural clays, for example, halloysite, laponite, kaolinite, vermiculite, and Pal (Aguzzi et al., 2007; Carretero and Pozo, 2009; Chrzanowski et al., 2013; Rodrigues et al., 2013; Yang et al., 2016).

In the following section, more detailed description of their application as drug carriers for NSAIDs is given.

As can been seen in Table 8.1, investigations on several NSAIDs [acetylsalicylic acid (ASA), diclofenac sodium (DS), ibuprofen (IBU), naproxen, FB, and 5-aminosalicylic acid (5-ASA)] have been carried out to examine the possibilities for their application within drug–clay composites. A poor water solubility

TABLE 8.1 An Overview of Literature Data on Application of Natural and Modified Clays as Carriers for NSAIDs

Clay	Drug	Modification	Preparation of drug–clay composite	Drug release testing	References
Bentonite	Naproxen	None	Adsorption from drug solution	Apparatus: not specified Dissolution medium: 0.1 M sodium phosphate buffer (pH 7.4) containing different 0.2–1.0 M NaCl Time: 6 h	Tabak et al. (2011)
MMT	5-ASA	CS	Adsorption from drug solution on CS–MMT biocomposites	Apparatus: USP apparatus 2 (paddle stirrer) Dissolution medium: 0.1 M HCl Time: 2 h	Aguzzi et al. (2010)
MMT	IBU	None	Adsorption from drug solution	Apparatus: dialysis membrane bags in a shaker bath Dissolution medium: simulated gastric fluid (pH 1.2)(for 120 min) and simulated intestinal fluid (pH 7.4)(up to 600 min)	Zheng et al. (2007)
		CS-g-lactic acid-	The drug-loaded novel nanohybrid films and porous scaffolds have been prepared by solvent casting and freeze-drying of the grafted polymer solution	Apparatus: not specified Dissolution medium: phosphate buffer (pH 7.4) Time: 8 h	Depan et al. (2009)
		Polypropylene amine	Adsorption from drug solution on polyoxypropylene–MMT composites	Apparatus: not specified Dissolution medium: phosphate buffer solution at (pH 5.4 and 7.4) Time: 6 h	Salahuddin et al. (2012)

Material	Drug	Modifier	Method	Details	Reference
MMT modified with a quaternary ammonium salt	IBU	PEG	Hot melt extrusion	Apparatus: USP apparatus 2 (paddle stirrer) Dissolution medium: phosphate buffer (pH 7.2) Time: 4 h	Campbell et al. (2014)
MMT	DS	PLGA	Double emulsion solvent evaporation technique	Apparatus: dialysis bag method Dissolution medium: simulated gastric (pH 1.2) and simulated intestinal fluid (pH 7.4) Time: 8 h	Kaur and Datta (2013)
		None	Adsorption from drug solution	Apparatus: dialysis bag method Dissolution medium: simulated gastric (pH 1.2) and simulated intestinal fluid (pH 7.4) Time: 8 h	Kaur and Datta (2014)
		Alginic acid	Gelation method	Apparatus: dialysis bag technique Dissolution medium: simulated intestinal fluid (pH 7.4) Time: 8 h	Kevadiya et al. (2010)
MMT	FB	Aminopropyl grafted	Adsorption from drug solution	Apparatus: USP apparatus 2 (paddle stirrer) Dissolution medium: pH 1.2, 4.0, and 6.8 buffer and water Time: 2 h	Yang et al. (2013)
Pal	ASA	Pyrrole	In situ electropolymerization of pyrrole monomer in the presence of Pal as the modifier and ASA as the drug source	Apparatus: not specified. The release of ASA was triggered by external electrical stimulus, in which a negative potential of −0.6 V was applied at the aspirin-Pal PPy nanocomposites and a solution of phosphate buffer (pH 7.4) was used as dissolution medium. Time: 3 h	Kong et al. (2014)

5-ASA, 5-aminosalicylic acid; ASA, acetylsalicylic acid; CS, chitosan; DS, diclofenac sodium; FB, flurbiprofen; IBU, ibuprofen; MMT, montmorillonite; Pal, palygorskite; PLGA, [poly(D,L-lactide-co-glycolide)].

of these drugs is a common problem that affects their bioavailability. It has been, therefore, continuously required to develop an efficient drug delivery system that would enhance bioavailability in addition to reduction of NSAIDs side effects. The application of new techniques for drug–clay composites preparation is also encouraging for researches in this area. Tabak et al. (2011) investigated the structural properties of the naproxen–bentonite (with the high MMT content) composites prepared by liquid drug adsorption. The samples were investigated by means of XRD, thermal analysis (TG, DTA, and DSC), and FTIR spectroscopy in addition to drug release testing. The data revealed that the drug penetrated into the interlayer spacing of the bentonite as the neutral molecule, displacing water species. The higher stability of naproxen–bentonite than raw-bentonite in the temperature range of 200–700°C signified the binding strength between the naproxen molecules and the clay sheets. The amount of the drug released at pH = 7.4 (up to 80 %) increases in line with the ionic strength of the medium. This result is ascribed to the release mechanism governed by unrestricted diffusion controlled repulsive interaction between the negatively charged bentonite surface and the anionic naproxen species. Another example of drug (IBU) intercalation into unmodified MMT as a sustained release drug carrier is presented in paper of Zheng et al. (2007). The in vitro release experiments revealed that IBU release from IBU/MMT composite was pH dependent and steadily during 6 h.

Kaur and Datta (2014) investigated the adsorption behavior of DS onto MMT as a function of pH of the aqueous drug solution, contact time, initial drug concentration, and clay dosage. Additionally, mechanism of drug–MMT interaction and in vitro release of DS from the synthesized clay–drug composites under simulated gastric and intestinal conditions was investigated. The high adsorption capacity (497 mg/g) was ascribed to physical and chemical sorption of the drug on MMT. The DSC results confirm the presence of crystalline form of the drug in the synthesized clay–drug composites. A prolonged release of the DS was observed in the simulated intestinal fluid (PBS 7.4) with 76% release in 8 h from the intercalated clay–drug composite with no burst release. A clay-based drug delivery system comprising of [poly(D,L-lactide-co-glycolide)] (PLGA)/MMT nanocomposite has been explored for the oral sustained release of DS using double emulsion solvent evaporation technique (Kaur and Datta, 2013). A drug encapsulation efficiency of 98% was obtained for the synthesized PLGA/MMT nanocomposite system, while the particle size of the drug-loaded PLGA/MMT nanocomposite was found to be in the range of 10–20 nm as analyzed by high resolution transmission electron microscopic (HRTEM) technique. The drug was found to be intercalated in the PLGA/MMT nanocomposite as confirmed by the XRD studies. The thermal analysis shows the crystalline nature of the encapsulated drug in the nanocomposite. The in vitro drug release studies of DS encapsulated PLGA/MMT nanocomposite showed a sustained drug release (up to 51%) under simulated intestinal condition (phosphate buffer saline, PBS 7.4) during 8 h.

In numerous investigations, modifications of the outer clay surface were performed in order to design materials with novel surface properties and higher drug loadings in drug–clay composites. Biocomposites of CS and MMT were prepared by solid–liquid interaction of the components to be used in modified release of 5-ASA (Aguzzi et al., 2010). It was shown that CS was effectively retained by MMT particles through cation exchange and that a synergic effect between the clay mineral and the polysaccharide was relevant for high drug loading in the 5-ASA/CS/MMT compared to both 5-ASA/MMT and 5-ASA/CS interaction composites. In addition, slower drug release with almost linear release profile from the drug-modified clay composite supported possibility of their application in modified release formulations. The nanohybrids of CS-*g*-lactic acid and sodium MMT were investigated as biomaterials for modified drug (IBU) release and tissue engineering applications. The drug-loaded nanohybrid films and porous scaffolds have been prepared by solvent casting and freeze-drying of the grafted polymer solution, respectively, from which the significant difference in drug release was observed (Depan et al., 2009). Alginic acid (AL), an anionic polysaccharide, was used for preparation of DS–MMT–AL composites by gelation method (Kevadiya et al., 2010). DS encapsulation efficiency in the MMT-AL composite beads increases with an increase in the MMT content. The controlled release of DS from DS–MMT–AL composite beads was observed to be better as compared to DS–AL. Campbell et al. (2014) investigated composites of the poorly water soluble drug IBU with layered silicates (nanoclays) and a poly(ethylene glycol) (PEG) prepared by hot melt extrusion. Addition of layered silicate retarded IBU release from the PEG matrix, even though the crystalline content of PEG was reduced. This study therefore indicates that drug release in solid dispersion systems may be modified or indeed tailored by the inclusion of layered silicates. Salahuddin et al. (2012) developed the polyoxypropylene–MMT (POP–MMT) nanohybrid as IBU carrier. Stabilized in the POP–MMT hybrid, IBU could not be released out at pH 5.4, due to the low swellability of POP–MMT in low pH domains, while the release rate at pH 7.4 was significantly increased due to the enhanced swelling behavior of this organo-MMT.

Yang et al. (2013) attempted to intercalate FB, into saponite clay modified with aminopropyl group (FB–AMP–clay). 3-Aminopropyl functionalized magnesium phyllosilicate (AMP clay) was synthesized by a one-pot direct sol–gel method, and then FB was incorporated into AMP clay (FB–AMP) at different drug/clay ratios. FB–AMP–clay showed a significant increase in release rate, that is, FB was completely released at pH 6.8 for 2 h. According to the pharmacokinetic animal study after an oral administration, the FB concentration in plasma for FB–AMP–clay was twice larger than that for intact FB, and the time to reach the peak plasma concentration was also reduced, indicating that this AMP–clay system is useful to enhance the bioavailability of FB.

A clay polymer nanocomposite (CPN) based on ASA-loaded Pal-modified polypyrrole (PPy) prepared by in situ electropolymerization of pyrrole monomer in the presence of Pal as the modifier and ASA as the drug source was proposed by Kong et al. (2014). The resulting CPN was characterized by TEM, XRD, cyclic voltammetry (CV), chronocoulometry, electrochemical impedance spectroscopy (EIS), and FTIR. The CPN was used as a new platform for aspirin delivery, which could significantly enhance aspirin loading capacity of the system and control aspirin release by external electrical stimulus. The results indicated that the proposed novel drug delivery system might be promising as an implantable device where drug release could be electrically tuned according to the patient's requirement.

Zeolites, as another representatives of aluminosilicates (both natural and modified), were also considered for application in drug delivery (oral and topical) of several drugs (metronidazole, sulfamethoxazole, erythromycin), but mostly representatives of NSAIDs (ASA, DS, diclofenac diethylamine (DDEA), and IBU) (Table 8.2).

Initial investigations related to use of zeolite (in particular, mineral CLI) for drug adsorption (for further application as drug carriers) of ASA were theoretical (Lam et al., 1998). It was demonstrated through theoretical approach that the NZ is able to bind aspirin (ASA) molecules on its surface, allowing a modulation of drug activity by its slow availability. In the following papers regarding the use of CLI (modified with surfactant molecules) as ASA carrier both theoretical and experimental studies were performed (Lam et al., 2001; Rivera et al., 2003). The results indicated that the cationic surfactant (benzalkonium chloride) is well adsorbed on the CLI model unlike the anionic surfactant (sodium lauryl sulfate) and that the presence of surfactant in the external surface of CLI improved the drug adsorption, without producing structural changes of the starting material.

The reported results (Table 8.2) of investigation on SMZs in delivery of DS, DDEA, and IBU reveal the possibility of their potential use as prospective excipients for pharmaceutical application. However, it should be emphasized that the formulation of a final dosage form includes further investigation of its overall composition and possible interaction of SMZs (as one of its components) with other auxiliary substances.

The most commonly drug used in the reported papers (Table 8.2) was DS. Diclofenac is a NSAID of the phenylacetic acid class with anti-inflammatory, analgesic, and antipyretic properties and is one the most widely prescribed NSAID worldwide (McGettigan and Henry, 2013). The usual oral or rectal dose (DS) is 75–150 mg daily in divided doses (Brayfield, 2014). Diclofenac is rapidly absorbed when given as an oral solution, sugar-coated tablets, rectal suppository, or by intramuscular injection and the terminal plasma half-life is about 1–2 h. Because of the side effects associated with its administration (gastrointestinal disturbances including discomfort, nausea, diarrhea, and occasionally bleeding or ulceration) and its short half-life, it is an ideal candidate for modified-release dosage forms where the rate and/or place of release of the active substance(s) is different from that of a conventional-release dosage form

TABLE 8.2 An Overview of Literature Data on Application of Natural and Modified Zeolites in Drug Delivery

Zeolite	Drug	Modification	Preparation of drug–zeolite composite	Application	Drug release testing	References
CLI	ASA	Theoretical study		Drug adsorption on zeolite	—	Lam et al. (1998)
CLI	Metronidazole	Theoretical study		Drug adsorption on zeolite	—	Lam et al. (2001)
CLI	Sulfamethoxazole ASA Metronidazole	Benzalkonium chloride Sodium lauryl sulfate	Theoretical study	Improvement of drug adsorption	—	Lam and Rivera (2006)
CLI	Erythromycin	Zn^{2+}-conditioning	Solvent evaporation method	Topical treatment of acne	Apparatus: USP apparatus 2 (paddle stirrer) Dissolution medium: 0.05 M KH_2PO_4/Na_2HPO_4 buffer Time: 6 h	Cerri et al. (2004)
CLI	Erythromycin	Zn^{2+}-conditioning	Adsorption onto the micronized rock by vacuum drying	Topical treatment of acne	Apparatus: USP apparatus 2 (paddle stirrer) for preliminary test and diffusion Franz cell with 20 mm diameter for powder and its formulations in inert bases Dissolution medium: phosphate buffer at pH 6.5 for the release of erythromycin and at pH 5.0 for the release of zinc Time: 6 h	Bonferoni et al. (2007)

(Continued)

TABLE 8.2 An Overview of Literature Data on Application of Natural and Modified Zeolites in Drug Delivery (*cont.*)

Zeolite	Drug	Modification	Preparation of drug–zeolite composite	Application	Drug release testing	References
CLI	Sulfamethoxazole ASA Metronidazole	Benzalkonium chloride	Adsorption from drug solution onto modified zeolites	Drug delivery support	—	Rivera et al. (2003)
CLI	Sulfamethoxazole Metronidazole	Benzalkonium chloride Sodium lauryl sulfate Tween 80	Adsorption from drug solution onto modified zeolites	Prolonged drug release	Apparatus: not specified Dissolution medium: 0.1 N HCl Time: 24 h	Rivera and Farías (2005)
CLI	Metronidazole Sulfamethoxazole	Benzalkonium chloride	Adsorption from drug solution onto modified zeolites	Drug delivery support	—	Farías et al. (2010)
CLI	Sulfamethoxazole	Benzalkonium chloride	Adsorption from drug solution onto modified zeolites	Prolonged drug release	Apparatus: not specified Dissolution medium: 0.1 M HCl Time: 12 h	Farías et al. (2011)
CLI	DS IBU DDEA	Benzalkonium chloride Hexadecyltri-methylammo-nium bromide	Adsorption from drug solution onto modified zeolites	Prolonged drug release Improvement of the excipients functionality	Apparatus: USP apparatus 2 (paddle stirrer) Dissolution medium: phosphate buffer solutions pH 6.8 for DS; pH 7.2 for IBU, and pH 7.4 for DDEA Time: 8 h	Krajišnik et al. (2010)
CLI	DS	Cetylpyridinium chloride	Adsorption from drug solution onto modified zeolites	Evaluation of drug sorption	—	Krajišnik et al. (2011)

CLI	DS	Cetylpyridinium chloride	Adsorption from drug solution onto modified zeolites	Investigation of drug adsorption and release from drug-modified zeolites composites and physical mixtures of drug and modified composites	Apparatus: USP apparatus 2 (paddle stirrer) Dissolution medium: phosphate buffer pH 6.8 Time: 8 h	Krajišnik et al. (2013a)
CLI	DS	Hexadecyltrimethylammonium bromide	Adsorption from drug solution onto modified zeolites	Investigation of drug adsorption and release from drug-modified zeolites composites and physical mixtures of drug and modified composites	Apparatus: USP apparatus 2 (paddle stirrer) Dissolution medium: phosphate buffer pH 6.8 Time: 8 h	Krajišnik et al. (2013b)
CLI	DS	Hexadecyltrimethylammonium bromide	Modified zeolite–drug physical mixtures containing DS and HB-modified zeolite in different (mmol HB/mmol DS) ratios were prepared	Utilization of ANN models for prediction of DS release from drug-modified zeolites physical mixtures	The antiedematous activity of DS-modified zeolites mixtures was assessed by quantification of the rat's paw swelling by plethysmometry (in vivo investigation)	Krajišnik et al. (2014)

(Continued)

TABLE 8.2 An Overview of Literature Data on Application of Natural and Modified Zeolites in Drug Delivery (*cont.*)

Zeolite	Drug	Modification	Preparation of drug–zeolite composite	Application	Drug release testing	References
CLI	IBU	Benzalkonium chloride Cetylpyridinium chloride	Adsorption from drug solution onto modified zeolites	Prolonged drug release	Apparatus: USP apparatus 2 (paddle stirrer) Dissolution medium: phosphate buffer pH 7.2 Time: 8 h	Krajišnik et al. (2015)
CLI	DS	Cetylpyridinium chloride	Adsorption from drug solution onto modified zeolites	Prolonged drug release	Apparatus: not specified Dissolution medium: simulated intestinal fluid (USP 25) Time: 6 h	de Gennaro et al. (2015)
PHI CHA	DS	Cetylpyridinium chloride	Adsorption from drug solution onto modified zeolites	Prolonged drug release	Apparatus: not specified Dissolution medium: simulated intestinal fluid (USP 25) Time: 1500 min	Serri et al. (2015)

ANN, artificial neural network; CHA, chabazite; CLI, clinoptilolite; DDEA, diclofenac diethylamine; PHI, phillipsite.

administered by the same route. Nowadays, attempts have been made in the field of pharmaceutical technology to modify the pharmacokinetic properties of diclofenac, leading to the creation of novel drug products with improved clinical utility (Altman et al., 2015).

In the study of Krajišnik et al. (2010), two cationic surfactants (benzalkonium chloride and hexadecyltrimethylammonium bromide) were used for modification of the zeolitic surface in two levels (equal to and twice as ECEC of the zeolitic tuff). Prepared samples were characterized by FTIR spectroscopy, thermogravimetric and HPLC analysis, while functionality-related characteristics of SMZs were evaluated by powder flow determination. The prepared SMZs were used for additional investigation of three model drugs: DDEA, DS, and IBU by means of liquid drug adsorption. Investigation of the model drugs adsorption on the obtained composites revealed that a variation between adsorption levels was influenced by the surfactant type and the amount present at the surface of the composites. Determination of flow properties showed that modification of zeolitic surface reflected on powder flow characteristics. In vitro drug release profiles of the drugs–SMZs composites revealed a sustained drug release over a period of 8 h. In another study (Krajišnik et al., 2011), the contribution of adsorption and partition to the overall sorption of DS onto NZ modified with cetylpyridinium chloride was described using a mathematical analog method.

An additional investigation of DS release from drug–SMZs composites at three different levels of cetylpyridinium chloride (CPC) (corresponding to 100, 200, and 300% of zeolitic ECEC, denoted as DS/ZCPC 10-30) was performed and the obtained results were compared with the DS release from corresponding physical mixture, as well as from physical mixture of NZ and DS (Krajišnik et al., 2013a). Results showed that the prolonged release of DS from all the three composites, as well as from physical mixture containing ZCPC-10 (modified with the lowest CP amount) and DS was achieved over a period of 8 h. The drug release from both DS/ZCPC-10 (max 55%) and corresponding physical mixture (max 38%) was remarkably lower than that from the physical mixture of NZ and DS (max 85%) (Fig. 8.6). Taking into account the different CPC amount and its organization on the zeolitic surface (monolayer vs. bilayer), the authors proposed schematic representation of the possible DS release from the ZCPC 10–30 composites (Fig. 8.7). The kinetic analysis of the DS release data for all the three composites, and for the physical mixture of ZCPC-10 and DS, showed that drug release profiles were best fitted with the Korsmeyer–Peppas and Bhaskar release models, indicating a combination of drug diffusion and ion exchange as the predominant release mechanisms in the dissolution medium.

de Gennaro et al. (2015) studied adsorption of DS by zeolite–CLI modified with the same surfactant–CPC in amount above ECEC of CLI (150% of ECEC). Kinetics experiments showed a very fast loading of the DS at the surface of CPC-modified zeolite. Light scattering (LS) and confocal scanning laser microscopy (CLSM) analyses have shown a wide distribution of volume

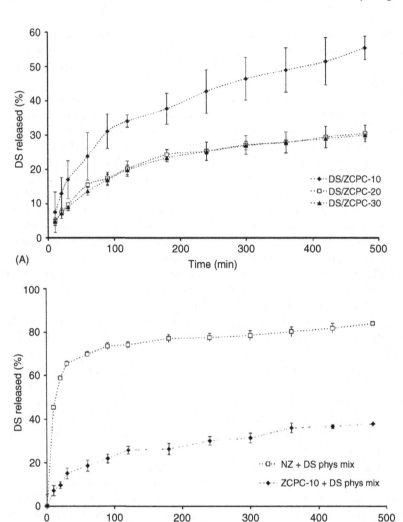

FIGURE 8.6   (A) In vitro drug release profiles of *DS* from the *ZCPC 10–30* composites. (B) In vitro drug release profiles of *DS* from *DS/ZCPC-10* and *DS/NZ* physical mixtures. *(Reprinted from Krajišnik D, Daković A, Malenović A, Milić J: An investigation of diclofenac sodium release from cetylpyridinium chloride-modified natural zeolite as a pharmaceutical excipient, Micropor Mesopor Mater 167:94–101, 2013, with permission from Elsevier)*

diameters of SMZs particles that, along with their irregular shape, make them cohesive with scarce flow properties, suggesting that a granulation process is most likely required during production procedure of a dosage form for oral administration. In addition, CLSM observations have enabled the discovery of the localization of different molecules in/on SMZs according to their chemical

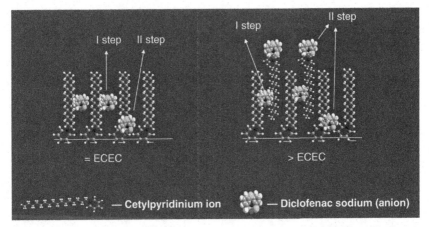

FIGURE 8.7 Schematic representation of the possible DS release from the ZCPC 10–30 composites. *(Reprinted from Krajišnik D, Daković A, Malenović A, Milić J: An investigation of diclofenac sodium release from cetylpyridinium chloride-modified natural zeolite as a pharmaceutical excipient,* Micropor Mesopor Mater *167:94–101, 2013, with permission from Elsevier)*

nature. DS release in anionic medium, such as simulated intestinal fluid, could be sustained for about 5 h through a mechanism prevalently governed by anionic exchange with a rapid final phase probably ascribed to the release of DS fraction within the patchy bilayer of SMZs.

The two other NZs—phillipsite (PHI) and chabazite (CHA)—modified with CPC were studied as novel excipients for DS modified drug release and obtained results were compared with the results of commercial CLI (Serri et al., 2015). Kinetics experiments showed a fast adsorption of DS at the surface of the three different SMZs. The results indicated that SMZ–CLI powder had the best flow properties, followed by SMZ–CHA and SMZ–PHI. DS release was controlled by particle drug diffusion in the case of SMZ–CLI and SMZ–PHI, as for SMZ–CHA, a combined (film + particle diffusion control) mechanism was envisaged.

Utilization of artificial neural network (ANN) models [static—multilayer perceptron (MLP) and generalized regression neural networks and dynamic—gamma one-layer network, and recurrent one-layer network] for prediction of DS release from drug–SMZs zeolites physical mixtures comprising different surfactant/drug molar ratio (0.2–2.5) (Krajišnik et al., 2014) was performed as a continuation of previous investigations (Krajišnik et al., 2013b). The inputs for ANNs trainings were surfactant hexadecyltrimethylammonium bromide (HB)/drug (DS) molar ratios, that is, drug loadings in the drug-modified zeolite mixtures, whereas the outputs were percentage of drug release in predetermined time points during drug release test (8 h). The obtained results revealed that MLP showed the highest correlation between experimental and predicted drug release. The safety of both natural and cationic SMZs as a potential excipient was confirmed in an acute toxicity

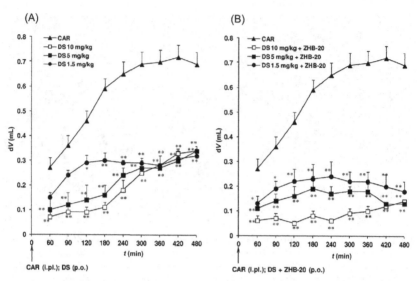

FIGURE 8.8 Time course of the antiedematous effect of diclofenac sodium *(DS)* (A) and DS-modified zeolite *(DS + ZHB-20)* mixtures (B), expressed as volume differences in milliliters (dV) between carrageenan *(CAR)* treated (inflamed), and a basal paw volume. Basal paw volume was obtained before treatment (CAR i.pl. and DS or DS + ZHB-20 p.o.; denoted by *arrow*). Each point represents the mean ± SEM of volume differences (dV) obtained in six to eight animals. Statistical significance was determined by comparison with the curve for CAR alone (*$p < 0.05$, **$p < 0.01$, one-way ANOVA followed by LSD test). *(Reprinted from Krajišnik D, Stepanović-Petrović R, Tomić M, Micov A, Ibrić S, Milić J: Application of artificial neural networks in prediction of diclofenac sodium release from drug-modified zeolites physical mixtures and antiedematous activity assessment, J Pharm Sci 103:1085–1094, 2014, with permission from Elsevier)*

testing during 72 h. DS (1.5, 5, 10, mg/kg, p.o.) as well as DS-modified zeolites mixtures produced a significant dose-dependent reduction of the rat paw edema induced by proinflammatory agent carrageenan (Fig. 8.8). The antiedematous effect of DS was intensified and prolonged significantly by modified zeolite suggesting the potential improvement in the treatment of inflammation by DS-modified zeolite mixtures.

IBU, another representative of NSAIDs with a good safety profile and different polarity (practically insoluble in water) compared to DS (sparingly soluble in water) is also a candidate for investigation of prolonged release formulations. The sorption of IBU by SMZs containing different amounts of benzalkonium chloride and cetylpyridinium chloride (100–300 % of zeolitic ECEC value) was performed (Krajišnik et al., 2015). The biopharmaceutical performance of SMZs as drug formulation excipients was evaluated by in vitro dissolution experiments from the composites with medium surfactant contents. The drug sorption was influenced by the surfactant type and amount used for the zeolite modification and prolonged drug release over a period of 8 h (up to ~40%) was achieved with both groups of samples.

8.3   MODIFIED BIOSILICA STRUCTURES FROM DIATOMITE FRUSTULES: PREPARATION, PHYSICOCHEMICAL CHARACTERIZATION, AND APPLICATION

8.3.1   Diatomite Processing and Its Physicochemical Characteristics

Diatoms are microscopic unicellular, colonial, or filamentous algae found in marine and freshwater ecosystems as well as in brackish water, soil, or even on moist surfaces. Diatom's protoplast, containing recognizable golden-brown chloroplasts, is enclosed in a distinguished cell wall called a frustule (Fig. 8.9). Diatoms frustules vary in size from less than 1 µm to more than 1 mm, but are typically 10–200 µm across (U.S. Geological Survey, 1997) and they appear in a broad variety of elaborate forms with ornamental perforations. Generally, frustule comprises two parts that fit together like a lid and a base of a pill-box and it represents a highly porous, yet rigid, amorphous silica framework. Frustules provide a remarkable example of three dimensional organizations in hierarchical porous structures where pores are organized in functional arrangement

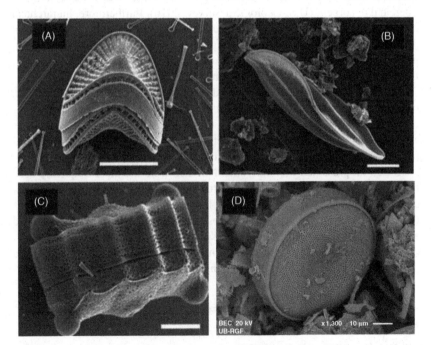

FIGURE 8.9   **Extraordinary structures in nature.** Frustules of *Campylodiscus* sp. (scale bar, 50 µm) (A), *Entomoneis* aff. *pulchra* (scale bar, 10 µm) (B), *Biddulphia biddulphiana* (scale bar, 20 µm) (C), and centric frustules found in diatomite from Kolubara (Serbia) coal basin (D). *(Part A–C, Gordon R, Tiffany MA: Possible buckling phenomena in diatom morphogenesis. In Seckbach J, Kociolek JP editors: The diatom world, Dordrecht, 2011, Springer Science and Business Media, pp 253, 255, with permission of Springer)*

at different levels exhibiting macro-, meso- and microporosity. At the end of diatoms' life-cycle, frustules settle and accumulate on the ocean and freshwater floors creating a siliceous sedimentary rock—diatomite.

With regard to deposit form, depth and topographic constraints, recovery of diatomite can be achieved through open-pit or underground mining. Diatomite is often processed near the mine to reduce the cost of hauling the crude ore, which can contain up to 65% water. Typical diatomite processing involves a series of crushing, drying, size-reduction, and calcining steps, using heated air for conveying and classifying within the plant. The analysis of oven-dried crude ore blocks typically shows 80–90% silica (SiO_2) plus alumina (2–4% attributed mostly to clay minerals) and hematite (0.5–2%). Apparent block density is 320–640 g/L with 80–90% voids. In-place ore contains from 10% to as much as 65% water (2–10% in the opaline structure). Dry powdered natural rock has an apparent density of 80–250 g/L. The melting point of diatomite ranges from 1400 to 1750°C (U.S. Geological Survey, 1997).

Unique physicochemical properties of diatomite (low density, high porosity, large surface area, high absorptive capacity, low thermal conductivity, and chemical inertness) enable its commercial use as filter aid, cement additive, filler, and absorbent (U.S. Geological Survey, 2016). Furthermore, hierarchical porous structure of frustules inspired research on their potential application in the fields of optics (Butcher et al., 2005), photonics (Fuhrmann et al., 2004), microfluidics (Losic et al., 2009), chemo- and biosensing (Setaro et al., 2007; De Stefano et al., 2009), micro- and nanofabrication (Losic et al., 2007).

In addition to previously mentioned desirable physicochemical properties, other relevant features of diatomite, such as modifiable surface chemistry, biocompatibility, and nontoxicity, impose this abundant and low-cost material as an excellent candidate for a drug carrier. Literature reports on diatomite potential in drug delivery are presented in Table 8.3.

Based on presented literature data, NSAIDs were the most frequently used model substances for diatomite-based drug carrier. In addition to DS, indometacin was also employed, but as a model for water insoluble/hydrophobic drugs (Aw et al., 2011; Bariana et al., 2013; Losic et al., 2010). Diatomite (unmodified and modified) was investigated as a prospective carrier for different drug delivery routes and detail description of this material in its potential application as a drug carrier will be given in the following sections.

8.3.2 Applications of Natural and Modified Diatomites in Drug Delivery

The possibility of employing unmodified diatomite for drug delivery has been indicated in some literature reports. Aw et al. (2012) used purified Australian diatomite for the loading of indometacin by an incipient wetness method. Prolonged drug release over 2 weeks from indomethacin-loaded diatomite was observed and it occurred in two stages: initial burst release (in the first 6 h),

TABLE 8.3 Literature Reports on Diatomite as a Prospective Drug Carrier

Diatomite (origin)	Modification	Drug	Application	References
Purified Australian	None	Indometacin Gentamicin sulfate	Oral and implant drug delivery	Aw et al. (2011)
Purified commercial (Fossil Shell Flour)	None	Mesalamine Prednisone	Oral drug delivery	Zhang et al. (2013)
Purified Australian	Organosilanes (APTES, mPEG-silane, OTS, GPTMS) Phosphonic acids (2 CEPA, 16 PHA)	Indometacin Gentamicin sulfate	Oral and implant drug delivery	Bariana et al. (2013)
Purified Australian	Oligo(ethylene glycol) methacrylate copolymers	Levofloxacin	Thermo-responsive drug delivery	Vasani et al. (2015)
Commercial calcined (provided by DEREF Spa, Italy) processed to obtain micro- and nanoparticles	APTES + sulfo-GMBS [+ poly(D-arginine)]	Small interfering ribonucleic acid (siRNA)	RNA delivery	Rea et al. (2014)
Commercial (provided by DEREF Spa, Italy) processed to obtain nanoparticles	APTES + HOOC–poly(ethylene glycol)–NH$_2$ + CPP	Sorafenib	Targeted drug delivery	Terracciano et al. (2015)
Purified Australian	APTES + graphene oxide	Indometacin	pH sensitive drug delivery	Kumeria et al. (2013)
Purified Australian	Caprylocaproyl macrogol-8 glycerides + lecithin and propylene glycol + caprylic/capric triglyceride	Carbamazepine	Oral drug delivery	Milović et al. (2014)
Purified Australian	Dopamine modified Fe$_3$O$_4$ nanoparticles	Indometacin	Magnetically guided drug delivery	Losic et al. (2010)
Purified food grade	Dopamine and human serum albumin modified iron oxide nanoparticles	None (proof-of-concept study with dye molecules as drug mimics)	Magnetically guided drug delivery	Todd et al. (2014)
Peruvian food grade	Partially neutralized aluminum sulfate	DS	Oral drug delivery	Janićijević et al. (2014)
Purified diatomite from Kolubara coal basin	Partially neutralized aluminum sulfate	DS	Oral drug delivery	Janićijević et al. (2015)

which was attributed to the release of surface deposited drug, followed by a slow release assigned to the release of drug from pores and internal structure of the frustules. Gentamicin sulfate could also be loaded in/on purified Australian diatomite using the same procedure as for indometacin (Aw et al., 2011). Drug release profile of gentamicin-loaded diatomite appeared similar to that of indomethacin-loaded diatomite, comprising initial burst release (in the first 6 h) described by first-order kinetics followed by slow release (from 8 h until complete release at the end of 2 weeks) which fitted well to zero-order kinetics.

Zhang et al. (2013) utilized purified commercial diatomite to load separately mesalamine and prednisone by an immersion method. The release of both drugs under simulated gastrointestinal conditions from the corresponding loaded diatomites was prolonged. Drug permeation across Caco-2/HT-29 cocultured monolayers was enhanced for both mesalamine and prednisone after their loading on/in diatomite frustules. Enhanced drug permeability probably resulted from the opening of intercellular tight junctions and the facilitation of paracellular transport as indicated by the changes in transepithelial electrical resistance.

However, in order to obtain a material of a desired functionality, that is, a material with optimal drug loading and drug release characteristics which would deliver therapeutic dose of a drug at a desired/planned rate and even to a proper site, modification of diatomite with organic or inorganic compounds may be necessary.

Surface modification with organic compounds is one of the approaches used for the preparation of potential diatomite-based drug carrier. Bariana et al. (2013) performed surface modification of purified Australian diatomite by covalent attachment of selected organosilanes and phosphonic acids (Fig. 8.10). Model drugs indometacin (practically insoluble in water) and gentamicin sulfate (freely soluble in water) were loaded on/in modified diatomite by an incipient wetness method and differences in drug loading capacities (14–24%) and release periods (13–26 days), depending on functional groups present on the surface of modified diatomite, were observed. Hydrophilic surfaces (rich in amino, carboxyl, or epoxide functional groups) were found to favor prolonged release of indometacin, while hydrophobic surfaces (long hydrocarbon backbone of the modifying substance) favored extended release of gentamicin sulfate. Biphasic release of indometacin as well as gentamicin sulfate, from the loaded modified diatomite included initial burst release (first 6 h) accompanied by sustained release over 13–26 days.

Another interesting research exploited graphene oxide (GO) decorated diatomite microparticles as potential drug microcarriers (Kumeria et al., 2013). Firstly, silanization of purified Australian diatomite was performed with (3-aminopropyl)triethoxysilane (APTES), after which APTES-modified diatomite was covalently coupled with GO sheets through the formation of amide bonds from primary amino groups of APTES-modified diatomite and carboxyl groups of GO sheets. Covalent crosslinking was 1-ethyl-3-(3-dimethylaminopropyl)carbodiimide (EDC) and N-hydroxysuccinimide (NHS) assisted: EDC coupled NHS to

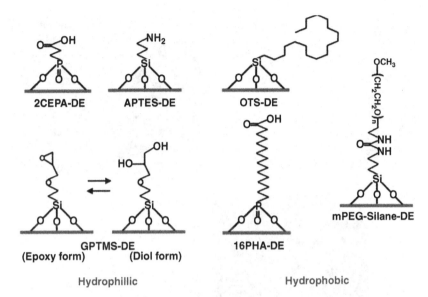

2CEPA-DE   APTES-DE   OTS-DE

GPTMS-DE
(Epoxy form)   (Diol form)   16PHA-DE

mPEG-Silane-DE

Hydrophillic   Hydrophobic

FIGURE 8.10 Schematic representation of diatomite surface covalently modified with organosilanes (APTES, GPTMS, OTS, and mPEG-silane) and phosphonic acids (2-CEPA and 16-PHA). *(Reprinted from Bariana M, Aw MS, Kurkuri M, Losic D: Tuning drug loading and release properties of diatom silica microparticles by surface modifications, Int J Pharm 443:230–241, 2013, with permission from Elsevier)*

carboxyl groups of GO sheets forming an NHS ester which afterward reacted with primary amino groups of APTES-modified diatomite to form stabile amide bonds with the release of NHS. The decoration of modified diatoms' frustules with GO patches was nonuniform, random, and partial with some uncovered areas as revealed by SEM analysis. The structure comprising GO sheets on modified silica particles was identified by Raman spectroscopy and the amide bond formation within this structure was evidenced by FTIR spectroscopy. The loading of a model drug indometacin and in vitro drug release studies were conducted on APTES-modified diatomite decorated with GO as well as on APTES-modified diatomite. Significantly higher drug loading (28.5%) and encapsulation efficiency (95%) were achieved after the attachment of GO onto modified diatomite. When tested in phosphate buffer pH 7.4, sustained release of indometacin over 8 days from APTES-modified diatomite was further extended to 12 days for APTES-modified diatomite decorated with GO. Even more prolonged release of indometacin (37 days) was noted from APTES-modified diatomite decorated with GO at pH 3.5. The authors also prepared and characterized GO decorated diatomite microparticles through electrostatic self-assembly of GO sheets with APTES-modified diatomite, but they did not test it as a drug carrier.

Inorganic nanoparticles have also been employed for the surface modification of diatomite. Purified diatomite from an Australian mine was functionalized with dopamine modified iron oxide (Fe_3O_4) nanoparticles through electrostatic

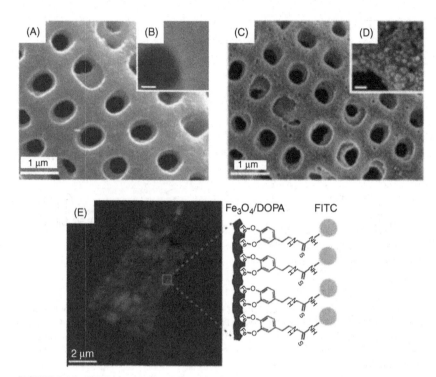

FIGURE 8.11 SEM micrographs of diatomite frustules before (A, B) and after functionalization with dopamine modified iron oxide nanoparticles (*Fe₃O₄/DOPA*) (C, D) and confocal 3D image of functionalized diatomite labeled with fluorescein isothiocyanate (*FITC*) (E). *(Adapted from Losic D, Yu Y, Aw MS, Simovic S, Thierry B, Addai-Mensah J: Surface functionalisation of diatoms with dopamine modified iron-oxide nanoparticles: toward magnetically guided drug microcarriers with biologically derived morphologies, Chem Commun 46:6323–6325, 2010, with permission of The Royal Society of Chemistry)*

self-assembly and high resolution SEM images (Fig. 8.11C–D) confirmed the presence of a dense, ultrathin layer of nanoparticles on the frustule's surface (Losic et al., 2010). The magnetic properties of this functionalized diatomite were demonstrated by strong response of the suspended functionalized diatomite particles to an external magnetic field. Indometacin was used as a model drug for loading on/in the functionalized diatomite. Dissolution of the loaded drug comprised fast release during the first 8 h followed by slower sustained release over 2 weeks. Furthermore, successful labeling of amino groups from dopamine modified Fe_3O_4 nanoparticles attached to frustules with fluorescein isothiocyanate was shown by confocal fluorescence microscopy (Fig. 8.11E) proving that amino groups of functionalized diatomite are accessible for covalent coupling with biomolecules.

Purely inorganic modification of diatomite was also investigated as an approach to increase the loading of model drug DS and to provide an extended drug release. Food grade diatomite was modified with the precipitation product

FIGURE 8.12   SEM micrographs of the starting (A) and modified diatomite (B). *(Reprinted from Janićijević J, Krajišnik D, Čalija B, Dobričić V, Daković A, Krstić J, Marković M, Milić J: Inorganically modified diatomite as a potential prolonged-release drug carrier,* Mater Sci Eng C *42:412–420, 2014, with permission from Elsevier)*

of partially neutralized aluminum sulfate solution at three levels (mass ratios) (Janićijević et al., 2014). The modification procedure was relatively simple, non-time consuming, and environmental friendly. The original diatomite structure was retained after the modification process as shown by SEM (Fig. 8.12) and FTIR analyses (Fig. 8.13). All three inorganically modified diatomite samples achieved significantly higher adsorbent loading with DS (up to 13 times higher) than the starting diatomite during adsorption batch experiments, but only the sample showing high adsorbent loading at the lower level of modification

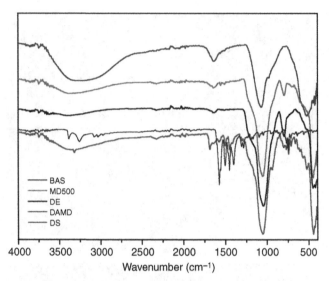

FIGURE 8.13 FTIR spectra of the starting diatomite *(DE)*, modified diatomite *(MD500)*, partially neutralized aluminum sulfate (BAS), DS and DS adsorbed on MD500 *(DAMD)*. *(Reprinted from Janićijević J, Krajišnik D, Čalija B, Dobričić V, Daković A, Krstić J, Marković M, Milić J: Inorganically modified diatomite as a potential prolonged-release drug carrier, Mater Sci Eng C 42:412–420, 2014, with permission from Elsevier)*

(i.e., the sample prepared at the medium modification level) was chosen as a carrier for in vitro drug release studies. High adsorbent loading of the selected modified diatomite sample (~250 mg/g in 2 h) enabled the preparation of comprimates containing adsorbed DS in the amount near to its therapeutic dose (~55 mg per 300 mg comprimate), which is very important feature for potential therapeutic application of this drug carrier in various pharmaceutical dosage forms. In vitro drug release studies in phosphate buffer pH 6.8 demonstrated prolonged drug release over 8 h not only from comprimates containing DS adsorbed onto the selected modified diatomite sample (DAMD–18% after 8 h), but also from comprimates containing physical mixture of DS with the selected modified diatomite sample (PMDMD–45% after 8 h) (Fig. 8.14). During drug release from DAMD, desorption occurs. Strong interactions between DS and the modified diatomite have to be overpowered during drug's desorption and this may be the explanation for much slower rate and smaller extent of drug release in 8 h time from DAMD compared to PMDMD. Prolonged DS release from PMDMD may result from equilibrium between two processes: the dissolution of DS particles and adsorption of dissolved DS onto MD500 because, as shown by adsorption experiments, modified diatomite has high affinity for DS. For comparison, in vitro drug release studies were also performed from comprimates containing physical mixture of DS with the starting diatomite (PMDD) and they released 90% of the drug in 90 min (Fig. 8.14).

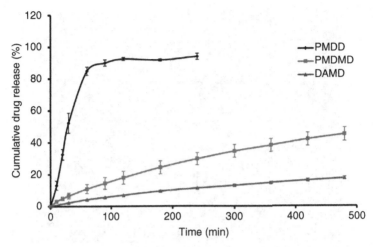

FIGURE 8.14   Drug release profiles from *PMDD*, *PMDMD*, and *DAMD* comprimates. *(Reprinted from Janićijević J, Krajišnik D, Čalija B, Dobričić V, Daković A, Krstić J, Marković M, Milić J: Inorganically modified diatomite as a potential prolonged-release drug carrier, Mater Sci Eng C 42:412–420, 2014, with permission from Elsevier)*

In vivo acute toxicity testing of inorganically modified diatomite samples (2000 mg/kg administered via oral route to mice) was engaged to evaluate safety of those materials intended for pharmaceutical applications and during the testing period (72 h) no death or any kind of toxicological reaction in animals was observed.

These results encouraged further looking into application of purely inorganic modification on domestic diatomite from Kolubara coal basin in Serbia (Janićijević et al., 2015). Diatomite from Kolubara coal basin, after being purified by thermal treatment (550°C, 4 h) and sieving (particle size fraction lower than 125 µm) (Fig. 8.15A), complied with the limit test A for heavy metals and pharmacopoeial (European Pharmacopoeia, 2008, Ph. Eur. 6.0) requirements for microbiological quality. Inorganic modification was performed by precipitation of partially neutralized aluminum sulfate in diatomite suspension at the level that was chosen as optimal in previous work (Janićijević et al., 2014). Modification of refined Kolubara's diatomite with partially neutralized aluminum sulfate increased adsorbent loading with DS 8.8 times (373 mg/g). DS was adsorbed onto the starting diatomite (i.e., refined diatomite from Kolubara basin) most likely in an amorphous form as pointed by XRPD analysis (Fig. 8.16) and this process involved drug's carboxylate group according to FTIR spectrum analysis. Adsorption of DS onto modified diatomite resulted in the alteration of the drug's XRD pattern (Fig. 8.16) and FTIR spectrum. Further analyses and literature review revealed the compliance of diffraction pattern and FTIR spectrum peaks of this new phase to those of the diclofenac acid. Therefore, it was estimated that DS was adsorbed onto modified diatomite in its acidic form. In vitro drug release

FIGURE 8.15 SEM micrographs of the starting diatomite (A) and modified diatomite with adsorbed DS (B). *(Reprinted from Janićijević J, Krajišnik D, Čalija B, Nedić Vasiljević B, Dobričić V, Daković A, Antonijević MD, Milić J: Modified local diatomite as potential functional drug carrier—a model study for diclofenac sodium,* Int J Pharm *496:466–474, 2015, with permission from Elsevier)*

studies in phosphate buffer pH 7.5 demonstrated prolonged release of diclofenac over 8 h not only from comprimates containing DS adsorbed onto the modified diatomite (MDD–37% after 8 h), but also from comprimates containing physical mixture of the modified diatomite with DS (PMDD–45% after 8 h) (Fig. 8.17). Conversely, rapid drug release during the first hour (82% of DS released in 60 min) was observed for comprimates containing DS adsorbed on the starting diatomite (DD) (Fig. 8.17). Drug release profiles from all three types of comprimates (DD, MDD, and PMDD) were best described by Korsmeyer–Peppas

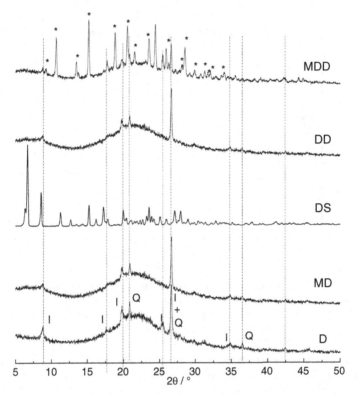

FIGURE 8.16   X-ray diffractograms of the starting diatomite (*D*), modified diatomite (*MD*), DS, DS adsorbed on D (*DD*) or MD (*MDD*). *(Reprinted from Janićijević J, Krajišnik D, Čalija B, Nedić Vasiljević B, Dobričić V, Daković A, Antonijević MD, Milić J: Modified local diatomite as potential functional drug carrier—a model study for diclofenac sodium, Int J Pharm 496:466–474, 2015, with permission from Elsevier)*

model. The value of Peppas release exponent *n* indicated that non-Fickian diffusion was the mechanism of DS release from MDD and PMDD, while Fickian diffusion governed DS release from DD comprimates.

Based on all previously mentioned, diatomite seems as a promising drug carrier and its suitability for a desired purpose can be further improved by modification (either organic or inorganic). In addition to its potential functionality, diatomite has a GRAS status (when used as filtering and processing aid in food industry). In vitro studies demonstrated that diatomite (comprising frustules of 10–20 μm in length) can be considered as a noncytotoxic biomaterial at concentrations up to 1000 μg/mL (Zhang et al., 2013) and even diatomite nanoparticles (obtained by processing commercial diatomite; average particle size lower than 450 nm) can be regarded as noncytotoxic at concentrations up to 300 μg/mL (Rea et al., 2014). In vivo acute toxicity testing of purified diatomite from Kolubara coal basin performed on mice (at the dose of 2000 mg/kg given via

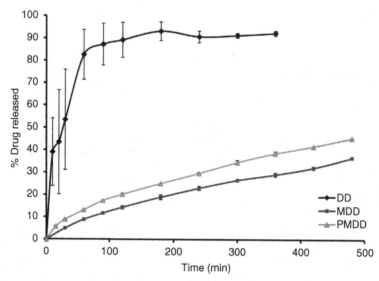

FIGURE 8.17   Drug release profiles from *DD, MDD,* and *PMDD* comprimates. *(Reprinted from Janićijević J, Krajišnik D, Čalija B, Nedić Vasiljević B, Dobričić V, Daković A, Antonijević MD, Milić J: Modified local diatomite as potential functional drug carrier—a model study for diclofenac sodium, Int J Pharm 496:466–474, 2015, with permission from Elsevier)*

oral route) also pointed on possible safety of this material in pharmaceutical applications (Janićijević et al., 2015).

8.4   CONCLUSIONS

As representatives of natural silica–based materials, clays (typically phyllosilicates) and zeolites (as representatives of tectosilicates) are found as versatile materials for a wide range of applications in the pharmaceutical technology, due to their favorable physicochemical and functionality-related characteristics in addition to their inertness and low toxicity. Diatomites (as natural biosilica structures) may be a low cost alternative to synthetic mesoporous silica in drug delivery and this area of diatomite application has just begun to emerge thus offering many possibilities for further exploration. In addition, the possibility of surface modification of these materials and their application in preparation of composites with various drugs has been attracting great attention in the pharmaceutical field due to synergistic characteristics regarding its biopharmaceutical and technological features.

The literature data regarding the application of both natural and modified silica-based materials in drug delivery showed their ability to modify (extend or delay) and/or target (site-specific) drug release or even improve drug solubility. Additional reported advantages, such as reduction of drug toxicity and therapy-related side effects are particularly important for their use as drug carries for NSAIDs. Further research on application of these natural-based silica materials in drug delivery, in addition to investigations of their safety and biocompatibility will be focused on tailoring their structure by appropriate modification, which would with a detailed analysis of drug–carrier interactions, contribute in achievement of improved drug carriers.

ACKNOWLEDGMENT

This work was realized within the framework of the projects TR 34031 and ON 172018 supported by the Ministry of Education, Science and Technological Development of Republic of Serbia.

REFERENCES

Aguzzi C, Capra P, Bonferoni C, Cerezo P, Salcedo I, Sánchez R, Caramella C, Viseras C: Chitosan–silicate biocomposites to be used in modified drug release of 5-aminosalicylic acid (5-ASA), *Appl Clay Sci* 50:106–111, 2010.

Aguzzi C, Cerezo P, Viseras C, Caramella C: Use of clays as drug delivery systems: possibilities and limitations, *Appl Clay Sci* 36:22–36, 2007.

Altman R, Bosch B, Brune K, Patrignani P, Young C: Advances in NSAID development: evolution of diclofenac products using pharmaceutical technology, *Drugs* 75:859–877, 2015.

Aw MS, Simovic S, Addai-Mensah J, Losic D: Silica microcapsules from diatoms as new carrier for delivery of therapeutics, *Nanomedicine* 6:1159–1173, 2011.

Aw MS, Simovic S, Yu Y, Addai-Mensah J, Losic D: Porous silica microshells from diatoms as biocarrier for drug delivery applications, *Powder Technol* 223:52–58, 2012.

Bariana M, Aw MS, Kurkuri M, Losic D: Tuning drug loading and release properties of diatom silica microparticles by surface modifications, *Int J Pharm* 443:230–241, 2013.

Benkli YE, Can MF, Turan M, Çelik MS: Modification of organo-zeolite surface for the removal of reactive azo dyes in fixed-bed reactors, *Water Res* 39:487–493, 2005.

Bhattacharyya KG, Gupta SS: Adsorption of a few heavy metals on natural and modified kaolinite and montmorillonite: a review, *Adv Colloid Interface* 140:114–131, 2008.

Bonferoni MC, Cerri G, de' Gennaro M, Juliano C, Caramella C: Zn^{2+}-exchanged clinoptilolite-rich rock as active carrier for antibiotics in anti-acne topical therapy. In-vitro characterization and preliminary formulation studies, *Appl Clay Sci* 36:95–102, 2007.

Bowman RS, Haggerty GM, Huddleston RG, Neel D, Flynn MM: Sorption of nonpolar organic compounds, inorganic cations and inorganic oxyanions by surfactant-modified zeolites. In Sabatini DA, Knox RC, Harwell JH, editors: *Surfactant-enriched subsurface remediation, ACS symposium series 594*, Washington DC, 1995, American Chemical Society, pp 54–64.

Brayfield A, editor: *Martindale: the complete drug reference*, ed 38, London, 2014, Pharmaceutical Press, pp 48–49.

Brooks PM, Day RO: Nonsteroidal antiinflammatory drugs: differences and similarities, *N Engl J Med* 324:1716–1725, 1991.

Butcher KSA, Ferris JM, Phillips MR, Wintrebert-Fouquet M, Jong Wah JW, Jovanovic N, Vyverman W, Chepurnov VA: A luminescence study of porous diatoms, *Mater Sci Eng C* 25:658–663, 2005.

Campbell KT, Craig DQM, McNally T: Modification of ibuprofen drug release from poly(ethylene glycol) layered silicate nanocomposites prepared by hot-melt extrusion, *J Appl Polym Sci* 131:40284, 2014.

Caputo D, Pepe F: Experiments and data processing of ion exchange equilibria involving Italian natural zeolites: a review, *Micropor Mesopor Mater* 105:222–231, 2007.

Carretero MI, Gomes CSF, Tateo F: Clays, drugs and human health. In Bergaya F, Lagaly G, editors: *Handbook of clay science, part B: techniques and applications*, ed 2, Amsterdam, 2013, Elsevier, pp 711–764.

Carretero MI, Pozo M: Clay and non-clay minerals in the pharmaceutical industry. Part I. Excipients and medical applications, *Appl Clay Sci* 46:73–80, 2009.

Carretero MI, Pozo M: Clay and non-clay minerals in the pharmaceutical and cosmetic industries part II. Active ingredients, *Appl Clay Sci* 47:171–181, 2010.

Cerri G, de Gennaro M, Bonferoni MC, Caramella C: Zeolites in biomedical application: Zn-exchanged clinoptilolite-rich rock as active carrier for antibiotics in anti-acne topical therapy, *Appl Clay Sci* 27:141–150, 2004.

Cerri G, Farina M, Brundu A, Daković A, Giunchedi P, Gavini E, Rassu G: Natural zeolites for pharmaceutical formulations: preparation and evaluation of a clinoptilolite-based material, *Micropor Mesopor Mater* 223:58–67, 2016.

Cervini-Silva J, Nieto-Camacho A, Ramírez-Apan MT, Gómez-Vidales V, Palacios E, Montoya A, de Jesús ER: Anti-inflammatory, anti-bacterial, and cytotoxic activity of fibrous clays, *Colloids Surf B* 129:1–6, 2015.

Chrzanowski W, Kim SY, Abou Neel EA: Biomedical applications of clay, *Aust J Chem* 66:1315–1322, 2013.

Colella C: A critical reconsideration of biomedical and veterinary applications of natural zeolites, *Clay Miner* 46:295–309, 2011.

Daković A, Kragović M, Rottinghaus GE, Sekulić Z, Milićević S, Milonjić SK, Zarić S: Influence of natural zeolitic tuff and organozeolites surface charge on sorption of ionizable fumonisin B1, *Colloids Surf B* 6:272–278, 2010.

Daković A, Matijašević S, Rottinghaus GE, Dondur V, Pietrass T, Clewett CFM: Adsorption of zearalenone by organomodified natural zeolitic tuff, *J Colloid Interface Sci* 311:8–13, 2007a.

Daković A, Tomašević-Čanović M, Dondur V, Rottinghaus GE, Medaković V, Zarić S: Adsorption of mycotoxins by organozeolites, *Colloids Surf B* 46:20–25, 2005.

Daković A, Tomašević-Čanović M, Rottinghaus GE, Matijašević S, Sekulić Z: Fumonisin B1 adsorption to octadecyldimethylbenzyl ammonium-modified clinoptilolite-rich zeolitic tuff, *Micropor Mesopor Mater* 105:285–290, 2007b.

de Gennaro B, Catalanotti L, Bowman RS, Mercurio M: Anion exchange selectivity of surfactant modified clinoptilolite-rich tuff for environmental remediation, *J Colloid Interface Sci* 430:178–183, 2014.

de Gennaro B, Catalanotti L, Cappelletti P, Langella A, Mercurio M, Serri C, Biondi M, Mayol L: Surface modified natural zeolite as a carrier for sustained diclofenac release: a preliminary feasibility study, *Colloids Surf B* 130:101–109, 2015.

De Stefano L, Rotiroti L, De Stefano M, Lamberti A, Lettieri S, Setaro A, Maddalena P: Marine diatoms as optical biosensors, *Biosens Bioelectron* 24:1580–1584, 2009.

Depan D, Kumar AP, Singh RP: Cell proliferation and controlled drug release studies of nanohybrids based on chitosan-*g*-lactic acid and montmorillonite, *Acta Biomater* 5:93–100, 2009.

European Pharmacopoeia sixth edition, Strasbourg, 2008, Council of Europe.

European Pharmacopoeia eight edition, Strasbourg, 2013, Council of Europe.

Farías T, de Ménorval LC, Zajac J, Rivera A: Adsolubilization of drugs onto natural clinoptilolite modified by adsorption of cationic surfactants, *Colloids Surf B* 76:421–426, 2010.

Farías T, de Ménorval LC, Zajac J, Rivera A: Benzalkonium chloride and sulfamethoxazole adsorption onto natural clinoptilolite: effect of time, ionic strength, pH and temperature, *J Colloid Interface Sci* 363:465–475, 2011.

Fuhrmann T, Landwehr S, El Rharbi-Kucki M, Sumper M: Diatoms as living photonic crystals, *Appl Phys B* 78:257–260, 2004.

Godelitsas A, Armbruster T: HEU-type zeolites modified by transition elements and lead, *Micropor Mesopor Mater* 61:3–24, 2003.

Gualtieri AF, Passaglia E, Galli E, Viani A: Rietveld structure refinement of Sr-exchanged phillipsites, *Micropor Mesopor Mater* 31:33–43, 1999.

Hrenovic J, Rozic M, Sekovanic L, Anic-Vucinic A: Interaction of surfactant-modified zeolites and phosphate accumulating bacteria, *J Hazard Mater* 156:576–582, 2008.

Janićijević J, Krajišnik D, Čalija B, Dobričić V, Daković A, Krstić J, Marković M, Milić J: Inorganically modified diatomite as a potential prolonged-release drug carrier, *Mater Sci Eng C* 42:412–420, 2014.

Janićijević J, Krajišnik D, Čalija B, Nedić Vasiljević B, Dobričić V, Daković A, Antonijević MD, Milić J: Modified local diatomite as potential functional drug carrier—a model study for diclofenac sodium, *Int J Pharm* 496:466–474, 2015.

Joshi GV, Kevadiya BD, Mody HM, Bajaj HC: Confinement and controlled release of quinine on chitosan–montmorillonite bionanocomposites, *J Polym Sci A* 50:423–430, 2012.

Kaur M, Datta M: Synthesis and characterization of biodegradable clay–polymer nanocomposites for oral sustained release of anti-inflammatory drug, *Eur Chem Bull* 2:670–678, 2013.

Kaur M, Datta M: Diclofenac sodium adsorption onto montmorillonite: adsorption equilibrium studies and drug release kinetics, *Adsorpt Sci Technol* 32:365–387, 2014.

Kevadiya BD, Patel HA, Joshi GV, Abdi SHR, Bajaj HC: Montmorillonite-alginate composites as a drug delivery system: intercalation and in vitro release of diclofenac sodium, *Indian J Pharm Sci* 72:732–737, 2010.

Kong Y, Ge H, Xiong J, Zuo S, Wei Y, Yao C, Deng L: Palygorskite polypyrrole nanocomposite: a new platform for electrically tunable drug delivery, *Appl Clay Sci* 99:119–124, 2014.

Krajišnik D, Daković A, Malenović A, Djekić L, Kragović M, Dobričić V, Milić J: An investigation of diclofenac sodium release from cetylpyridinium chloride-modified natural zeolite as a pharmaceutical excipient, *Micropor Mesopor Mater* 167:94–101, 2013a.

Krajišnik D, Daković A, Malenović A, Kragović M, Milić J: Ibuprofen sorption and release by modified natural zeolites as prospective drug carriers, *Clay Miner* 50:11–22, 2015.

Krajišnik D, Daković A, Malenović A, Milojević-Rakić M, Dondur V, Radulović Z, Milić J: Investigation of adsorption and release of diclofenac sodium by modified zeolites composites, *Appl Clay Sci* 83–84:322–326, 2013b.

Krajišnik D, Daković A, Milojević M, Malenović A, Kragović M, Bajuk Bogdanović D, Dondur V, Milić J: Properties of diclofenac sodium sorption onto natural zeolite modified with cetylpyridinium chloride, *Colloids Surf B* 83:165–172, 2011.

Krajišnik D, Milojević M, Malenović A, Daković A, Ibrić S, Savić S, Matijašević S, Radulović A, Daniels R, Milić J: Cationic surfactants-modified natural zeolites: improvement of the excipients functionality, *Drug Dev Ind Pharm* 36:1215–1224, 2010.

Krajišnik D, Stepanović-Petrović R, Tomić M, Micov A, Ibrić S, Milić J: Application of artificial neural networks in prediction of diclofenac sodium release from drug-modified zeolites physical mixtures and antiedematous activity assessment, *J Pharm Sci* 103:1085–1094, 2014.

Kumeria T, Bariana M, Altalhi T, Kurkuri M, Gibson CT, Yang W, Losic D: Graphene oxide decorated diatom silica particles as new nano-hybrids: towards smart natural drug microcarriers, *J Mater Chem B* 1:6302–6311, 2013.

Lam A, Rivera A: Theoretical study of the interaction of surfactants and drugs with natural zeolite, *Micropor Mesopor Mater* 91:181–186, 2006.

Lam A, Rivera A, Rodrídguez-Fuentes G: Theoretical study of metronidazole adsorption on clinoptilolite, *Micropor Mesopor Mater* 49:157–162, 2001.

Lam A, Sierra LR, Rojas G, Rivera A, Rodríguez-Fuentes G, Montero LA: Theoretical study of the physical adsorption of aspirin on natural clinoptilolite, *Micropor Mesopor Mater* 23:247–252, 1998.

Lee WF, Chen YC: Effect of bentonite on the physical properties and drug-release behavior of poly(AA-*co*-PEGMEA) bentonite nanocomposite hydrogels for mucoadhesive, *J Appl Polym Sci* 91:2934–2941, 2004.

Lee WF, Fu YT: Effect of montmorillonite on the swelling behavior and drug-release behavior of nanocomposite hydrogels, *J Appl Polym Sci* 89:3652–3660, 2003.

Levis SR, Deasy PB: Characterisation of halloysite for use as a microtubular drug delivery system, *Int J Pharm* 243:125–134, 2002.

Losic D, Mitchell JG, Lal R, Voelcker NH: Rapid fabrication of micro- and nanoscale patterns by replica molding from diatom biosilica, *Adv Funct Mater* 17:2439–2446, 2007.

Losic D, Mitchell JG, Voelcker NH: Diatomaceous lessons in nanotechnology and advanced materials, *Adv Mater* 21:1–12, 2009.

Losic D, Yu Y, Aw MS, Simovic S, Thierry B, Addai-Mensah J: Surface functionalisation of diatoms with dopamine modified iron-oxide nanoparticles: toward magnetically guided drug microcarriers with biologically derived morphologies, *Chem Commun* 46:6323–6325, 2010.

Lvov YM, Shchukin DG, Möhwald H, Price RR: Halloysite clay nanotubes for controlled release of protective agents, *ACS Nano* 2:814–820, 2008.

McGettigan P, Henry D: Use of non-steroidal anti-inflammatory drugs that elevate cardiovascular risk: an examination of sales and essential medicines lists in low-, middle-, and high-income countries, *PLoS Med* 10(2):e1001388, 2013.

Milić J, Daković A, Krajišnik D, Rottinghaus GE: Modified natural zeolites–functional characterization and biomedical application. In Tiwari A, editor: *Advanced healthcare materials*, Hoboken, Salem, 2014, John Wiley & Sons, Inc., Scrivener Publishing LLC, pp 361–403.

Milović M, Simović S, Lošić D, Dashevskiy A, Ibrić S: Solid self-emulsifying phospholipid suspension (SSEPS) with diatom as a drug carrier, *Eur J Pharm Sci* 63:226–232, 2014.

Mumpton FA: La roca magica: uses of natural zeolites in agriculture and industry, *Proc Natl Acad Sci USA* 96:3463–3470, 1999.

Rawtani D, Agrawal YK: Multifarious applications of halloysite nanotubes: a review, *Rev Adv Mater Sci* 30:282–295, 2012.

Rea I, Martucci NM, De Stefano L, Ruggiero I, Terracciano M, Dardano P, Migliaccio N, Arcari P, Taté R, Rendina I, Lamberti A: Diatomite biosilica nanocarriers for siRNA transport inside cancer cells, *Biochim Biophys Acta* 1840:3393–3403, 2014.

Rivera A, Farías T: Clinoptilolite-surfactant composites as drug support: a new potential application, *Micropor Mesopor Mater* 80:337–346, 2005.

Rivera A, Farías T, Ruiz-Salvador AR, de Ménorval LC: Preliminary characterization of drug support systems based on natural clinoptilolite, *Micropor Mesopor Mater* 61:249–259, 2003.

Rodrigues LADS, Figueiras A, Veiga F, de Freitas RM, Nunes LC, da Silva Filho EC, da Silva Leite CM: The systems containing clays and clay minerals from modified drug release: a review, *Colloids Surf B* 103:642–651, 2013.

Rowe RC, Sheskey PJ, Quinn ME, editors: *Handbook of pharmaceutical excipients*, London, Washington DC, 2009, Pharmaceutical Press, American Pharmacists Association.

Rožić M, Ivanec Šipušić D, Sekovanić L, Miljanić S, Ćurković L, Hrenović J: Sorption phenomena of modification of clinoptilolite tuffs by surfactant cations, *J Colloid Interface Sci* 331:295–301, 2009.

Salahuddin N, Kenawy ER, Abdeen R: Polyoxypropylene-montmorillonite nanocomposites for drug-delivery vehicles: preparation and characterization, *J Appl Polym Sci* 125:E157–E166, 2012.

Serri C, de Gennaro B, Catalanotti L, Cappelletti P, Langella A, Mercurio M, Mayol L, Biondi M: Surfactant-modified phillipsite and chabazite as novel excipients for pharmaceutical applications? *Micropor Mesopor Mater* 224:143–148, 2015.

Setaro A, Lettieri S, Maddalena P, De Stefano L: Highly sensitive optochemical gas detection by luminescent marine diatoms, *Appl Phys Lett* 91:051921, 2007.

Simon LS: Actions and toxicities of nonsteroidal anti-inflammatory drugs, *Curr Opin Rheumatol* 8:169–175, 1996.

Sinha Ray S, Okamoto M: Polymer/layered silicate nanocomposites: a review from preparation to processing, *Prog Polym Sci* 28:1539–1641, 2003.

Sullivan EJ, Bowman RS, Legiec IA: Sorption of arsenic from soil-washing leachate by surfactant-modified zeolite, *J Environ Qual* 32:2387–2391, 2003.

Tabak A, Yilmaz N, Eren E, Caglar B, Afsin B, Sarihan A: Structural analysis of naproxen-intercalated bentonite (Unye), *Chem Eng J* 174:281–288, 2011.

Takahashi T, Yamada Y, Kataoka K, Nagasaki Y: Preparation of a novel PEG-clay hybrid as a DDS material: dispersion stability and sustained release profiles, *J Control Release* 107:408–416, 2005.

Terracciano M, Shahbazi MA, Correia A, Rea I, Lamberti A, De Stefano L, Santos HA: Surface bioengineering of diatomite based nanovectors for efficient intracellular uptake and drug delivery, *Nanoscale* 7:20063–20074, 2015.

Todd T, Zhen Z, Tang W, Chen H, Wang G, Chuang YJ, Deaton K, Pan Z, Xie J: Iron oxide nanoparticle encapsulated diatoms for magnetic delivery of small molecules to tumors, *Nanoscale* 6:2073–2076, 2014.

U.S. Geological Survey: Minerals yearbook, vol. I, metals & minerals. Reston, Virginia, 1997, U.S. Geological Survey, pp 24.1–24.6.

U.S. Geological Survey: Mineral commodity summaries 2016. Reston, Virginia, 2014, U.S. Geological Survey, pp 58–59.

Vasani RB, Losic D, Cavallaro A, Voelcker NH: Fabrication of stimulus-responsive diatom biosilica microcapsules for antibiotic drug delivery, *J Mater Chem B* 3:4325–4329, 2015.

Viseras C, Cerezo P, Sanchez R, Salcedo I, Aguzzi C: Current challenges in clay minerals for drug delivery, *Appl Clay Sci* 48:291–295, 2010.

Viseras C, Lopez-Galindo A: Pharmaceutical applications of some Spanish clays (sepiolite, palygorskite, bentonite): some preformulation studies, *Appl Clay Sci* 14:69–82, 1999.

Wang X, Du Y, Luo J: Biopolymer/montmorillonite nanocomposite: preparation, drug-controlled release property and cytotoxicity, *Nanotechnology* 19:065707, 2008.

Wang X, Nguyen AV: Characterisation of electrokinetic properties of clinoptilolite before and after activation by sulphuric acid for treating CSG water, *Micropor Mesopor Mater* 220:175–182, 2016.

Wingenfelder U, Furrer G, Schulin R: Sorption of antimonate by HDTMA-modified zeolite, *Micropor Mesopor Mater* 95:265–271, 2006.

Yang L, Choi SK, Shin HJ, Han HK: 3-Aminopropyl functionalized magnesium phyllosilicate as an organoclay based drug carrier for improving the bioavailability of flurbiprofen, *Int J Nanomed* 8:4147–4155, 2013.

Yang JH, Lee JH, Ryu HJ, Elzatahry AA, Alothman ZA, Choy JH: Drug–clay nanohybrids as sustained delivery systems, *Appl Clay Sci* 130:20–32, 2016.

Yang L, Shao Y, Han HK: Improved pH-dependent drug release and oral exposure of telmisartan, a poorly soluble drug through the formation of drug-aminoclay complex, *Int J Pharm* 471:258–263, 2014.

Zhang H, Shahbazi MA, Mäkilä EM, da Silva TH, Reis RL, Salonen JJ, Hirvonen JT, Santos HA: Diatom silica microparticles for sustained release and permeation enhancement following oral delivery of prednisone and mesalamine, *Biomaterials* 34:9210–9219, 2013.

Zheng JP, Luan L, Wang HY, Xi LF, Yao KD: Study on ibuprofen/montmorillonite intercalation composites as drug release system, *Appl Clay Sci* 36:297–301, 2007.

Index